PHILIP AUGAR

The Bank That Lived a Little

*Barclays in the Age of the
Very Free Market*

ALLEN LANE
an imprint of
PENGUIN BOOKS

ALLEN LANE

UK | USA | Canada | Ireland | Australia
India | New Zealand | South Africa

Allen Lane is part of the Penguin Random House group of companies
whose addresses can be found at global.penguinrandomhouse.com

First published 2018
003

Copyright © Philip Augar, 2018

The moral right of the author has been asserted

Set in 10.5/14 pt Sabon LT Std
Typeset by Jouve (UK), Milton Keynes
Printed and bound in Great Britain by Clays Ltd, Elcograf S.p.A.

A CIP catalogue record for this book is available from the British Library

ISBN: 978–0–241–33597–0

To my sources, with gratitude
and to my supporters, with love

Contents

List of Illustrations   ix

Author's Note   xi

PART I

The Rise and Fall of BZW, 1983–97

1. Lord Camoys' Dream, 1983   3

2. The Golden Ticket: BZW, 1985–95   20

3. The Scholar's Tale, 1986–93   31

4. The Changing of the Guard, 1994   40

5. A Dark Night in Essex, 1995   49

6. The Dumb Money, 1996   57

7. In Memoriam BZW, 1997   68

PART II

Groupthink, 1998–2007

8. Diamond's Halo Slips, 1998   81

9. Middleton's Law, 1998   95

10. Matt Barrett's Master Class, 1999   105

11. Diamond or Varley, 2003   127

12. The Big Vision, 2004   134

13. Dutch Courage, 2007   154

PART III

Coronation, 2008–11

14. Twilight of the Gods, 2008   177

CONTENTS

15. Night Falls, 16 September–13 October 2008   199

16. When Amanda Met Roger, 2008   226

17. Antiques Roadshow, 2009   242

18. Crown of Thorns, 2010   257

PART IV

Humiliation, 2011–17

19. Thin Ice, 2011   279

20. A Boardroom Row, 2012   291

21. Here Today, Gone Tomorrow, 2012   307

22. A Complete Mess, 2012   327

23. 'Barclays is not the place for you,' 2015   337

24. The Second Coming of Jes Staley, 2016   359

Epilogue: And Then   373

Appendices
   i.   Barclays Board Members, 1986–2017   379
   ii.   Barclays Share Price, 2007–17   385

Notes   387
Index   409

List of Illustrations

1. Bar Don Quijote, San Antonio (Welcometoibiza.com)
2. Lord Camoys (Rex Shutterstock)
3. 54 Lombard Street, 1906 (Historic England)
4. 54 Lombard Street, 1980s (Associated Newspapers/Rex Shutterstock)
5. 54 Lombard Street, 2000 (John Sturrock/Alamy)
6. 1 Churchill Place (Jacob Carter/Rex Shutterstock)
7. 41–43 Brook Street (Openoffices.com)
8. Sir Timothy Bevan (The Times/News Licensing/Tim Bishop)
9. John Quinton (Trevor Humphries/Rex Shuttestock)
10. BZW Trading Floor (Mike Abrahams/Alamy)
11. Harry Enfield as *Loadsamoney* (ITV/Rex Shutterstock)
12. Andrew Buxton and Martin Taylor (UPP/TopFoto)
13. Matthew Barrett and Sir Peter Middleton (Sean Dempsey/PA Images)
14. New York Racquet and Tennis Club (BeyondMyKen/Wikimedia Commons)
15. Bob Diamond playing golf (Getty Images)
16. Carol Vorderman advertises FirstPlus (The Advertising Archives)
17. John Varley and Rijkman Groenink (EPA/Rex Shutterstock)
18. Gordon Brown on holiday (Darren Staples/PA Images)
19. Lord Myners (Mark Harrison/Camera Press, London)
20. Baroness Vadera (Charlie Bibby/Financial Times, 2016. Used under licence from the Financial Times. All rights reserved)
21. Lehman Brothers before the Barclays takeover (Richard Levine/Alamy)

22. After the Barclays takeover (Photoshot/TopFoto)
23. Amanda Staveley (© Siddharth Siva)
24. Roger Jenkins (Bloomberg/Getty Images)
25. Front pages of the first and second editions of the *Financial Times*, 27 March 2009 (Used under licence from the Financial Times. All rights reserved)
26. John Varley, Bob Diamond and Marcus Agius (ED/CVA/ Vismedia/Camera Press, London)
27. Alison Carnwarth (Micha Theiner/CityAM/Rex Shutterstock)
28. Lord Turner (PA/TopFoto)
29. Demonstration at Canary Wharf (Suzanne Plunkett/Reuters)
30. Demonstration at Barclays AGM (Oli Scarff/Getty Images)
31. Hector Sants, Paul Tucker and Baron King (Bloomberg/Getty Images)
32. Rich Ricci (David Hartley/Rex Shutterstock)
33. Jerry del Missier (Jane Mingay/Rex Shutterstock)
34-36. Bob Diamond at the Treasury Committee (Gavin Rodgers/ Rex Shutterstock)
37. Sir David Walker (Leon Neal/AFP/Getty Images)
38. Antony Jenkins (Simon Dawson/Bloomberg/Getty Images)
39. Lucknam Park (VisitBritain/Getty Images)
40. John McFarlane (Fairfax Media/Getty Images)
41. Jes Staley (Tolga Akmen/AFP/Getty Images)
42. Evening Standard advertisement (Author's own photograph)
43. Lord Mandelson and Bob Diamond (Private collection)

Author's Note

It was in 1978, forty years ago this year that I started in the City: I spent twenty years working there and (so far) have spent twenty more writing about it. I was at the centre of the action as City institutions and people seized the commanding heights of the economy and then from a different vantage point I watched it all go wrong. I never meant it to be like this but a fascination with the City and what it stands for has become who I am.

I think of my forty working years as four distinct decades. When I began as a trainee investment analyst in the late 1970s (with aviator glasses, hair slightly too long and just one suit), stockbroking, which was mainly what the City did then, was thought to be a genteel pastime. To the person in the street, stockbrokers wore bowler hats and pinstripes, drank a bit too much and lived in big houses in Surrey. Not much of that was true, but it didn't really matter because the City was a quiet corner of national life and kept itself to itself.

That changed in my second decade, after the financial deregulation in 1986 known as Big Bang. Perceptions of the pink-cheeked, gin and tonic brigade were replaced by images of excitable young men in striped shirts and braces yelling into their phones as markets raged. It was good television, but away from the cameras something less visual and more dangerous was happening. Smart investment bankers were pulling the strings in corporate and institutional boardrooms and encouraging governments to let market forces rip. The culture of money and the marketplace took hold of national life and the City was in charge. I doubted it would have a happy ending so in 1999 I left, and instead started describing it in books and articles and on television and radio.

In my third decade, as I wrote my first books, markets were in their pomp. These were years of steady growth and low inflation and the liberated financial markets, created by Margaret Thatcher and John Major and sustained by Tony Blair and Gordon Brown, were credited with being responsible for the economic miracle. Bankers proclaimed that risk had been transformed and encouraged financial institutions, governments, businesses and households to load up with debt. The City of London became the world's international financial services capital and was praised as a shining light for the UK economy.

That changed in 2008, the beginning of my fourth decade, with the banking crisis and the subsequent years of austerity. The poster child became a demon and popular discontent with the unequal distribution of wealth and opportunity was expressed in volatile and unexpected election results in the victim economies.

This book is the story of that rise and fall told through the fortunes of one institution, and I see it as a paradigm for what happened to banking, the City and the British economy during my working life. Barclays' journey from an old Quaker bank to a full-throttle capitalist machine makes it a perfect example of my underlying theme but the truth is I stumbled upon it. I never worked there myself but spent a few years at its less grand rival NatWest. After I left the City, my interest in Barclays was piqued in 2000 by Martin Vander Weyer's memoir *Falling Eagle*. As a writer and commentator I followed with – let me simply say – great interest, the bank's frequent changes in strategy and chief executive. Then in 2013 at a dinner organized by the Centre for the Study of Financial Innovation, I fell into an argument with Bob Diamond, who had been deposed as Barclays' chief executive the year before. We continued the discussion afterwards, which prompted me to explore how Barclays had got into such a mess. This book is the result.

A word on sources and methodology. I have dramatized events and reconstructed dialogue based on more than 400 hours of interviews with over one hundred people closely involved in the story described. Many have also shared material from their personal archives, including file notes, emails, internal presentations and contemporaneous notes of meetings. Most of those who spoke to me did so on condition that they could not be identified as a source. Out of deference to their wishes and to avoid giving undue emphasis to others, interviews are not individually referenced. Readers should not assume that I have spoken to everyone mentioned in the book, or that the persons whose words, thoughts, actions or feelings are described were necessarily the source of that information. In many cases they were, but sometimes other people – present either in person or on the call or who were briefed afterwards – provided me with information. Statements given to parliament, official reports, court records, memoirs, articles, other books and my personal experience as a practitioner, non-executive board member, adviser and writer have also been used to supplement interviews. Citations to written sources are given in the Notes at the end of the book.

A number of individuals met and talked to me, sometimes extensively, on condition that their names did not appear in the book. Charles Bycroft and Karl Edwards are pseudonyms for two of them. Both are still practising in their respective fields and may be identifiable to some of those who know them; if so, I hope that their wish for privacy will be respected. Roger and Carol are pseudonyms for middle-ranking Barclays' employees who appear in the story and it will be obvious to the reader why their names have been changed. 'The Thinker', William, is intended to represent a type of investor and is based on conversations with a hedge fund manager who spoke to me on the condition of strict anonymity. I also spoke to a close colleague of William's and used my knowledge of the hedge fund sector to complete the picture. I have respected these interviewees' wishes by changing many details, including locations and appearances.

I am deeply grateful to all of those who spoke to me but a number of people deserve special thanks. Margaret Roddan has been a constructive influence throughout, correcting drafts, offering me ideas and pushing me into new directions. Rachel Hopcroft and Richard Wyatt have given me insight and expertise into their respective fields. Sarah White's eye for detail has been invaluable. The research skills of Dominic Lindley and Abbie Edwards have unearthed important evidence I would otherwise have missed. I am deeply appreciative of the painstaking work of my copy-editor, Bela Cunha, and the resourcefulness of my image editor, Cecilia Mackay. Martin Vander Weyer commented on a draft with wit, wisdom and a deep knowledge of the subject. The book would not have happened without Stuart Proffitt and Ben Sinyor, his diligent number two at Penguin. Stuart combines patience and persistence with deep insights into a wide range of subjects. I think of him as André Previn to my Eric Morecambe in the sketch in which the exasperated conductor tells the ham-fisted pianist: 'You're playing all the wrong notes.' The great comedian replies: 'I'm playing all the right notes. But not necessarily in the right order.' Stuart, I am eternally grateful to you for teaching me both the notes and the order. Finally, I wish to thank those close to me for sharing their lives with me and with Barclays these past few years; your love and support kept me going.

Philip Augar
Cambridge, 2018

PART I

The Rise and Fall of BZW, 1983–97

I

Lord Camoys' Dream, 1983

On a sweltering evening in July 1983 a battered Land Rover bumped round the coast road and stopped in San Antonio on the west side of the island. The driver, a stocky middle-aged man wearing a bush shirt and crumpled chinos, mopped his brow and crossed into the cool interior of the Bar Don Quijote, a white stucco building on the corner of the street. The German barman greeted him warmly: Ralph Thomas Campion George Sherman Stonor, seventh Baron Camoys – Tom to his friends – was a regular.

Camoys and his young family had been spending summer holidays at his mother-in-law's house in the nearby hamlet of Casa Galera since 1967. The clubbing crowds had not yet discovered Ibiza. Cheap travel, broadband and mobile phones were still to come and the island was a perfect retreat for those who knew about its picturesque charms.

The previous day's English papers had just arrived. Sitting at his favourite corner table, Camoys ordered a glass of white wine. In the absence of the *Financial Times*, off the streets since 1 June because of industrial action, *The Times* was his main source of business news. The headline that day was: 'Stock Exchange reforms may end legal action' and the article below reported an agreement between the Stock Exchange and Margaret Thatcher's recently re-elected Conservative government. He lit a cigarette and read: 'The Government has said it would call off the legal action against the Stock Exchange in return for reforms which will alter the way stocks and shares are bought and sold in Britain.'[1]

3

Faced with a government that disliked anti-competitive price agreements and the threat of a Restrictive Practices Court case, the Exchange had dramatically agreed to abolish its tariff of fixed commissions on share dealing by the end of 1986. In the cosy world of bankers and brokers in which Camoys worked, this was sensational news. But neither he nor anyone else realized then that it would have bigger consequences for British society than any change in business practices since the Industrial Revolution 200 years before.

This agreement, the blue touchpaper that lit the explosion which became known as Big Bang, changed the City of London from a tired old lion into a roaring dragon. It breathed fire into the economy but later burned it badly. In a quarter of a century it transformed culture, values and attitudes to money throughout the whole country. It fuelled a housing boom, created unprecedented prosperity but then blew it all away. It made governments' reputations before leaving them in ruins. Its heroes made millions, yet many ended up in disgrace. And the bank that Camoys worked for was at the heart of it all.

Camoys was a modern English aristocrat. He was a distant descendant of King Charles II but had neither the inclination nor the means to live a life of idleness. Educated at Eton and Balliol College, Oxford, with a keen brain but little money – at least by the standards of many of his class – he needed a career of his own, and banking ran in the family. His great-great-grandfather Watts Sherman had been a partner in a New York bank that in 1858 had taken on one John Pierpont Morgan as a junior banker. Watts Sherman quickly decided that the ambitious young man's risk appetite was too much for the firm and suggested he find other employment. Disappointed but undeterred, J. P. Morgan moved on, returning later to recruit Sherman's finance partner. The bank he founded would come regularly in and out of the Barclays story over the period covered in this book.*

By the time Tom Camoys inherited the title in 1976 and bought Stonor Park, the crumbling family seat from his impoverished father's executors, he was a well-established banker, whose aristocratic

---

* Between 1959 and 1989, the bank was known as Morgan Guaranty but is referred to as J. P. Morgan throughout this book.

background gave no indication of his bustling energy. He had run Rothschild's money markets department, a business that involved trading based on interest rate movements. He went on to become chief executive of Amex Bank Ltd after it bought Rothschild's euro-market interests. In that capacity he got to know the most senior Englishman on Wall Street, Dennis Weatherstone, chairman of J. P. Morgan's executive committee. The English aristocrat and the son of a London Transport clerk were a contrasting pair but ironically, given his great-great-grandfather's history, it was from the J. P. Morgan man that Camoys learned how modern international banks worked. In 1978 Barclays, the grandest of Britain's High Street banks, recruited him to be managing director of its merchant banking sub-sidiary, a position he still held in 1983.

Barclays was a curious mixture of tradition and adventure. It had been founded as a joint stock bank in 1896 through the amalga-mation of twenty country banks, many of them owned by Quaker landowners, and the families' influence remained strong.[2] When Camoys joined, the chairman was Anthony Favill Tuke, son and grandson of previous chairmen, and there was a strong reverence for tradition.[3] Lord Carrington, who first became a non-executive dir-ector at Barclays in 1967, left when he became a cabinet minister in 1970 and rejoined in 1982, described board meetings as 'High mass without the vestments'.[4] This characteristically pithy remark encap-sulated the formality, grandeur and ritual of a great British institution. The head office, 54 Lombard Street, although completed only in 1969, felt like a time warp. Inside were portraits of the founders and East Anglian landscapes. There were squash courts and even a rifle range in the basement.[5] Trusted retainers and descendants of the bank's founding fathers discreetly enforced arcane dining-room pro-tocols. In Tuke's time, board meetings lasted only an hour and were followed by lunch ('damned good lunches', recalled one family mem-ber many years later) before the directors disappeared back to the country.

Tuke's board included representatives of five other founding fami-lies, among them his successor as chairman, Sir Timothy Bevan.[6] Although Barclays had been a quoted company since 1902, they treated it as though it was still all their own, with a directors' flat in

Pall Mall and privileges for those in the 'Special List' of family members and their circle.

It was wonderfully genteel and not at all like the business Camoys wanted it to be. He let his frustration show, pressing colleagues for action and answers. Soon after he arrived, a senior director was sent to have a word with him. 'Tom, we're slightly worried about you. You don't seem to realize that you have joined a club. We are all very nice to one another here.'

However, Barclays was not simply a timeless relic; it had always been a bank that lived a little. Before the Second World War a judge in Chancery reprimanded it for pursuing its own interests as a lender at the expense of clients for whom it was a trustee. In the same period Barclays allowed branch managers to keep the commissions it received for selling insurance policies to customers. It was a perquisite that enabled Barclays to keep down the cost of their salaries and pensions but which presented branch managers with a conflict of interest that had uncomfortable echoes several decades later.[7] In the 1970s and 80s, its involvement in apartheid-practising South Africa made Barclays a target for protesters in the UK and although public pressure eventually forced it to withdraw, the perception remained that it had stayed on as long as was commercially convenient.

There was, however, a more attractive side to living a little because Barclays could also be commercially innovative and daring. In 1925 it had diversified abroad by forming Barclays Bank – Dominion, Colonial and Overseas (DCO) – an imperial foray described by the *Financial Times* as a 'bold and inspiring conception'.[8] By 1980, the overseas bank contributed a fifth of group profits and employed over a third of Barclays' staff in its 2,000 branches.[9] This entrepreneurial spirit popped up time and time again throughout Barclays' history. In 1966 it was the first British bank to introduce a credit card, Barclaycard, which proved to be an important source of profits for the bank and transformed consumer credit in the UK. A year later it installed Britain's first cash machine, outside a Barclays branch in Enfield, north London.

The formation of the merchant bank in 1975 came in the midst of a great upheaval in the banking sector, and was another example of Barclays' determination to keep up with the times. Until the 1970s banking was a very comfortable business. Between the end of the Second World War and 1970, Barclays' average annual return on shareholders' funds was a fat 4 per cent above the Bank of England's base rate, and it didn't have to work very hard to achieve it.[10] The odd cash machine apart, banks looked much as they had in the 1950s. There were no laptops, no internet, no telephone banking – that started in 1984 – and staff spent the days filing and entering data onto ledgers. Lending was based on the manager's personal knowledge of the customer, fees were charged for operating current accounts and deposit rates were generous. Opening hours were short and the same at every bank, none opened at the weekends and banks politely declined to compete too hard with each other or even to advertise on that racy modern medium, television.

The explanation for this easy way of life was a tacit understanding between the authorities and the banks. The Bank of England capped the amount banks could lend and made them hold capital as a contingency against bad debts, but in return the banks were effectively allowed to collude over interest rates and conceal their true profits. No one rocked the boat.

This changed after the 1970 general election in which Edward Heath's Conservative Party unexpectedly ousted Harold Wilson's Labour government. With his chancellor of the exchequer, Anthony Barber, the new prime minister embarked on a 'dash for growth', cutting taxes and interest rates. Banks became an instrument of this policy and to encourage them to lend more, controls on lending and capital requirements were eased in 1971. In return, the banks agreed to end collusion on interest rates and to publish more informative financial statements.[11] The end of the cartel shattered the industry's equilibrium. Competitive pricing and a push for market share replaced friendly rivalry: in 1972 bank advertisements finally appeared on television.[12]

The consequences for both the economy and the banking sector were disastrous. The 'Barber boom' led to inflation, while freedom from control led the banks to lend wildly to credit-hungry consumers and businesses. The government slammed on the brakes to slow down the economy and in 1973 introduced emergency measures for banks – known as 'the corset' – to bring bank lending back under

control. But it was too late to save either the government, the economy or the banks. A major oil crisis – crude oil rose from $3 to $12 a
barrel – added to the inflationary pressures and property prices collapsed. The economy plunged into recession and Labour returned to
power in the general elections of February and October 1974 to face
recession, trade union problems and inflation running at 16 per cent.

Twenty-six secondary banks had to be rescued between 1974 and
1978 in a Bank of England organized operation dubbed 'the lifeboat'.[13] NatWest, one of the big four clearing banks, had to issue a
statement to quell rumours that it was in trouble.* Barclays, which
was the biggest UK bank and not itself in difficulty, was required as
a good citizen to contribute a quarter of the total lifeboat funds in
line with its market share.[14]

Responsible citizenship aside, banks were now competing more
vigorously than ever before and also faced a challenge from a different quarter. Innovative banks such as Morgan Stanley, Warburg and
the Industrial Bank of Japan were raising funds for clients in capital
markets through bond issues – parcels of debt that could be traded by
investors. This new form of finance was marketed as a cheaper alternative to conventional loans from banks' balance sheets, and it
directly threatened corporate banking, a very profitable part of their
business.

Sir Anthony Tuke – he was knighted in 1979 – Barclays' chairman
between 1973 and 1981, therefore had to deal with more competition, closer scrutiny from shareholders who could now see exactly
how much or how little the bank was making, a weak economy and
erratic government policy. It was a daunting list for a man who had
grown up in more stable times but who in many respects personified
the contrast between Barclays' style and substance.

Tuke was a shy man but his reserved demeanour concealed an
impatient streak. He hated lengthy discussions at board meetings and
was intolerant of delay, for example, preferring to be driven hundreds
of miles if his flight was delayed because he liked to be on the move.
It was the same in business. In retail banking, he cut the UK branch

---

* It was called the National Westminster Bank until the 1990s when it changed to
NatWest. The latter is used throughout this book.

network to save costs but grew the domestic loan book to maintain market share. Overseas, he simply expanded aggressively, adding staff, opening branches and increasing the balance sheet.

In corporate banking, to replace the lending business lost to the capital markets, he set up Barclays Merchant Bank in 1975, pulling together corporate finance activities from various parts of the bank. Charles Ball, a senior corporate financier, was hired from Kleinwort Benson to run it in 1976, but Tuke didn't drive through the organizational changes necessary to support him. Perhaps reflecting Barclays' origins as an amalgamation of many smaller banks, its culture was tribal. Local head offices guarded their clients from the corporate lending division in London, which in turn denied access to the merchant bank. It was all very political. Ball left after little more than a year, saying there were 'too many signs around the place saying "keep off the grass" '.[15] Camoys was recruited to replace him in 1978.

In most parts of the business, Tuke's aggressive strategy paid off. Profits took a hit in the recession years of 1974–6, but the crucial average annual return on shareholders' funds remained 4 per cent above the Bank of England's base rate in the 1970s, just as it had been in the days of the cosy cartel.[16] Flattering comparisons were drawn with Walter Wriston's fast-growing US banking conglomerate, Citigroup, already aspiring to be a universal bank selling every kind of financial service to blue chip clients, and Wriston acknowledged the British bank as a serious global competitor. Tuke appeared on the cover of the American magazine *Business Week* – an accolade usually reserved for go-getting chief executives of the modern age – photographed in front of the antique-looking brass doors of 54 Lombard Street.

It was a fitting image. To Camoys' frustration, Barclays never quite knew whether it was part of the new age or the old and his merchant bank was caught in the dilemma. Barclays' traditional corporate bankers ignored the threat from the capital markets and just hoped it would go away. They seemed happy to offer loans from the bank's own resources at ever decreasing margins and regarded 'Bumble', as the merchant bank was nicknamed, with hostility, guarding Barclays' clients and balance sheet for their own business.

Camoys was sure the capital markets were here to stay. With a career to build and a dilapidated stately home to restore, he had no time to waste. On that July 1983 evening in Ibiza, he decided that his moment had come. He put down his newspaper, walked over to the bar's single telephone and gave his London office instructions to prepare a report on the Stock Exchange's deal with the government, ready for his return.

THE BANKER, THE BREWER
AND THE BARON

It was only when Camoys got back to London a few days later that he discovered the City had already concluded that reform would go much further than the abolition of minimum commissions. A distinctive characteristic of the London Stock Exchange was that market makers in shares – known as jobbers – were not allowed to talk directly to investors. That was the preserve of agents – known as brokers – who were not allowed to make markets themselves. The latter would be commercially unviable with lower commissions and this would surely lead to the end of 'single capacity' firms. City bars and restaurants were agog with speculation and excitement, but behind closed doors in boardrooms and round partners' tables, serious plans were being laid.

Merchant banks such as Morgan Grenfell and Kleinwort intended to expand their existing business of lending money and advising corporate clients by opening trading arms to buy and sell securities to investors. Such banks, combining trading securities with advice to corporations and governments, already existed in the US where they were called investment banks and the business they were in was investment banking. Even staid British High Street clearing banks such as Barclays' deadly rival NatWest, liked the look of this business which would soon be open to them for the first time. Revolution was in the air and Camoys was determined that Barclays would not get left behind.

As the summer turned into early autumn, Camoys developed a plan to transform Bumble. Why not jump over the pack by doing things bigger, better, faster and sooner? It would require acquisitions, capital and an increase in Barclays' risk appetite. Would the bank go for such a daring strategy?

Camoys first presented his plan to Deryk Vander Weyer, the bank's deputy chairman, a man he knew to be a progressive banker and clever strategic thinker. Vander Weyer had joined Barclays at the age of sixteen and had been a candidate to take over from Tuke as chairman in 1981. He had a lot of support from Barclays' insiders but a succession agreement had been fixed some years earlier and the family-dominated board appointed the Eton-educated, ex-Welsh Guardsman Timothy Bevan, great-grandson of Barclays' first chairman, who had been at Barclays since 1950. The consolation prize of UK chairman and group deputy chairman was not enough for a man of Vander Weyer's talents and by the time Camoys approached him, he was close to joining British Telecom as deputy chairman. [17]

Intrigued by Camoys' plan but knowing he was likely to leave the company soon, Vander Weyer told him to see Bevan. That meeting would shape the next crucial phase of Camoys' career. As he navigated the corridors connecting Barclays Merchant Bank offices in Gracechurch Street with Barclays' imposing head office at 54 Lombard Street, he was wary.

Bevan currently had a lot of problems to deal with. When he had taken over from Tuke – who remained on the board as a non-executive director – another wave of banking deregulation was already underway. It had begun immediately after the general election in 1979. The abolition of foreign exchange controls under the new prime minister, Margaret Thatcher, and chancellor of the exchequer, Geoffrey Howe, allowed British institutions to invest more easily overseas and made London a more attractive place for foreign banks, but that meant more competition for Barclays. The emergency corset restraint on bank lending imposed in 1973 was ended in 1980 and the year after that, in Bevan's first year, the Bank of England further eased controls on banks' balance sheets. Hire purchase controls were ended in 1982 and an interest rate cartel among member-owned building societies was ended in 1983.

Competition was bursting out everywhere, and as a market leader Barclays had a lot to lose. Bevan's task was made harder by a global recession and a Latin American debt crisis. The results, now all too plain for people to see with transparent reporting, were poor and in his first full year pre-tax profits fell; it would be 1984 before they exceeded the £539 million earned in 1981.

Little, if any, of this was Bevan's fault. He illustrated both the strengths and weaknesses of family leadership. He was imperious in manner, dismissive of his board and protective of the Barclays' families, but for all this he had the bank's long-term interests at heart. His hobbies included ocean sailing, parachute jumping and plunging head first down the icy Cresta Run, but in business he was cautious, with the single aim of handing the bank on to his successors intact. Instead of trying to match the push for market share being made by other clearing banks and building societies, Bevan warned his bankers not to lower credit standards and stood his ground.

Camoys and Bevan moved in the same circles but did not know each other particularly well. As Camoys took the lift to the sixth floor and was shown into the chairman's fusty office, he knew he would have to judge this conversation carefully. Bevan was unpredictable, swore a lot and could be abrupt under pressure. Camoys explained that he wanted to create an investment bank at Barclays along the lines of Wall Street houses such as Goldman Sachs, Merrill Lynch and Morgan Stanley. He said this would enable Barclays to raise money for clients on the capital markets by selling and trading debt and equity securities to investors. This was how investment banks were challenging the traditional lending business of banks such as Barclays. His plan would be a defence against such predators and if it worked would compensate for any decline in corporate lending, just as Tuke had intended when Bumble was first formed eight years before.

Bevan listened carefully, occasionally jotting down notes in fountain pen on the large blotter on his desk. The way Camoys told it, this would not be a huge gamble. The sums involved would be relatively small for a bank still making profits of £500 million a year and if everyone else was doing it, Barclays would look foolish to be left behind. But Camoys already had a reputation within the bank for impatience and Bevan did not yet trust his judgement. He looked round for someone he knew better to give a second opinion and chose Barclays' UK managing director, Andrew Buxton.

Buxton was forty-four at the time, a year older than Camoys, and like him, an experienced banker. He had joined Barclays, in 1963 with a classic Barclays' background: Winchester, Oxford and the Grenadier Guards. Although brewing not banking was the Buxton family business, reassuringly for Bevan, Buxton had a distant Quaker family connection with Barclays. His family had helped Barclays rescue the failed Gurney bank in 1866. His stepfather was a regional director at Barclays, and within the bank Buxton was regarded as 'core' family.

Thus it was that these three scions of the British upper class, the banker, the brewer and the baron, with backgrounds from public schools, ancient universities and the best British regiments, came together to pit their wits against Wall Street's sharpest talent.

Once again, Camoys went through his pitch. He explained to Buxton that his idea was to replicate the American investment banks' model by adding trading and corporate advice to Barclays' traditional business of lending. The previously separate activities of market making and agency broking would soon be combined and Camoys planned to buy both a jobber and a broker and merge them with Barclays Merchant Bank. As head of banking for Barclays' big business customers, Buxton had seen for himself the threat that the capital markets posed. He endorsed Camoys' plan and recommended it to Bevan, who, after several meetings, told them: 'I've decided that we should do it.' Camoys would be chief executive but Bevan considered it improper for him to negotiate financial terms when hiring the people he would be leading; that would be done by Buxton.

The Barclays board at this time numbered over thirty – all men – including family members, a smattering of the great and the good, the heads of the regional head offices and a few senior professional bankers. Quite what they would have made of the exotic new world conceived by Camoys and Buxton is hard to imagine but they were never given an opportunity to express an opinion. Bevan reported the decision to go into securities trading at a hastily convened board meeting. The move would soon transform Barclays' business model, risk profile and culture but the board were simply told about what would turn out to be the biggest change in the bank's corporate life. It was an innocent misjudgement of the complexity and consequences of the path down which they were starting.

Between 1983, when the agreement between government and City was first struck, and 1986, when Big Bang was implemented, there was a scramble to buy up Stock Exchange firms. At the time, the Stock Exchange was a village community of barely a hundred firms, employing fewer than 20,000 people in total.[18] The largest firms had only a few hundred staff each and most were much smaller than that, using what would soon come to look like tiny amounts of capital. When the big banks came calling, the partners of these little brokers and dealers could scarcely believe their luck. Many of them had nearly gone out of business during the oil crisis and stock market slump in 1973–4 and now they were being courted from all sides. They entered frenetic negotiations, usually selling themselves to the highest bidder, the most senior partners making a million or two pounds each - quite a lot of money in the mid-1980s.

The prize catch was the prestigious broking firm Cazenove, whose blue-blooded partners listened politely to pitches from Barclays and other banks before deciding to remain independent. In the merry-go-round of mergers and acquisitions the merchant bank Warburg pulled ahead with the strongest line of acquisitions, but by Big Bang day, 27 October 1986, Barclays was not far behind. It bought two of the larger Stock Exchange partnerships, Wedd Durlacher (which made markets in securities) and De Zoete & Bevan (which advised financial institutions and corporations but did no trading of its own) for a total of £129 million, merged them with Bumble into a new investment bank and called it Barclays De Zoete Wedd - BZW.[19] Barclays had seen off serious competition, secured two of the best firms available and sewn them into its own merchant bank. What could possibly go wrong?

'ONE OF THE SMARTEST MEN YOU'LL EVER MEET'

In Manhattan, 3,000 miles from Ibiza, another bank had also been having big ideas in the summer of 1983. Morgan Stanley was the kind of business Tom Camoys wanted Barclays' merchant bank to be. It was an integrated investment bank, combining trading in securities markets for wealthy individuals and financial institutions, advising big corporations on financial and strategic matters and raising money for them in the capital markets. Like J. P. Morgan, the bank from which it had evolved, it too laid claim to the slogan 'first-class business in a first-class way'.

In 1983, Morgan Stanley was still a partnership and had just navigated a turbulent decade following Wall Street's own version of Big Bang on 1 May 1975. With the loss of fixed commissions, the industry-wide tariff of set prices for buying and selling securities, the traditionally genteel world of white shoe investment banking (named after the light buckskin footwear popular in Ivy League colleges and with their Wall Street alumni) got much more competitive. Commissions on share trading were slashed and the industry's business model was ripped up. But under the leadership between 1973 and 1982 of Robert Baldwin, a decisive man who wanted no truck with the old white shoe ways, Morgan Stanley quickly adapted.[20]

As May Day 1975 loomed, banks that had never poached each other's clients or staff suddenly competed head on. Morgan Stanley had broken one of Wall Street's taboos in 1974 when it became the first bank to lead a hostile takeover of one major company, Electric Storage Battery, by another, International Nickel. Later, it was on the receiving end of another break with tradition when one of its main clients, IBM, snubbed it as lead adviser by choosing Merrill Lynch and Salomon Brothers to run its first bond issue. It was a rare setback for a bank that was constantly searching for new opportunities.

As Camoys pored over his day-old *Times* in San Antonio town, a little-known 44-year-old New Yorker, William Bernard Cook, was toiling away deep inside Morgan Stanley's operations building at 55 Water Street in Manhattan's financial district. Cook was a computer expert who had helped a Connecticut medical equipment firm, US Surgical Corporation, grow rapidly, until in 1979 he had caught the eye of a Morgan Stanley managing partner, Thomas C. Melzer.

Melzer, himself a graduate in electrical engineering, was in charge of trading securities issued by the US government and saw that computers could give Morgan Stanley an edge. He persuaded Robert Baldwin that they needed a technologist who really knew what he was about and hired Cook as the firm's global head of technology. It was a big call to make on a man with no experience of Wall Street but, as we shall see, it paid off in more ways than one. By 1983, Cook was in the final stages of developing TAPS (Trade Analysis and Processing System), a computer system that automated parts of share trading and settlement.

This was at a time when traders in the City of London were still doing deals on a handshake and recording the details in pencil in notebooks. It is doubtful whether Camoys, Bevan or Buxton had ever seen a computer, let alone had one on their fine mahogany desks. Even while they were laying their plans, their understanding of investment banking was out of date. Technology would soon turbocharge the developments in financial services brought about by Big Bang. The world Barclays was intent on entering was about to become unimaginably complex and the paths of Bill Cook and Barclays would cross during the next two decades in a surprising way.

In 1977, Cook, who had already gained a reputation at US Surgical for developing bright graduate talent, went back to his alma mater, the University of Connecticut, on a hiring trip. There he met a young economics lecturer who was planning an academic career. Robert E. Diamond was the second of seven surviving children born to second-generation Irish immigrants. He was a New England boy born and bred but definitely not white shoe. The son of a mathematics teacher, he spent his early years in Westport, Connecticut, and then moved to Concord, Massachusetts, when his father became a school principal there.

It was a step up for the family. They moved into a detached home in a nice part of town. Bob walked every day to Concord-Carlisle high school, where he worked hard and played hard. But money was tight and his father worked as a milkman during the school holiday to make ends meet. If the boy wanted a new baseball bat, he had to buy it himself, so he cleared snow, mowed lawns and baby-sat for neighbours.

Much was expected of the eldest son of an American family in the 1960s. At school Bob was good with numbers so he decided to aim above the state universities his parents had attended and won a place at Colby, a small private liberal arts college up in Maine. Diamond's father told him that he would have to pay his own way. He received some financial aid and loans from Colby and topped this up with work in the campus library, bartending in town and mending roads back home in Concord.

Colby is one of those idyllic colleges set in a beautiful wooded campus with spacious lawns separating the college buildings from the residential fraternity houses, where young Americans who are clever and fortunate enough to go there learn about life, each other and themselves. He was a model student: well organized and hardworking, he played in the football and baseball teams and excelled at his major, economics.

After graduating in 1974, Diamond moved to the University of Connecticut, where he came top of his MBA class. He wanted to do a doctorate on organizational behaviour but first he needed to pay his debts and get some real-world experience. He started reading the employment pages of the *Wall Street Journal* and saw Cook's US Surgical advertising for smart, confident graduates looking for a challenge. He attended the firm's recruiting roadshow, where he heard Cook make an unusual pitch to the prospective applicants: 'It will be tough. You will work in the computer room punching cards from midnight till eight a.m. You can have eight hours to sleep and then I want you back here at four p.m. for another eight hours in the classroom. Half of you won't make it. Those that do will be all set for a career in the computer industry.' This was the kind of challenge the young Diamond relished.

With a shared interest in management and a passion for sports, Cook and Diamond hit it off. Diamond cancelled interviews at IBM and joined Cook's team at US Surgical for the modest salary of $10,800. Diamond was methodical, accurate and disciplined, well cut out for Cook's boot camp. The other guys liked him and after six months Cook put him in charge of the computer room. Diamond's academic plans were already receding when eighteen months later Cook took him aside and told him he was leaving US Surgical to build a technology platform for Morgan Stanley. Diamond knew little about Wall Street but he was intrigued by Cook's description and persuaded Cook to recruit him for the second time.

The move from Main Street to Wall Street was a big shock. US Surgical was not exactly sleepy hollow – some managers at the firm later had to give back bonuses earned on overstated sales figures going back to 1979 – but it was a world away from investment banking. Morgan Stanley was in Manhattan not Connecticut. People started work earlier, shouted louder and got paid more. They were quick to judge and had no time for losers. The winners made a lot of money.

They dressed differently too. US Surgical computer staff worked in shirts, ties and slacks but rarely business suits. Diamond had always liked to dress nicely but his wardrobe didn't have the right clothes for Wall Street. He took himself off to Richards of Greenwich, his local family-run tailor, and bought two blue suits to wear at Morgan Stanley, the place where in August 1979 his Wall Street career began.

On his first day, he left the rented house he shared with friends in Greenwich, took the sixty-minute train ride to Grand Central Station and then the downtown 4 train to Wall Street. It was shaping up to be another hot summer's day and Diamond was nervous. As the train pulled in, a smart young man looked at him and asked if it was his first day. Diamond was taken aback. Was it so obvious? He admitted it was. 'Then you should probably take the price tags off your jacket.' Welcome to Wall Street.

Diamond was a born leader. Just as at US Surgical, he was put in charge of the computer room, and it wasn't long before he was offered a job working for Jerry Lloyd, Morgan Stanley's chief administrative and operations officer. Diamond thought carefully before accepting. The CAOO was an important man who sat on the bank's executive committee but Administration and Operations was unglamorous. Trading was where the money and excitement were and he was now nearly thirty years old. If he was going to move into trading it would need to be soon. So he struck a deal: another year in Operations and then he could become a trader. The promise was kept and at the end of 1981 he moved into bond trading as a junior trader, working for Thomas C. Melzer, the man who had hired Cook.

Cook's star was also rising. Baldwin introduced modern management techniques into an industry in which management was something the rainmakers did in their spare time. Cook thrived and became known within the firm as 'one of the smartest men you'll ever meet'. Cook persuaded Morgan Stanley to invest heavily in graduate recruiting. Dick Fisher, Baldwin's successor as Morgan Stanley's president in

1984, told the magazine *Business Week* that Cook was responsible for a stream of the best and brightest young talent arriving at the firm. According to another Wall Street big hitter, David E. Shaw, founder of the eponymous investment business, Cook was 'a remarkable manager ... He combined active guidance and candid critical feedback with a kind and supportive demeanor and a contagious enjoyment of his work.'[21]

Cook was not only a talented manager and hirer: his TAPS computer system paid for itself within a couple of years. Other Wall Street firms rushed to copy it. Between 1979, when he joined Morgan Stanley, and 1986, when he left to join one of the new breed of dynamic investment houses known as hedge funds, Cook and a few likeminded souls transformed Wall Street. Computers were programmed to execute trades automatically when pre-drawn lines were crossed. Sophisticated risk models supplemented traders' feel for markets. Trade processing became automated and paper was on the way out. Faster communications linked America with the rest of the world. At the same time, Ronald Reagan, tax cuts, deregulation and a squeeze on inflation rebooted the American economy and the US financial services industry boomed.

For British firms like Barclays the timing was very unfortunate. Between July 1983, when the run-up to Big Bang started, and October 1986, when it ended, the Americans moved the finishing line. As 1986 dawned, Morgan Stanley announced that it would be getting a stock market listing to enable it to raise more capital. It and many of the other big Wall Street firms were already becoming well-capitalized forerunners of modern investment banks, with professional management, rapidly developing technology and a global reach, while Barclays and the other British banks were still on the starting grid.

2

The Golden Ticket: BZW, 1985–95

'IS THIS KIND OF THING LEGAL?'

Charles Bycroft lowered his long, lean frame into seat 21A. It was just before six in the evening of Monday 19 February 1996 and flight BA 179 to New York's JFK airport would be taking off shortly. He watched the cabin crew hang his suit carrier in the centre aisle locker and glanced at the *Evening Standard* as the last few passengers passed through Club Class on their way to the back of the plane.

He declined the pre-flight champagne but asked for a glass of wine to be brought to him after take-off, a familiar drill for a man who had been plying his trade between London and New York for over a decade. As the plane taxied across the runway and then climbed over the west London suburbs, he pulled out his briefing notes.

After leaving public school, the quick-witted but academically uninterested Bycroft had started work in 1972 as a junior dealer at the London Stock Exchange, on whose cavernous floor between Old Broad Street and Throgmorton Street all trading in British stocks and shares had to take place. It was a man's world, full of jolly japes, cigarette smoke and the whiff of boozy lunches, but amid the banter serious work was done too. At hectic moments the senior dealers would shout 'Blue!' and young men like Bycroft, wearing the Blue Button badge signifying their junior dealer status, would be dispatched to carry messages between their firms' hexagonal trading booths. It required a quick brain, fleetness of foot and a degree of physical strength to force a way through the crowds clustered around the pitches when trade was busy. But after the oil crisis and throughout the 1974 recession the market floor was quiet. It turned out to be a horrendous year for the stock market. In November, the *Financial Times* index of leading shares, the FT30, which had peaked at 544 in 1972, stood at just 150. Investment business dried up and the Stock Exchange firms laid off staff.[1]

Bycroft was one of the many who lost their jobs, but as one career door closed another opened. Young men of his type had an adventurous streak. Africa called, first of all in the form of a big mining company and then with a British bank in South Africa. In the 1980s, however, upper-class Englishmen fell from favour in colonially rooted banks now seeking to leave their pasts behind. So it was back to London and a career crisis. What could a well-connected young man with enterprise and social skills but few formal qualifications do in Prime Minister Thatcher's get-ahead, survival-of-the-fittest Britain? He was in a tight spot but got lucky: he was introduced by a friend to an American executive search firm opening up in the UK, became their sixth employee in London and was told to specialize in financial services.

Executive search was well established in the US but British industry was only just emerging from its long post-war slumber. In the sedate world of men in grey suits, jobs were for the boys and for life. Young executives had to use their connections and wait their turn. The idea that you might hire a search firm to fill a vacancy rarely occurred to British business leaders in the early 1980s.

Bycroft and his firm helped to break this mould. He was one of the pioneers of executive search in Britain, patiently building his contacts and explaining his trade to a bemused audience. Once he was asked, 'Is this kind of thing legal?' But as British industry in the 1980s deregulated, de-unionized and became more results orientated, hiring and firing became routine and search took off.

One sector above all depended on head hunters to find qualified staff. As we have seen, the end of the Stock Exchange's closed shop triggered a scramble for qualified people among the many financial institutions trying to build investment banks. The partner-run firms that would seed these new trading factories were tiny relative to the ambitions of the banks. The big banks bolted the partnerships together between 1983 and 1986 but they were still too small. As the powerful new owners raided rivals in a desperate attempt to bring themselves up to critical mass there was a hiring frenzy. Analysts who researched investment ideas, sales people who passed those ideas on to investors, traders who used their firm's own money to meet client orders – demand for them all far outstripped supply. Corporate financiers with access to the boardrooms of big companies wanting to raise capital were also much sought after. Pay rates were bid higher and higher. Signing-on fees – golden hellos – were sometimes used to induce staff to jump ship.

It was an easy sell for the recruiters. The paternalistic bond between the City's employers and employees had been broken by the mass redundancies of 1974, and the search firms that sprang up at the time of Big Bang found a receptive audience among the brokers and dealers. The 'marzipan' layer of talented young women and men just below partnership level, so called because they were below the icing but above the cake, were especially keen to talk. Expectations of big bucks, lock-ins and incentives replaced gratitude for a 10 per cent bonus and a turkey at Christmas. The executive search industry whipped up the fervour and bagged its fees – often a third of a successfully placed candidate's first-year compensation.

Bycroft was the right man in the right place at the right time. He built a portfolio of banking clients but did not act for one client against another. Ambitious banks with an appetite for hiring were particularly prized and Bycroft's firm carefully nurtured a relationship with Barclays as they felt their way into investment banking.

His first involvement had been back in 1985 and came direct from Camoys, by this time chief executive of the new investment bank. Camoys had spent the previous year and a half with Buxton negotiating the purchase of Wedd Durlacher and De Zoete & Bevan. Integrating the two was a torturous process because people who had run their own businesses found it hard to adapt to corporate life, and Camoys had to settle frequent turf wars between warring tribes. Technology systems, client coverage and reporting lines – the brokers, traders and bankers – would argue about everything. It was energy sapping and time consuming and deflected management from keeping up with developments across the Atlantic, where Bill Cook at Morgan Stanley and other Bill Cooks at other Wall Street firms were busy developing the computer-based trading systems that would raise the bar for the rest of the world.

Camoys needed help, ideally a chairman of BZW who could deal with clients and regulators and keep track of the ever-changing industry. He raised the idea with Bevan, who said: 'You are quite right. As it happens, I've already approached someone.' Camoys was affronted: 'Without speaking to me first? Who is it?' Bevan mentioned the name of a leading businessman and Camoys snapped back: 'He's not an investment banker. I can't run the business and teach a novice.' He told Bevan that if the proposed appointment went ahead, he would leave. It was a threat that would be used often by Camoys' successors without being meant but this headstrong aristocrat clearly did mean every word. It was only a year until Big Bang and for Barclays to lose the architect of the investment bank at this stage would be a disaster. Bevan backed down and told Camoys to come up with some ideas of his own.

It was a situation tailor made for Bycroft's firm. Top of their list was a former tax barrister, Sir Martin Jacomb.[2] Jacomb was fifty-five, already a City grandee, vice-chairman of Kleinwort Benson, an adviser to the governor of the Bank of England and a recent member of the Takeover Panel, the City's most prestigious regulator. They knew that he was disappointed to have been passed over for Kleinwort's chairmanship two years previously.

Jacomb was a shrewd reader of the banking industry. Like Bevan and Camoys, he could see the tide flowing from old-style lending to the bond markets. He also appreciated that only the best-capitalized investment banks had a chance of competing in this new world and that simply by virtue of its size, Barclays had some advantages over Kleinwort. On 21 May 1985 Jacomb's appointment as chairman of BZW and deputy chairman of Barclays plc was announced. He started work on 1 July.

It had been a sweet moment, plucking a man of Jacomb's eminence from a blue-blooded house like Kleinwort and slotting him into a clearing bank. Bank watchers said it showed that Barclays, not to mention Bycroft and his firm, were forces to be reckoned with in the new world of investment banking. But on 12 July, not a fortnight after Jacomb started at Barclays, the old City adage 'If you can't take a joke, don't work in the stock market' came into play and this time the joke was on him, Bycroft's firm and Barclays.

The day started innocuously enough. Jacomb was still finding his feet in his new office when he received a telephone call from Michael Hawkes, the veteran banker who had beaten him to the chairman's job at Kleinwort. Hawkes asked if they could have a chat that morning, there being something that Jacomb ought to know. It was a five-minute walk between Kleinwort's offices near Fenchurch Street station and Gracechurch Street, where Jacomb was based. To the casual observer Hawkes looked every inch the sober banker he was, silver-grey hair, silk tie and pressed handkerchief peeping from the breast pocket of his beautifully tailored suit, but closer inspection would have revealed a spring in his step.[3] For while Jacomb had been on garden leave in June, Kleinwort had been negotiating with several partners of Wedd Durlacher, the trading firm Barclays had just bought. The previous day negotiations had been completed and Kleinwort had signed them up.

This was the most dramatic raid on one bank's staff by another that the City had ever known. Trading skills were crucial to the successful transition from old-style lending to modern-day investment banking: that was why Barclays had bought Wedd. Kleinwort had been priced out of the auction for Wedd but they now simply marched in and recruited eight of their most able traders. It was a stunning reply to those who had regarded Jacomb's departure to a bigger rival as a sign that Kleinwort could not compete with the big investment banks that were being formed.

Hawkes had joined Kleinwort straight from Gray's Inn in 1954, when men wore bowler hats in the City streets and rival firms treated each other with respect. In his world, gentlemen dealt with each other face-to-face and Hawkes felt that on a matter of this sensitivity a chairman-to-chairman discussion was appropriate.[4] It must have been an irony-clad meeting. The two lawyers turned financiers, only recently competing as colleagues for the chairmanship of Kleinwort, were now meeting as representatives of rival firms a matter of weeks after one of them had told the other of his own departure.

Word quickly spread through Barclays that an enormous hole had been knocked into its trading operation. BZW's top management, including Jacomb, were summoned to Lombard Street to explain what had happened and Barclays insisted on renegotiating the price they were to pay for Wedd from £100 million down to £80 million.[5]

The Kleinwort raid showed how fluid able people could be in the fast deregulating City. Big Bang was now little more than a year away. No one knew quite what to expect as trading moved from direct contact on the Stock Exchange floor into the anonymous electronic dealing rooms that banks such as Barclays now had to design and construct. Fortunately for Bycroft, there were plenty of teams to build and for head hunters with his connections, these were prosperous years.

27 OCTOBER 1986

Tension was high at BZW on the first day of trading under the new system. Parties had been held the previous Friday to mark the end of dealing on the Stock Exchange floor, and after weekends of rehearsals all the technology was in place. Now it was for real. From now on, deals would be done over the telephone and by computers: face-to-face trading where people elbowed each other across the floor and could see each other's expressions ended very suddenly. With it went some of the trust, obligation and long-term relationships which had sustained the sleepy City of London for decades.

On the first day of Big Bang, BZW's staff were told to be ready for work at seven in the morning, an hour and a half earlier than before. Timetables were studied to check out the early trains, hotel rooms were booked and commuters from the outer suburbs wondered if they would have to move closer to London. As the day developed, it all became real and the teams Camoys had put together started to function as one. De Zoete's salespeople had to negotiate commission rates with clients and then persuade Wedd's traders to buy or sell at a competitive rate. It was less clubby and more aggressive, but people learned quickly.

Lower dealing costs, government privatizations of state-owned industries, a cut in stamp duty in the 1986 budget and the Thatcher–Reagan feel good factor boosted stock market turnover. The value of shares traded doubled and then trebled in the months after Big Bang. The markets and the technology coped with the revolution, the City was euphoric and the business Tom Camoys had built immediately established itself as one of the leading firms.

It was all going smoothly when in June 1987 BZW had some terrible news. The strain and the lifestyle had told on Camoys and at the age of forty-seven, he suffered a stroke. It was a great shock to both the firm and the family. Stonor Park was not yet paying its way, BZW was at a critical stage and both businesses required Camoys' attention, but he had to step down as chief executive of BZW, later to return as deputy chair. A new chief executive was urgently required, and Jacomb turned to Bycroft's firm for help.

Camoys' illness left a huge gap but it also presented an opportunity to bring in a banker with different skills. Many corporate clients still regarded Barclays principally as a lending bank and preferred to use more established investment banks – Goldman Sachs, Morgan Stanley and Merrill Lynch, for example – to raise money in capital markets and the old City merchant banks such as Warburg, Kleinwort and Schroders for corporate finance advice. Although BZW was functioning well, Barclays was actually not much nearer solving the strategic problem that had first drawn it into investment banking. The next chief executive would need to be someone who could persuade big corporate clients to do capital markets business with Barclays as well as being able to manage the trading business.

It was still only a year after Big Bang. British corporate financiers had little direct experience of capital markets since the merchant banks where they learned their craft had until 1986 been prevented by Stock Exchange rules from working directly in securities markets. As a result, they lacked first-hand knowledge of running a capital markets deal. American investment bankers understood exactly how such markets worked but few of them knew their way around the City or the UK's corporate boardrooms. Bycroft needed to find someone familiar with both the City and the capital markets. It was a small field but he thought he knew just the man.

David Band was the son of an Edinburgh doctor, educated in the

1950s at Rugby, the English public school made famous by *Tom Brown's Schooldays*, and emerging with confidence and good connections to study French and German at Oxford. From there he joined J. P. Morgan in London in 1964 and soon demonstrated an ease with clients and an instinctive feel for the bond markets. His star rose rapidly. By 1976, he was running J. P. Morgan's South-east Asian operations from Singapore. He moved as general manager to Paris and then to New York as a senior vice-president in charge of international capital markets. In 1987, when Bycroft came calling, he was running J. P. Morgan in London. [6]

It was quite an honour. The great John Pierpont Morgan and the bank he founded dominated American corporate and banking life in the late nineteenth and early twentieth centuries and was still a force to be reckoned with. It chose both its clients and its staff carefully. J. P. Morgan exuded discreet power. The bank's traditional headquarters at 23 Wall Street bore no name; everyone knew the building simply as the House of Morgan. The culture was calm, considered and meticulous. Trainees of a previous generation were taught the rudiments of banking and even how to fold the *Wall Street Journal* lengthwise on a crowded subway train to be able to read it while other travellers sweated away. To become a J. P. Morgan client said something about a firm's quality; to become an employee suggested you were a person of integrity and discretion.

Senior people rarely left J. P. Morgan but Bycroft had noticed that Band had lost out in a management reshuffle at the end of 1986 and thought that he was worth approaching. If Band could be tempted to leave J. P. Morgan, BZW would capture a man reputed to have the skills it needed to make the next step in investment banking.

Band was a keen skier and tennis player, stayed slim and tanned and was always beautifully dressed in expensive shirts and suits. With bright eyes, a Roman nose and light brown swept-back hair, he cut an impressive figure. He proved to be an easier hire than Bycroft or Jacomb expected. Band enjoyed a drink, which did not sit well with J. P. Morgan's discreet style, and his career there had already peaked. They politely expressed their regrets at his resignation but did not get in the way. On 10 February 1988 BZW announced Band's appointment as its new chief executive.

'LOOK AT MY WAD!'

The late 1980s and early 90s were the years when most of the British public first became aware of the City. Prime Minister Thatcher's vision of a share-owning democracy had led to the privatization of state-owned enterprises such as British Telecom and British Gas. Millions of people became stock market investors for the first time, lured by the prospect of shares at a discount and television advertisements exhorting them to let their friends in on the story: 'If you see Sid, tell him,' ran the punchline of a famous commercial for British Gas shares.

Global stock markets ripped up and down as the British and American governments' deregulation of business and markets and reduced taxation of personal and corporate income allowed the animal spirits to run loose. It was the age of the yuppies and their Sloane Ranger girlfriends. They drank and they drove Flaming Ferraris. News bulletins showed agitated young men in fashionable striped shirts and braces yelling down their phones in dealing rooms the size of football fields. The action was gripping, especially at moments such as Black Monday, 19 October 1987, when after an unexpected rise in US interest rates from 8.75 to 9.75 per cent – with London paralysed after freak winds – markets fell by nearly a quarter in two days.

Publicized by the government's privatizations, the drama of volatile markets and the theatre of the dealing room, the City infiltrated popular culture. Buying and selling, working hard and playing hard, looking after number one replaced old-fashioned attitudes such as loyalty, commitment and community. In pre-Thatcher, pre-Big Bang Britain, it was poor form to speak openly about money; after Big Bang, it was exactly what everyone was talking about. In 1988 the comedian Harry Enfield's first words as a plasterer on the topical satire show *Friday Night Live* were: 'Look at that! Look at my wad! I've got loadsamoney.' The phrase promptly entered the national lexicon.[7]

It was exciting, racy and looked very glamorous. But after a promising first year, Big Bang stopped working for the firms that were trying to take advantage of it. Lower charges encouraged investors to deal more but the increase in trading volume was not enough to compensate for the reduction in commission on each share traded, nor was market making the profitable business the new firms hoped it would be. Combined with rising staff costs and expensive technology this meant that few of the businesses that had been put together made money and BZW was no exception. Between 1987 and 1991, it barely covered its costs. It never made an acceptable return on the £1 billion of capital it employed, let alone justified the amount of time that Barclays' senior management had to spend on it. In 1991, under pressure from the board and shareholders, Band took an axe to the sprawling BZW empire, closing some businesses, including the only recently expanded US equities operation, and laying off 10 per cent of the staff.[8]

This surgery was accompanied by the transfer of all of Barclays' money market and treasury operations from the clearing bank into BZW, a sleight of hand that made the investment bank look better and briefly took the pressure off. Treasury and money markets involved low-risk trading of IOUs issued by governments and financial institutions in return for short-term cash. It was an old bank business, staffed by old City dealing types and more akin to traditional banking than new investment banking and the gift of such a profitable business increased the hostility felt by the traditional corporate bankers towards BZW. But the move had the effect of boosting BZW's published results for 1992 to £304 million, more than the total it had earned during the rest of its existence, and BZW suddenly felt good about itself. It felt even better in 1993, when favourable markets, privatization work and some clever corporate finance deals helped it to profits of £501 million and a return on capital of over 40 per cent.[9] These were spectacular results: every £100 that had been invested in the business produced a return of £40 that year. If that could be sustained, BZW would have paid everything back to shareholders in a couple more years.

Band had a slight Scots accent with an American euro-banker drawl and a manner of speaking in mangled sentences that sometimes baffled his audience but he knew his way around the UK corporate circuit. He had a good instinct for customers' needs and understood the bond markets. His vision for BZW, like that of its founder Camoys, was for it to become a global bank like J. P. Morgan, and by the end of 1993 it looked as though he had pulled it off.

If the story had stopped then, everyone would have been happy. Band, although now drinking heavily, was delivering. Barclays' board was enjoying the plaudits from shareholders for sticking with investment banking. BZW's staff had grown from 1,300 at the time of Big Bang to nearly 6,000 and shared a £100 million bonus pool; Bycroft's firm had recruited over one hundred of them. Search had become a big business and Bycroft and his ilk had used the demand for qualified people to ratchet up pay in the City. In the 1970s, partners lived in nice houses in Kent and took holidays in Tuscany; others travelled in from the suburbs and went on package holidays. In the 1990s, twenty-somethings with three years' experience were demanding six-figure compensation and thought nothing of flying off to Vegas for a stag weekend, while their bosses now lived in Chelsea and holidayed in yachts off the Côte d'Azur. For those on the inside, be they brokers, bankers or the search consultants who placed them, every ticket was golden.

3

The Scholar's Tale, 1986–93

HOGG'S APPRENTICE

For most people, however, Britain was a miserable place in the chilly winter of 1992–3. Unemployment was rising to 3 million, the hoped-for economic recovery that had helped John Major's Conservatives win the general election of April 1992 had yet to materialize and an IRA bombing campaign was causing fear on the streets. Bookmakers slashed the odds on the monarchy's survival after the Prince and Princess of Wales announced that they were to separate. The establishment was creaking and the nation sensed it.

But in an elegant second-floor office deep in London's Fitzrovia just north of Oxford Street, one of the country's most promising young managers pondered his own future with optimism. He was widely admired in the City and in Fleet Street and was tipped for business stardom. He stared out over the busy junction of Margaret Street and Great Titchfield Street, aware that he would soon need to make an important career decision; one opportunity in particular intrigued him.

John Martin Taylor was born in Lancashire in 1952, the son of a Burnley accountant. His father died suddenly when Martin (he never used his first name) was eight years old, leaving his mother to bring up him and his younger brother and Martin was sent away to boarding school a week after his father's death. Despite these traumas he stood out as the brightest boy in his year, coped easily with schoolwork and at the age of ten was in a class of twelve-year-olds, isolated from his own age group but ready to take the entrance exams for the schools that educated Britain's elite.

He had to wait two years until he was old enough to do so, and then sat the Election to College at Eton. He was awarded one of the King's Scholarships for the brightest candidates, which not only brought help with the fees but special status within the school: the King's Scholars lived and ate together 'in College' and wore distinctive black gowns.

It was an unusual childhood, giving rise to both resilience and vulnerability. The rarefied atmosphere of College might have destroyed him but Taylor flourished. Back home in Burnley, his brother teased him for having become a posh southerner but he took it in good part.

His interests were eclectic and he was intellectually confident. After specializing in physics, mathematics and chemistry at school, he switched subjects completely when he sailed into Balliol, one of the premier Oxford colleges and nursery of statesmen, to read English. According to one alumnus, the former prime minister H. H. Asquith, Balliol bred 'the tranquil consciousness of an effortless superiority'. Less than a year in, Taylor changed again, this time to oriental studies, an audacious move which required him to learn Mandarin, and probably cost him the first-class degree to which he had otherwise seemed destined.

Taylor looked for a job straight after graduation. At Oxford he had dabbled in student journalism, which helped him get a place on the sought-after training scheme run by the Reuters news organization. He specialized in financial journalism and after four years joined the *Financial Times*, eventually becoming the lead writer on *Lex,* the paper's sharpest and most acerbic business column. He was fluent and witty in print and in person and by 1982 had established himself at the cutting edge of business journalism.

Working at the *Financial Times* brought young Taylor into contact with many of Britain's top business people, including Christopher Hogg, chief executive and chairman of Courtaulds. An old conglomerate with interests in textiles, paints and packaging, Courtaulds like many such businesses, was facing huge problems. Britain was in recession, the Thatcher government was battling inflation and the unions and Courtaulds' portfolio needed reshaping. Taylor often commented in *Lex* on the problems of such industrial companies, and Hogg persuaded him that it would be more fulfilling to manage one than write about them. In 1982 he resigned from the *Financial Times*, turned down several lucrative City jobs and at the age of thirty joined Courtaulds as Hogg's assistant, taking a pay cut to do so.[1]

From the outset, Taylor knew that this would be a long haul. Hogg had already been at Courtaulds for over ten years and he expected a similar commitment from his protégé. Hogg made him learn textiles from the factory floor, moving him around the departments and progressively promoting him. In 1987 Taylor became managing director of the textiles group and in 1990, as chief executive, led its demerger from the rest of Courtaulds with Hogg as his chairman.[2]

Taylor was a success as chief executive of the new Stock Exchange listed company, raising productivity, investing in new technology and holding profits steady in tough markets. In the 1992 annual report he told shareholders: 'The story of Courtaulds Textiles over the last few years is essentially one of a smaller number of better qualified people working harder in more difficult circumstances to produce similar returns.'[3] Shareholders and the press loved his analytical approach but in reality this was a medium-sized business facing intractable strategic issues.

Courtaulds Textiles was a manufacturer but the future was in branded clothing, which would require a total transformation of the business. At the time of the demerger, Taylor had told Hogg that he would do a further three years and the board was cautious about embarking on such a radical change with a chief executive who was now in the later stages of his time there. As he stared out over Fitzrovia in March 1993 it began to feel right to get out of the way, and Taylor let the search firms know that he was ready to move on. His phone had already started to ring with some interesting offers but the one that really tempted him was the chief executive's job at Barclays.

'IN THE POO BY '92'

From his *Financial Times* desk at Bracken House in the shadow of St Paul's Cathedral and then his office in Fitzrovia, Taylor had been watching Barclays with bemusement for nearly twenty years.

Thatcher's free market economy was in full swing, institutional shareholders were demanding changes in corporate governance, yet as late as 1986, the penultimate year of Timothy Bevan's time in the chair, Barclays seemed to be in denial.

The challenges at this stage came in the corporate and retail bank rather than BZW. Competition, which had stepped up in the 1970s following the end of the cartel, intensified in the 1980s. Now that banks had to disclose more information, shareholders were able for the first time to compare their financial performance, and the banks responded by competing for market share and profits. In 1984 Midland revolutionized retail banking by waiving bank charges for customers who stayed in credit. Customers flocked to Midland and by the end of the year all banks had to follow suit. The 'shareholder value' revolution – companies should be run in the interests of shareholders rather than other stakeholders – was in full swing and was being modelled most famously by 'Neutron Jack' Welch, chairman of GE.[4] Encouraged by reward schemes that paid out if share price targets were reached and by professional fund managers who were themselves measured on the quarterly performance of their share portfolios, executives sought to emulate Welch, sometimes sacrificing longer-term shareholder value in the interests of immediate profits. This was dangerous in every industry but especially so in banking. Banks could boost short-term profits by lending to less creditworthy borrowers but this left them vulnerable to defaults whenever the economy turned down.

This is exactly what happened in British banking in the 1980s, though not to Barclays under Bevan, who stood resolute and refused to chase market share. But then in August 1986 the banks released their results for the first half of the year and National Westminster's profits of £482 million turned out to be 10 per cent bigger than Barclays'. It was a shock to a bank that had been top of the pile ever since true banking profits had been published in 1970. Critics said Barclays under Bevan was drifting sideways at a time when the rest of the industry was reinventing itself, that it was stuck in a paternalistic time warp with no idea where to go next or who to turn to – traits allegedly personified in its chairman.

Such criticism was too harsh. Bevan's conservative lending policies saved Barclays from loading up the balance sheet at the top of the economic cycle. The bank had kept pace with innovative retail developments such as free-if-in-credit current accounts, Saturday opening and a more relaxed atmosphere in branches.[5] Nor was he a stuffed shirt who couldn't look beyond the immediate circle. Andrew Buxton was waiting in the wings but Bevan thought Buxton was too young to succeed him. In his opinion the best candidate was John Quinton, a grammar school and Cambridge-educated son of the manager of a Barclays' branch in Norfolk. With the board's agreement, Bevan declared overwhelming support for Quinton and in 1987 he became the first non-family chairman of modern times.

Quinton had worked in a Barclays' branch during the university holidays when he was a student. Bespectacled and slightly overweight, he looked like a 1950s bank manager even as a youth. He joined Barclays straight from university in 1953 and moved smartly up the ladder to the manager's job at Barclays' King's Cross branch. He was seconded to the civil service but returned to take up board membership from 1982 and in 1985 became a vice-chairman under Bevan.

Bevan's conviction that his duty was to the bank's long term enabled him to resist the temptation to chase market share but Quinton, although no less of a company man, saw things differently. The mood in the bank was for action to recapture market leadership from National Westminster and Quinton decided that this could be achieved by further improving customer service and liberalizing the bank's lending policy. Barclays' branch staff were encouraged to greet customers with the kind of welcoming 'open for business' smile that McDonald's was bringing to the fast food industry. In 1987 Barclays introduced Connect, Britain's first debit card. Soon Barclays trumpeted that it had more cash points, longer opening hours and a better in-branch experience than any of its rivals.[6]

Its more modern image was also projected by sponsorship of the Football League (and later the Premier League) as football cleaned up its act after the hooligan-besmirched 1980s. Quinton, a Tottenham Hotspur season ticket holder, was shown presenting trophies to the championship-winning teams. The timing was good: Barclays' logo was frequently picked up by the television cameras, including those of Sky, the aggressive new station making the running in sports broadcasting. As far as the outside world was concerned, Barclays was on the up.

While modernization was a success, however, the second part of Quinton's plan, a more liberal lending policy, proved to be a serious error. Banking chiefs have to decide whether the economy is at a stage when it is safe to put 'risk on' by encouraging customers to borrow or whether it is time to take 'risk off' by adopting a more cautious approach to lending. Quinton got this badly wrong. He decided that it was not too late to join the residential and commercial property lending boom that Bevan had wisely avoided. With Quinton determined to catch up, Barclays' exposure to property, construction and housing more than doubled in 1987 and 1988.[7]

Some of the money Barclays lent came from shareholders in a deeply unpopular rights issue in March 1988 and they were getting restless. In the last quarter of the twentieth century, financial institutions managing pension funds and pooled savings replaced private individuals as the main owners of stock market listed companies. These asset managers – sometimes called 'fund managers' or simply 'institutions' – were well organized and, empowered by the theory of shareholder value, expected to be listened to. Many were sceptical about what they saw as Barclays' ill-timed dash for growth, a perception exacerbated by Quinton's slogan of 'Number 1 by '91', a reference to his determination to overtake National Westminster. 'In the poo by '92', replied the cynics. There was nearly a shareholders' revolt against the rights issue, but in the end the big institutions decided that it would be more damaging to their investments to cancel the issue than to proceed with it.

The rights issue had barely been completed when, in May 1988, just as shareholders had feared, the Thatcher government raised interest rates to slow down the UK's overheating economy. Quinton imposed a partial cap on lending to the property sector but it was too late. The housing and commercial property markets crashed and it was clear that Quinton had expanded at the top of the credit cycle. Barclays' results for 1991, released early in 1992, showed profits down 30 per cent, a flat dividend for shareholders and £1.5 billion of provisions against bad debts.[8]

Shareholders complained to analysts, the press and Barclays' non-executives about the poor results. Analysts made unfavourable comparisons with their new pin-up, Lloyds, led by the down-to-earth Brian Pitman and his brilliant chairman, Sir Jeremy Morse. Quinton, who had himself been knighted in 1990, was further criticized for accepting a request from his friend Eddie George, governor of the Bank of England, to release his able finance director, Brian Pearse, to rescue Midland Bank following its calamitous acquisition of a US bank appropriately named Crocker, and again when he took on extra work (even though he had undergone heart by-pass surgery in 1990) by becoming chairman of the Premier League. There were members of the board who felt that he should be spending more time on Barclays, not less.

Buxton was now clearly the heir apparent. After thirty years at Barclays he had certainly been waiting for a long time. He had joined the bank on the Special List in 1963, done his time in the branches, worked with distressed borrowers after the lending boom of the early 1970s and acted as BZW's chief executive following Camoys' stroke.[9] Bevan appointed him to the board in 1984 and made him vice-chairman of the bank in 1985; in 1988 Quinton made him managing director, with responsibility for all domestic banking matters.[10]

Shareholder discontent, Quinton's distractions and Buxton's presence as a viable alternative finally told. By 1992, the Barclays board was only just over half the size of the thirty-one-member body that had waved through the investment banking proposal ten years before. The UK's newly powerful institutions expected boards to include independent non-executives capable of challenging the executive directors on their behalf but Barclays was a halfway house between the old and new styles. Most of the family members and time-serving directors had gone but they had been replaced by the great and the good drawn from the upper echelons of the public sector and the bank's client base. The nineteen members included Sir Peter Middleton, a former permanent secretary at HM Treasury, who would come to play an important part in Barclays' history; Sir Michael Franklin, another former permanent secretary, though from a rather less prestigious Whitehall department, the Ministry of Agriculture, Fisheries and Food; Sir Peter Wright, a former head of the diplomatic service; and the star turn, Lord (Nigel) Lawson, Margaret Thatcher's chancellor of the exchequer from 1983 until 1989, when he resigned after a disagreement on exchange rate policy. It was not quite the dynamic board envisaged by the institutions though the nineteen members did include at least three heavyweight businessmen of the kind they wanted.

Sir Denys Henderson, who had been on the board since 1983, chaired Barclays' Compensation Committee. He was a plain speaker who, as chairman of ICI, had fought off Hanson Industries in 1991. His Compensation Committee included another blunt businessman, Sir Derek Birkin, a grammar school boy from the Yorkshire coal-fields, who became chairman of the mining company RTZ and had been a Barclays' board member since 1990. The third heavy hitter was Sir Nigel Mobbs, a Barclays' board member since 1979, who was chairman of his family property company, Slough Estates, and whose amiable manner hid forthright views.

These three did exactly what non-executive directors were meant to do in this new world by representing shareholders' interests; in the matter of the chairmanship, however, they could not entirely shake off old habits and turned to the family. Quinton, who would complete forty years' service in mid-1992 thus entitling him to a full pension, was told that Buxton would take over immediately as chief executive before adding the chairmanship at the end of the year when Quinton retired. By appointing Buxton as chief executive and chairman designate Barclays were defying the Cadbury Committee, an official inquiry into corporate governance, which had recently recommended that such roles be split. Buxton was warned that in due course Barclays would have to comply.[11] Taylor's successors at the *Lex* column regarded Buxton's appointment as 'perplexing' and said he 'must take a share of the blame for the lax cost control which has been a substantial part of Barclays' problem.'[12]

Buxton did not hold both roles for long, though it was bad debts rather than corporate governance or poor cost control that precipitated further change. When the results for 1992 were released, the dividend to shareholders was cut to below the level paid in 1988 and bad debt provisions of £2.5 billion dragged the bank into loss. Buxton had been in charge of domestic banking at Barclays when many of these loans were made; if he didn't know about them at the time, said critics in Fleet Street and the City, then he should have done. What followed was a brutal demonstration of how power at Barclays had finally shifted from family custodians to cold-eyed shareholders and professional non-executive directors. The route led straight to Martin Taylor's office in Fitzrovia.

4

The Changing of the Guard, 1994

THE MESSENGER IN THE NIGHT

He zipped the white cotton overalls over his pinstriped suit and drew the hood tightly round his head. Rubber boots next, then a mask. He never wore gloves for such purposes. He stepped through the door onto the roof of the Bank of England building, moved cautiously towards the box he had left in the corner, watching and listening intently, hardly daring to move. Then, joy: not one but two, three and four bees flew into the hive.

It was an early summer day in 1993 and Robin Leigh Pemberton was in the last weeks of his ten-year stint as governor. By the time the honey was ready he would have retired to his farm in Kent. This ruddy-faced gentleman banker had impressed the City through decency and common sense. He had dealt with the wreckage of two failed banks, Johnson Matthey in 1984 and Bank of Credit and Commerce International in 1991. He had guided the Bank of England through the taming of inflation in the Howe–Lawson years, Big Bang and the sterling crisis of 1992, in which interest rates were raised to 15 per cent. He was too modest a man to claim the credit but he had been a steadying influence and it had been a successful governorship.

A few hundred yards away stood 54 Lombard Street where Barclays' head office was in the last stages of another major reconstruction. Leigh Pemberton's City contacts told him that the company itself also needed a make-over, and with no wish to preside over another banking rescue, he had made his views known to the non-executives.

A few hundred yards in the other direction at 33 King William

Street were the shiny new offices of Mercury Asset Management. The glass and steel lifebelt round the midriff of its stone tower symbolized the Thatcherite functionalism, at the cutting edge of which stood Mercury, that had been founded as Warburg Investment Management in 1969 by the merchant bank Warburg. Over the next twenty years, it and other financial institutions managing the savings and pension contributions of millions of people created the whole new industry of institutional fund management. Mercury was one of the stars. Following Warburg's flotation of 25 per cent of the business in April 1987, it was a quoted company itself; by 1993, its pension fund clients owned 5 per cent of all the other companies listed on the London Stock Exchange.[1]

Mercury's fund managers were bright and challenging, none more so than Carol Galley, the head of its UK pension fund business. Galley had started at Warburg as a graduate librarian and had worked her way to the top of a male-dominated City. Elfin and elegant, she was reputed to be the highest-paid woman in Britain. She was formidably incisive, dismissive of time wasters but had an engaging sense of humour. She was known as 'the Ice Maiden' for her coolness under pressure, and colleagues said that nothing annoyed her more than an incompetent chief executive.

After observing the bad business decisions of the last few years and a flat share price, she had come to view Barclays' top management with disdain. To her practised eye, it looked a throwback to the worst of pre-Thatcher British management. Mercury's analysts and fund managers discussed the matter. They decided that it would be better for both Mercury and the bank to engage with it and to speak to other shareholders about a joint approach to the board rather than simply sell the shares.

One fellow institution that Mercury knew very well was the Prudential's fund management arm. Like Mercury, it was one of the UK's largest stock market investors and took a similar approach to large underperforming companies. Its chief executive was Mick Newmarch, who had joined the Prudential as a clerk straight from school. He was a burly man, nicknamed 'the Bruiser' for his direct style of doing business. In the winter of 1992–3 Barclays was in the Prudential's sights too.

Barclays' results for 1992 were expected to be poor and the institutions were clearly fed up. Buxton's appointment as both chairman and chief executive in defiance of the Cadbury Report gave them their opening. 'The Bruiser', 'the Bee Keeper' and 'the Ice Maiden' reached the same conclusion: something or someone would have to change at the top of Barclays.[2]

The protagonists asked David Mayhew, a senior partner of Barclays' stockbrokers Cazenove, to raise their concerns with the board. Mayhew was the 'messenger in the night' in many City dramas and at the time the single most influential intermediary between British companies and their shareholders. In 1988 he was one of several people arrested in connection with a scheme to keep the Guinness plc price high in support of its bid for Distillers. Three people went to jail but the case against Mayhew was dropped in 1992. Throughout this long ordeal, Cazenove stuck by him and he remained at the centre of many significant corporate transactions while he was under investigation. It was typical of his discretion that few people at Barclays ever knew that he was a distant member of one of their founding families, the Tukes, and had been brought up by his Quaker grandmother on the Friends' prayers and principles.

Mayhew's market judgement was exceptional and he had an open line to the City's top investors. He told one of Barclays' corporate heavyweights, Mobbs, that some of their heavy hitters were unhappy. With the warning coming from a man such as Mayhew, Mobbs needed no second bidding and briefed Henderson and Birkin. In March, with the Bank of England pressing in the background and the leading shareholders demanding action, they told Buxton that the time had come to split his role.

A DIFFERENT KIND OF BANKER

Executive search had matured since Bycroft's early days. He made a very good living moving traders and investment bankers around the City, but his own industry had stratified and there was now a super-league of headhunters who controlled entry into British boardrooms. One of these was Spencer Stuart, a well-established global partnership which was close to Barclays. David Kimbell, chairman of its London office, was a jovial former British Leyland executive who had done work for ICI, where Denys Henderson was chairman. It was therefore perhaps not surprising that Henderson should call Kimbell to say that Barclays would be splitting the roles of chairman and chief executive. 'Come and meet the board and give us your thoughts. We are looking for a different kind of banker.'

Kimbell wanted to give Barclays some international options and brought Dayton Ogden, a US colleague, over for the pitch. They produced a short list of three external candidates: Michael Carpenter, a senior executive at GE in the US; Charles Miller Smith, at the time finance director of Unilever; and 41-year-old Courtaulds' chief executive Martin Taylor. The list rapidly shrank: Carpenter would be too expensive and Miller Smith soon withdrew. Taylor, however, was an interesting proposition, so Kimbell took up some informal references, then told Barclays he was a strong candidate.

Taylor's first interview was over breakfast with Henderson in a pretty eighteenth-century townhouse owned by ICI in Smith Square, round the corner from head office in Millbank. They already knew each other because ICI had just spun off its pharmaceutical business and Courtaulds had provided friendly advice based on its own demerger experience. Nonetheless Taylor was nervous. He had put his own name forward, saying to another head hunter: 'Why don't they tap me up for Barclays?' Sitting across the table from Henderson, Taylor was not sure whether in this situation he was the hunter or the hunted. He was very keen to get the job.

Taylor has a light, agile voice and words usually tumble out in well-constructed bursts, but that morning he said very little. While his guest tucked into scrambled eggs and bacon, Henderson described Barclays as 'in a pickle' and mentioned the pressure from the institutions. After talking solidly for an hour and a half, he suddenly said: 'We don't know what to do. Could you be of any use to us?' It was the first question Taylor had been asked. 'Yes, probably,' he replied and agreed to meet Buxton.

Buxton had just been leant on by the board and told to separate the two parts of his job. After initially playing for time, he had agreed with good grace. Now the tall, upright, handsome Guardsman, thirty years a banker, was meeting the clever journalist-turned-businessman who had no direct banking experience. It could have been awkward but was surprisingly easy. If he was sceptical, Buxton was too well mannered to let it show.

Buxton was the last serving board member of the Barclays Quaker line and the last of the old-school bankers for whom lending was a relationship business. His passion was shooting and other country sports. Weekend house guests in Suffolk would be wakened on a Saturday morning by blasts from a .22 rifle as Buxton, still in his pyjamas, shot rabbits from his bedroom window. When in London, he liked to swim at the RAC club's lovely pool in Pall Mall. He was a decent man – too decent in many ways for the world of pushy shareholders and aggressive investment bankers in which he was now operating.

Taylor was also a good-looking man but in a different way. Women fell for his lively intelligence, blue eyes and fair hair – slightly longer than military length. His slender frame did not look as though it could handle a shotgun, let alone a Guards' assault course. Temperamentally he and Buxton were from different planets: the London intellectual and the East Anglian countryman; the lover of classical music and the Tory squire; Picasso and Constable.

After first meeting at Spencer Stuart's offices close to Marble Arch, they had dinner and some nice wine at the flat the Buxtons used above Barclays' Sloane Square branch. Jane Buxton cooked supper, Andrew Buxton asked Taylor some questions, they discussed how they would work together and over coffee, Buxton suggested that they announce everything the following week with the bank's results. Though he did not say it, the vacancy – which had been rumoured since early March and confirmed later that month – had been around for too long and they were terrified of a leak. Taylor was taken aback. It seemed premature, terms had not been agreed and he wanted time to reflect. He was about to go on a family holiday to a remote part of the Massif Central in France. He needed to breathe deeply and discuss with his family what life would be like in the spotlight. He would give a decision when he returned in two weeks.

While Taylor was away, Henderson also did some thinking. Taylor had a good reputation in the City. He was witty, fluent and thoughtful and handled questions calmly and confidently – but he would be a high-risk appointment. Courtaulds was a small company in a different industry. Its profits were less than £50 million and it employed only 22,000 people; Barclays made fifteen times as much money and employed five times as many.[3] Courtaulds was important in its own industry but otherwise insignificant; as far as the press were concerned, it was a curiosity whereas Barclays was an obsession. Could Taylor make the step up?

Henderson told Kimbell to double-check his references, so he went to see Sir Christopher Hogg, by this time chairman of Reuters. 'Would this be the right move for Martin and the right move for Barclays?' Kimbell asked. Hogg was emphatic: 'It's right for both. Martin needs a challenge and Barclays needs a fresh mind. It's a fantastically clever idea. Anything I can do to help, I will.'

Kimbell reported back to the board, who were unanimous. Taylor returned from France and confirmed his acceptance. Buxton, who had opposed some other candidates, pushed for Taylor as hard as anyone. His appointment was announced on Thursday 19 August 1993: he would join the board on 1 November and become chief executive on 1 January 1994. As the *Sunday Telegraph* remarked: 'he may not be a banker but then just look at the mess bankers have made of banking in the last two decades.'[4]

A BREATH OF FRESH AIR

Martin Taylor strode briskly past the joggers and dog walkers enjoying the grassy mounds of Greenwich Park in mid-August 1993. He did a lot of his thinking in the park's leafy acres, and in the days before his appointment to Barclays was announced, he pondered carefully the approach he would take. He believed that banking was stuck in the past and decided to demonstrate from the start that under his leadership, things would change. On the day his appointment became public, he wore the conventional bankers' uniform of dark suit, striped tie and laced brogues. But the following day, for his media interviews he had changed into a designer suit, soft blue shirt and flowery tie.[5]

He attended two board meetings and an executive committee away day as chief executive designate and spent an anxious Christmas in Blackheath shocked at what he had seen. When he finally took over as chief executive he laid down a marker: 'If at the end of two years – and two years is a deliberate time frame – the bank has no direction, then that will be my fault.'[6]

He was appalled by the ad hoc practices he had observed: 'I am absolutely astonished that what seems to me to be ordinary management principles are not yet established in this industry.' Barclays was 'stuffy, pompous and snobbish', lacked a 'strong group identity', was 'far too status conscious' and had 'old fashioned military traditions'.[7] His frankness excited younger staffers at Barclays, but other observers wondered about the inner thoughts of chairman Buxton, the board and senior management, who had presided over the practices Taylor so despised.

It was also a very confident call from a man who had no practical experience of banking. His induction into Barclays was perfunctory compared to his eleven-year journey at Courtaulds. He had never worked in a branch, sat at a till or helped old ladies fill out cheques. He had never been hunched over a terminal, had his gut wrenched by swings in markets or felt the pressure from a desk head screaming for profit before the markets closed. He was a critic and businessman, albeit a very good one, rather than a banker. He could easily see what was wrong but had no operational experience of banking to guide his solutions.

For three years, this did not seem to matter. The British economy recovered from the 1991–2 recession and Barclays' results recovered with it. Taylor played it well, being careful not to claim credit for work done before he had arrived and stating that profit should be treble the £664 million reported a few weeks after he started.[8]

He got the 'risk on or risk off' decision right, telling his bankers to expand the loan book as the economy recovered and cut back as it peaked.[9] He introduced computer models to manage risk and stronger processes to monitor performance. The years 1994–6 were the centre of his reign, as he rebuilt profits through asset disposals, reductions in staff numbers and lower provisions for bad debts. The most dramatic year was the first, 1994, when just as he had promised, profits trebled as the economy recovered. Reflecting on the year that had just been completed, Taylor said: 'So far, the improvement has been largely accounted for by making the bank smaller. But now we have a real chance of making the business strong. There is real momentum developing.'[10]

1995 was a harder year. City analysts said that other banks, notably Lloyds, were cutting costs and growing revenues faster, but Taylor had a card up his sleeve.[11] Asset reductions and the sale of businesses had enabled Barclays to build up a capital reserve.[12] Unlike conventional bankers, who often squandered spare capital on questionable acquisitions, Taylor used his in a series of buy backs of the company's own shares, which had the effect of increasing the value of those that remained in circulation. The last of these, in August 1996, followed a 15 per cent increase in interim profits, strong growth across the business and signs that Taylor's strategy was working.[13] The Bank of England was impressed with Barclays' direction and even encouraged it to consider buying the struggling NatWest. Discussions were held but the NatWest board was resistant, and Barclays had neither the appetite nor the money to mount a contested bid.[14]

It also had its hands full with one part of the group that was still occupying a disproportionate amount of senior management's time: BZW. Taylor of course knew that its record-breaking profits of £501 million in 1993 had been flattered by the inclusion of Barclays' Treasury profits. But there were also signs of progress, if not yet substantial profits, in the newer businesses. BZW had achieved success lead managing sterling denominated bond issues, privatization work at home and abroad, and had earned praise as well as revenue from an innovative tax scheme it had developed for corporate clients. Taylor wondered whether it might be on the verge of a breakthrough.

That was certainly what he heard in the boardroom, where he and Alastair Robinson, chairman of UK banking, were the only two executive directors without direct involvement, past or present, in the BZW camp. The chairman, Andrew Buxton, had helped to broker the deals that put BZW together between 1983 and 1986; the deputy chairman, Sir Peter Middleton, was also chairman of BZW; David Band was the chief executive of BZW; and Oliver Stocken, the group finance director, had joined Barclays Merchant Bank in 1979 and held several senior positions at BZW.

BZW was often discussed at board meetings in late 1993 and early 1994 and raised a lot of bullish enthusiasm. A little more investment, the BZW men argued, would see the investment bank pull clear of its British rivals and truly challenge the leading American firms. Taylor listened carefully and studied the numbers. He was much less convinced. Soon after he started he was forced to take a closer look at what would become the defining problem of his tenure.

5

A Dark Night in Essex, 1995

'LONG TALL SALLY'

In his first few weeks at Barclays Taylor received a stream of middle-aged Englishmen, all telling him what a great bank he was taking over and how their particular part of the business was the biggest jewel in the crown. There was one memorable exception. The head of human resources at BZW was female, American and about Taylor's age. Sally Bott was engaging, funny and very direct and had only just arrived at BZW from Citigroup, where she had worked in the tough environment of the trading floor. She had wound up in human resources because she was a good judge of people. She was slim and stylish and the bankers called her 'Long Tall Sally'.

In August 1993 she had taken a call from Bycroft's New York partner. She was expecting a pitch for business but instead he told her about an interesting job in the UK with an investment bank wanting a head of human resources. Would she be interested in meeting one of his London colleagues to discuss the situation?

Sally Bott had been at Citigroup for nearly twenty years and wanted to test herself somewhere else. It was now or never. She agreed to meet Bycroft on one of his regular visits to New York in one of his firm's meeting rooms high above Grand Central Station in what New Yorkers still call the Pan Am building.

Bycroft's crowd were traders and bankers but human resources were the gatekeepers to his business and he had met many of them. Sally Bott was something else. She was from the kind of firm Barclays wanted to be and would give the tree a much needed shake. She understood the business and knew it inside out: she talked numbers, detail and follow through and was streets ahead of anything he had heard from British HR people. Her directness shocked and excited him. 'The guy's a total jerk,' she had unhesitatingly said about one of Wall Street's most esteemed figures.

Bycroft set up a meeting for her with BZW's chairman, Middleton, and deputy chairman, Camoys, at the St Regis hotel off New York's 5th Avenue. He wasn't sure if they were ready for Sally Bott's brand of HR, but if the meeting went well he would get her to see their chief executive, Band.

When she arrived at the St Regis, Bott was directed up to the bedroom floors. It wasn't how Americans did things, but she smoothed her skirt and knocked on the door. The man who opened it introduced himself enthusiastically as Tom Camoys and ushered her into the sitting room of a grand suite, where Middleton, leaner and quieter, was waiting. They were all old-world charm and Bott tempered her style. They described BZW as the leading UK investment bank, owned by a well-capitalized and highly regarded parent and ready to tackle the established US players. Middleton told her: 'We are looking for a bit more than an HR person. We want someone to help us reach out for global talent.' She thought it was worth talking further and agreed to see Band a few days later.

That meeting took place over breakfast in the restaurant of another of New York's best hotels, the Carlyle. If nothing else, Bott thought, these guys do things in style. Band smoked, drank a lot of coffee and listened for half an hour while she ran through her CV. He asked no questions, but after she finished said suddenly: 'You've got the job.' It was far too quick and it made her suspicious. Did this bank always make decisions on such scant evidence? She insisted on meeting more people and on going to London to see things for herself.

She met more of BZW's senior managers on the London trip, then went back to New York and thought about it for a couple of weeks. She accepted the job in October and left Citigroup at Christmas, after tidying up for the bank's year-end.

She was invited to a BZW offsite meeting at another smart hotel, the Lanesborough in London, to observe the annual compensation meeting. This was one of the most important events in an investment bank's calendar. Department managers spent weeks preparing their pitches for staff bonuses. Their demands always exceeded the available pot and human resources and senior management would then moderate the claims.

It was an excitable meeting. Usually in British investment banking in the early 1990s bonuses came out of shareholders' funds because there were no profits to distribute. However, 1993 had been the best year in BZW's history, partly – but only partly – due to the continuing inclusion of Barclays' old-fashioned Treasury profits. Department managers had got wind of this and had submitted some ambitious bonus demands. The data sheets to back up the claims were thin, though, and the discussion about financial performance was superficial. Sally asked everyone present whether they knew how much capital they used, whether each unit was profitable and what the returns were like if they were adjusted for risk. The human resources managers seated round the table looked uncomfortable. They explained that with the American firms trying to hire all the best people, they had to take a strategic view and pay the market rate irrespective of the financial results.

When she had resigned from Citigroup, colleagues had told her that she was crazy and needed to see a psychiatrist if she was contemplating going somewhere like BZW. Her bosses recommended that she take a holiday to think it over, offered her a posting to any overseas location she cared to name and asked her to do anything but what she was intending. The Americans said she would talk too fast for them, that the British spoke a different language and that she would lose patience with their bumbling ways. After the Lanesborough meeting, she thought her old colleagues might be right, but it was too late to turn back. She reported for work at BZW in Swan Lane, EC4 on 3 January 1994 two days after Taylor's official starting date. The main building was smaller and dowdier than she had been used to but at least it was recognizable as an investment bank. That, however, was not where her office would be. She was taken across the street to another building where the 'support functions' were located; human resources and operations were crammed onto one floor. There was no air conditioning, the windows were sealed shut and the lighting was poor. Left alone in her office, she saw a mouse scurry across the floor, screamed and leapt onto the sofa.

There was a lot to do quite apart from dealing with the rodents. Bott started work at half-past six in the morning and was leaving at half-past ten at night. She had no idea the UK was that dark. She was advised to lengthen her skirts when walking the trading floors. Citigroup kept calling and offering her the old job back. She could see that people in the City were deluding themselves, thinking they were playing in the big league, but it was like taking a college baseball team to the World Series. They had no idea how far ahead the US firms were, and were just not experienced enough to compete with hardened Wall Street professionals. They had an inflated opinion of themselves, behaved like imperial lords and put tribal vendettas above the company's best interests. No one could beat Wall Street acting like that: you had to be lean, mean and together.

Her first sight of BZW's trading floor worried her. Bott asked herself: 'Where are the Pakistanis? Where are the Indians? Where are the Chinese? Where are the women?' Wall Street in the early 1990s was certainly not in perfect gender or ethnic balance but this was something else. She wondered what such lack of diversity said about the bank's underlying culture. How could a bank managed and staffed by men of a similar background compete in an industry that was already multi-cultural and global?

She was properly trained in financial analysis and studied the results. There were huge gaps in the numbers. Where was foreign exchange's contribution? Where was the bond business? Where were derivatives, the new financial instruments that were the talk of Wall Street? Could BZW's profits really be just the old Barclays' Treasury business? Did all the profits from trading equities, which happened in a separate department from trading fixed income bonds, get paid back to the staff? Was there no tie between financial performance and individual remuneration?

There were processes in place but nothing was as rigorous as she had been used to at Citigroup. She met staff who had failed pre-employment screening for drugs and alcohol but had been hired anyway and young people who had been thrust onto the trading floor without proper training. The New York office, where she discovered weak governance and compliance, problems with the regulators, overpaid staff and ongoing sexual harassment suits, was a particular concern to her. Sally wanted to tell someone and the new chief executive looked like exactly the right man.

REALITY DAWNS

Taylor and Bott met for the first time at the end of January 1994. She spoke about the lack of diversity and the old boy network. She told him that the City was living in the past. Band wanted BZW to be like J. P. Morgan but she warned Taylor that that would not happen without a transformation in people, process and culture. BZW was better than many other British banks but it was not in the global league and under present management never would be. At first Taylor thought she was a drama queen. Her message contrasted with the consistent bullishness he heard round the board table and he thought she must be exaggerating. A few days later, though, he was forced to change his mind.

An increase in US interest rates in February 1994 caught traders everywhere by surprise. Even the mighty Goldman Sachs felt the pain, reporting a sharp fall in profits and cutting back its London operations. But far from being the street-smart leader of the pack Taylor had heard about from the management, BZW seemed equally flat-footed and its profits halved in 1994. It was the following year that really persuaded Taylor there was a major problem. At one level Big Bang was proving a glorious success. London was firmly established as the global capital for cross-border financial services, with huge market shares in sectors such as international equities (64 per cent) and currency trading (27 per cent). The City contributed nearly a tenth of the government's tax receipts and had used that fact to secure enormous political influence. The number of people working in financial services had soared since 1986 to over half a million. They earned well above average salaries and stimulated the housing market in the commuter towns around London.

Despite the fact that the City's social and economic importance had been transformed by Big Bang, many of its institutions were still struggling. American banks were cross-subsidizing their entry into London from their hugely profitable home market, driving up staff costs and committing vast amounts of capital. The crunch came in 1995 when the investment banking strategies that the old merchant banks had dived into in 1986 unravelled spectacularly. In February, the venerable house of Barings was brought down by the fraudulent activities of a junior trader in Singapore, Nick Leeson. In May, Warburg, which had unwisely expanded its bond business in 1994 just as the markets crashed and then bungled an attempted merger with the American bank Morgan Stanley, sold itself to the Swiss Bank Corporation. In June, Kleinwort concluded that it was, after all, too small to compete and agreed to sell itself to the German bank Dresdner. The same month, Smith New Court reached the same conclusion and announced that it was to be taken over by the Wall Street giant Merrill Lynch.

This was a dramatic unfolding of the corporate strategies of the mid-1980s and it caused Taylor to reflect on what Barclays was trying to do. The assumption had been that British investment banks would be able to mount a direct challenge to the Americans, at least in the European markets. The bear market of 1994 exposed the fragility of this argument, and the bull market that began in 1995 confirmed it. The US investment banks swung smartly back into serious profit but BZW did not and Taylor privately started to question the future of his investment bank.

He decided that Bott was right: BZW was indeed delusional and had fooled itself into thinking that its time had come. The expensive recruits were failing to deliver, technology needed big investment and cultural tensions between the warring tribes had to be settled. Radical action was required.

An evening in December 1995 hardened his resolve. BZW was holding an offsite meeting for its senior management, with country heads flying in from all over the world to join their London colleagues. Band asked Taylor if he would join them, make a speech and answer a few questions and he agreed. The atmosphere over drinks and the meal was convivial and Taylor spoke for ten minutes outlining his vision for the bank. He knew how touchy BZW's senior management were and deliberately emphasized the importance of each of Barclays' four pillars of retail, commercial and investment banking and asset management. It was a mature and reflective speech that deserved a full discussion and Taylor invited questions.

After a few seconds, a hand went up. One of BZW's country heads asked: 'What are the prospects for our bonuses?' It was a crass question that told Taylor all he needed to know about the priorities of BZW's senior people and their commitment to the wider group. He groaned inwardly but gave a better answer than the question deserved, explained that the board recognized it had to build a business at BZW, that it had to put money in before getting returns but that the business had to do its bit too. In that context, he was concerned that BZW's results for the year were substantially behind budget.

No one said anything but the atmosphere changed. Suspecting that this information was new to the audience, he decided to check for himself and asked who was aware that they were a long way behind budget. Only the management committee raised their hands. The rest of the fifty or so people present were indeed unaware of the true level of profitability because Band held some costs centrally. With only a few days of the year remaining, Taylor knew that BZW's results were £150 million behind plan and only marginally better than 1994's slump – in contrast to the performance of its Wall Street rivals.[1]

Taylor tried to improve the meeting's mood before he and Band were driven back to London but he left behind a chastened crowd. Sitting in the back of the car as they drove through the dark Essex countryside, Band turned to Taylor: 'You shouldn't have told them all that, it will demoralize them.'

'Well, David,' said Taylor, 'the person who is most demoralized at the moment is me. I can see what you have done and I understand the need to keep morale up but actually we are fooling ourselves. The outside world isn't fooled and I'm the piggy in the middle between the demands of the shareholders on the one hand and the voracious expectations of your colleagues on the other. This kind of thing really doesn't help.'

Band paused. 'I know,' he admitted. 'I'm desperately worried about it. And I need to talk to you about it in the New Year. We need to make some plans.'

They began a review of the business in January 1996, and within a few weeks Charles Bycroft was on flight BA 179 to New York. He was quick off the plane, the late-night queues at immigration were short and he was in the plush art deco surroundings of the Carlyle hotel on New York's Upper East Side before midnight.

After a short sleep, and grateful for his overcoat in the Manhattan cold, he walked up 76th St, turned right along Park Avenue and strode in twenty minutes to No. 370, the grand Renaissance-style building that housed the New York Racquet and Tennis Club, one of Manhattan's most exclusive venues. He made his way into the imposing lobby, hung up his coat and was shown into a side room to wait for the man he had come all this way to meet: Robert E. Diamond.

6

The Dumb Money, 1996

A FISHING TRIP ON PARK AVENUE

At half-past seven on the morning of Tuesday 20 February a black town car drew up outside 370 Park Avenue. Bob Diamond got out, not wearing an overcoat but still warm from his early-morning workout. He asked his driver to come back in an hour, walked briskly into the New York Racquet and Tennis Club lobby, acknowledged the doorman's greeting and collected Charles Bycroft from the waiting room.

They climbed the marble stairs to the club's first-floor dining room and were shown to Diamond's favourite table, overlooking Park Avenue. A formally attired waiter brought water, juice and pre-printed order cards. Bycroft chose scrambled eggs and tea. Diamond went for his usual plate of cut fruit and coffee, made a note of it all and handed the card to the waiter.

The dining room, like the rest of the club, was for men only and the tables were generously spaced to allow for private conversation. A few members sat on their own and pairs talked quietly over breakfast, careful to respect rules that forbade business papers in the dining room. Over by the window, Bycroft began one of the most important hours of his year.

He had managed to get a meeting with Taylor the previous December and used it to float an idea. Wall Street's fixed income departments – those buying and selling parcels of debt issued by companies and governments, also known as bond trading – were booming in 1995 but BZW's were not, and Bycroft had noticed. 'Are you convinced,' he had asked Taylor, 'that the existing management team in fixed income is up to the job and if not can I help out?'

Taylor had seen for himself, when American investment banks such as Goldman Sachs, J. P. Morgan and Morgan Stanley pitched business propositions to him, that the top US firms had a greater depth and quality of management than he saw at BZW. The current head of fixed income, Sam Marrone, a former US Marine who had served in Vietnam prior to working on Wall Street, was no slouch. But was he, Taylor pondered, one of the really top people that could transform the business? He thanked Bycroft for the idea, promising to think about it, and a few days later attended Band's away-day in Essex. After reflecting over the Christmas break, Taylor called Bycroft: 'There is no retainer on this and no formal mandate. It is no win, no fee. But you can have the usual terms if you find us a new head of fixed income.'

Bycroft did not like fishing trips but the usual terms were a third of the first year's compensation. For a global fixed income head, this could be worth half a million dollars and was too good to miss. There were only three or four people in the world capable of doing the job to the level Taylor had in mind and fewer still would countenance moving to London to a firm with a retail banking culture. Bycroft knew from the outset that Diamond was his man.

A CAREER AT A CROSSROADS

Diamond's career had blossomed since he first travelled to Wall Street on the downtown train back in 1979. Chauffeur-driven cars were now his preferred means of travel. He had a wardrobe full of suits and his Church's shoes were highly polished. He was already a wealthy man, with a reputation as one of the world's best managers of a fixed income business. But surprisingly Diamond was currently out of work and at a career crossroads. After a long run of uninterrupted success, he had found his way blocked by two Wall Street titans, and if he was to make it to the summit of investment banking, his next move was crucial.

In 1981, Morgan Stanley had honoured its promise of a job on the trading floor, albeit in a junior position on what was known as the Repo desk, arranging short-term borrowing for dealers in government securities. Overnight rates rarely moved unexpectedly and Diamond was more of a bookkeeper than a trader. After six months, he was already frustrated. He grumbled to his girlfriend (and wife-to-be) Jennifer that he had been the top performer at US Surgical, was the only person Cook took with him to Morgan Stanley, had won the respect of Morgan Stanley's chief operating officer, but here he was, reconciling overnight trades. Cook's trade processing system had not yet kicked in, there were no computers to automate the process, no mobile phones to ease communications, just a lot of paper and coloured cards. He had mastered all there was to know about overnight Repos and was bored.

Then he got a break. Early in 1982, a senior trader announced that she was taking maternity leave. Her job required her to take a view on longer-term interest rates, which was the kind of trading that Diamond wanted to do. Luckily for him, Thomas Melzer, the man who had recruited him and Cook from US Surgical, was her boss too. Melzer gave Diamond a temporary promotion on the understanding that no matter how well he did, the senior trader would get her job back when she was ready. When the maternity leave ended, however, the trader decided to stay at home and Diamond's temporary job was made permanent.

Over the next few years he proved to be a very good trader and leader. He saw things from other people's point of view. He joined in the banter, stood his round in the pub, but never got stupidly drunk or went on to the girlie bars. He was hard but fair and people wanted to work for him. He progressed up the management ladder and in 1988 moved with his young family to London in order to take charge of all Morgan Stanley's fixed income trading outside the US. He stayed there until 1992 as the American firm built its business in Europe and Asia and worked its way into the British financial establishment.

One of the traders who worked for Diamond was the son of Jack Hennessy, chief executive of Credit Suisse First Boston (CSFB), which, like Morgan Stanley, was in the 'bulge bracket', the handful of leading US investment banks whose names very often appeared together on the front page of deal prospectuses. Hennessy kept hearing good things about Diamond and in 1991 unsuccessfully invited him for dinner several times. They finally met in New York late that year. 'Would you be interested,' Hennessy wanted to know, 'in running CSFB's Asian business from Tokyo?' The hook was a seat on CSFB's executive board, a position that was blocked at Morgan Stanley by Diamond's boss, the head of fixed income, John Mack.

Mack, eight years older than Diamond, was the son of first-generation Lebanese immigrants. After graduating from Duke University and working his way around the broking circuit for four years, he landed a job in bond sales at Morgan Stanley in 1972. By 1992 he was chairman of Morgan Stanley's operating committee and had a reputation as a tough, hard-charging business leader. He was already one of the leading investment bankers on Wall Street and was spoken of as a future chief executive of Morgan Stanley. But Diamond did not like his management style and was not sure whether Mack rated him either. If Mack did become chief executive, Diamond doubted that Morgan Stanley would be a place he wanted to work. He decided to meet the top Credit Suisse management in Zurich and informed Mack of what he was doing.

Diamond in recruiting mode at a rival firm would be a threat. Morgan Stanley offered him a lot of money to stay, said he would in due course join the management committee and floated the idea that he might eventually become the firm's chief operating officer. It did not sound like his idea of the dream job and nothing firm was on the table. Six weeks later, in January 1992 he handed in his resignation to join CSFB in Tokyo.

Losing Diamond was bad enough, but what soured the relationship was that he recruited a bunch of people to move with him, just as Morgan Stanley had feared. Mack claimed that a raid on this scale was underhand and destabilizing, but Diamond dismissed it as an accepted part of investment banking – as they both knew full well.

The move to CSFB brought Diamond up against the second titan. By the time he joined CSFB in 1990, two years before Diamond, Allen Wheat, the son of a nuclear scientist, was already a Wall Street legend. He was one of the founders of over-the-counter derivatives, a lucrative branch of the financial services industry developed in the 1980s in which investment banks devised intricate securities to solve clients' financial problems and sold them directly to customers away from the regulated glare of the public markets.

Wheat had made his name at Bankers Trust, which under his leadership came to dominate the new industry. But Bankers Trust's low credit rating put off some clients, and there were rumours that Wheat was unhappy with the provisions the bank insisted on making against his team's trades. In a devastating move – from which Bankers Trust never fully recovered – Wheat left for the AAA-rated CSFB, taking a team of twenty which had been responsible for about a quarter of Bankers Trust's profits. At CSFB, he created Credit Suisse Financial Products (CSFP), a firm within a firm, and the model of what he thought a global derivatives business should be: multi-product, managed globally and giving an unprecedented slice of revenues to its team. As an extra sweetener to their star recruit, in addition to running derivatives, Wheat was put in charge of Asia – a role that was also promised to Diamond.

Derivatives touched all product areas, including Diamond's bond and foreign exchange business. Disagreements about how much revenue Wheat's team would take on complex trades and about valuations of custom-built over-the-counter derivatives – let alone the fact that they had both been promised the same job – got their relationship off to a bad start, and although CSFB moved Diamond back to New York in the summer of 1994 as global head of fixed income and foreign exchange, an uncomfortable situation was developing.

Diamond had spent four years wrangling with Wheat, who was expected to become the next chief executive of CSFB. He struck Diamond as a man who was unlikely to let bygones be bygones. In January 1996 Diamond had enough money and a big enough reputation to resign without a job to go to.

After CSFB, Diamond had wondered whether he should return to teaching. He had the wealth to live a comfortable life on a teacher's pay but investment banking had changed him, as it changes everyone who works in it for any length of time. Anyone in the middle levels and above in investment banking earns enough money to live a different life from that lived by other people of their age: bigger houses, more exotic holidays, nicer clothes, better restaurants, priority lines at airports, the best hotels. The power is alluring too. You are at the centre of the action, working with dynamic people in an electric environment. You meet corporate chief executives, big investors and people from Washington. Tom Wolfe wrote of the hubristic Sherman McCoy in *The Bonfire of the Vanities*: 'On Wall Street he and a few others – how many? Three hundred, four hundred, five hundred? – had become precisely that . . . Masters of the Universe.'[1] Diamond was no Sherman McCoy but he was in the upper reaches of the real life top 300 and it was both too late and too soon to return to the quiet life. That was how he found himself sitting across the breakfast table from Bycroft in the New York Racquet and Tennis Club in February 1996.

Diamond had initially taken Bycroft's call coolly, but inwardly he was excited. Diamond thought that the City in 1996 was on the verge of a boom: the launch of the euro and European monetary union at the beginning of 1999 would lead to huge growth in European bond markets. This would be good for all banks, he believed, but particularly for the European firms, who at long last would have a domestic market comparable in size to the US bulge bracket's vast home market. The Europeans presently traded bonds issued by European governments and corporates in their own local currencies. The market was fragmented and none of its parts was big enough to attract the very largest issuers. Monetary union, Diamond thought, would change all this and was the Europeans' chance to create a market with real depth.

There would also be a boost to trading from Asia, where Diamond believed the capital markets were still in the early stages of lift-off. Europe was in the right time zone to do their investment banking business and to tap into the wealth of the Middle East. The city that would benefit most from this would be London. Paris and Frankfurt had aspirations but they did not have enough financially experienced people to challenge the City. If ever there was a time for a British bank to break into the big league, he thought, this was it.

Diamond was careful to give nothing of this thinking away to

Bycroft. 'What's the story?' he asked as their food arrived. Bycroft barely touched his breakfast while he outlined the opportunity at BZW. He took it gently, leaving plenty of room for Diamond to make up his own mind. It was very artfully done, portraying BZW as a talented but mixed-up teenager needing guidance. As Bycroft finished his pitch, though not his eggs, Diamond pursed his lips and stared hard at him for just a moment too long. 'I've blown it,' Bycroft thought. Then Diamond nodded. 'OK. Let me talk to them.'

The first meeting on Diamond's exploratory trip to Barclays at the end of February 1996 was with Sally Bott. They met for coffee before breakfast in a meeting room at the Dorchester in London's Park Lane – two Americans with over thirty years of Wall Street experience between them and inside knowledge of how the top investment banks worked. They were both straight speakers and pulled no punches. 'The place is a mess,' Bott told him. 'So I hear,' replied Diamond. 'But can it be turned round?' She thought carefully. 'Let's just say that there is a big opportunity.'

An hour later Diamond went downstairs to meet Taylor over breakfast. He struck Taylor as in a class above anyone at BZW and much more like the investment bankers from other firms who came pitching for Barclays' business. He was calm and controlled. He could be forceful but knew what he was talking about. Taylor could see that Diamond had done his homework. He said he would want to replace nearly everyone and that the money was not important to him, what mattered was the opportunity.

As he flew home, Diamond mulled over what he had heard. He felt that Barclays was a great bank that needed a capital markets arm if it was to remain great. It had a famous brand name and a strong credit rating, but the merchant bank's fixed income model was that of a pre-Big Bang broker dealer making no money outside the UK and focused on old products. He believed that a modern European investment bank should be global and integrated, whereas BZW was domestic and fragmented. Would Taylor give him the freedom to redesign BZW's fixed income division along modern lines? It was worth a try. After discussing with Jennifer whether the time was right to move their family to London again, in May 1996 he called Taylor: 'I'll come.' It was a turning point in Barclays' history.

'IT'S HOW THEY DO THINGS HERE'

Diamond spent the Fourth of July holiday with his family on the island of Nantucket off the New England coast, waved them goodbye as he boarded the Cape Air shuttle to Boston and then took an overnight flight to London, landing in the morning of Sunday 7 July. He was due to attend the men's tennis singles final at Wimbledon that day with BZW's deputy head of fixed income, Alex von Ungern-Sternberg, and some BZW clients. It rained, there was a streaker and the unseeded American, MaliVai Washington, lost to Richard Krajicek. It wasn't the result Diamond had hoped for but it was a civilized way to begin his career at Barclays.

Diamond's first day in the office was Monday 8 July. His assistant, Caroline Bews, who had moved with him from Morgan Stanley to Credit Suisse and now to Barclays, had been there for a week to set up his office and find out how everything worked. He walked in, took the lift to the trading floor and a few minutes later she brought him a pot of coffee on a tray with a cup and saucer. He was not used to such formality. 'It's how they do things here,' she told him.

By mid-morning he had a fair idea of what he had let himself in for. The BZW building in Ebgate House was an uninspiring 1970s construction with low ceilings and not enough natural light. It was the worst environment on a trading floor Diamond had ever encountered. The morning meeting of senior staff took place at nine in the morning, when there was more coffee and people chatted. For Diamond, nine was the middle of the day, and meetings had to be properly analytical, with people going through lists and proposed actions. The coffee and conversation culture was totally alien to him.

Coffee was not the only thing they drank. The fixed income boys on Wall Street knew how to party, but not during working hours. The City had been a boozy place before Big Bang, but by 1996 sparkling water had replaced gin and tonic at lunchtime, except, it appeared, at BZW. Leader of all this good cheer was one of BZW's most senior sales people, Roger.

Clients liked him and he would disappear with them for three hours in the middle of the day. In Diamond's world it was not acceptable for senior people to have their judgement impaired by alcohol or to be unavailable during working hours. He suggested to Roger that it would be in everyone's interests if he moderated his drinking. If a client expected a long liquid lunch he should take the rest of the day off and leave a message as to where he could be found.

A few days later, Roger was missing again and none of his colleagues owned up to where he was. The trading book had stock that needed placing and Roger had the contacts to do it. Meanwhile, bond prices were moving against them and every minute's delay was costing money. Roger returned mid-afternoon very drunk, bursting loudly into the glass office in the middle of the trading floor that Diamond had built. Diamond suggested he go home early and that they meet again in the morning.

That evening he considered how to handle things. Roger was popular with clients and colleagues, but BZW had no future if it carried on the way it was. Next morning Roger came in looking pale and sheepish. Diamond reminded him of their agreement. 'Instead, you came in clearly intoxicated and confronted me in front of the entire trading floor. I have no option. You can't stay.'

Sally Bott had warned Diamond about BZW's tribalism and he witnessed it for himself soon after he joined. He had come to know people at the Bank of England when he was in London with Morgan Stanley and the Bank's dealers now made a 'welcome back' gesture, asking him to sell some British government bonds to investors. A deal from the Bank of England would get the fixed income department and its new leader off to a flying start if it could be carried out successfully. Diamond wanted to make sure that BZW's US clients were offered some of the bonds and asked the sales heads in London how much they were holding for the firm's US sales team. The reply shocked him: 'Why would we hold something for them? They've never done anything for us.' Diamond gave them a long icy stare: 'They are us. That's the whole point.'

Diamond made connections that other people missed. He probed and challenged, asking different questions until he got the whole picture. He wondered why BZW's interest rate derivatives business used the same amount of capital as Morgan Stanley's equivalent yet made only a fraction of the profit. He and his head of derivatives sat in a

meeting room while Diamond scrawled big ideas and potential linkages on a whiteboard. Diamond kept asking questions about the cost
base, risk management, product design, sales team but he still couldn't
work out why BZW was less profitable to such an extent than its
competitors. Finally he asked: 'Who are our top five clients?'

The answer was: 'Goldman Sachs, Morgan Stanley, J. P. Morgan,
HSBC, Citibank.' Diamond whistled softly. 'My God. We really are
the dumb money. These are our competitors. We are the guys they all
come to when they are in trouble. They are using our balance sheet to
clear up their messes. They are making fifteen basis points on every
trade, we're making one.' BZW was being given the crumbs from the
table.

It was a devastating realization, and Diamond decided to find a
new head of derivatives. He rang Bycroft, who produced a string of
derivatives experts, but none fitted. Then Diamond had a tip-off from
another search firm: he told Bycroft to talk to a young Canadian at
Bankers' Trust in London, Jerry del Missier.

They met one evening at the end of 1996 in a second-floor conference room at Royal Mint Court, where BZW's Treasury team were
based. At precisely six o'clock the lights went out. Diamond went
outside to get help but the entire building was dark: the lights were on
a timer. Del Missier asked: 'Do people really all leave here at six?' But
he liked Diamond and joined his crusade.

For BZW 1996 had not been a good year. The competitive cost
pressures that had driven out many of the other British investment
banks in 1995 remained severe, and revenue in Diamond's fixed
income and foreign exchange business had been disappointing. Consequently, the bonus pool was small. It was not really his year, though,
and not yet really his firm, so Diamond decided to sit back and watch
the process. He left the detail to Mike Keegan, known on the trading
floor as 'the Prince of Darkness', who he had brought over from
CSFB as chief operating officer. Keegan ran the numbers and came
in to Diamond's office looking even more downbeat than usual. 'It's
not good news,' he said. 'There's no way that this bonus pool will
work. A third of the people are getting a zero bonus. They will leave.'

Diamond gave him the stare and said: 'We can't have that. We need
people to staff this business. Go back and do the numbers again.'

Keegan went away and worked again with human resources and the desk heads, then returned, looking even more gloomy. 'It's worse than we thought. On the latest numbers, 40 per cent of our people are in for a zero bonus. And 90 per cent of them got no bonus last year or the year before.' It was another Damascene moment for Diamond. 'Then we are employing the people who can't get jobs anywhere else. They are unemployable. They have nowhere to go. They have had no bonus for years, there's a hiring frenzy going on out there and they're still with us. That tells me all I need to know.'

7

In Memoriam BZW, 1997

A DEATH IN THE FAMILY

On a cool afternoon in early May 1996, the Gothic arches of South-wark Cathedral rang to the rare sound of BZW singing in harmony. People had come in their hundreds to remember David Band, BZW's chief executive, who had died of a heart attack in France on 28 March while on a skiing holiday. Colleagues, competitors, clients and friends had trudged from the City across London Bridge to pay their respects.

An anxious wait for the Band family, stuck in heavy traffic, delayed the start of the service. Then Donald Brydon, the founder of BZW's asset management business and a close colleague of Band, read from *The Pilgrim's Progress*, the chaplain of Rugby School led the prayers and Band's old boss and Camoys' inspiration, Sir Dennis Weather-stone, knighted in 1990 and only recently retired as chairman and chief executive of J. P. Morgan, gave the address. The *Financial Times'* obituary summed up the mood: 'David Band will be indelibly associated with the development of BZW into perhaps the first successful experiment in integrating investment banking into a UK clearing bank.'[1]

At least one member of the congregation doubted that success: Martin Taylor. He had grown to like Band. After their frank discussion on the way back from the senior management meeting in Essex in December 1995, they had been working together to strengthen the investment bank's management. Diamond had been earmarked to lead fixed income, and another of Bycroft's recruits, Bill Harrison, a top City investment banker, would lead corporate finance. In the event both joined after Band's death and Harrison became his successor. It was the strongest leadership team BZW had ever put together, but as Taylor ate cake and made small talk after the service, he wondered whether the occasion would be remembered as a memorial for Band or for BZW itself.

During the second half of 1996 Diamond moved relentlessly on the bond business and Harrison, a whirling dervish Brummie, created havoc in corporate finance. Diamond reported to him, their skills were complementary and although Harrison was unnerved when Taylor gave Diamond a place beside him on the Barclays executive committee, they were an effective pair.

Despite the efforts of this unusual couple, Taylor's attitude was changing. He had originally believed that BZW's problems could be fixed by better management, but he now had deeper concerns. The competitive gradient had steepened as the Americans poured in more resources. He asked himself whether Barclays' ambition to be an integrated investment bank combining the trading of equities – shares which offered ownership rights in the company that issued them – and fixed income bonds – securities which were forms of debt and conferred no ownership rights in the company that issued them – was still realistic given the scale of the US competitors. He asked the same question about corporate finance, where the US firms could offer companies in need of finance more capital and more experience.

He thought again about the original strategic rationale, which was to protect Barclays' lending business. Somehow a defensive move had morphed into a full-throttle attempt to join Wall Street's elite. If that narrow objective was re-established and grandiose plans to compete with Goldman Sachs and their kind were abandoned, equities and equity-related corporate finance could be ditched. That was appealing because, although these businesses were liked by clients, any profits went out of the door with the staff. With the retail bank and Barclaycard performing well and BZW falling away after a promising start, 1996 was following a familiar pattern. The investment bank contributed little to Barclays' profits, yet he was spending most of his time on this troublesome and now questionable business. Taylor kept these thoughts to himself during the autumn of 1996, partly because there was no one he trusted to share them with. In contrast to the close relationship he had enjoyed with Courtaulds' chairman, Hogg, he had no rapport with Buxton. They were metropolitan chalk and country cheese and never really understood each other.

Buxton was struggling as chairman. He found Taylor's quick brain and eloquence intimidating, but it was defining his own role that he found most difficult. Barclays had never had a separate chief executive so there was no precedent to guide him. At times he obsessed about details, at other times he seemed disinterested. He was, in fact, an essentially shy man searching for a role in a world he no longer understood. On one occasion they had dinner together at the RAC, the Pall Mall club where Buxton liked to swim. Buxton seemed withdrawn and confessed that he wished he had been a farmer. Taylor wondered whether he regretted taking the chairman's position.

They never had a cross word but scarcely ever engaged either. Taylor thought Buxton's image of Barclays as a great bank that would be there for ever was outdated. He suspected Buxton of undermining him – incorrectly – and gave little away to him. Middleton, Barclays' deputy chairman, who had seen his fair share of politics at the Treasury, took an office midway between the chairman and chief executive in an attempt to build bridges. In the end he found it easier to hold a separate weekly meeting with each one rather than have the three of them awkwardly together.

Taylor liked to debate with people who would stretch him in the way that Hogg had done. For the corporate governance arrangements to work as envisaged by Cadbury, executives needed to reach out to the non-executives, and non-executives needed to commit sufficient time to understand the business. But at Barclays under Taylor and Buxton neither happened, in part because the business of banking had outgrown the means of managing it.

The old model of lending money and keeping the loans on the balance sheet was being changed by the financial technique of securitization, whereby banks made loans, then parcelled them up into smaller chunks and sold them on to other financial institutions. The creation of BZW added a new dimension to Barclays' business, introducing equities and equity derivatives, a fancy new product based on future share price movements that was scarcely known in London when Camoys conceived the investment bank. The 1983 annual report was forty-eight pages long and the bank's assets – loans to customers and securities held for trading purposes – were £65 billion; the comparable figures for 1997 were 166 pages and £235 billion.

Such a business needed tight management and an engaged board with the time and expertise to understand the risk; it was no longer a game for gentlemen amateurs. While they themselves had grown up in the old world, Birkin, Henderson and Mobbs had at least done what shareholders expected of non-executives in ousting Quinton and splitting Buxton's roles, but of this triumvirate only Mobbs remained. Taylor regarded their successors as adding little value. To his disgust, board discussions were often leaked to the press and he wondered: 'Why would anyone with the bank's interests at heart do such a thing?' He decided that, since he couldn't rely on the board either for guidance or to keep confidential information to themselves, he would share his thinking with them only when absolutely necessary.

THE FIRST TIME OF ASKING

Over Christmas 1996, Taylor spent his daily walks around Greenwich Park working out how to solve the investment banking problem. As the temperatures dropped, so did his mood. Shareholders and the press were obsessed with it, the investment bankers were high maintenance and the business was risky: wouldn't life be simpler without it? He decided to float the idea of withdrawing from investment banking at the January 1997 board meeting and briefed Harrison a few days before. Harrison had been at the bank for only four months and this was a terrible shock to him. He was convinced that success was just round the corner and insisted on using the board meeting to state his case.

Harrison in full flow was a nigh irresistible force. Little more than five feet tall and barrel chested, he paced the boardroom, finger jabbing, eyes blazing, spitting passion. According to him, it was all taking shape just beautifully. Diamond was shaking up fixed income, the sales, trading and research team in equities was the best in London and just needed a bigger flow of corporate finance deals to put through the pipeline. 'And that, gentlemen and lady,' he assured them, looking across at Mary Baker, a board member of ten years' standing, 'is my business. Leave that one to me.' The Birmingham accent got broader as he became more excited: 'You have waited a long time to get in this position. This is the wrong time to give up.'

He was an extraordinary performer. In his career as a corporate financier, he had won over many boards with clever arguments and bravado and he did so again that day. Taylor listened glumly as the board asked all the wrong questions. There were no questions about capital and risk, nor about the rapidly developing derivatives business which would soon make beached whales of Harrison's generation. A few asked about profits and the effect of BZW on Barclays' stock market valuation, but most bought Harrison's story that a few more good people and his personal contacts would make the difference. Later in the meeting, during the chief executive's report, Taylor said he was open-minded about BZW's future, a clear warning that he was a sceptic, but for now Harrison carried the day and Taylor had to accept the board's decision.

The next day, however, his doubts were reinforced by news of a planned $10 billion merger of two American investment banks, Morgan Stanley and Dean Witter. A few weeks later, Bankers Trust bought the mid-sized investment bank Alex Brown for $1.7 billion. All around them sizeable institutions were getting together, whereas BZW's US business was tiny and weak. Taylor travelled to New York to discuss potential tie-ups with Wall Street partners, including Sandy Weill and Jamie Dimon's acquisitive financial services conglomerate Travelers Group, and explored a joint venture in investment banking with the French bank Paribas. As 1997 wore on, he became more and more certain that BZW should be sold or dramatically shrunk. Its poor performance in 1996 stood out in contrast to the rest of Barclays and was criticized by shareholders at the annual general meeting in April 1997 – as was the news that Harrison's remuneration for four months' work (including a £1.5 million cash sum upon arrival to compensate for deferred pay lost when he left Fleming) had been £3 million.[2] After the meeting, as usual, Taylor visited the largest institutional shareholders for private meetings; nearly every fund manager he met demanded that Barclays follow the example of Lloyds and focus on traditional banking for retail and corporate customers.

Two months later NatWest, which had been following a similar strategy to Barclays, announced that it was reviewing its own investment bank following losses in derivatives. Taylor calculated that BZW, accounting for roughly a tenth of Barclays' earnings, took up 70 per cent of board time, 85 per cent of audit and risk time and 98 per cent of the Remuneration Committee's time. Harrison was not landing well in corporate finance, missing meetings, shouting and swearing and not making good on promises. The breakthrough in winning new corporate deals looked no nearer and that raised questions about equity sales, research and trading, which was unprofitable without them. Taylor had seen enough. He decided that it would be right to exit from both businesses and leave Diamond's fixed income department as Barclays' sole representative in investment banking.

THE SECOND TIME OF ASKING

It was a huge decision, reversing the strategic direction Barclays had been following since 1983. For fourteen years, the board and senior management had been focusing on creating a full service investment bank, spending huge amounts of time and shareholders' money to the neglect of other parts of the bank. They still believed that Barclays had to be able to react to the needs of large corporate customers which were using the money and bond markets rather than traditional bank borrowing. The possibility of some partial exit from investment banking had been discussed at several board meetings, but many directors believed a modern Barclays needed the geographical diversification once provided by its old flag-planting international bank, Dominion, Colonial and Overseas. They felt enlarged by their association with BZW and diminished by the idea that it might be cut back. Shattering that illusion would be traumatic, so Taylor thought carefully about how to break the news.

The first thing he did was to brief Buxton and then his advisers, Goldman Sachs, asking them to prepare the sale of BZW's equities and corporate finance businesses. He needed to tell one or two senior people at BZW, but knowing when and how much to tell the full board was problematical. He was certain that he would have share-holders' support but realized that it would be at the very least difficult and potentially impossible to win over the board. They had no under-standing of the way that investment banking was changing or of Barclays' real role in the world.

Every board discussion of any note was followed by a leak to the *Daily* or *Sunday Telegraph*. After one board away-day in Harrogate, Taylor told the board that there was a leaker and that as a result he could not be completely open with them. He added: 'I can't imagine what Carol Galley would think if she knew.' A couple of months later, in Buxton's office, Taylor confronted the chief suspect, who denied responsibility but turned bright red. 'That went pretty well,' said Buxton afterwards. 'I don't think so,' replied Taylor. 'I have just made an enemy.' It was an awful dilemma. He and the shareholders were in agreement, but an out-of-touch and indiscreet board was not. Deciding that it would be too risky to wait for the board's approval, he took an executive decision.

Early on the morning of Monday 22 September Taylor told Mid-dleton, the BZW chairman, that he intended to find a buyer for the equities and corporate finance business. Though they had discussed this in outline, Middleton was surprised to learn that the chief execu-tive's thinking had progressed so far. Later that morning Taylor broke it to Harrison, who took the news much less calmly than Middleton. There followed ten days of bitter and emotional discussions as Har-rison fought to change Taylor's mind.

Jonathan Davie, a charismatic BZW senior executive, was asked to chair a new company that would contain the businesses up for sale under the direction of Goldman Sachs. Davie brought a handful of colleagues into the secret and rumours circulated round Barclays that something big was afoot. The non-executives were outraged. Sir Nigel Rudd was one of the biggest stars on the UK corporate circuit at the time. He had been on the board only a year but was furious and insisted that a full board discussion take place at the next meeting. Taylor had played it cleverly, though, and by then it was too late to turn back. At the meeting on Thursday 2 October Goldman Sachs presented a sale plan, which the Barclays board, having been brought into the process so late, had little choice but to endorse.

That evening, BZW's staff were told that Barclays would be selling the corporate finance, equities and Australian businesses. Taylor had got his way and his successors at the *Financial Times* supported his decision in a brutal *Lex* column: 'Faced with a choice between pouring perhaps billions of dollars into BZW to take it into the top division or cutting loose, Barclays' board had a fairly easy decision.'[3] A few days earlier, Sandy Weill's Travelers Group had bought the investment bank Salomon Brothers for $9 billion and merged it with the retail broker Smith Barney. Taylor's analysis that the stakes had got too high for Barclays appeared to have been vindicated.

What followed was an embarrassment. Advised by Goldman Sachs, Taylor believed that it would be easy to sell BZW, but a serious crisis in Asian financial markets in the late summer and autumn of 1997 made buyers cautious. BZW's Hong Kong, Singapore and Tokyo businesses had been reckoned a star prize but they lost value overnight as Asian markets and currencies plunged. With the market falling and potential investment banking buyers falling away, BZW's senior staff ran the sale process for their own benefit. They selected Diamond's old firm, CSFB, as their preferred destination, which offered a nominal sum to Barclays. In early November there was a tense discussion between Taylor and Lukas Muehlemann, his counterpart at Credit Suisse, during which Taylor threatened to pull the plug on the entire sale unless an acceptable price was paid. Muehlemann agreed a face-saving £100 million and the deal was announced on 12 November.[4]

It was subsequently revealed that Barclays was liable for write-offs and operating losses of £688 million, while Harrison himself received more than £4 million for his thirteen months at Barclays.[5] NatWest sold its own European equities business to Bankers Trust in December 1997 for £129 million and the High Street banks' Big Bang experiments were over.

DIAMOND CIRCLES THE WAGONS

While Taylor was clearing out equities and corporate finance, Diamond had his own worries in fixed income, letting go most of the existing senior management in his first few months. His predecessor, the Vietnam veteran Marrone, saw the way the wind was blowing and departed early. His deputy, von Ungern-Sternberg, who had taken Diamond to the tennis at Wimbledon, went the same way. Fifty staff were made redundant on a single day early in 1997, cleansing BZW of the nowhere-else-to-go, zero-bonus brigade. To replace them Diamond hired carefully, looking into the backgrounds of candidates and identifying people like del Missier, who still had something to prove. These included a slew of people from his old firm, CSFB, and just as Mack had done when Diamond had taken people from Morgan Stanley to CSFB, Allen Wheat rang up to complain. He told Taylor that such behaviour was unacceptable, but Taylor went along with it and sanctioned the offer of two-year contracts to entice people to a bank whose parent looked ambiguously committed at best.

Diamond realized that the news that equities and corporate finance were to be sold would fuel rumours of a plan to get out of investment banking entirely. He himself was confident but staff, clients and potential recruits would now be even more sceptical. So he did three things.

First, in late September 1997, just after Middleton and Davie had been told what was happening, he spoke to Taylor, who agreed to support an investment bank based on fixed income bond trading and to help Diamond sell the proposition. He also agreed that equity derivatives and Structured Capital Markets, a tax business run by Roger Jenkins and Iain Abrahams, would be exempted from the sale and be given to Diamond to manage.

Second, he worked out how to persuade the media, clients and staff that this was a positive development. He would point out that no European firm had ever been able to break into the mergers and acquisitions and equities markets that were dominated by the bulge bracket. What Taylor was doing was realistic and logical. Fixed income bonds were just another kind of debt, which was a natural

Barclays' business and with the advantages of a European time zone, the advent of the euro and Barclays' huge balance sheet, the new business had a competitive advantage.

Third, on 2 October 1997, once the equities news had broken, he gathered together his senior team and convinced them to buy in to the strategy. They would call the new business Barclays Capital Group and banish all talk of it being the rump of BZW. Their first press notice was headed BCG until someone pointed out that one of the world's top management consultancies used those same initials. It was not the only mistake they were to make in their first few months.

PART II

Groupthink, 1998–2007

8

Diamond's Halo Slips, 1998

A DIFFICULT AFTERNOON

May 1998, 54 Lombard Street: the chief executive's conference room was carefully laid out for a meeting of the Barclays Credit Committee. This was the body responsible for setting the bank's global credit limits, and the risk managers in head office liked to create an appropriately menacing atmosphere. One side of the long polished wood table was reserved for Taylor and committee members and opposite were places for presenters, who on this occasion were from Barclays Capital. It was a formal meeting with papers, an agenda and minutes – far removed from the febrile environment of the Canary Wharf trading floor – and ever so slightly intimidating.*

Diamond dashed in at the last minute, recognized Patrick Perry, Barclays' group treasurer, and sat down next to him. It was the wrong side of the table. The secretariat at the bottom of the table looked anxious but Taylor signalled to let things be.

It was barely six months since the traumatic dismantling of BZW. Taylor was pleased with Barclays Capital, which had shrugged off malicious gossips in the City predicting it was next for the chop. The investment bank's staff watched Taylor closely for signs he might flinch but he had been supportive, attending their management away-days and walking the trading floor. The May Credit Committee meeting would be the first significant test of the relationship.

Diamond had identified the emerging markets of east Europe,

---

* The investment bank moved to Canary Wharf in 1997; head office moved there in 2005.

particularly Russia, as a priority area and had recruited a team including Noreen Harrington, a former Goldman Sachs managing director, to build the investment bank's presence there. Barclays Capital believed they needed a fivefold increase in their trading limits with Russia, an increase that was opposed by Barclays' risk department. To resolve the issue, Taylor would need to balance prudence with diplomacy – the kind of exercise he enjoyed.

Diamond introduced the Barclays Capital paper. He said Russian companies needed to raise capital, financial institutions wanted to provide it and Barclays Capital was ready to build on its sterling base. It all added up, he said, to a strong case for increasing the amount of capital they could commit to Russian counterparties.

Malcolm Forster, a Barclays' man since graduating from the University of Kent in 1971, and by now the credit policy director, then set out the risk department's views. He dispassionately explained their methodology. Countries were graded on a scale according to economic and political risk, which in this case led them to take a more cautious line on Russia than Barclays Capital wanted.

Taylor opened the meeting up. There was one strong dissenter to Barclays Capital's request: Christopher Haviland, a senior executive in Barclays' international banking business and an independent-minded banker who had just witnessed the Asian financial crisis of 1997 at first hand. He was convinced that it would spread to Russia and was firmly set against any increase in the limit.

Forster's boss, Alan Brown, another Barclays' veteran, had just also become a vice-chairman of Barclays Capital. He suggested a compromise, capping the Russia country limit at £500 million, more than double the existing limit but far short of the £1 billion that the Barclays Capital team were requesting.

Taylor listened carefully and asked a few questions. The requested limits were very high, and coming so soon after the BZW closure costs of £469 million, Barclays could scarcely afford another write-down in its investment bank.[1] Taylor had lost much of the goodwill he had earned from shareholders for closing BZW because of the badly handled sale process. His reputation would be damaged by another mistake and he decided that a fivefold increase was too much. He endorsed Brown's proposal of a £500 million limit but added that the position had to be hedged as far as possible. This meant using derivatives to insure the Russian exposure against unexpected movements in interest rates, currencies and securities markets. Seeking such protection was expensive but was standard practice. Taylor looked along the table for approval.

Everyone nodded agreement with the exception of Haviland, a precise speaker who left no one in doubt about his views: 'I am sorry, chairman, but I cannot support this increase. Russian guarantees are worthless. The country has no money.'

Taylor said that he wished to reach a unanimous decision. 'Is there any more information, Christopher, that would help you understand the situation better?'

'I understand it perfectly, chairman,' Haviland replied. 'Russian guarantees are worthless. There is nothing you can do to induce me to change my mind.'

It was a disappointing outcome both for Taylor, who wanted consensus and for Diamond, who wanted bigger limits. Taylor concluded the meeting by sanctioning Brown's compromise, but reminded Barclays Capital that they should not go too fast too soon and that of course the overall limit had to be observed.

Diamond was gracious, thanked Haviland for his input and briefed the rest of the team back at Canary Wharf. The emerging markets people were furious. Why had they been hired if they were not going to be allowed to take advantage of the wonderful prospects for fixed income investors in Russia and the other emerging markets?

RUSSIAN DOLLS

As it turned out, the traders were wrong. Barclays' conservatism proved well judged and the investment bankers' enthusiasm reckless. The Asian financial crisis of 1997 spilled over into Russia in exactly the way Haviland had feared. On 17 August 1998, the Russian government devalued the rouble, defaulted on its debt obligations and abandoned support for its currency altogether on 2 September.

In Barclays' group risk, Brown, Forster and colleagues were watching developments calmly. Their biggest Russian positions were with well-established trade banks and they believed their overall exposure was within the £500 million limit. Any potential losses would be manageable and consistent with the kind of volatility expected from a trading business. Then they suddenly heard of a previously unreported Russian trading book position of £100 million, which broke the new limits. They could not get a clear explanation of what it was from Barclays Capital traders and suspected that lines of authority had been breached.

Barclays was about to raise some capital in the bond markets. This was a routine funding matter but had to be accompanied by an update on current trading. Statements had already been sent to investors stating that current trading was in line with general expectations; now Barclays would have to reveal the substantial losses or postpone the issue, which would have led to market rumours. In any case, there would have to be full disclosure and the bank would have to make a very conservative provision – perhaps as much as £250 million – in its accounts against potential losses.

Taylor was in Toronto about to speak at a conference organized by Barclays Global Investors when he took a call from treasurer Perry telling him that there was bad news from Russia. 'At least,' said Taylor, 'we know that the extent of the loss is well under control.' There was a moment's silence. 'Not quite,' replied Perry. 'It seems that Barclays Capital have a bigger exposure than the country limit we agreed. It looks like they have been marking some Russian counterparties as Swiss or American and their true exposure is much greater than we had thought.'[2]

Taylor paused to allow this startling news to sink in. It was only four months since the Credit Committee discussion. Diamond knew bond markets inside out and had brought in some top bond people to help. How could they have broken the group's risk rules? Was it incompetence or deceit? As the Barclays Capital people met at Canary Wharf, had they said to each other – or thought – 'Let's just take no notice of those guys'?

He would need answers to these and many other questions, but more immediately he had to make a statement to the Stock Exchange so that the planned capital raising could go ahead. He would also need to tell Barclays' regulators, the Financial Services Authority, which had just been formed as part of the new Labour government's regulatory shake-up. He told Perry to find out what level of provision would be needed and caught the next flight back to London.

Perry and Forster immediately summoned a meeting of senior Barclays Capital executives, risk managers and traders. They wanted to be certain that there were no more unreported positions in the trading book and to work out how far the rogue position might fall. They decided to take a 30 per cent provision against potential losses in the overall Russian trading book and to assume that virtually all of the additional unexplained £100 million exposure would be lost. It was harsh treatment. Diamond said that the actual losses would be much less (as indeed they proved to be) but with the capital call imminent, he understood the need to present a pessimistic scenario to investors.

There was one more embarrassing task to be done before the news was made public: the Bank of England had to be informed. The Bank sent three senior officials round to investigate; their report was never made public.

In the first week of September Barclays announced that it would be taking a charge of £250 million against its total Russian banking and securities trading exposure, which had now reduced to £340 million. The Russian situation had also impacted other markets: in July and August, Barclays Capital had lost approximately £75 million elsewhere in the trading book. The share price immediately dropped 5 per cent and continued to sink over the next few weeks. Investors and commentators wondered whether this new investment banking strategy was all that it was cracked up to be and the Barclays' board, still furious at having been outflanked on the equities sale, seriously questioned their chief executive's judgement.

Taylor's investigations revealed what had happened. Harrington's team had developed a relationship with a large Russian financial institution, Renaissance. To get business going, Barclays Capital agreed to lend them £100 million and to accept a portfolio of Russian securities as collateral, a standard capital markets Repo transaction. As Taylor had instructed them to do at the Credit Committee, Barclays' traders took out an insurance policy against a collapse in the rouble, offset this against the position and did not report it because they believed it was hedged. But the hedge failed because at the end of a long chain the ultimate counterparties were not Swiss or American but Russian; far from offsetting the risk and keeping it within the country limit, the hedge was worthless.

Taylor had observed similar things going on elsewhere. He was angry. The rules were clear: to do business with a foreign entity, management needed to be sure there was room in the country limit. But in this case the traders had used a loophole by excluding hedged positions from the running total. No one would have found out in normal times but the unusually high levels of fragility and instability in 1997–8 had revealed their subterfuge. Taylor concluded that traders would do whatever they could get away with. There was no sense of duty to the bank – their own pay packet would always come first. He insisted that people were fired, and Harrington abruptly announced that she would be leaving.

The remaining question was whether Diamond had been complicit. Taylor summoned him to his office. Diamond was very emotional and offered to resign. He said the traders had behaved terribly but he had discussed the situation with his family and had decided to take full responsibility.

Taylor was faced with a binary choice: either he decided that Diamond was part of it and that he had to go, or he gave him the benefit of the doubt and let him stay. The advantage of firing him was that it would draw a line under the episode. The disadvantage was that Diamond's leadership of Barclays Capital was so important that there was a real risk the business would unravel, a situation that would jeopardize the entire bank. If Barclays Capital failed so soon after the death of BZW, major shareholders would turn and Barclays would be in play. Royal Bank of Scotland under its ambitious chief executive George Mathewson was circling both NatWest and Barclays. This was not the moment to appear vulnerable.

Behind these strategic questions were those of trust. On the one hand, Diamond's apology sounded as though it came from the heart. On the other, Taylor felt that when you are dealing with someone who is a very close colleague and find yourself wondering if they are telling you the truth or not, you have to part company. Obviously

Diamond was financially incentivized to stay at Barclays. A nagging voice inside Taylor warned: 'Well, he would say that, wouldn't he?'

It was another existential moment for Barclays and as before the investment bank was the cause of it. In the end Taylor decided to believe Diamond, but emerging markets activity would have to be curtailed, proprietary trading groups disbanded and credit limits cut.[3] He told him that it was his responsibility to ensure that people in his division stuck to the rules. One more instance of Barclays Capital breaching its limits or breaking the rules in any other way would be the end of Diamond's career at Barclays. 'And probably mine too,' he thought.

Three weeks later there was more bad news. One of Wall Street's most prestigious funds, Long Term Capital Management, which boasted a roster of smart investment bankers, Nobel Prize-winning economists and rocket-scientist traders among its principals, became insolvent. They used computer models to predict market movements and borrowed huge amounts of money to leverage their bets. Barclays and other banks had been falling over themselves to provide LTCM credit, taking a small fee while LTCM's investors made huge returns. After a four-year winning streak, the Russian crisis prompted a sell-off in other emerging markets, the LTCM models failed and the hedge fund was bust. The whole house of cards collapsed and the US Federal Reserve organized emergency funding. Because Barclays was one of LTCM's twelve biggest counterparties, it contributed $300 million – the only UK bank to have been asked by the Fed to contribute.

Taylor spun the news hard, pointing out that unlike some other British banks it had not invested in LTCM, and portrayed the $300 million contribution to its recapitalization as an act of responsible financial citizenship. In due course, he said, Barclays would get all its money back – as indeed it did. But investors were not convinced. It seemed a pretty expensive entry fee for a seat at the credit casino.[4] Barclays' share price fell 10 per cent in a day to half the levels seen just six months earlier. Investors believed that Barclays Capital, the latest iteration of the bank's investment banking strategy, was just like the last one – accident prone and more likely to spring an unpleasant surprise than to succeed.

A DISASTROUS BOARD MEETING

Taylor's confidence in Barclays Capital was badly shaken. He believed that he was dealing with people who were putting the company at risk because of the nature of their business. He saw recklessness and unreliability built into their behaviour by 'take the money and run' short-term incentives. He could live with that if he doubled up on controls and if shareholders were supportive, but his meetings with them revealed real hostility to the investment bank. He calculated that the retail bank on its own would be worth more than the current stock market value of the entire group; investors actually appeared to be placing a negative worth on the investment bank. Would it be possible to release value for shareholders by splitting up the bank?

On Thursday 1 October, shortly after the Russian debt and LTCM imbroglios, Barclays had scheduled a board meeting in New York. Taylor decided that in his regular chief executive's report he would raise the possibility of demerging consumer and small business banking from corporate and investment banking. On this model, Barclays would become a High Street bank like Lloyds and the investment bank would be sold. Unrealistic ambitions to become a universal bank would be consigned to the history books. He hoped that floating this idea would finally bring about a realistic board discussion and formal review of the options.

The meeting was at the St Regis, the elegant midtown Manhattan hotel favoured by Barclays. The board meeting was to be in the morning, Barclays Capital would host a seminar for hedge fund clients to be addressed by Eddie George, the governor of the Bank of England, at lunchtime and in the evening there would be a party at the Frick Museum, a spectacular art gallery in a neo-classical 5th Avenue townhouse.

In a fully functional relationship, Taylor would have discussed this plan in detail with Buxton, but their mutual engagement had not improved. A few days before leaving London, Taylor had told Buxton that his report would call for serious consideration of a break-up of the group. Buxton was familiar with the direction of the chief executive's thinking but did not realize it had gone this far. Having avoided confronting Taylor for so long, he now believed he had little option but to intervene or look a fool, and he decided to give the non-executives advance warning of the proposal.

First he briefed Rudd in London, who was apoplectic at what he regarded as – following the carve-up of BZW – the chief executive's latest madcap scheme. Buxton's regular pre-board meeting with the non-executive directors was held on the evening of 30 September 1998. He outlined Taylor's plan and told them that at the board meeting he would be going round the table asking each of them in turn for their views.

By the following morning board opinion had hardened against the chief and his plan. Taylor had connected particularly well with one board member, Lord Lawson, but he had recently retired, leaving seven non-executives, including three senior businessmen considered close to Buxton: David Arculus, chairman of Severn Trent and IPC, and former head of the EMAP publishing empire; Peter Jarvis, a former Whitbread chief executive and chairman of Debenhams; and Rudd. The remaining non-executives were Middleton, the former Treasury mandarin and one of two deputy chairmen; the veteran property man Mobbs; and two leading businesswomen: Mary Baker, a past president of Women in Management, and Hilary Cropper, chief executive of FI Group, a technology services company.

The executive directors included Sir Andrew Large, who had joined the board on 1 May of that year and was the other deputy chairman. Insiders assumed that he had been recruited not just to add prestige and industry expertise to the board – which as a senior investment banker and former chairman of the Securities and Investment Board he undoubtedly would – but to become chairman of Barclays Capital when Middleton stepped down from the role on 1 May 1998. However, neither Taylor nor Diamond wanted a group deputy chairman with a foot in the investment bank and Large was underemployed in his four days a week executive directorship. Perhaps searching for a role, over the summer he had sent a stream of notes and queries to senior executives and had annoyed Taylor and others with these interventions.[5] Taylor expected no support from him.

The other executive directors were the finance director Oliver Stocken, who had been with Barclays Merchant Bank and BZW before taking the group job; and John Varley and Chris Lendrum, heads of retail and corporate banking respectively. Apart from the secretariat, there was only one other person seated at the board table that morning: Bob Diamond, who was in town for the governor's seminar, had attended the board for the chief executive's report.

After routine board matters had been dealt with, Buxton invited Taylor to give his report, which he did orally, supported by a short paper entitled 'Consequences of Russia: Portfolio Options'. The paper set out the events of the previous months, the remedial action taken and the 40 per cent fall in Barclays' share price since the Russian turmoil. The crisis had affected all bank shares but, said Taylor's paper, Barclays' was a worse performance than all but a handful of international banks and the diminution in value equated to 'roughly seventy times the net Russian loss'. It took Barclays' share price to a dangerously low level. 'The fundamental valuation problem is the same as it has been for the whole of my time at Barclays. The risk characteristics and low return of the capital markets business have a depressing effect on the multiple of the group as a whole and thus potentially detract from the value of the retail businesses.' According to the chief executive, the stock market valuation had 'now reached a level which is vital to our optionality and perhaps to our independence'. Taylor presented the board with two options: 'Sharply reduce the capital markets business or separate our retail interests completely.' His paper concluded with a request and an appeal: 'Formally I am coming to the Board to ask for permission to explore the possibility of demerger and advice as to how to go about it. I am also hoping for the broadest possible response – emotional and rational – to the issues set out in this paper.'[6]

It was a dispassionate analysis deserving of full discussion, but he had not pre-sold it to the board. The atmosphere was uncomfortable as he outlined his thoughts, occasionally glancing at some notes on an index card. Middleton glanced across the table and saw Mobbs looking glum with his head in his hands. Lendrum had only recently joined the board and was shaking his head in disbelief. Were all board meetings going to be like this? Arculus, sitting next to Taylor, was heard to mutter: 'Three hundred years of history' and was seen wringing his hands. No one looked Taylor straight in the eye.

Buxton said that before taking the non-executives' views, he wanted to hear what the executive directors thought. Varley had sat next to Rudd on the flight to New York. Rudd was about as far away from Taylor in interests and background as it was possible to get on a FTSE 100 board. He was a grammar school boy from Derby with no degree, a love of golf and shooting and no time for smart boys like Taylor, who he regarded as being all brains and no judgement. Rudd's instinctive feel for business and Taylor's analytical approach had already clashed. Rudd sensed that Taylor did not like the board and raged against him the whole way across: 'He stuffed us on BZW and he's bloody well not going to do it again.'

Varley, however, knew a lot about Barclays' investment banking history. An Oxford graduate with a first-class degree in history and a qualified solicitor, he had started at Barclays in 1982 as an assistant director in the corporate finance department of Barclays Merchant Bank. He worked with Buxton on Barclays' strategy for Big Bang and after it became BZW stayed until 1994, eventually becoming deputy chief executive of the global equities division. He then took a year out to join a hedge fund run by his wife's brother-in-law Crispin Odey before Taylor persuaded him to come back to Barclays to chair asset management. He had witnessed Barclays' difficulties in breaking into corporate finance, the in-fighting at BZW and the problems of integrating the different parts of the new investment bank. In 1998 Taylor had put him in charge of global retail banking and Barclaycard with a seat on the board. Varley repaid that loyalty in New York, speaking out in support of Taylor's proposals. But he was alone in doing so.

Lendrum had discussed the idea with Diamond before the meeting and dismissed Taylor's proposal out of hand. Large and Stocken were also opposed to a demerger. Diamond contrasted the diversity of a broadly based retail, commercial and investment bank like Barclays with retail banks such as Lloyds. He described Taylor's plan as like putting all the chips on black. Buxton went round the table. The non-executives were of the same mind: they believed that Taylor was panicking, insisting that Barclays remain a big global player and that Barclays Capital added to its prestige. Emotions ran high. The atmosphere was absolutely venomous.

At the end of the meeting Taylor said: 'I don't believe problems can be solved by failing to confront them. If that's the way you want to work, I can't go along with it.' He left alone and visibly shaken. With the exception of Varley, not a single director had shown any sign of understanding what he had said. None had said: 'Look, we may have to do this but let's not overreact to short-term events. Let's park the issue for a few months and come back to it.' On the contrary one director insisted: 'I want to be part of a big international bank. I don't care what the shareholders think.' The identification between man and bank was total. Taylor shot back: 'You simply don't have the right not to care. It's not your bank.'

A PARTY AT THE FRICK

Once the meeting broke up, Taylor went to meet Pattie Dunn, chief executive of Barclays Global Investors, the bank's fund management division, and some of its clients. Diamond and several directors hurried over to the Windows on the World restaurant on the 107th floor of the World Trade Center for the Barclays Capital lunch with Eddie George. A good discussion between the governor and the guests from the hedge funds about the implications of LTCM, not to mention the spectacular views, helped take their minds off the disastrous board meeting. But there was one more piece of awkwardness to endure: the party at the Frick. Many of the leaders of New York's financial community, Barclays' clients and central bankers, in town for IMF and World Bank meetings, were there. As expert guides chaperoned Barclays' guests around the art treasures and ushered them on to drinks and dinner, it looked like a relaxed evening, but among the Holbeins and Vermeers the bank's non-executive directors were muttering in little huddles.

The following morning Mobbs and Rudd discussed the previous day's events as they were driven in a stretch limo – Mobbs liked to do things in style – to play golf at Pine Valley Golf Club in New Jersey. Taylor had cut across the board's authority when he had closed BZW without giving them time to respond and now he had introduced another radical proposal with minimal consultation or explanation. Mobbs said: 'We just cannot allow this to go on. We must do something about it.' They agreed to talk to deputy chairman

Large, who they believed to be unhappy with Taylor, and drum up support for removing their troublesome chief executive.

THREE STRIKES

On the flight home, Taylor anxiously turned everything over in his mind. The evidence of the New York meeting was that he and the board had completely different objectives. He had lost their support and unless he compromised would probably be pushed out at the next opportunity. On the other hand, equally he could not defend a business and a strategy that he did not believe in. He wondered whether to force the issue again, this time backed up with a full paper. But Barclays might then descend into civil war and he doubted his right to inflict that on the bank. Or should he resign? He was feeling the strain of holding the ring between hostile shareholders opposed to the investment banking strategy, aggressive investment bankers incentivized to roll the dice and a board that he considered to be in a fantasy land where Barclays belonged at the top table of global banking.

The following Monday Taylor made a rare visit to his next-door-but-one neighbour's office. 'Andrew,' he said, 'it's clear to me that we cannot continue at strategic loggerheads. We've tried to paper over this for eighteen months but the disagreement over the investment bank is very deep. We need to end it. If you would like me to leave, let's talk about it.'

Buxton panicked. He knew that he had let relations with Taylor drift for far too long and that his own position was not secure. Some board members had wanted him out of the business altogether when Taylor was appointed and he was still under pressure. There would be hell to pay with the board, shareholders and the media if Taylor left in the wrong way.

'It would be terrible if you left. That's not what I want at all,' he replied.

Taylor read Buxton's alarm and knew that he had to do the right thing by Barclays: 'Look, when I came I indicated that I would do seven years, until the end of 2000. That's two years away and it's no longer realistic for me to stay that long. I can serve the business for one more year to give you time to find a successor and organize an orderly transition but there would have to be certain conditions.'

Buxton perked up. 'What are the conditions?'

Taylor said: 'I have three. First, get rid of Andrew Large. He is undermining my position. I can't stay if he stays. Second, we would need to agree departure terms that are fair to me and to the bank. I'm not going to put myself in the position of being pensioned off on the cheap once you no longer need me. Third, you must allow me to manage Diamond. I have lost Barclays Capital's trust and there must be no ambiguity about reporting lines if they come to you for approval.'

Buxton was pleased. The conversation with Large would be awkward but nothing else on Taylor's list looked difficult. He agreed to sort out terms immediately and did so within two days. Taylor left on a business trip to Hong Kong and Tokyo feeling cheerful and looking forward to a change in direction. His buoyant mood stayed with him during the following week's half-term holiday break with his family.

But upon his return in early November, Buxton asked to see him. He announced abruptly: 'I have spoken to Large. I have decided not to remove him from the board but he will step down as an executive director and consequently his compensation will be cut.[7] I told him that you wanted me to fire him.'

'That is not going to help, is it?' said Taylor, thinking to himself, 'one down, two to go'.

A few days later, Barclays Capital surprised Taylor with an announcement he was not expecting. He questioned Diamond about it. 'Oh, I've mentioned it to the chairman,' Diamond said. The subject was not especially important but the breaking of the chain of command, by his lights, was deadly. 'Two down, one to go', thought Taylor.

He went straight in to see Buxton an hour later. 'We agreed three conditions and two have already been broken. This is not going to work. We need to expedite things.' Buxton, who had a reputation for being frugal in such matters, replied: 'The terms we agreed were for two more years. If you go now, they no longer apply.' Taylor was not surprised by his chairman's inconstancy. He remembered childhood cricket with his brother where the rules were 'three strikes and you're out'.

9

Middleton's Law, 1998

'WHAT ON EARTH IS GOING ON?'

At nearly noon on Monday 23 November 1998 a tall neatly dressed man of late middle age was walking along the Strand in central London. From his domed forehead, his hair, whiter now than shades of grey, had receded. A pair of wire-framed spectacles was perched on his nose. He looked thoughtful and unobtrusive, like Peter Cushing's Sherlock Holmes taking the midday air. The Strand was busy with office workers out to beat the queues in the sandwich shops and others making their way to Covent Garden for some early Christmas shopping. He stopped suddenly, causing the crowds to swerve round him, reached inside the breast pocket of his overcoat and took out his mobile phone.

'Hello. This is Peter Middleton,' he said.

It was his assistant, Gill Herbert, utterly reliable and very old school, who would never divulge important information over the phone. 'Sir Peter,' she said, 'can you come in this afternoon?' Middleton was baffled. 'Why? I don't think I have anything on there today.' Gill Herbert was insistent: 'Why don't you come in and pay a few bills?' Middleton still wasn't getting it. 'Gill, there really is nothing I have to do.' They had worked together for a long time and she knew how to handle him. 'You really do need to be here at once. Something serious has happened.'

Gill Herbert, he knew, was not one to panic, so he took a taxi over to Lombard Street. A posse of senior executives were waiting for him when he got out of the lift at the sixth floor where he, Buxton and

Taylor had their offices. Middleton asked them: 'What on earth is going on?'

'Martin has resigned.'

'What do you mean he's resigned?'

'He's resigned. Would you go and see him?'

Middleton protested: 'I'm really the wrong person. There is a chairman, another deputy chairman and non-executive directors who chair the board committees. One of them should talk to him.'

'The chairman is in the Middle East at a meeting with the Emir of Qatar, Andrew Large is in Australia and Nigel Mobbs is entertaining the Queen as deputy lieutenant of Buckinghamshire.'

'Well, it should be Peter Jarvis, then,' said Middleton. 'He's chairman of the Nominations Committee.'

'He's at another board meeting. It has to be you.'

Reluctantly Middleton agreed. He settled his spectacles and went to knock on the door of Taylor's office. The chief executive was sitting behind his desk, looking strained. 'You won't be able to persuade me,' Taylor said immediately.

Middleton said: 'Look Martin, I have had a lot of experience of resignations and I am not going to try to talk you out of it. But you can't just resign in abstract and expect something to happen. You need to resign to the board, they can accept it, everything is properly done and we can make an announcement to the Stock Exchange. Have you got a lawyer?'

Taylor was not his usual composed self. 'This is perfectly straightforward. I want to go. Why do I need a lawyer?', he asked.

Middleton reminded him that there would be terms to settle and notices to draft and that it would be in everyone's best interests to get the lawyers involved. He was already worried about the number of people Taylor had evidently spoken to and added: 'Whatever you do, Martin, don't tell anyone else. You have told quite enough people already. Now write a proper letter setting out what you want to do.'

Middleton left Taylor to draft his resignation letter and contact his solicitor and went outside to speak to the bemused executive team. He told them that he was going to get Mobbs to come in to talk to Taylor and that he would see the rest of them shortly.

Middleton collected his thoughts. The 64-year-old veteran had experienced many crises during his career as a civil servant so he knew that it was essential to play for time. Fevered stories of mergers in the banking sector, some actual, others imagined, were intriguing the stock market. The board had turned against Taylor and a faction certainly wanted him out but it had to be seen to have happened in the right way or Barclays would be in play. Everything would probably be settled within twenty-four hours but he wanted to give Jarvis and Mobbs time to talk to the chief executive. Meanwhile, there were far too many people in the know and he had to keep as many of them as possible out of the way to prevent the news spreading. He decided to gather the senior executive team together at his west London home to ensure that they held firm while they waited for news from Lombard Street.

Early the following morning a trickle of middle-aged men in suits climbed the steps to Middleton's front door. They were shown into an elegant ground-floor drawing room and waited for Middleton to begin. He explained that Taylor would probably be going and that they should make contingency plans. They discussed what had happened, talked through various possible scenarios – what to do differently if Taylor stayed, what to do if he left – and waited for news. A carriage clock chimed the half hours but the morning passed without news and by lunchtime the conversation was getting thin. Middleton dispatched his wife to bring in sandwiches. At the same time, a few miles east, a last-ditch lunch between Taylor and Mobbs was taking place.

Buxton had received Taylor's resignation by fax in the Middle East. The peace he thought he had brokered with his chief executive had not lasted long and this would mean trouble. He called a board meeting for his return and hired a private plane to fly back to London immediately. While it was refuelling in Athens, Mobbs tried to persuade Taylor to slow down his departure; by the time he landed in Stansted, it was too late. Taylor was resolute that he wished to leave immediately and by then stories were flying round head office. Mobbs decided that the situation was irretrievable and that Barclays needed to work out terms with Taylor and make a timely announcement.

Given the fragility of the situation, the question of who would take over was pressing. During the afternoon, Mobbs and Jarvis consulted with the other non-executives and discussed whether any of the executive directors were ready to step up. Finance Director Oliver Stocken was close to retirement and the only other full-time executive directors on the main board were John Varley, the head of retail banking, and Christopher Lendrum, the head of corporate banking. Lendrum had never worked in investment banking; Varley knew both investment banking and retail banking but he was forty-two, only a few months older than Taylor when he had taken the job. The experiment with a young chief executive had not ended well and the board decided it would not repeat it. With both Scottish banks – the Bank of Scotland and the Royal Bank of Scotland – known to be on the lookout for takeover targets, they could not afford another mismatch. Finding the right man would take time, so there had to be an interim solution. Their thoughts turned to Barclays' two deputy chairmen, Large and Middleton.

Large had a high standing in the City but internally would not have been a popular choice. His attempts to carve out a bigger piece of the action had not gone down well with many senior executives and he had just been dressed down by Buxton.

Middleton, on the other hand, had been deputy chairman since 1991 and was an interesting proposition. He was numerate, having studied economics at Sheffield University and statistics at Bristol University. He had done his National Service in the Royal Army Pay Corps and was also a skilled political operator as his long career in the civil service showed. He had joined the Treasury in 1962 and worked his way up, becoming permanent secretary in 1983 in the halcyon days of Margaret Thatcher's premiership. It was an exceptional position, second only to the cabinet secretary in the Whitehall pecking order. For six years his boss had been Chancellor of the Exchequer Nigel Lawson – they met again on the board of Barclays – who remembered his 'quickness, his intelligence and his political sensitivity', as well as 'his habit of cultivating the press'. He felt that 'he was at his best as a troubleshooter, taking a grip of a complex specific issue in a way few others could have done.[1] Others knew him for Middleton's Law: 'Even if you have a badly functioning economy – which in many ways we still do – it is always possible to make it worse by government initiatives.'

When he joined Barclays, he made it clear that he regarded banking as a second career, not a retirement job, and devoted himself to it. He had been briefly considered in 1993 as a replacement for Buxton as chief executive but at that time had not yet built his base and the board had made its unexpected choice of Taylor. Five years later, it was now his time: on Friday 27 November, the board invited him to become interim chief executive.

There was an additional twist. Taylor had made it clear when he resigned that his relationship with Buxton was one of the problems and the board, who were now as cross with Buxton as they were with Taylor, decided that he would have to resign too. Would Middleton, the board asked him, also take over as chairman when Buxton retired in April 1999? And so it was that the former civil servant found himself acting chief executive and chairman designate of Britain's grandest bank just a few months before he was entitled to collect his old age pension, while the wunderkind nearly twenty years his junior departed.

WHOEVER WOULD HAVE THOUGHT IT?

Middleton was quietly spoken, with a soft Yorkshire accent and had a habit of chuckling to himself at the apparent absurdity of situations. The chuckle seemed to be saying: 'Blow me down. Whoever would have thought it? Now what on earth are we going to do about that?' but actually it was a device to disarm his interlocutors; the wily Middleton saw the angles and consequences of every action. He embarked on the second phase of his professional life with enthusiasm and more than a little guile.

His predecessor had proved to be not just a different kind of banker but a good one too. Taylor had introduced sophisticated modelling into Barclays' risk and credit analysis, which, Russia and LTCM apart, had brought the balance sheet under control. Middleton knew that he would do well to be his equal at judging the economic cycle. He would also need to win over the City and Fleet Street, where Taylor had a strong following.

Unsurprisingly, however, his priority was the boardroom. In Whitehall, Middleton had learned how to get ministers and other government departments alongside through logic, charm and cunning. At Barclays, the dysfunctional relationship between chairman, chief executive and the non-executives had resulted in an exceptionally able chief executive flaming out in a spectacular and unnecessary fashion. The board had asserted itself and Middleton was determined that on his watch corporate governance would work as it was meant to. He met the non-executives for half an hour before every board meeting, kept close to the various board committee chairmen and consulted them on important decisions.

He let the executives know that he was going to act like the chief executive and that no one would get very far by treating him like an interim. He amended Middleton's Law for the private sector: 'If there is a problem, the one thing to avoid is changing the organization; the right thing to do is to make the existing organization work better.' He announced that he was not going to change the senior staff, that Barclays was going to have one of its best years in 1999 and that everyone had to make it so.

One of the most important decisions Middleton had to make was what to do about Diamond. Barclays Capital had swung round from a quarter of a billion pounds profit in 1997 into a quarter of a billion pounds loss in 1998, and for several months its chief executive was a chastened man. When they met, Diamond told Middleton he had learned the lessons of the Russian losses. With Taylor, he had made a distinction between using the bank's own money in proprietary trading, and trading to execute client orders. He had closed proprietary trading straightaway and was committed to building a great business.

Taylor had barely trusted Diamond but Middleton took a different line. He had come across plenty of brash Americans in his time but Diamond was different. He decided Diamond owed the bank one and would repay straight dealing with straight dealing. He did not believe that the investment bank had wilfully smashed the Russian country limits. He was convinced that the 1998 results were an aberration and that Barclays Capital would bounce back. The board had rejected Taylor's break-up strategy and were committed to investment banking and that being so, Diamond was the best person to run it. He told Diamond to get on with the job and that he didn't want to see him again outside routine meetings unless there was a problem.

THE BEST CHIEF EXECUTIVE
BARCLAYS NEVER HAD?

Finding a permanent successor to Taylor was high up the board's priorities. Middleton had been exploring the feasibility of creating a combined 'bank-assurance' group by merging Barclays and the Prudential with Sir Peter Davis, the insurer's chief executive, and took the idea to the board. Davis would have become chief executive of the combined business, but the board vetoed the idea before serious negotiations were even started. Despite the way that Taylor's tenure had ended, they once again turned to Spencer Stuart and David Kimbell. They told him they were looking for a career banker with first-hand experience of running a big firm in the public eye. Kimbell came up with a short list of two potential chief executives, both American.

Robert Joss, chief executive officer of Westpac Banking Corporation, had modernized one of Australia's largest banks but seemed reluctant to engage. The other American was Michael O'Neill, fifty-two years old at the time, who had risen to become chief financial officer at BankAmerica. He was a solid, pragmatic, no-nonsense career banker who liked to understand balance sheets and enjoyed forensic analysis of financial problems. NationsBank had just merged with BankAmerica: O'Neill knew that he was not going to be the chief executive of the joint enterprise. He was ready to move and he and his wife liked London. He also checked out well with Barclays' contacts in the US. His appointment was announced on 11 February 1999. Middleton would move up to become chairman as intended.

O'Neill bought a house in Mayfair, the family's dogs were booked into quarantine and plans were laid for their children's education. The Barclays machine went into overdrive producing presentations and explanations for the new chief executive and setting up a programme of visits for soon after his arrival. Then, in the middle of the week before O'Neill was due to join, Middleton was asked to take a call from California. It was a shaky sounding O'Neill. He had passed out when watching the news on television and had been rushed into the Emergency Room at his local hospital. Tests had revealed a cardiac arrhythmia and defibrillators had to be used to reset his heart rate. The doctors said he would eventually be fine but he wanted to delay his starting date for a couple of weeks. The board at Barclays was still leaky and Middleton decided not to share this information with them. A brief announcement stated that it was taking longer than expected to make the right education provisions for O'Neill's children and that his start date would be slightly delayed.

Two weeks later Middleton received another Californian phone call. O'Neill was still very ill and asked for a further two weeks' postponement. Middleton put out another notice announcing that the education issues were taking longer to resolve but that the new chief executive would be starting shortly. Speculation had been low level after news of the first delay but now ratcheted up a notch. Middleton kept his fingers crossed and maintained a confident façade. A further few days passed and then there was another phone call. O'Neill's condition was serious and he would not be able to come to London after all.

Middleton now called the board together to give them the news, but they wanted to hear from O'Neill himself and asked him to come to London to see them. At first he was reluctant to take the long flight, but after consulting his doctors and accompanied by his wife, he flew to London. All were shocked at how unwell he looked: he was clearly still very ill. Barclays' doctor confirmed the diagnosis of the American specialists and agreed that it would not be wise for O'Neill to take up a high-pressure role at that moment. He handed back the envelope with his share options and returned to the US. On 12 April 1999 it was announced that he would not, after all, be joining Barclays.

Middleton had one last line to pursue before he commissioned another search. Could Joss yet be tempted to London? But it turned out Joss was about to leave banking to become dean of Stanford Business School. The reason for his diffidence a few months before was now clear.

Kimbell went back to work. From the short list he produced, the board decided that Peter Burt, chief executive of the Bank of Scotland, was their man. A deal was agreed, an announcement was prepared and then it transpired that Burt would want to merge Barclays with Bank of Scotland and move the headquarters to Edinburgh. Middleton hastily convened a board meeting one Sunday evening, at which the directors predictably opposed the idea, and Burt withdrew.

In public Middleton was stoical, but in private the heat was on. The search for a new chief executive at one of the UK's biggest and most prestigious companies was turning into a long-running farce. Barclays was being ridiculed in the media, the board looked inept and the shareholders were getting restless. As Taylor had pointed out in his board paper, the stock market now valued the whole group at less than the stand-alone value of the consumer bank, making it vulnerable to a takeover.

Buxton chaired his last annual general meeting a week after it was announced that O'Neill would not be coming. Middleton's advice to Taylor that he should consult his lawyers before resigning proved to be valuable to the departing chief executive for he received a pay-off of £1.6 million, which was criticized at the meeting. Questions were asked about press speculation of a bid from the Royal Bank of Scotland but Buxton briskly sidestepped round them.

Away from the public eye, Middleton was being continually pressed by George Mathewson, chief executive at the Royal Bank of Scotland, to do such a deal. The longer Barclays went without a permanent chief executive, the more frequent and more insistent Mathewson's calls became. Middleton was also under pressure from below as Barclays' retail banking boss Varley proposed a merger with the Halifax Building Society. A permanent appointment could not wait much longer.

At this moment a surprising option appeared on the table: O'Neill. His heart condition had been diagnosed and treated and he would soon be fit to work. While Middleton deliberated, the press speculated, and O'Neill was quoted as saying: 'I would love the job. It's not impossible, though there are a lot of hurdles that need to be cleared.'[2] Middleton was tempted but the civil servant's caution cut in. He and the bank would look foolish if O'Neill were to be taken ill again and the risk was just too high.

O'Neill has gone on to live a healthy life and his record as a banker suggests that he would have been a positive appointment for Barclays. Once he received the all clear from his doctors, he became chief executive of the sprawling Bank of Hawaii, where he refocused the business, rebuilt the balance sheet and saw the share price quadruple. In 2009 he campaigned unsuccessfully to be chief executive at Bank of America by promoting the idea of breaking it up. Instead he joined the board of Citigroup and became chairman in 2012, promptly ousting Vikram Pandit as chief executive and inserting Michael Corbat in his place. In October of that year *Forbes* ran an article on O'Neill entitled 'Meet the man who is really running Citigroup'. It was a happy outcome for the man who nearly ran Barclays.[3]

IO

Matt Barrett's Master
Class, 1999

There was no alternative but to resume the search. The bank was in a delicate position. Investors had no faith in a board that had presided over the bungled sale of BZW, the departure of a popular CEO and the accident-prone recruitment of his successor. The strategy was unclear. Did Barclays want to be a retail bank serving High Street customers or a universal bank selling all manner of financial services to corporates, financial institutions and private individuals in all parts of the world? If it was to be a retail bank, it was underperforming against Lloyds and other British banks. If it still had ambitions to be a universal bank, why had it closed BZW? No model existed anywhere for a large investment bank that dealt in fixed income bonds but not in equities. Barclays' experiment still seemed more likely to disappoint than please.

The board knew that after the sudden departure of Taylor and O'Neill's withdrawal, they could not afford to make a mistake – if the Barclays share price took another dent, the bank would be vulnerable to the hostile takeover bid they so feared. By the middle of 1999, with the help of Kimbell they had settled on a long list of eight, including four internal candidates. Diamond was one, but he needed to rebuild trust after the mishaps of 1998 and he was an outsider. So too was Varley, the head of retail banking, who at the age of forty-three was still considered too young. But Middleton, who was leading the search himself, wanted a politically astute proven chief executive with retail banking experience and favoured the external candidates, one of whom particularly intrigued him.

RESTLESS IN TORONTO

The Bank of Montreal's (BMO) Bay Street headquarters in downtown Toronto, Canada's tallest office block, was all decked out for Christmas 1997. Up on the sixty-eighth floor guests at BMO chairman Matt Barrett's Christmas party were enjoying the views over Lake Ontario along with a festive glass of punch. All the leading lights of Toronto's financial community were there, including John Cleghorn, the chairman of the Royal Bank of Canada (RBC), BMO's biggest rival. A lively topic of conversation among the guests was how Canada should respond to the march of the big American banks into their territory. Cleghorn was worried that Canada's banks were getting left behind in the global race for banking scale. In a quiet corner, he and Barrett agreed to have a longer chat in private to see what could be done about it.[1]

The outcome was dramatic. Barely a month later, on 23 January 1998, BMO and RBC announced plans to merge. If all went to plan, the merged bank would become the tenth largest financial institution in North America and the twenty-second in the world; it would be Canada's largest employer, with 85,000 workers, $453 billion in assets and a stock market valuation of $39 billion. Barrett admitted that the opportunity to 'create one of the great banks of the world is a banker's dream'.

However, the proposal posed a problem for the Canadian government. Paul Martin, finance minister in Canada's Liberal government, had already set up a task force to advise him on competition and concentration in the financial services industry, and he did not like being jumped on in this way. He had a cautious approach to financial deregulation and doubted whether Canada needed to emulate the likes of Citigroup, Chase and Bank of America. After deliberating for several months, he blocked the RBC–BMO deal on the grounds that putting together the first and third largest banks in Canada would be anti-competitive.

The government's veto left Canada with a different kind of financial services industry from the one that Barrett and Cleghorn had in mind. At odds with the spirit of the age of deregulation, Canada would not be joining the global financial services race and would be maintaining a more controlled and regulated banking sector. It was a decision that eventually worked out well for Canada, but it left Matt Barrett disappointed. The prospect of a transformational merger that would give Canada a globally competitive financial behemoth had excited him; another period of organic growth in a country where the regulators were financially conservative did not. In February 1999 he decided to resign as chief executive of the Bank of Montreal and told journalists that he planned to spend some time in the sun, write a book, grow a ponytail and find his karma.

Chilling out was not what Barrett had originally intended to be doing that year. His private life wasn't going according to plan either. A marriage of nearly thirty years that had produced four children had ended in divorce in 1995. Barrett was a charming and witty man, good looking, with deep-set eyes, bouffant silvery hair and a rakish moustache, and an A-lister on the Canadian social scene. Still in his early fifties, he was unlikely to remain single for long.

In 1997, he was invited to a party at the Toronto house of Peter Munk, founder and chairman of Barrick Gold, the world's largest gold-mining corporation. Anne-Marie Sten, a beautiful six-foot-tall former model, wearing what one guest described as a 'nipple-grazing' black sheath dress, dominated the room. Barrett fell for her. Five weeks later, despite friends warning that she had expensive tastes and had spent eight years as the 'pleasure wife' of an international arms dealer, he donned white tie and tails and became her third husband. Even those closely involved thought it was a bit quick. Sten herself later said: 'The priest who married us suggested that before we marry, maybe we should try therapy for a while. I would have done that. I like to figure things out. But Matthew said, "No. Just look at her!" '[2]

Exactly as Barrett's friends had predicted, the infatuation did not last. In less than two years, the couple separated and Sten went to Europe. While the lawyers wrangled over the divorce and Bank of Montreal's shareholders digested the news of their chief executive's retirement, Barrett went house-hunting in the fashionable beach suburb of Conchas Chinas in Puerto Vallarta, Mexico. But then, in mid-June, on a gorgeous Mexican morning, he took a call from Spencer Stuart. He never got to write his book or grow his hair.[3]

Barrett had kept his eye on the global banking scene during his sabbatical and knew all about Barclays. Kimbell's New York colleague Dayton Ogden flew south to meet him. The pitch was that Barclays could be the kind of bank that Barrett had wanted to build in Canada. Why walk away from unfinished business? Why not go over and talk to them? Barrett put away his snorkel, returned to Canada, packed his suits and ties and headed over to London to meet Middleton and the board.

Barrett had come up the hard way. He was born in Ireland in 1944, the son of a bandleader, and had attended a strict church school where the discipline and the education were raw. He left at the age of eighteen and found a job as a bank clerk at the Bank of Montreal, which had set up in London during the war to pay the Canadian troops. It had only two branches in the UK and Barrett worked in the one just off Pall Mall in Waterloo Place, London. His first job was in the walks department, trudging round the City delivering cheques. When his father died soon afterwards, Barrett took on some of the responsibilities of providing for his mother and sister. He worked hard, learning banking from the bottom up and after five years was marked out as a young man with management potential and was posted to Canada on a BMO trainee scheme. On 15 January 1967 he walked off the plane with a borrowed C$100 in his pocket.

He impressed senior management by turning round one of the bank's worst branches in Alexis Nihon Plaza, a shopping centre in downtown Montreal. He was unusual in not having a degree and was desperate to make up for the disadvantage this caused. When the bank established a fast-track scheme for graduates, Barrett promptly ordered the necessary books and studied for a degree, and at the first opportunity he took a short course at Harvard. Combining hard work with charm and vision, he was appointed chief executive of Bank of Montreal in 1989 and chairman the following year at the age of forty-five.

Under Barrett's leadership, Bank of Montreal delivered nine years of record profits and the share price quadrupled. He expanded Harris Bank, a Chicago retail bank, through acquisition, grew Nesbitt Burns into one of Canada's leading investment banks and kept costs in the retail bank under firm control. But Barrett's BMO was not just a profit machine. It introduced a balanced scorecard tracking employees' performance with all stakeholders: shareholders, customers, colleagues and communities. In 1994 he created the bank's Institute for Learning to keep staff abreast of new ideas and developed active programmes to encourage the employment of women and ethnic minorities.

A sleepy Canadian bank became one of the industry's leaders. Its chief executive was a big star on the Canadian business scene: in 1994, Barrett was made an Officer of the Order of Canada, the country's highest civilian honour, was named the country's 'Outstanding chief executive of the year' in 1995 and won the Canadian Catalyst Award for fostering the advancement of women in banking.

By the time he left, BMO had a strong position in everything it did: retail, commercial and investment banking and private banking for high net worth individuals. It made over half of its earnings outside Canada and was indeed a mini-version of everything that Barclays wanted to be. Could Barrett do it again on a bigger stage?

The country boy who had started by carrying cheques around the City in 1962 was now a thoroughly modern chief executive. The Irish lilt had been overlain by a Canadian accent, as he discussed shareholder value, economic profit (profits adjusted for the cost of capital) and other fashionable business concepts. Middleton's Nominations Committee – himself, Arculus, Jarvis, Mobbs and Hilary Cropper – could not make him out. He spoke a lot of good sense but was very laid back and smoked throughout the interviews at Spencer Stuart's no smoking offices. He took his time to answer a question, first tapping a cigarette out of the packet, lighting up and drawing deeply before replying through the faint blue haze. In the absence of an ashtray, he stubbed his cigarette butts in a coffee cup, pausing occasionally to flick stray flecks of ash off the table.

After the shambles of Taylor's departure and the near misses of 1998, Barclays needed to find a cool head who knew banking inside out, which Barrett obviously did. They decided that although he might give them a few unpredictable moments, Barrett was capable of picking up the battered crown. In July 1999, barely a month after he was first approached, his appointment as chief executive was announced.

'SWISS TONI' COMES TO TOWN

As chief executive's landings go, Barrett's could have been better. The media calculated that, if certain performance targets were met and his options kicked in to their maximum value, his £1.7 million annual package would eventually be worth £30 million. The press recycled provocative photos of his estranged wife from her modelling days. Stories circulated about Barrett's love of the nightlife and the Barclays wags swiftly dubbed him 'Swiss Toni' after a fifty-something car dealer in a popular British television series whose quiff and moustache bore a striking resemblance to Barrett's. Toni regarded any opportunity in life as 'like making love to a beautiful woman'.

To begin with, Barrett did not go down well at head office. He appeared uninterested in the copious briefing packs that had been prepared for him. His move to the UK was complicated by North American expectations of living allowances and Barclays had to send a human resources manager to Canada to arrange the details of shipping his belongings. He occasionally appeared to doze off in meetings, called for frequent smoking breaks and made politically incorrect wisecracks. It was not how Sally Bott liked to do things and she left soon after he joined.

Chief executives on the move often bring their support team with them, in Barrett's case an organizational psychologist named Gary Dibb. In time this worked out well, but initially Barclays' existing head office staff resented Dibb's presence and his rumoured compensation. Barrett's personal life kept popping up in the gossip columns too, causing embarrassment to the staid Barclays establishment. The pictures of Anne-Marie Sten kept resurfacing and the popular press decided to give him another moniker, 'the £7 million bonk manager'. In the first few weeks senior Barclays executives like Varley, the head of retail banking, and David Allvey, the recently recruited finance director, were heard asking: 'How could we have done this?'

Nor was business going well. Results for the first half of 1999 announced shortly after Barrett's appointment were down 25 per cent after a £345 million restructuring charge, a provision for bad debts of £320 million – mainly at the retail bank – and a £117 million loss on the sale of Merck Finck, a German bank that had been bought during Quinton's expansionist days. In contrast, Barclays' principal rivals, HSBC, Lloyds and NatWest all reported profit growth of above 10 per cent. Barrett gave himself one hundred days to work out what to do and in the meantime left the existing management team to get on with running the business.[4]

He was unimpressed by their efforts, particularly those of the retail banking chief Varley. Varley's full head of white hair, rimless spectacles and chubby face gave him the air of an Oxford don. He spoke thoughtfully and gently in carefully constructed sentences, and sometimes attended mass at the Brompton Oratory on his way to work. The most flamboyant thing about him was the bright-coloured braces he used to hitch up his high-waist trousers. Varley presented himself as an old-fashioned English gentleman and Barrett heard that he had married into one of the Barclays families. To the poor boy from Ireland, it sounded like a soft ticket. His scepticism soon hardened further.

Barclays had just joined Link, a consortium of banks for sharing cash machines. With Varley's approval, in March 2000, Barclays proposed to charge non-customers to use its machines, a move that would have disadvantaged the smaller banks. The public was in uproar and Donald Cruickshank, a former regulator who was conducting a review of banks for the Treasury, cited it as an example of banks' profiteering: the service cost 30 pence per transaction to provide, yet customers were charged £1. Barclays had to back down.

There was another public relations goof over Barclays' branch closures. The entire industry was readjusting to a new world of telephone and internet banking. Most banks were quietly closing branches in unprofitable or over-banked locations, and analysts criticized Barclays for being slow to follow. It responded clumsily in April 2000 by announcing the closure of 171 branches on a single day – the same day as it was revealed that Barrett had been paid £1.3 million for his first three months' work. Simultaneously, Barclays was running an advertising campaign based around a 'big bank' theme, using stars such as Sir Anthony Hopkins and intended to show that 'big is also friendly'. Given the closures, redundancies for staff but high pay for top executives and the publicity around the Cruickshank report, the media regarded this as crass bragging. Some of the branches Barclays closed were the last ones remaining in rural communities; wreaths were hung over them by activists, and Barclays' reputation sank still further. After the April 2000 board meeting, Varley went into Barrett's office and offered to resign. Barrett replied: 'When I want you to resign, I will tell you.' He promptly ordered a discreet search to find a replacement.

Barrett, however, was becoming familiar with Barclays' unusual culture and with the UK's way of doing things. He impressed the board with his strategic grip and deep understanding of banking. A natural communicator, he took to the road to meet 20,000 staff at town hall meetings across the country. He would place a stool on the stage and invite his audience to 'ask anything you want'. His easy manner won people over and his one-liners became part of Barclays folklore. One recruit told how he had been given a two-year-old uniform; Barrett was furious: 'It'll be like a kid in his father's army suit.' At another meeting he apologized for giving a lengthy answer, likening it to Lady Astor on the *Titanic*: 'I asked for ice but this is ridiculous.' After a presentation in Birmingham, staff tore posters from the wall and asked him to sign them and got him to pose for photographs.[5] Swiss Toni was in town.

'COOL BRITANNIA'

Barrett picked up the reins at Barclays on 1 October 1999 at a time when the UK was also going through a change in style. A couple of years before, on 2 May 1997, a youthful Tony Blair had stood on the steps of 10 Downing Street with his professionally successful wife and three children waving to the cameras, the first Labour prime minister since 1979. He was forty-three years old and his New Labour had just trounced John Major's tired Conservatives, a party that the electorate decided had simply been in power for too long.

Blair's vision of Britain was more exciting than his predecessor's idyll of cricket on the village green, warm beer and old maids cycling to holy communion. This was now the age of 'Cool Britannia', when icons such as the rock band Oasis were invited to 10 Downing Street by the electric guitar-playing prime minister. He was snapped playing football with a star footballer of the time, Kevin Keegan, and often appeared in public without a tie.

It was the time too of the dot.com revolution, which gave the public access to the internet for the first time. Emails replaced letters and online shopping began turning into a national obsession. Department stores moved out of town and coffee shops and mobile phone retailers transformed the High Street. It wasn't just the look of the country that changed either; so too did government priorities. As the City had prospered, other parts of Britain had been left behind: some of those High Streets started to fill with pound shops or were boarded up. Blair tried to put this right, pouring money into the National Health Service, increasing welfare payments and introducing the Sure Start children's programme in the poorest parts of Britain.

But this was still a government that was overtly friendly to business and the financial services industry. In 1996, Blair had briefly flirted with the idea of a 'stakeholder economy' in which 'we shift the emphasis in corporate ethos from the company being a mere vehicle for the capital market to be traded, bought and sold as a commodity, towards a vision of the company as a community or partnership in which each employee has a stake'.[6] The City, which New Labour had been wooing for the previous four years, was aghast and made its views known. As one of Blair's advisers explained: 'Company directors were concerned that they would be made accountable to people other than shareholders, and institutional investors were frightened that it would destroy shareholder value.'[7] The idea was dropped and senior Labour figures such as Secretary of State for Trade and Industry, Peter Mandelson, widely regarded as the Svengali behind the election victory, went out of their way to be reassuring. 'We are intensely relaxed about people getting filthy rich,' Mandelson famously said, adding the often forgotten rider 'as long as they pay their taxes'.[8]

Blair's chancellor of the exchequer, Gordon Brown (MP for Kirkcaldy, birthplace of Adam Smith), a believer in the market economy, was equally business-friendly. He relied on the City's overseas earnings and tax payments to keep the economy in balance and was popular there. Immediately he took office, the new chancellor handed over responsibility for setting interest rates to the Bank of England, and the City was delighted that this key decision would now be taken on economic rather than political grounds. Brown also moved responsibility for supervising the banks from the Bank of England to a new regulator, the Financial Services Authority, which was given a dual brief of promoting as well as regulating the sector. Investment bankers and fund managers were warmly welcomed into numbers 10 and 11 Downing Street. They told the government that the economy worked best when markets were left to get on with things, and encouraged the authorities not to intervene. It led to light touch regulation, a laissez faire attitude to takeovers and a continuation of the City's supremacy over other global financial capitals and within the UK economy.

For Barrett's Barclays, the political and regulatory environment for a bank could scarcely have been better. In contrast to the restrictive regime he had just left behind in Canada, Barrett found the British regulators taking seriously their new mission to promote the City, giving banks a free hand to run their businesses.

He was also lucky with the British economy. Gordon Brown's 'golden rule' that over the course of the economic cycle the government would borrow only to invest and not to fund current expenditure had earned him the nickname 'Iron Chancellor' and was the basis of the 'Goldilocks economy' – neither too hot nor too cold, with high employment, rising house prices, low interest rates, steady growth and low inflation – which prevailed for all of Barrett's time at Barclays.

These conditions were particularly good for banks, with interest rates at a 5 per cent sweet spot. Retail banks make their money simply by lending at a higher rate than they offer to depositors and the difference is the net interest margin. In contrast to later years when low interest rates made customers sensitive to any slight change, rates of about 5 per cent gave banks room to make a generous net interest margin by trimming deposit rates and adding a bit to borrowing rates. When conditions were like this, all chief executives had to do was to avoid overlending, keep a lid on costs and not do anything stupid. There was a wobble in the global economy in 2001 after Wall Street's dot.com bubble burst and the terrorist attacks on the World

Trade Center in New York affected investor confidence, but the UK economy motored on, outperforming the US, France and Germany.

A SMALL BUSINESS IN BIRMINGHAM

A casually dressed man in his late twenties, with tidy shoulder-length brown hair and a neatly pressed Ben Sherman shirt hanging loose over his smart jeans, shook hands with an older man in a grey suit and Barclays' tie. They were in the bank's Colmore Row branch, one of Birmingham's most prestigious business streets, just up from Snow Hill station. Karl Edwards, a successful small businessman of the kind held up as role models by Blair and Brown, was there to meet a Barclays' commercial mortgage adviser and had been shown into a small meeting room. The man in the grey suit asked: 'How can we help you today?'

Edwards had started October House Records in 1988 when he was eighteen. At that time he was living at home with his parents on the Chelmsley Wood council estate, the largest in Europe. The estate had a reputation for petty crime and drug dealing, but Edwards detested all that and wanted to make money the right way, taking a job as a DJ at the Solihull ice rink, where he often played dance records from his own collection. After the session ended, skaters would ask where they could buy the tunes he had played, and it gave Edwards the idea of starting a mail order record business from his bedroom.

House music was all the rage and Edwards knew where to find the hottest sounds from dealers in America and Europe. The business built up, his bedroom was soon overflowing with stacks of vinyl and he needed a place to keep his stock. In 1994 he rented space in a Portakabin alongside Birmingham's National Exhibition Centre and an office in town from which he sold records to callers. The following year he started a website and the year after that opened a proper shop in Birmingham. Local DJs hung out there listening to records, so Edwards started selling DJ equipment too and October House Records thrived.

By 1999, he faced a tricky decision. He needed more warehouse space and rents were expensive. It made more sense to buy a purpose-built storage facility but that would mean taking out a mortgage and he hated the idea of being in debt. He thought about it carefully. His customers had plenty of money to spend, there was a good atmosphere in the country and Blair's government seemed to know what they were doing. He discussed it with his wife, Barbara and they decided that although they had a young family, it was now or never. He made an appointment at Barclays where he had been banking since 1993.

The mortgage adviser listened to Edwards' proposition, looked over his bank statements and gave him a form to fill in. He was helpful and Edwards felt he was on his side. The mortgage was approved, Edwards bought a small warehouse and got on with growing his business, grateful to Barclays and happy that he was with such a supportive bank.

'BOBTIMISTIC'

A hundred miles from Birmingham, after Taylor's tortures, Barrett made running Barclays look easy. It was his second stint as a banking chief executive and it showed in his style. The intensity that had seen him work ferociously as a young banker and hands-on chief executive had gone. He no longer had a great appetite for detail but he knew the right questions to ask. After his 100-day review period, he set a target of achieving £1 billion of cost savings by 2003 and focused on the shape of the group. He intended Barclays to become a top ten global bank and there was no more talk of splitting retail and investment banking. He divided his businesses into two categories, regional and national. Barclays' retail banks around the world would always be a series of national businesses and would be managed as such. Investment banking was an international business and would be run on a global basis. Barrett looked carefully at what Diamond was doing.

The sale of BZW's equities business in 1997 and the acrimonious departure of its chief executive, Harrison, were widely assumed by observers to be the end of Barclays as a serious investment bank. However, Diamond had surprised them, using Barclays' strong brand, credit rating and balance sheet to build a different kind of business.

Like Camoys fifteen years earlier, Diamond believed that Barclays' traditional lending relationships could be extended into the newer capital markets in which companies raised money by issuing securities, and he had made stunning progress.

He had something to build with and the economic environment helped. Among the BZW crowd were people who would make the grade in a different environment. Some strategically important units such as the tax structuring and equity derivatives teams had been salvaged from Taylor's fire sale. Barclays had an existing infrastructure and regulatory approval in many global financial centres. A long period of falling interest rates from the late 1990s onwards triggered record levels of activity in the bond market. In Europe, the introduction of the euro and a single set of regulations created a huge common currency capital market, as Diamond had predicted. These were boom times for bond markets but it took inspirational leadership to exploit the benign conditions.

Diamond was always positive – colleagues called him 'Bobtimistic' – but there was a lot to do. He needed people, technology and capital. There were only about 50,000 people working in front-line roles in the global fixed income industry at that time. Diamond needed a few thousand to come to Barclays – and they had to be the right ones.

Choosing who to let go was easy, as Diamond knew many of the employees, himself. On his first walk across BZW's trading floor in New York he had met three people he had fired at previous firms, including one he had fired twice. In his first year alone, 500 people were removed from the payroll.

The hiring was harder. By no means all of the 50,000 were good enough; of those who were, not all would take a punt on Bob. Money helped but there had to be a story to follow too. Diamond looked for people on the rise, such as the Bankers Trust derivatives expert del Missier; a nineteen-year veteran of J. P. Morgan with a passion for military strategy, Tom Kalaris; the brilliant Salomon Brothers banker Naguib Kheraj. He brought in his old mentor Bill Cook to advise on technology, people development and culture. (Cook devised a clever graduate recruitment scheme with IQ tests and cash prizes to encourage students to consider the unfashionable house of Barclays.) Diamond's inner circle developed a 'no jerks' rule for new hires.

Cook remained in New York but flew to London frequently. BZW was a web of different technology systems but at Barclays Capital he insisted that all systems would be properly integrated. Recruits were told they would not be able to build parallel systems and there would be a technology committee to test proposals. They called it 'techno-fascism'.

Expansion was pay-as-you-go. Every new initiative had to pay for itself: there would be no loss leaders. Sterling products had to be profitable before they moved into the euro, and euro products had to be profitable before an attack was made on dollar markets. It was disciplined, remorseless and, in London, unprecedented.

They took no prisoners inside or outside the bank. In 2000, Richard Meddings, the group financial controller, carried out a review of Barclays Capital's capital consumption. The results were startling: according to Meddings, Barclays Capital was not paying the full price for the capital employed in its £50 billion of risk weighted assets, a third of the group total.[9] Meddings sent a paper to Diamond and set up a meeting to discuss it. As he made his way to Canary Wharf, he knew it would be a difficult meeting, but he was not expecting to be confronted by a panel of academic experts with detailed arguments challenging the paper. The investment bank's attitude was: 'We're right. What are you going to do about it?'

Results backed up this aggressive attitude. In 1999 Barclays Capital rebounded from a loss of £270 million in the Russian year of 1998 to an operating profit of £316 million with revenues of £1.2 billion. That recovery put Barclays Capital back on its feet, though it was still not much bigger than BZW had been in its best years. The outside world remained doubtful, with headlines like 'Barclays would be better off in bits'.[10]

But in the next four years Barclays Capital ripped up history. Between 1999 and 2003 staff numbers rose from 3,900 to 5,800 and revenues and profits more than doubled to £2.7 billion and £782 million respectively. Its profits now constituted a fifth of the whole bank's total and the influential trade magazine *Euromoney* named Barclays Capital 'The World's Most Improved Investment Bank' for 2002. Extraordinarily it had been done without corporate finance or equities, causing the magazine to opine: 'the ideal model for the investment bank is no longer certain. It may well be that, by accident or design, the Barclays Capital model is the one that will be vindicated by the market shift taking place around us.'[11] It had been won the hard way, piece by piece, person by person, without a single acquisition. London had never seen anything like it.

Diamond's personal standing in the industry was rising. He was no longer a divisional head whose way had been blocked by a couple of Wall Street titans, but there were disappointments too. In February 2001, on a late-night flight back to London from New York, he felt like a dismal failure. He pulled the blanket up to his chin, fastened his seat belt and put on his eyeshades. He wanted the world to go away. An audacious attempt to land a team of bond specialists from CSFB had just collapsed when his old rival Allen Wheat turned them round at the last minute.[12] Diamond's plan to fix one of Barclays Capital's long-standing problems, the lack of a credible US dollar bond business, had ended in defeat and every First Class seat around him on that BA flight was occupied by CSFB's senior management team celebrating their success.

Wheat's apparent triumph that night was to be his last at CSFB. Within months he was ousted as chief executive and replaced by Diamond's other nemesis, Mack, who had just lost out in a power struggle at Morgan Stanley. Diamond's career resumed its upward trajectory and his photograph appeared more and more often in the press. *Forbes* proclaimed 'Diamond comes up trumps' in March 2003 and two months later a headline in *Euromoney* described him as 'the man who achieved the impossible'.[13]

SQUARE PEGS IN SQUARE HOLES

With Barclays Capital in recovery mode, Barrett turned his attention to fixing his main national business, UK retail banking. The big High Street banks faced increasing competition from the building societies, many of which had changed from member-owned mutual societies into shareholder-owned companies listed on the Stock Exchange.

For a bank like Barclays that was losing market share, buying a mortgage bank was a quick way of catching up. There was also another motive for bulking up. The board were aware that the competition authorities had raised no objection to the merger in 2000 of NatWest, the competitor that Barclays historically measured itself against, with the Royal Bank of Scotland. The board wondered whether Barclays would be next to go.

Barrett decided that Barclays' retail bank needed strengthening. It required assets, management and technology and in August 2000 agreed a £5.4 billion deal to take over the Woolwich, one of the leading building societies. At a 25 per cent premium offer to the share price, Woolwich did not even try to negotiate a better deal for its shareholders. Barrett responded in typically colourful fashion to criticism that Barclays was overpaying: 'I don't believe in Ouija boards but the timing was right. It is an understatement to say that we are pleased by this deal.'[14] When asked why he had not gone for something less expensive, he said that companies are cheap for a reason and he had no interest in taking over another bank's problems.

The acquisition filled out Barclays' weakness in mortgages and took it out of reach of all but the biggest bidders. It brought a big book of assets, a smart internet banking platform, known as 'Open Plan', which enabled customers to flip between their mortgage and current accounts, and a chief executive in John Stewart who had the experience to run Barclays' entire retail banking operation.

That left the problem of the incumbent Varley. Barrett realized that there was obviously more to him than a silver spoon. He was hard working, experienced and intelligent but Barrett did not rate him as a retail banker. In August 2000 he told Varley that Woolwich boss Stewart would be running the retail bank and that he would be in charge of integration. Varley could see the writing on the wall and began to look outside for jobs. A few weeks later, though, Barrett sprung a surprise by making him finance director, a role for which Varley's skills and experience were well suited.

His successor as head of retail, Stewart, was undoubtedly a very good banker. He had joined Woolwich as a branch manager, had worked his way up the organization and front-line staff loved him. He would talk to customers in branches and pick up the phone in call centres. He had turned Woolwich round and was expected to do the same at Barclays. But the Barclays retail bankers were ready for him.

He was a practical man rather than a political operator and the Barclays machine wrapped him in red tape. Meetings were mysteriously difficult to arrange, were cancelled at the last minute or flooded with officials. The Barclays bureaucrats raised obstacles to integration and many senior Woolwich managers left in frustration. Stewart himself stayed only three years before moving to the National Australia Bank.

Despite the high price, the purchase of Woolwich gave Barclays momentum and restored self-confidence. Barrett declared that Barclays would achieve returns for shareholders that would be in the top quartile of its peer group and double economic profit every four years. This would be achieved through managing by value, a consulting technique that involved analysing every business for profit potential, cutting those that could not cover their cost of capital, and by a relentless drive for efficiency.

This was the kind of modern management that Galley, Newmarch and other shareholders had wanted to see from Buxton ten years before, and investors loved it. Less discussed and equally important was an increase in Barclays' leverage, the use of borrowed money to ramp up the bank's returns. In times of low interest rates and rising asset prices it made sense to borrow cheaply and lend that money on at a higher rate or use it to play the markets. It was an easy way to make money and every bank did it, in the process often lowering the credit standards they required of borrowers, particularly in the housing market.

In 2000, the big international banks borrowed an average of twenty times their equity capital – essentially shareholders' reserves – to lend to customers and trade in the markets. When Barrett took over in 1999 Barclays' leverage was in line with the market average. By 2004, the leverage ratio of Barclays' peer group had crept up to twenty-two times but Barclays' had soared to over thirty. A 3 per cent fall in asset prices would have wiped out its equity capital and the bank would have been technically insolvent. But the global economy was flying, the revered Fed chairman Alan Greenspan was setting the direction, and the prospect of such a large fall in apparently widely diversified collections of assets seemed inconceivable to bankers, regulators and their boards.

Using these methods of leverage and modern management, Barrett achieved his target of getting Barclays to be a top ten global bank at the end of 2003, when it was ninth in the world measured by market capitalization. Over Barrett's first four years to the end of 2003, total shareholder return – the increase in the share price plus dividends reinvested in Barclays' shares – was 31 per cent, double that of its peers and in contrast to a 28 per cent fall in the FTSE 100 which, despite a strong real economy, was depressed by carnage in technology and internet-related stocks. In 2004, the first year of the next cycle, Barclays topped the peer group. The role of leverage in this achievement was scarcely noticed or questioned.

Barrett's run of success was briefly interrupted in May 2002 when he and the chief executives of two other High Street banks, Fred Goodwin of the Royal Bank of Scotland and Peter Ellwood of Lloyds, appeared before the House of Commons Treasury Select Committee. They were asked about the Competition Commission's recent finding that the big British banks had made £725 million of 'excessive profits' over the past three years. Barrett batted the question away, saying: 'I do not know what "excess" profits means' and gave the committee a technical explanation of the cost of equity capital. The other bankers were equally dismissive of suggestions that their organizations were profiteering, but the following morning the *Daily Telegraph* newspaper reported the session under the headline 'Not us mate – we're only doing our job'.[15]

However, the banks' high profits were an issue that kept popping up. A year later, called in by the same committee to answer questions about credit card charges, Barrett was unable to explain a complicated Barclaycard offer which claimed to give consumers a zero interest rate but in reality did no such thing and was later banned by the Office of Fair Trading. When challenged, he said: 'I do not borrow on credit cards because it is too expensive,' and added that he also did not advise his children to use credit cards. 'Barclays chief executive Matt Barrett candidly criticised his own product, suggesting that the astute consumer would do well to steer well clear of it,' said the BBC.[16] Other banks also attracted criticism for their charges, lack of transparency and (in the case of Fred Goodwin's RBS) for sending a credit card application form to a dog called Monty.

Such stories seemed only to add to the fun. These were the

go-getting days of the free market and unfettered shareholder value in which the intervention of quasi-public bodies such as the Competition Commission were dismissed in favour of market solutions. Competition, it was believed, would protect the consumer, and light touch regulation rather than prescriptive interference was the order of the day. Barrett and the other chief executives saw off the complaints and got on with the job of making money for shareholders.

Barrett saved Barclays. He came in at a time when the bank was vulnerable after the bloody departure of Martin Taylor. The retail bank was underperforming and the investment bank was in disgrace after the Russian calamity. Middleton had calmed things down but when Barrett took over, Barclays would have been swallowed up if it had stumbled. Barrett's sure touch took that issue off the table. During his first year, 1999, despite the weak first half, group profits were up by 30 per cent to £2.5 billion. When these were announced in February 2000 and discussed at the annual general meeting in April, they took away some of the heat that the public relations blunders of clumsy closures and proposed charges for cash machines had generated. The following year saw pre-tax profits up by £1 billion to £3.5 billion, with Woolwich kicking in for the first time. After the dot.com crash, a slowdown in the global economy and weak stock markets saw profits stagnate in 2001 and then dip to £3.2 billion in 2002, but the UK remained strong, the US recovered and in 2003 profits grew again to £3.8 billion.

It was Matt Barrett's master class. He had learned the business of banking from the bottom up and had been a chief executive before. He did not need to read the copious briefing packs: this was a business that he already understood. Not only did he know what was wrong, he knew how to fix it. He was a banker not a commentator, a streetfighter not a toff. He had operational feel and could implement. He was shrewd, smart and strong. He saw Varley's strengths and put him in the right slot. He did not care if he paid a full price for Woolwich; it was a good business, filled a strategic hole and would be worth it. The boardroom purred, shareholders were happy and employees were well paid and proud to work at Barclays. It all seemed too good to be true – and unfortunately it was.

BARRETT'S TIME BOMBS

Retail banking changed in the 1990s. Before then, selling was very amateurish, just a casual conversation when there was an opportunity to be helpful: 'You're going to Spain for your holiday? Have a lovely time and would you like some pesetas to take with you?' For branch staff, banking was a service to customers and profit was the last thing on their mind. Branch banking worked like the army. At Barclays there was a series of nine grades from managers' assistant to the most senior branch manager, grades five and above being entitled to a company car. Promotion involved timeserving, training courses and rotation around the business. At the end of the year there was a bonus that depended on the bank's overall results rather than individual performance. Everyone got the same and the sums were not life changing – 10 per cent of salary would represent an excellent year – but the scheme encouraged corporate spirit and discouraged thoughts of personal aggrandizement. People were proud to work for Barclays, felt that it belonged to them and they to it.

By the early 1990s, however, as competition and pressure to deliver results increased, branches were being reorganized into marketing units with senior sales roles filled by people with no banking background. It was a sign that branch bankers were expected to sell and that expectation soon became critical. In the scruffy staff rooms behind the smart banking counters, whiteboards appeared, showing who had sold what that day and how many sales points they had earned. As real time data became available to management, the pressure to perform every day increased, sales targets were introduced and profit replaced service as the industry's objective. These were industry-wide trends – Lloyds in particular was a real machine, priding itself on sales management. But if Lloyds was the leader, the other big banks, including Barclays, were determined to catch up, and incentives would be how they did it.

Soon after he joined Barclays, Barrett replaced existing share option schemes with a plan 'designed to provide more leverage for exceptional performance creating higher shareholder value'. Executive directors' performance bonus was 'explicitly linked to Economic

Profit' – profit adjusted for the cost of capital used by the business.[17] In 2001 he widened the circle, introducing a Performance Incentive Plan for all staff, one that 'enables people to see a direct link between their contribution to Barclays' performance and their own compensation'. Public statements spoke of embedding a high performance culture with stretching standards for employees and 'variable pay-for-performance incentives directly tied to economic profit generation'.[18]

Linking pay with performance was common in business. From the 1980s, backed by academic theory, management consultants promoted the idea that the interests of employees and shareholders should be 'aligned'.[19] All banks did it but Barclays under Barrett was unusually explicit in doing so. It was the same with another fashionable concept, the sales techniques of 'cross-selling' and 'up-selling'.

These practices originated in fast-moving consumer businesses such as cinemas, where staff were told to encourage moviegoers to buy high-margin soft drinks and popcorn along with their standard entry ticket, but they were new to banks. Once the idea caught on, the banks pushed it hard; again Barclays was unusually upfront. When it reached an agreement with Legal & General to sell its insurance policies, Barrett explained that 'cross-sell and up-sell is the mantra',[20] a clear message to staff that was reinforced by the pay incentives that had just been put in place.

One product that could be easily up-sold and cross-sold was payment protection insurance (PPI), policies that were meant to insure borrowers against loss of earnings through sickness or redundancy. The banks' profits on each PPI policy were very high and staff were given extra sales points for closing a sale. Thus incentivized, staff went to work on PPI with a will. By 2005 Barclays had the highest market share of all the banks; between 2001 and 2005, PPI formed between 32 per cent and 42 per cent of Barclays' UK retail and business profits. Nearly 70 per cent of borrowers from the bank in these years bought a PPI policy with their loan.[21]

The combination of share options, sales-related pay, performance-related bonuses and cross-selling was potent. Regional managers, branch managers and sales staff in the branches could earn a lot of money if they pumped out the products. The numbers were not the life-changing sums that Diamond's investment bankers could earn, but for branch staff earning £30,000 a year a 10 per cent bonus could pay for a holiday and a 25 per cent bonus could look after the mortgage for a year. For branch and regional managers earning between £50,000 and £100,000, the rewards were even greater and they urged their staff to sell, sell, sell. In the most aggressive branches, the cry would go up on a Friday afternoon: 'We need to sell three more policies this afternoon to hit our weekly target. Double sales points on every one sold.' The temptation to stuff the client was, for some, irresistible.

At one level, Barrett understood this risk and emphasized the importance of treating customers fairly. The experience of the French bottled mineral water Perrier in 1990, when a badly cleaned pipe contaminated the water and damaged the brand, had made an impression on him; he wanted to know how Barclays' pipes were cleaned. He established a Brand and Reputation Committee and devoted part of Barclays' annual November planning meeting to matters such as employee satisfaction, customer grievances and the bank's reputation.[22] However, the bulk of such meetings were spent discussing how top quartile shareholder returns could be delivered and the connection between staff incentives and the way customers were treated was missed.

Consequently neither he, the rest of the executive team nor the board delved very far into the detail of exactly how the money was being made. It all looked fine on paper. Away from head office, though, out in the branches, more than a few target-driven managers responded to the incentive plans by putting themselves and the bank above their customers' interests. This proved to be a costly mistake.

II

Diamond or Varley, 2003

THE ENFORCER CALLS

In the early summer of 2003, Barclays chairman Middleton received a visit from the boardroom enforcer. Despite the twinkling eyes in his ruddy face, Nigel Rudd was a tough cookie. He had been on the Barclays board since 1996 and chaired several major companies. His golfing friend Nigel Mobbs had just retired and he was now the dominant figure on the board, as he tended to be wherever he worked. He was deputy chairman designate to replace the retiring Sir Brian Jenkins, a Woolwich import. Having already been instrumental in the departure of one generation of Barclays' top brass, he now had his sights on another.

Middleton had been on the board for twelve years and had his feet comfortably under the table. In 1999, the year he had been both chairman and chief executive, he had earned £1.75 million, more than ten times his salary as a senior civil servant; as chairman alone since 2000, his annual earnings exceeded half a million pounds. He and Lady Middleton acted as ambassadors for the bank and enjoyed the lifestyle. Barrett had recently told the board that he wanted to go and that he wanted to do so immediately. It was Middleton's job, as chairman, to lead the search for his successor, but behind the scenes the board was disconcerted. They liked what Barrett had given them and did not want to contemplate life without him. Middleton was sixty-nine years old and had been chief executive and then chairman for nearly five years. He was still on top of his game but he couldn't go on for ever. How would it be if Middleton stepped down and Barrett replaced him in the chair?

Rudd was sent to sound out Barrett. At first the chief executive was adamant that he wanted to retire to the sun. The English winters were long, the summers unpredictable and he wanted to go back to the kind of life he had contemplated before he came to Barclays. But Rudd was persuasive, played the loyalty card and refused to go away. Finally he was able to tell the board: 'I've got Matt.' Next, he had to tell Middleton.

Rudd was always direct and to the point. His view was that if you had bad news to give, it was best to get it out there straight away. He told Middleton: 'Look, Peter, the board feel that it is time for you to go.' He said there was nothing personal nor any criticism of his performance but that it was a matter of succession planning. It was usually hard to read what Middleton was really thinking but this time there was no doubt: he was very cross. After some discussion, it was agreed that he would leave in eighteen months' time, at the end of 2004, handing over to Barrett.

Leading the search for a new chief executive was therefore Middleton's last job for Barclays. There were five internal candidates and the board decided that all should be interviewed separately over dinner, which was the way the officer class traditionally sorted things out – in the Mess.

HIS TO LOSE?

Varley was busy preparing the group's mid-year results for 2003 when his email pinged with a message from Gill Herbert, Middleton's assistant. 'Sir Peter and the board invite you to an informal discussion over dinner next Tuesday.' Varley groaned. 'Informal, my hat,' he thought. This was an interview for the chief executive's job and would be as important as any meeting in his career. Just three years previously he had thought he was being eased out; now he was within sight of the summit. He still had work to do finalizing the results' announcement. It would be a busy few days.

As finance director he saw many shareholders and came across well with them. He had a fine brain and made a good combination with Barrett. With direct experience of most parts of the bank and an overview of the whole business he had a strong CV. Many on the board thought the post of chief executive was his to lose, but as he prepared for the interview with typical thoroughness, Varley knew that he had one serious rival.

As the results flowed in, Diamond's reputation within Barclays rose. In addition to running Barclays Capital, in August 2002 he was appointed chairman of Barclays Global Investors, the second largest asset manager in the world measured by funds under management but currently underperforming in profits.[1] By 2003 Diamond was not just a credible candidate to replace Barrett as chief executive; to many external Barclays watchers he was the favourite to do so.

EAT BEFORE YOU COME

One by one the five aspiring chief executives came to dinner with the non-executive directors. A dining room in the basement at 54 Lombard Street, slightly too small for the numbers present, was laid out formally with an array of cutlery and glasses on a polished round table. Drinks were served in the corner as the group assembled.

It was a domestic affair with no external candidates. The five candidates revealed a variety of styles. Varley was careful and precise; Diamond was charismatic. Roger Davis, who ran business banking, was confident and forceful; the Barclaycard chief, Gary Hoffman, obviously knew how to run a business; David Roberts, a former Welsh international athlete who had joined Barclays as a graduate trainee in 1983 and was now head of the retail bank, was the youngest man in the field.

After the waiting staff had withdrawn, the evening's candidate made a five-minute vision statement, while the non-executives ate – the candidates all knew that they should eat beforehand – and then asked questions.

The Irish-Canadian chairman-elect was excluded from the interviews by governance protocol and seven of the eight non-executive directors were British. The six men and two women included a past Lord Mayor of London, Brian Jenkins; a future High Sheriff of Cambridgeshire, David Arculus; three knights, Richard Broadbent,

Jenkins and Nigel Rudd; and a Cambridge professor of management studies, Sandra Dawson. Hilary Cropper and a former chief executive of Boots, Stephen Russell, were the other British non-executives. Quite what the eighth member, Jurgen Zech, a German who had recently retired from the insurance industry, thought of this very British process is not known.

In reality, however, it was a two-horse race. Varley had been talking to investors for the past two years and his presentation was calm and controlled. He was comfortable in the dinner setting and exuded authority. Diamond, by contrast, was mystified by the idea that a great bank like Barclays would choose its chief executive in this way. Why on earth would the board combine a crucial business decision with a semi-social occasion? It was an alien environment for him so he had prepared for the evening with professional help. Realizing that for this audience he would have to present a conservative image, he played the judicious banker to demonstrate he could run a large business and emphasized the importance of culture and values. His replies to questions were courteous, well informed and with a dash of wry humour. He finished his pitch: 'Barclays is a great bank with a proud history. It would be an honour to lead it.'

After the final dinner, Middleton assembled the non-executives together to collect their impressions. They agreed that Davis, Hoffman and Roberts were all good men but they were not chief executive material here and now. Diamond had his supporters but the attitude of traditional elements on the board was: 'An American investment banker as chief executive of Barclays? That really won't do.' Others asked: 'Why are we seeing him, then?' They were told: 'He's very important and he wants the job.'

Varley also divided the board. Some considered him too pedestrian to run Barclays and pointed to what they thought was his poor judgement when he ran the retail bank. They also doubted his ability to run the investment bank were Diamond to leave and argued that not appointing Diamond was just too risky. Others felt Varley had the intelligence, experience and bearing to carry it off in the style that Barclays required. With no clear consensus, Middleton said he would take the board's assessment to Barrett and seek his views.

FINALLY, THE CHAIRMAN SPEAKS

Diamond, meanwhile, was wondering what was going on. Some weeks had passed since his interview and the trail had gone cold. The signs were not good. If he was going to get the job, he thought, surely conversations would be taking place about compensation and succession planning at Barclays Capital. Why wouldn't anyone tell him what was happening?

Late in September he and Middleton were in Dubai attending an IMF and World Bank meeting at which the UK's chancellor of the exchequer Gordon Brown would be speaking and many central bankers, policy-makers and big Barclays' clients would be present. Diamond looked for an opportunity to have a few words with Middleton but he always seemed to be with other people at the formal sessions so Diamond arranged to see him at his hotel. The usually imperturbable Barclays chairman seemed uncomfortable and reluctant to engage. They talked in general but Diamond left the meeting without having asked him directly how far the board had got in reaching a decision about the next chief executive. On the way back to his own hotel, he was annoyed with himself for not having pushed things further. He feared the message was clear: they were going for someone else. He figured that if the board were considering him, there would by now have been an interview with Barrett and discussions about compensation. The silence was all too revealing.

Middleton took Barrett carefully through the board's deliberations, reminding him that he was being consulted, not given a casting vote. Barrett saw Barclays' core business as corporate and consumer banking and knew enough about investment banking to be wary of the financial and reputational risks it carried. He liked Diamond but was aware that he could be headstrong. Varley had learned from his mistakes and would be a safe choice. Middleton reported back to the board: 'Matt wants John.'

Varley had already been given strong hints that the job was his by the time Middleton and Barrett called him in to tell him the good news. He was less pleased to hear that the unsuccessful candidates would be offered a seat on the board, but that was apparently not negotiable. He went away to plan the transition while the rest were told. Middleton and Barrett, meanwhile, had to work out how to tell Diamond. It would be a delicate conversation. Diamond would be disappointed, possibly upset, and, although the bank was not yet dependent on Barclays Capital, it needed his continued commitment.

Diamond had not been back in London long when the call came summoning him to Middleton's office immediately. Barrett was there too to hear Middleton hesitantly reveal that Varley would be Barclays' next chief executive. Diamond said he was indeed disappointed with the outcome and the way they had dealt with it. 'You seem to assume that I will be fine with that but you have never asked me. This has been the silliest process I have ever been through. You haven't asked any of us for an application. We had a chat over dinner. There has been no communication and no explanation. It's no way to run a bank. Thank you for letting me know.'

He needed some time to think before returning to Canary Wharf, where his glass office on the trading floor was no place to hide disappointment and anger. The board had led him down the garden path before reverting to type and choosing one of their own. He wanted nothing more to do with them. He plugged his headset into his mobile phone and went for a walk.

As he paced around the City in that October afternoon, Diamond gradually calmed down and weighed up his options. He could do what he had done twice before at Morgan Stanley and CSFB and move out to get round an obstacle. His achievements at Barclays would make him a strong candidate to head up one of the big investment banks; and as there was always a rapid turnover at these institutions, he probably wouldn't have to wait long. Or he could make even more money by moving into private equity, where many of his friends worked. He was supporting a large extended family, and if you could not have status through the highest office, extraordinary wealth was the next best thing.

He sat down in a small coffee shop, ordered a frothy cappuccino and stared out through the condensation dripping down the window pane. Would leaving be seen as a failure? Would he be regarded as a man who had climbed the greasy pole but slipped down just before reaching the top? Or should he stay, finish the job he had started at Barclays Capital and wait to see if there would be another opportunity to get the position he so coveted?

Then there was Varley. Diamond and Varley had some history. Varley had supported Taylor's plan to demerge the investment bank in 1998. Diamond had often been frustrated by the constraints from Varley as finance director in head office. They had sorted it out but working with someone was different from working for someone. Diamond wondered whether he could trust Varley to support him as he took Barclays Capital to the next stage.

He decided to take counsel. His first call was to Jennifer and then he phoned del Missier, his key lieutenant at Barclays Capital. Del Missier was upbeat: 'Great. We've got a lot of work to do here. Let's get on with it.' Diamond called a couple more confidants at Barclays Capital and got the same response: none of them had truly wanted him to get the job while Barclays Capital was still a work in progress.

Nevertheless it still hurt. He was both disappointed and annoyed. He believed that he deserved the job. He felt he had been used, played with and then discarded. He had not been treated right. He was five years older than Varley and might never be offered the job again. The emotional side of him urged: 'Quit, go back to the US, get a top job on Wall Street.' The rational side countered: 'Stay here, finish what you have started and see how things play out.' He walked around the winding streets and dark alleys of the financial district for nearly two hours, dodging the City workers oblivious to the corporate drama inside the man threading his way between them. Then he took a deep breath, walked back into 54 Lombard Street and got the lift to the sixth floor.

John Varley's assistant was surprised to see Diamond appear at her desk. She wanted to warn her boss and give him a few seconds to prepare. Varley looked up quizzically as she entered his office. There was no time to brief him as Diamond walked straight into the room behind her.

12

The Big Vision, 2004

WITH OR WITHOUT?

Varley was in two minds about the investment bank. He had voted in favour of Taylor's demerger plan at the New York board meeting because he instinctively didn't trust the business, but as finance director he had seen Diamond turn it round and had been impressed. He could see a future for Barclays both with and without Diamond.

If he stayed, it would open up global possibilities. Following recent US legislation allowing US retail and commercial banks into full-scale investment banking, Chase had bought J. P. Morgan for $30 billion and Citigroup had added Schroders to its financial empire.[1] A breed of super-banks was emerging with investment banking at their core, and the continued presence of Diamond, the only man to have built a globally credible investment bank in London from the bottom up, would give Barclays the means of joining them.

If he left, Varley envisaged a more limited strategy and a less prominent place in the global banking hierarchy. Finding someone else with the charisma and operational grip to hold the business together would be nearly impossible. Varley had seen at BZW the drain on management time and financial resources that an underperforming investment bank involved: it worked only with Diamond at the helm.

Yet again, if he stayed it would not be easy. Diamond was ambitious and confident but difficult to deal with. His optimism was both a strength and a weakness, capable of driving himself and others to extraordinary achievements but also obscuring failings in those who reported to him. He was himself completely ethically straight, which led him to assume that others would be the same, a dangerous assumption on Wall Street. His cold stare and judgemental tone could crush those who displeased him and discouraged bearers of bad tidings from speaking up. If anything was amiss, he might be the last to know.

Barclays Capital was made in his image. They thought they always knew best, pushed things to the limit and argued ferociously if head office tried to interfere. They were on a mission to compete with Goldman Sachs, required lots of capital and the nature of their business involved unpredictable financial and reputational risk. Diamond could not possibly know all the people who had joined or even all of his managing directors. At times the investment bankers resembled adrenaline junkies on a roller coaster, enjoying the thrill and eager for the next ride. Every situation for them was an opportunity to buy or sell. They even traded an index, Vix, the Volatility Index, which enabled them to bet on how active the market would be. Varley distrusted volatility every bit as much as the investment bankers adored it. It was acceptable only if it was properly managed and Varley needed Diamond if he was going to keep such a business. He kept coming back to the same conclusion: without him, the investment bank might not be viable; with him, it might work.

As Varley's assistant retreated, Varley knew that Diamond's next words would determine Barclays' direction for a very long time. Diamond looked serious. Then he said, 'John, I want to offer my congratulations. This process has been terrible but that's not your fault. You deserve the job and you have my full support.'

Varley moved round his desk to shake Diamond's hand. They reached a deal late that afternoon. Varley would give Diamond the budget and the capital to double Barclays Capital's profits by 2007, a project known as the 'Alpha Plan'. Diamond would support Varley in his ambition to build one of the world's great banks and be his de facto deputy. They shook hands again, two very different but determined men with big ambitions.

APPLE-PICKING TIME

While Barclays' board were choosing Barrett's successor, 3000 miles away on a warm Saturday afternoon in September 2003 a crowd of casually dressed couples sipped cocktails in the grounds of a 1930s mansion at 444 Round Hill Road, Greenwich, Connecticut, an estate belonging to Sandy Weill, whose Travelers Group had merged with Citigroup in 1998 and where he was now chairman and chief executive. It was his annual apple-picking party to which Weill invited the bank's senior management and their partners to do some gentle work in the orchards and enjoy a fine barbecue prepared by his chefs. It was all a little awkward. The office wags joked that Sandy was too mean to pay proper apple pickers, but it was the closest Weill came to hosting a team event and invitations were coveted.

An English couple in their early forties stood on the edge of the group. Antony and Amanda Jenkins were easing their way in when they were approached by a large man with silver white hair. Jenkins, an Oxford graduate from the north-west of England, recognized him as one of Citigroup's most senior executives, Frits Seegers, who ran consumer banking for Asia-Pacific. Jenkins had joined Citigroup's middle management from Barclays fourteen years previously and after a series of promotions he was now running a large part of global cards, an important business just beyond the edge of Seegers' sprawling empire.

Seegers ignored Amanda, said abruptly: 'Antony, I'm hearing good things. We should talk', then moved on. Jenkins decided that the very brief encounter had been some sort of job offer, but it was one that he had no intention of taking up. Although Seegers was well in with Weill, he had a fearsome reputation inside Citigroup.

TAKING IT TO THE NEXT LEVEL

Beneath Varley's bookish demeanour lay a committed capitalist. This punctilious lawyer had learned banking as a corporate financier, trading and risk management at BZW and modern financial techniques at Odey Asset Management. He knew all about shorting (selling shares you didn't own in the hope that the price would fall and you could buy them back more cheaply before any money changed hands); leverage (borrowing money at low interest rates to invest in the markets); derivatives; and hedging risk. As Barclays' finance director, his interactions with investors showed him that shareholders of all kinds were demanding in their expectations. He knew that quick results were expected and he had no time to waste.

As he prepared for his first board meeting as chief executive designate in November 2003, he developed his strategy. Diamond's success in building Barclays Capital meant that something much more ambitious than the narrow bank he had supported in Taylor's day was now possible. He told the board that one-stop banking, in which corporate clients bought all manner of financial services from their bank, had finally taken off and his vision was for Barclays to become a universal bank, increasing the overseas contribution from a quarter to three-quarters of profits over the next ten years and completing the journey begun thirty years before under Tuke and Bevan. It would involve buying and selling businesses, leverage, using the capital markets to fund the business and paying top rates for people. He told them in a message later repeated to shareholders: 'The task of every generation of leadership is to take performance to the next level and that is what we are determined to do. I want the new era of leadership, building on the profound transformation of the last years, to be characterized by growth.'[2] There could be no halfway house. The big banks were dominating the industry and this was the moment to join them. It was a stupendous vision and it blew the board away.

THE WONDER YEARS

Varley formally took over as chief executive on 1 September 2004 and the results for that year and for 2005 were outstanding. In 2004, profits were up 20 per cent to £4,580 million, the dividend was increased by a stunning 17 per cent and the return on shareholders' funds was a juicy 19 per cent. Most parts of the business contributed; only UK retail was flat. There was a similar pattern in 2005 when profits rose by 15 per cent to £5,280 million and the dividend was increased by 11 per cent; UK retail managed just a 7 per cent increase. Even though Varley's first two years had gone very well, it was Diamond who became the globally recognized star as Barclays Capital roared ahead. It now made up a quarter of Barclays' profits, grew by

22 per cent in 2004 to exceed £1 billion and 25 per cent in 2005 to £1,272 million.[3] Diamond was the recipient of awards such as European Banker of the Year and was regularly touted as a candidate for the top banking jobs back in the US; Barclays Capital was named 2004, 'Bank of the Year' by the influential trade magazine *International Financing Review*.

The business had completely changed from the modest entity Diamond had originally put together from the ashes of BZW. In these two years, 4,100 people were added to the payroll nearly doubling its size to 9,900. It was impossible to apply the 'no jerks' rule or to instill Bill Cook's culture with recruitment of this scale. Barclays Capital was a melting pot of migrants from other investment banks united by the thrill of the chase and a love of money.

Given the importance of his business, shareholders asked why Diamond was not on the board, why he alone of the unsuccessful candidates had declined a board position. To join the board it would mean disclosing his pay. This was a situation made for no-nonsense Rudd. He told Diamond that 'people kind of know anyway' and even if there was much media interest, it would be a one-day wonder. After Diamond joined the board, on 1 June 2005, the accounts disclosed that he was paid £4.5 million, more than double the chief executive, with the explanation that 'his arrangements reflect general practice in the investment banking industry.'[4] The *Financial Times* confirmed Rudd's judgement: 'Mr Diamond's rewards are not outlandish when set alongside the most successful people in the transatlantic financial services industry and they are performance related.'[5]

When he was appointed to the board, Diamond was also given the title of Barclays' president with the expectation that he would have some overarching involvement in the affairs of the whole group. Day-to-day responsibilities for Barclays Capital passed to del Missier and Grant Kvalheim – who had joined from Deutsche Bank a few years before – but Diamond stayed in the Barclays Capital incentive plan 'to maintain close alignment of reward with Mr Diamond's contribution to the profit of Barclays Capital'.[6] He and Varley settled into a partnership reporting to an increasingly disengaged Barrett in the chairman's office. As Barclays Capital's business grew, its leader's influence became irresistible and his rewards exponential.

Barrett's interest lay not in the day-to-day issues of running a bank but in its strategic direction, particularly in whether merger and acquisition activity could accelerate Varley's vision. The question was partly prompted by an unsolicited approach from Sandy Weill's Citigroup, but Barclays had no interest in being a smallish part of someone else's grand plan and the board quickly rebuffed it. More interesting was a pan-European project led by Varley. Discussions about a three-way merger with Société Générale and Unicredit went some way but died after a disagreement between the prospective French and Italian partners over the allocation of the top jobs.

The most serious talks in 2004 and 2005 were with Bank of America. Barrett twice met Ken Lewis and James Hance, Bank of America's chairman and vice-chairman respectively, and Varley met them at various times in London and New York and once at their headquarters in Charlotte, North Carolina. Discussions lasted several weeks. Varley was pencilled in to become chief executive of the enlarged group and Diamond would run the investment bank. Talks fizzled out before the board was called upon to make a judgement on what would have been the end of Barclays as an independent business. But the merger and acquisition question continued to preoccupy the board and they would shortly return to it.

VARLEY SPLASHES OUT

Varley had not been pleased to see Davis, Hoffman and Roberts given board positions after his own promotion and the performance of the retail bank under Davis concerned him. In 2005 he planned to put Hoffman in charge of retail and recruit a new head of Barclaycard but first Hoffman had to recruit his successor. He knew the top managers in cards pretty well, including the former Barclays man and Weill apple picker Jenkins.

Jenkins was just on his way in to the Citigroup headquarters on Park Avenue in September 2005 when he received a call asking if he was interested in returning to Barclays to take charge of Barclaycard. As convention required, Jenkins initially expressed his reluctance to leave Citigroup and New York where he was very happy but Barclays were insistent. They assured him that under new chief executive Varley there was an exciting story emerging and offered to fly their recruiting team to New York to meet him. Jenkins decided there was nothing to lose and agreed to meet Barclays' chief operating officer, Paul Idzik, at New York's JFK airport. The meeting took place, bizarrely, in American Airlines' Admirals Club, a private enclave at the airport reserved for the airline's Gold Card holders. Idzik, a former management consultant responsible for finding and developing talent, sold the bank hard to Jenkins. After a couple of hours, he got back on a plane and returned to London.

Later that day Jenkins took a car round JFK to meet the head of human resources, Cathy Turner, and Hoffman. This time there was no Admirals Club, just an anonymous hotel on the edge of the airport. The meeting went well enough for Jenkins to agree to a formal interview the following day at Barclays Capital's offices at 200 Park Avenue and to meet Varley and Diamond in London on 31 October.

He met Diamond in the morning on the second floor of the Barclays Capital building at North Colonnade, Canary Wharf. Diamond in sell mode was captivatingly charming and reassuring. The afternoon was spent with Varley on the thirty-first floor of Barclay's newly opened head office, along the street in Churchill Place.* As they talked in a meeting room just off Varley's corner office, a storm brewed up to the west, smashing hard drops of rain into the plate glass windows. Jenkins wondered if it was a Hallowe'en omen.

Varley's pitch was that Diamond had done a great job at the investment bank but that consumer banking was lagging. The ambition was to become a top universal bank and to do that the consumer side of the business needed to be brought up to speed. If he came over, Jenkins would report directly to Varley and join the executive committee. Barclaycard would be managed separately from the rest of the consumer bank, Jenkins would have plenty of autonomy, and if all went well, who knows, there could be a succession to a higher level still.

* In 2001, Barclays announced that its head office would move to new premises in Canary Wharf and its registered address formally changed from 54 Lombard Street to 1 Churchill Place on 31 May 2005.

Jenkins flew back to New York to discuss the situation with Amanda. Meanwhile, back in London, Varley too was thinking. His original plan had been to retain the existing structure in which Barclaycard and retail banking were separately managed but now he had decided to have both businesses report to Hoffman, to whom Jenkins (if he came) would report. He wanted to break the news over lunch so he could see Jenkins' reaction himself and respond accordingly. He phoned Jenkins in New York: 'Antony, I'm sorry to interrupt you but there is something that I want to discuss with you. It's nothing to worry about but can you come over for a day or two?'

Despite Varley's assurances, Jenkins was unsettled. He and Amanda were flying over to spend Thanksgiving with their two children, who were at school in Kent, and were planning to be in London the next day. It would be possible to fit in a meeting and Varley obviously had something important to say.

Amanda drove them from Canterbury to a hotel in London and Jenkins took a train to Canary Wharf. As the Docklands Light Railway rattled through booming east London, Jenkins felt uneasy, wondering what news he was about to hear. Would the offer be withdrawn? Was there some top-secret plan that could not be imparted by telephone? He doubted that it would be good news; his resolve to join Barclays weakened with every stop.

He was shown to a dining room at the top of 1 Churchill Place, where Varley was waiting for him. Once the servers had left the room Varley came straight to the point:

'Look, Antony, this is slightly awkward but there is a snag with the arrangements that we were discussing. There are some leadership changes on the way and although I said that you would be reporting to me, you will in fact be reporting to Gary and through him you can make your views known to the executive committee. Then in six months that will change again and you can take your place on the executive committee.'

Jenkins was shocked. 'That's very surprising, not at all what we discussed. I need to think about this.'

Varley replied: 'We do appreciate that and there should be some compensation for the disappointment. If you join on these terms we will pay you a signing-on bonus of £1 million.'

Jenkins and Amanda had been due to dine with Gary and Nicola Hoffman that evening but it seemed inappropriate and so instead they went back to their hotel to reflect. The question in his mind was whether he really wanted to work for people who changed their minds at the last minute. He decided that on balance he did not and the following morning telephoned Varley to say that he would not, after all, be joining Barclays.

There was then a series of conversations with Varley and Idzik in which they emphasized the opportunity of being part of a universal bank that was going places. It was a persuasive pitch but the story had already changed once and Jenkins was wary. He suggested that Barclays offer some financial protection that would be triggered if certain conditions were not met. Varley considered the idea and consulted with colleagues. Barclaycard, once the jewel in Barclays' crown, was having a poor year and had lost its lustre. Jenkins would reinvigorate it and Varley knew that good managers in the world of credit cards were both expensive and hard to find. After more internal discussion, he made Jenkins an offer: if he was not on the executive committee by the end of 2006, Jenkins would be entitled to receive a further £6 million and would be able to leave with all the money then owing to him paid out in full. It was the kind of offer that would have been spectacular enough for an investment banker, but in the less exotic world of consumer banking, where the going rate for a head of cards was under half a million pounds a year, it was extraordinary. It was an offer Jenkins could not refuse and he agreed to join the bank with effect from 1 January 2006.

As 2006 began, with Barclays Capital outperforming both UK Banking and Barclaycard, Varley did some further thinking. The investment bank was becoming so successful that the balance of power within the group was wrong. Varley decided to reorganize the bank into two halves: the more traditional lending business which he called 'Group Retail and Commercial Banking', and the capital markets activities of Barclays Capital and fund management, which he called 'Investment Banking and Investment Management'. Diamond was already running the latter so Varley looked for a leader of equal calibre to run the former.

After a search led by Diamond, who had been given board

responsibility for talent management, the preferred candidate was
Jenkins' admirer at Citigroup, Frits Seegers. Frits was married to Kar-
tika Sukarno, daughter of the first president of Indonesia, and had
held various positions in Citigroup's consumer banking group in a
career of seventeen years. He achieved results by pushing himself and
his people hard and Citigroup's senior management loved him. He
was an international banker with a product knowledge that matched
Barclays' needs. Even so, at their initial meeting Varley was unsure.
Further research revealed a mixed reputation. He was certainly a
hard worker and a technically skilled banker but soundings revealed
a ruthless streak and a harshness with those who displeased him. Still
unsure, Varley took one further reference from Sir Deryck Maughan,
a former vice-chairman of Citigroup, who simply gave him the facts
about his record in a neutral way. Varley went ahead with the hire.
Seegers would become chief executive of Global Retail and Commercial Banking on 10 July 2006 with a pay, bonus and share package in
his first year totalling nearly £10 million.[7]

Before the move could be announced, Varley had to have one more
difficult conversation: Jenkins needed to be told. At the end of May,
Varley called him in to break this further news. 'Antony, I know this
wasn't the deal that we had but I have decided to cluster retail and
credit cards under one leader. You may know him from Citigroup.
His name is Frits Seegers.' Jenkins' style is measured and he was silent
for a moment but his stomach was churning as he thought back to
apple-picking day.

Jenkins looked hard at Varley. 'Yes, I do know him. Have you
checked him out?' Now it was Varley's turn to pause. Some members
of his own executive team had warned against hiring Seegers and
it looked as though Jenkins was of the same view. Varley replied:
'We have indeed taken references and have hired him to manage
all consumer services including Barclaycard. You will be reporting
to him.'

Jenkins said; 'I understand the merits of grouping everything
together but Frits will be a disaster. This triggers my exit. I will work
for a transition period until the end of the year but then I will go and
expect to be paid up in full as we have agreed.' Jenkins' departure
would leave a big hole in an important part of the organization and

be a step back from the ambition to be a top bank. Varley had anticipated Jenkins' reaction and had consulted human resources about
how to sweeten the package. Coolly he said: 'I think you should stay.
I will see what I can do about reporting lines. If you meet the targets
we have set, there will be another £6 million.'

That evening Jenkins returned to South Kensington to share the
news with Amanda. The latest £6 million would be performance
related and paid in shares over a period but still represented a life-
changing amount of money. Jenkins was already too far into
Barclaycard to give up easily. He had recruited a great number of
people and felt responsible to them. He was sure that Seegers would
not last long at Barclays and that new opportunities would appear for
him, though he was getting more doubtful about Varley's judgement
and Barclays' cavalier attitude to compensation. Diamond had the
reputation for being the hard-charging member of the team but Jenkins was now wondering whether Varley was in fact the driver of the
aggressive strategy. Anyway, they decided, that does not matter for
now: 'Let's sit tight, focus on Barclaycard and see what happens.'

Varley dealt decisively with those old rivals who had been promoted to the board against his wishes. Seegers' appointment was
followed by the departure of David Roberts, Barclays' head of retail
banking while Hoffman was moved to the less influential role of
group vice-chairman in charge of activities such as corporate responsibility. Davis had already left suddenly at the end of 2005. In 2003
they had been considered so important that they had been promoted
to the board; in 2006, they evidently did not pass muster in the
remorseless drive to become a top bank.

RELATIONSHIP BANKING IN
BIRMINGHAM, 2006

Karl Edwards' decision in 1999 to borrow money from Barclays to
buy a warehouse had paid off. Britain was booming under New
Labour and the leisure industry prospered. Consumers had money to
spend on records and visits to the clubs and DJs wanted the best new
sounds and equipment on which to play them. Edwards' friendly

store sold turntables, headphones and synthesizers to the industry, gave free advice to beginners and encouraged record buyers to browse. The warehouse had 1.7 million records in stock, the website was getting 150,000 hits every week and October House Records was flourishing.

As his turnover increased, Barclays paid him more attention. He was given his own relationship manager, a specialist in small business banking who took him out for nice lunches. If there were any minor cash flow problems, the bank was always there to assist and when cash balances built up, they helpfully pointed out where he could get the best deposit rates. Edwards' phone calls and emails were always dealt with by return and he felt like a valued customer. This was relationship banking at its very best.

One day Edwards was surprised by a phone call from his relationship manager. 'Karl, I want you to look at a competition we are running,' he said. It wasn't a good day for Edwards and in his flat West Midlands tones, he told the manager he was really too busy for stuff like that: 'I've got a business to run here. If I get time at the weekend I'll take a look at it.'

The relationship manager was insistent. 'The closing date is tonight, it won't take you a moment, I really think you should do it now.' Wanting to get on with his day and sensing that the Barclays man needed him to enter, he spent a couple of minutes filling out a simple form, then got back to selling records.

He forgot about the competition until a couple of weeks later he received another unexpected call from his man at Barclays. 'Good news, Karl. You remember that competition you entered? You've won first prize, an all-expenses-paid trip to New York, business class flights for you and your wife, spending money and three nights in the Four Seasons Hotel in Manhattan. How does that sound?'

It sounded pretty good and of course it further increased Edwards' warmth towards Barclays. They were looking after him and they were on his side. As 2006 progressed and the economy entered its ninth consecutive year of growth, Edwards decided to expand his warehouse space and look for new premises. If he found somewhere, he would need another mortgage and there was only one bank that he would contemplate borrowing from – Barclays.

HEADY DAYS

At Brocket Hall, a Regency stately home in Hertfordshire, and at other country house conference venues close to London's M25 motorway, they would arrive late in the afternoon, mostly in their chauffeur-driven cars from Canary Wharf and Heathrow, one or two screeching up at the last minute in their family saloons. For the eighteen men and one woman who comprised the Barclays board in 2006, offsite meetings were a regular event. There was butler service, log fires in the grates, fresh flowers in the hallways, first-night dinners in antique dining rooms and the next day presentation decks to take the board through the strategic options.

They were in confident mood. The global economy had delivered three successive years of strong growth and Barclays had outperformed its international peer group, pleasing shareholders with record profits and dividends. In 2006 Barclays delighted investors with a total shareholder return of 25 per cent.[8] In that year, profits grew by 35 per cent to £7,136 million, earnings per share by 32 per cent and the dividend was increased by a whopping 17 per cent. Economic profit – profit adjusted for the cost of capital – grew by a sensational 54 per cent. Barclays Capital's pre-tax profits doubled from £1,142 million in 2004 to £2,216, hitting the Alpha Plan targets a year early and getting a number one ranking in the international bond league tables.[9]

There had, however, been a marked increase in the risk in the business, increasing Barclays' leverage from thirty times equity capital at the start of Varley's time to nearly forty now. This was almost double the leverage ratio of comparable international banks but chairman Barrett, who would retire at the end of the year, and the board raised no objection. Only the regulators' barometer, tier one equity capital – equity capital raised from shareholders together with subsequently retained earnings – a thin 7.7 per cent, gave them any cause for concern. But still it was well within what were regarded as the safety margins at that time.

The wider landscape was pretty rosy too. Chancellor Gordon Brown, whose reputation for financial prudence had helped Labour

1. Where it all began: the Bar Don Quijote, San Antonio, Ibiza.

2. Tom Camoys, a modern English aristocrat – though one with neither the inclination nor the means to live a life of idleness – in the Barclays boardroom.

3–5. At the sign of the
Spread Eagle: the site where
Barclays' Quaker ancestors
traded from 1728 was later
numbered 54 Lombard
Street and, as Barclays' head
office, regularly rebuilt:
early twentieth century –
1969; 1969–90; 1994–2005.

6. Three and a half miles east and 156 metres high: the modern Barclays, at 1 Churchill Place, Canary Wharf.

7. The Barclays townhouse: 43 Brook Street, Mayfair.

8. Last of the old school: Sir Timothy Bevan, chairman 1981–7.

9. The first non-family chairman of modern times: Sir John Quinton, chairman 1987–92.

10. The BZW dealing room, Ebgate House, *c*. 1990. Bob Diamond called it the worst environment for a trading floor he had ever seen.

11. Harry Enfield, *Friday Night Live*, 1988: the Loadsamoney ethic of late 1980s Britain.

12. Country cheese and metropolitan chalk: Andrew Buxton, chief executive 1992–3, chairman 1993–9, and Martin Taylor, chief executive 1994–8.

13. Charisma and guile, formidably combined: Matt Barrett, chief executive 1999–2004, chairman 2004–6, and Sir Peter Middleton, chief executive 1998–9, chairman 1999–2004.

14. Breakfast with Bob: the New York Racquet and Tennis Club, 370 Park Avenue.

15. The big hitter: Bob Diamond, President, Barclays plc, at the Barclays Scottish Open, 2006.

16. The television maths expert Carol Vorderman advertises Firstplus, a Barclays' PPI product. It turned out to cost the bank rather more than 8.9 per cent APR.

17. All agreed? John Varley, chief executive 2004–10, and Rijkman Groenink, his counterpart at ABN AMRO, think they have a deal.

win a third general election in 2005, was expected to take over as prime minister from Tony Blair very soon. He had been a successful, pro-market chancellor and corporate leaders looked forward to him becoming premier in perfect economic conditions. Stock markets had recovered from the collapse of many internet-related stocks in 2000 and the trauma of the terrorist attacks on New York's twin towers in 2001. Investors were now dealing harshly with any managements they perceived to be under-performing, pressing them to deliver shareholder value and engineering takeovers for companies that failed to deliver. As we have seen, Barclays itself had merger discussions with several parties, and 2005 was also the year Proctor & Gamble bought Gillette for $57 billion; Bank of America swallowed MBNA for $35 billion and Telefonica took out O2 for $31 billion. Scarcely a month went by without a mega-merger between household names. Money was cheap – interest rates were still 5 per cent – corporate balance sheets were awash with cash and sharp-eyed investors were on the prowl. For private equity executives and hedge fund managers these were the crazy days in which fortunes were made in a few years that would previously have taken generations to build. Capitalism was triumphant, the champagne corks were flying and the very free market was the only club in town.

In June 2006 Gordon Brown used the Chancellor's annual speech to the City at the Mansion House to reflect on this happy state. He said : 'Government debt in Britain is lower than France, Germany, Italy, America and Japan,' and predicted that the economy would be 'stronger this year than last and stronger next year than this'.[10]

The City was in its pomp and the regulators helped it along. In the decade since its formation in 1997, the FSA had been more successful in delivering that part of its mandate which required it to protect the City's interests than it had been in its primary task of regulating it. It was admired as an exponent of light touch regulation which was regarded as a reason for the City's market share gains from New York where Wall Street lobbied for an equally light touch from its own regulators. In his June 2006 Mansion House speech, Brown claimed the credit for this: 'In 2003, just at the time of a previous Mansion House speech, the Worldcom accounting scandal broke. And I will be honest with you, many who advised me, including not a few newspapers, favoured a regulatory crackdown. I believe we were right not to go down that road which in the United States led to Sarbanes–Oxley, and we were right to build upon our light-touch system through the leadership of Sir Callum McCarthy – fair, proportionate, predictable and increasingly risk based.'[11] The FSA's confidence in light touch was demonstrated a few months later, in February 2007, when it merged its teams supervising RBS and Barclays under one senior manager. The team had just twelve staff keeping their eyes on two of the UK's largest banks which at that time had combined assets of £2 trillion.

The boom conditions of 2006 had bred total confidence in the banking industry. Northern Rock and HBOS were piling up mortgage market share, RBS was lending with astonishing confidence and gung-ho chiefs believed that 'big was good but bigger was even better'. Fund managers wanted to know why Northern Rock's asset and dividend growth was better than Barclays' and pressed Varley to get ahead of the pack. As the top of the industry consolidated around a smaller number of bigger players, Barclays dared not get left behind.

The Barclays board of 2006 had to map their bank's future in the midst of this euphoria. The moralistic boards of Barclays' founding Quakers and their families and Special List friends had long ago been replaced by a cadre of professional directors who followed carefully prescribed protocols. A crop of business scandals in Britain in the late 1980s and 1990s, including the publishing tycoon Robert Maxwell's looting of his firm's pension fund and Asil Nadir's theft from his company Polly Peck, had resulted in the introduction of the Combined Code of Corporate Governance in 1998. Following another spate of scandals in the early 2000s, this time in the US, where shareholders in Enron, WorldCom and Tyco fell victim to dodgy accounting and executives' greed, Congress tightened up boardroom practices through the Sarbanes–Oxley Act, and the UK strengthened its own code in 2003 after a review by a former investment banker, Derek Higgs.

Boards were required by Stock Exchange rules to follow these codes (or explain non-compliance). On paper the arrangements looked watertight: boards had to set strategic aims, review management performance and set corporate values. At least half the board had to consist of independent non-executive directors with an appropriate mix of skills and experience, who were expected to contribute to the company's strategy, display sound judgement and enquiring minds, understand the business and challenge the thinking of the executives from a detached point of view.

But these worthy aims were undermined by two factors. The first was specific to banking and followed the transformation of the industry in the last quarter of the twentieth century, the second was more general.

In the two decades since Tom Camoys persuaded Timothy Bevan and his quiescent board to build an investment bank, banking had become so large and complex that their successors in the boardroom, particularly the non-executives, could have little idea of what was really going on in the business they were meant to be overseeing. The group's report and accounts – 48 pages in Camoys' time, 166 pages in Taylor's – numbered 303 pages in 2006. Assets (loans to customers and securities held for trading) had grown from £65 billion in 1983, to £235 billion in 1997 and £996 billion in 2006. This growth was due not simply to a linear increase in the old businesses but also to the creation of a baffling array of new financial instruments in different currencies, interest rates and assets.

This was the world of derivatives, the business that was still in its infancy when Camoys founded BZW but that now underpinned Barclays' profits. Effectively bets on the future movements of stocks, currencies, interest rates, commodities and other assets, derivatives were used to hedge the bank's own risk, to create complex packages for clients and for proprietary trading. The sums involved were enormous: Barclays' derivatives based on the future movement of interest rates were, for example, £4 trillion. The real exposure was reduced by offsetting equal and opposite positions but the numbers were so large that any error could be fatal. Ten pages of the accounts were devoted to summarizing the derivatives book, but they were just headings and numbers on the page. The risk would have terrified Bevan and other conservative family members on his board. Their successors had to take comfort from a reassuring but impossible to verify figure showing the maximum amount that could be lost on any given day, the daily value at risk, to be £38.6 million.[12]

Even setting aside the extraordinary difficulty of the task, bank governance was weakened by the tiny circle from which boards of UK companies came. The original idea of having non-executives was that they should be different from the executives; in many ways, for all their faults, Barclays' family directors had met that criteria. They cared about the bank's past, present and future and saw themselves as custodians of the business for the long term. Their successors had many skills but intellectual diversity was not one of them. Non-executive appointments were rarely advertised and were controlled by the search industry, which ran a treadmill, recycling people with similar business beliefs round the UK's boardrooms. Like the executives running the show, they came from a world that believed in markets, prized growth above continuity and measured the future in quarters rather than years. Groupthink was becoming the fatal flaw in modern capitalism and the non-executives were the gene carriers. They all had the same DNA.

The Barclays board of 2006 was no exception. Of the executives, Varley, Diamond and finance director Kheraj had naturally spent much of their careers in investment banks. Deputy chairman Rudd's name had been made at the acquisitive conglomerate Williams Holdings. Sir John Sunderland had been chief executive and later chairman of Cadbury Schweppes during whose tenure the company had made a joint bid for the US food giant Nabisco, acquired the beverage company Snapple and constantly reshuffled the portfolio. Robert Steel, a former Goldman Sachs banker who advised on many such deals, was a board member until 11 October of that year. The senior independent director was the former Schroders corporate financier, Sir Richard Broadbent. With the partial exception of the academics Professor Dame Sandra Dawson (who ran the Cambridge Business School) and Sir Andrew Likierman (an accountancy expert), the rest of the board had similar mainstream business backgrounds.

The role of the chairman in guiding the board was crucial. Barrett's retirement left them with a dilemma. Varley and Diamond informally asked Rudd, who was in charge of choosing Barrett's successor, if he would consider taking the chair himself. Rudd was a properly qualified accountant, a commanding figure confident in his own judgement, usually right and well regarded by institutional shareholders. He would be a popular choice but he was not a banker and wisely knew his own limitations. He had been spoken of as a possible successor to Middleton a few years before but felt, now as then, that Barclays Capital had grown into something he no longer understood and believed that the next chairman should come from within the industry.

He told them that his choice was Broadbent, the only one of the non-executives who, in his view, had the knowledge and the capacity to get right inside the business. Broadbent had risen to a senior position in HM Treasury, the civil service's blue ribbon department, and had run the UK's tax department HM Customs & Excise, in between times advising corporates and trying his hand at management with Schroders. He would have the persistence and intellect to get inside Barclays Capital but his relentless questioning at board meetings had annoyed the executive directors and Diamond killed the idea. They moved on to one of the other investment bankers, Steel, who seemed interested until he was offered the role of under-secretary of the US Treasury.

With internal possibilities exhausted, Rudd briefed David Kimbell, kingmaker of the boardrooms. Kimbell tried to interest them in another former Schroders investment banker, Alison Carnwath, who had become a serial non-executive, but she had conflicts of interest. Then he and Rudd turned to Marcus Agius, one of the City's leading rainmakers in the lucrative world of mergers and acquisitions. He was chairman of Lazard in London and recent chairman of the FTSE 100 company British Airports Authority which had just been acquired by Ferrovial of Spain for the knock-out price of £10 billion.

Agius' stock was high and his background pure gold. The son of a distinguished soldier and Maltese diplomat, he had been educated at Cambridge and Harvard. He married Kate, the daughter of Edmund de Rothschild, loved shooting, ski-ing and fine art and was a member of White's, the oldest and most exclusive gentlemen's club in London. He networked hard and effortlessly on the corporate circuit. He was not the braying kind of corporate financier but listened carefully and was trusted by corporate boards. Diamond had his doubts but the rest of the board accepted that a corporate financier with experience of chairing a FTSE 100 company was what they were looking for. Agius agreed to take over as chairman on 1 January 2007.

The company now had two determined executive directors pursuing a growth strategy and a board of the same persuasion. Strong and informed challenge was required but the board had neither the inclination nor the knowledge to make it. The non-executives scarcely knew an equity swap from a mortgage-backed security or the difference between a CDO (collateralized debt obligation) and a CDS (credit default swap), all of which were products Barclays Capital traded.* The investment bankers on the board – Agius, Broadbent and, until October 2006, Steel – were advisers not traders, The rest were capable members of the corporate club who had excelled in their own fields but who were not qualified to govern a bank. After a whistle-stop induction that was little more than a briefing from business heads and a tour round the business, in less than a day per week they were expected to control a business that they had no hope of understanding.

Barclays' Charter of Expectations, prepared by the company secretariat and adopted by the board in 2004, wanted its non-executives to have 'a good understanding of the organisation's businesses and affairs to enable them to properly evaluate information and responses provided by management'.[13] But this was an unrealistic aspiration in a business with balance sheet footings of £1 trillion deployed opaquely in complex instruments. The business model had outgrown the means by which it was governed and this weakness was never challenged by shareholders, regulators or the government.

In November 2003, when Varley had so convincingly described the universal banking model, they decided that in a world of size and concentration its large corporations would require end-to-end banking from institutions that could serve their global needs. At the 2006 meetings, reassured by the exuberance of shareholders, politicians

---

* A mortgage-backed security is a financial instrument backed by a package of mortgages. A collaterized debt obligation is a security comprising pools of debt some of which might be mortgage-backed securities. A credit default swap is an insurance policy against a company defaulting. An equity swap is an agreement for two parties to exchange future payments from specified financial instruments.

and competitors and by relaxed regulators, Varley's strategy was reaffirmed but then taken even further than he had originally proposed. Analysis had shown that the biggest universal banks did even better than those in the second division. Clients, it appeared, rewarded scale with scale and that put the biggest banks in a virtuous circle. The board decided that Barclays had the financial and managerial resources to compete with them; and becoming not just one of the top ten but one of the top five universal banks became Barclays' strategic objective.

It was a huge commitment and it would mean emulating Citigroup, the US giant built by Walter Wriston in the 1970s, whose business model had inspired Anthony Tuke, and the much admired J. P. Morgan Chase, which Tom Camoys' great-great-grandfather had inadvertently seeded and Weatherstone, his inspiration, had run. Until Diamond came along, the lack of a successful investment bank had held back those aspirations but Barclays Capital's success completed that part of the jigsaw puzzle. What Barclays needed to finish the picture, the board decided, was an acquisition that would give it scale outside its home market.

13

Dutch Courage, 2007

BID ONLY

Varley pulled up the collar of his suit jacket and shoved his hands deep into his trouser pockets. The morning of Thursday 8 February 2007 was bitterly cold, overnight snow still lay on the ground. He was shivering and regretted leaving his chauffeur-driven BMW. But of course he had not expected to be walking anywhere. He was on his way to 199 Bishopsgate, the London office of ABN AMRO to see Rijkman Groenink, the Dutch bank's chairman, who had called him a few days earlier to suggest an urgent meeting on an unspecified subject. Varley thought that there could be only one reason for such a mysterious call: a proposal to merge their two banks.

A few minutes earlier, as Varley approached the revolving doors of 199 Bishopsgate, he had been surprised to see Simon Samuels, the City's leading bank analyst, leaving the building, followed by several other analysts whom he recognized. He realized that ABN's senior management had been presenting the bank's annual results and there would be dozens of people he knew. He cursed Groenink for his clumsiness. If any of them recognized Varley, they would reach the obvious conclusion and rumours of an ABN–Barclays merger would be all over the City. Varley turned right and went for a walk round the drab business district behind Exchange Square to give the crowd time to go. He was shivering and regretted leaving his overcoat in his chauffeur-driven BMW.

It was a wise precaution: Samuels' presence at the meeting had indeed been the result of market rumours that ABN might be subject to a bid and he was paying close attention to the Dutch bank's affairs.

Varley made his way back to 199 Bishopsgate, wondering whether Groenink's poor planning for the meeting was symptomatic of bigger problems. Groenink greeted him and apologized for the near miss. It was a short meeting, just long enough for Varley to warm his hands around a cup of tea. They had met twice the year before, the first time in London at a spring conference for bank investors at which Groenink had spoken bullishly about ABN's ambitions to be a global player and then again in the autumn, when he had seemed more subdued.

He was a man under pressure. He had been chairman since 2000 and was already on his third strategic plan. The first, growing his wholesale bank, had not delivered shareholder value. Neither did the next, targeting the mid-sized corporate sector. The most recent plan, to buy up smaller international banks, was deeply unpopular with ABN's shareholders.[1] He had just told the analysts that 2006 was 'a year of transition' and promised that 2007 would be 'a year of delivery', but it was not a convincing message.[2] Aggressive hedge funds were threatening to use their financial muscle to force a change in management or a break-up of the bank. Groenink came straight out with it: 'My board believes that we should talk.'

For a year Varley's strategists had been poring over ABN, a bank that was only slightly smaller than Barclays itself – at the end of 2006 Barclays' assets were £996 billion, ABN's €987 billion* - and it had featured on many of the presentation decks at the board offsite meetings. ABN was vulnerable and a good fit with Barclays. It offered a leading position in the Dutch market, which would give Barclays a base in the Eurozone, and its operations in over fifty countries would provide the global footprint Barclays' ambitions required. Its investment bank was weak and could be closed, sold or swallowed up by Barclays Capital. Its US retail bank, LaSalle, which was of little interest to Barclays, would be easily saleable. At the right price ABN would give Barclays the reach and scale to become a top five universal bank.

Varley was careful not to give too much away to Groenink but said that he would be interested in a further discussion. Mindful of the near miss in Bishopsgate, they decided to meet next at a secret

* The exchange rate was €1.50 to the pound.

location. Groenink was planning a skiing holiday in Switzerland and suggested that Varley meet him at the resort.

Varley flew alone to Geneva, rented a car at the airport and drove himself up the mountain. He was in English country wear – corduroy trousers, a sleeveless quilted jacket and leather-soled shoes – once again feeling cold, conspicuous and underdressed for a meeting with Groenink.

Groenink had arranged for a local museum to be closed for the day. Sporting smart après-ski gear, he swept up to its door in a chauffeur-driven 4x4 with a team of advisers. Amid the exhibits of past Swiss mountain life, the two men developed an outline plan for merging their banks in which Groenink would be chairman, Varley would be chief executive and the headquarters would be in Amsterdam. The Barclays eagle would have to go: Groenink's advisers said it would be considered too German by the Dutch bank's customers.

Varley reported back to the Barclays board in early March. They were a deal-doing group but not reckless acquirers and neither was Varley. His mantra was 'merger and acquisition should be the servant of strategy not its master' and this was not an acquisition that need be done at any price. The purchase would have to be made mainly in Barclays' shares to give some protection in the event of an across-the-board fall in bank shares and the cash element should be kept to a minimum.

Talks were set up for Monday 19 March but these plans were thrown by a story headlined 'Barclays in £80 billion offer to ABN AMRO' in that weekend's *Sunday Times*, which, along with the *Daily* and *Sunday Telegraph*, appeared for many years to have a hot line from the Barclays' boardroom. There were some testy exchanges between the two sides about who was responsible for the leak but when markets opened on the Monday, they issued a joint Stock Exchange announcement stating that they were in 'exclusive preliminary discussions' about a merger.

Barclays' resolve not to pay up or to pay cash was tested by a rapid counter-proposal for ABN from a consortium led by RBS and its ambitious chief executive, the feisty Scotsman Sir Fred 'the Shred' Goodwin. In these early months of 2007 the board certainly didn't want to be outmanoeuvred by its Scottish rival, which could have put Barclays itself back in play. Thirteen extra board meetings were held in 2007 and a Transaction Committee was set up comprising Varley, the driver of the deal; Agius, the M&A banker; Rudd, the experienced acquirer; and Broadbent, the corporate financier. It was twist or bust: do the deal and join the super-league or lose out to the Shred and risk getting shredded themselves.

Confidence in the City was still sky high in the summer of 2007, pumped up on Wednesday 20 June by a speech made by Gordon Brown, a week before he became prime minister. He told an audience of senior bankers assembled to hear the last of his Mansion House speeches: 'The City of London has risen by your efforts, ingenuity and creativity to become a new world leader.' In a recent study of the world's top fifty financial cities, London had come first, leading the chancellor to conclude: 'The financial services sector in Britain and the City of London at the centre of it, is a great example of a highly skilled, high value added, talent-driven industry that shows how we can excel in a world of global competition. Britain needs more of the vigour, ingenuity and aspiration that you already demonstrate.'[3] But one week later, on the very same day that he moved into Number 10, Northern Rock, one of the building societies that had taken advantage of financial deregulation by listing on the Stock Exchange and competing with the High Street banks, unexpectedly issued a profit warning. It caused only ripples in the City and Whitehall (and not even those in the country at large) and scarcely registered with the boards of Barclays and ABN who, with the bullish words of the prime minister-to-be ringing in their ears, simply pressed on with the battle.

With both sides jostling for position, by the middle of July ABN's shareholders had a choice: the RBS consortium's £71.1 billion nearly all in cash or Barclays' £67.5 billion mainly in shares. Barclays had potentially raised up to £13.4 billion from the China Development Bank and Singapore's Temasek Holdings largely conditional on the bid succeeding, and that was as much hard currency as they were prepared to offer. Varley toured the leading shareholders heading off criticism from a few investors by pointing to the protection of a mainly share offer: this was not a deal that could ever break the bank. However, he made it clear that it would be Barclays' final offer: 'We've put an enticing cream cake on the table for ABN shareholders. We are not going to top it up with more cream.'[4]

Barclays' chances of success depended on raising its share price above the value of the consortium's cash bid. On 24 July Varley took a break from Barclays business to attend an AstraZeneca board meeting where he was a non-executive director. During the morning he received an email from James Leigh Pemberton, Barclays' principal adviser at the investment bank CSFB, and a son of the bee-keeping former Bank of England governor. He reported that the Barclays share price had gone up to £7. 'We are bid only,' Leigh Pemberton told him, meaning that there were no sellers in the market, usually a sign that the price would go higher still. Leigh Pemberton thought that if the price reached £7.20, Barclays would be home and dry.

THE THINKER

A few days earlier, in a designer-styled office just off Grosvenor Square, a young man waited nervously for his bosses to arrive. An oval glass table with eleven chairs filled the room; the twelfth place, at the head of the table, was occupied by a statue of Rodin's *The Thinker*, which was always placed there for the hedge fund's weekly ideas meeting. A pair of contemporary Damien Hirst etchings hung on the walls. They had been bought with typical acumen just before the artist's reputation really took off. It was one of the new wave of fund managers that had surged through London in the past ten years, making fortunes for their founders. They charged 2 per cent of the assets they managed as a retainer and took 20 per cent of any investment gains they made for clients. In a rising market it had been easy money for everyone but this was one of the top firms, known for its edgy style, contrarian thinking and the stunning returns it made for investors.

Just after half-past four the traders and fund managers drifted in to the meeting as the markets closed and the day's deals were completed. Men like these had neither the time nor the appetite for conversation. No one looked at the young man, they just tapped away at their BlackBerries as they waited for the managing partner to arrive. He was the founder of the firm and the sole possessor of any semblance of social skills among a group of deep introverts.

At four thirty-five, five minutes late as usual, the managing partner eased cat-like into the final chair, his long black hair brushed back over his crown resting just above the open-necked collar of his light-blue shirt. He glanced at his Rolex, apologized for keeping them waiting and turned to the young man. 'William. What do you have for us today?'

William looked no more than a boy. Slight and pale, the dark rings under his eyes betraying the fact that he spent all day hunched over a computer screen and all night playing video games. He was twenty-five years old, had a first-class degree in computer sciences and a master's degree with distinction from the London School of Economics. He had been set for a career at HM Treasury but had disappointed his parents by turning down a safe and secure future in the civil service to look for a hedge fund to join. He got lucky with the first firm he wrote to and in three years had already shown an ability to extract smart investment ideas from the mass of data and company reports that he pored over hour after hour, seven days a week.

He spoke hesitantly at first, but as he got into his stride, there was a compelling logic about his arguments. 'Today it's about Barclays. It's one of the biggest positions we hold and I think it's on the edge of a cliff.' The traders and portfolio managers stopped tapping and ten pairs of eyes focused on him intently as William set out his case.

'I know we like Barclays. We've been in them all the way up from 500 pence when Varley took over. We love Diamond, we do a lot of business with Barclays Capital and they are one of our prime brokers. But I've been running the numbers. Barclays Capital have been using more and more capital to grow profits. The return on every dollar they invest gets lower every year, so they borrow more. They're growing profits by borrowing money at cheap rates and playing the markets with it. It's a dangerous game but no one is talking about it. By my calculations, Barclays are now the most highly leveraged bank in the market, borrowing forty times their equity capital. The US property market looks weak, the fixed income market has run out of juice and Barclays are heading for a fall. It's been an incredible ride but it's over.'

There was a moment's silence, broken only by the gentle hum of the air conditioning as it cut in. There was logic to what William had said but Barclays was idolized in the City. Had the fan club become so infatuated with Diamond and Varley that they had missed the evidence that Barclays was overstretched? Or was clever William simply calling it wrong?

Other voices were now heard round the table. The US market might be due a correction but it would be no more than that. Leverage was something everyone did, including their own firm, there was nothing wrong with it. Risk had been transformed by securitization and derivatives and Barclays was at the cutting edge of risk management. Any setback would be a buying opportunity. The fan club said that the stock had a long way to run; the jury was split.

Attention turned to the managing partner, who socialized with some of the senior management at Barclays and had nursed the holding all the way up. He asked a few questions about William's calculations, gave others the opportunity to speak and looked hard at the statue of *The Thinker*. He liked Barclays a lot and he admired Diamond and Varley but he had not made his first hundred million by letting sentiment get in the way. There were other things going on in the banking sector which worried him, Barclays' ABN bid looked badly timed and William had done exactly what he was paid to do: think, not groupthink.

He paused for a moment. William was certainly a bright young man but he was too inexperienced to be trusted on such a big call. The managing partner asked his senior portfolio managers to study William's idea, test it under various market scenarios and discuss it together. But that was not all. Before the meeting broke up, he looked across to his head trader. 'Just suppose we do decide to sell our long position. Could we short the stock too? Why don't you take a look?'

William's pulse quickened. Not only were they going to investigate the sale of a core holding, they were going to consider selling shares they did not own in the expectation of buying them back after the price fell. He had better be right or it would be the civil service after all.

BAD TIMING

ABN was not the only business Barclays was trying to buy in the early months of 2007. On 19 January it had announced an agreement to acquire EquiFirst, a US mortgage business with 9,000 commission-paid real estate brokers – estate agents' sales people in UK parlance – working on its behalf in forty-seven states. Buying a US mortgage originator was a departure for Barclays but as it cost only $225 million, it didn't require board approval and the City barely noticed.[5]

EquiFirst's specialty was in signing up low-income mortgage borrowers and it was a fast-growing business. Between 2000 and 2005 the US sub-prime mortgage market grew from $130 billion to $625 billion as a golden scenario of low interest rates and a strong economy tempted millions of Americans into home ownership. It seemed as though property prices would rise for ever, offering borrowers a sure way to build up a nest egg and giving lenders the illusion of protection against borrowers defaulting. Secure in this thought, mortgage originators didn't ask too many questions of 'sub-prime' borrowers, teased them in with attractive deals and then sold the loans off to other banks and investment banks, neatly taking any risk off their own balance sheets. It was a method of lending called 'securitization', or 'originate and distribute'.

The banks and investment banks were not too worried about the lowering of credit standards because they too sold on the loans, packaging them up and placing them in tranches with investors. This created a huge market in residential mortgage backed securities (RMBS) and mortgage linked derivatives. Over the same 2000–2005 period, the quantity of sub-prime loans packaged into bonds for resale grew from $55 billion to $507 billion.[6] Structuring, distributing and trading RMBS was done by investment banks' fixed income departments and all the big Wall Street players were deep into it.

Barclays Capital was late into the RMBS game. Diamond's rule that one initiative had to pay off before the next one began meant that it was 2001 before he sanctioned a big push into the US. The recruitment of Grant Kvalheim and a team of people from Deutsche Bank that year fired the starting gun. Kvalheim became co-head of Barclays Capital's US business, and as the fixed income market boomed, Barclays increased their commitment to it.

The investment bank's global assets – mainly loans to customers and securities held to facilitate customer orders – increased from £155 billion the year Kvalheim joined to £347 billion in 2004 and almost doubled again over the next two years, with much of the increase in US dollars.[7] It was time to make a serious play for RMBS business. Using money borrowed from other banks and investors Barclays Capital ramped up their involvement, leveraging the balance sheet in the process from under thirty in 2003 to over thirty in 2004 and almost forty in 2005.[8]

They did not originate the mortgages themselves but bought them up from the mortgage banks, briefly warehoused them on Barclays Capital's own books and then securitized them into SIVs, structured investment vehicles, in which they sold shares to investors. Like every other major bank on Wall Street, Barclays Capital traded RMBS shares and derivatives in its own and other financial institutions' SIVs.

In the second half of 2006, Barclays Capital bought a US mortgage servicing business, HomEq, adding 1,300 employees, and indicating its intention to step up its commitment to the sector. This strategy was confirmed by the acquisition of EquiFirst, which took them into mortgage origination for the first time. EquiFirst would be combined with HomEq's mortgage servicing business – sending out statements and processing payments – and Barclays Capital's capital markets capabilities to create what they called 'a vertically integrated mortgage franchise'. It would mean that in addition to buying up other banks' packages of mortgages and selling them on to investors, Barclays would now be dealing direct with US borrowers, offering them loans and servicing them with statements during the life of the loan. The idea was that by bringing mortgage origination in-house, Barclays would have more control over the quality of the loans it was buying and packaging.[9]

It proved to be a top of the market acquisition. During 2006 a few astute observers detected signs of sub-prime distress. Borrowers' late payments and default rates on interest repayments were climbing, lenders were repossessing properties and house prices were in decline. The price of credit default swaps – a form of insurance against bond failures – on mortgage backed entities increased dramatically towards the end of 2006. Eager to keep the party going for as long as possible, vested interests in the credit ratings agencies and investment banks kept this quiet but a handful of banks including J. P. Morgan and Goldman Sachs and smart hedge fund managers such as Steve

Eisman and John Paulson were gradually reducing their sub-prime exposure.[10]

Barclays Capital's fixed income team was not one of these: on the contrary, they were determined to make up for lost time. But over in London, Barclays' Risk Committee took a different view. Its role was to provide an independent oversight of the risk that the front line was running. It was now chaired by Broadbent, the senior independent director, and supported by the chief risk officer Robert Le Blanc, a veteran of J. P. Morgan, regarded as one of the best of his kind in London. They had developed Risk Appetite, a process which tested whether Barclays had enough capital to survive certain extreme scenarios, supplementing this with deep dives into areas that worried them.[11]

Towards the end of 2006 Broadbent and Le Blanc picked up the signals from the US mortgage market and commissioned a review. They stress-tested Barclays' US mortgage business to see what effect an increase in interest rates and a rise in unemployment would have on borrowers' ability to pay the interest on their mortgages. When this was modelled for its impact on Barclays' SIVs, the consequences were serious. This was driven home in February 2007 when HSBC revealed that due to rising defaults on loan repayments in the US sub-prime market, its charge for bad debt in 2006 would be $10.6 billion, 20 per cent higher than analysts were expecting. Broadbent and Le Blanc promptly ordered a cut in Barclays Capital's risk limits for the whole sub-prime business and its related areas.[12] Barclays Capital management argued that having come late to the party, they needed the bigger limits to catch up but the Risk Committee was insistent.

The board knew very little of this. They signed off the annual Risk Appetite conclusions but were not involved in the detail and did not understand the risk characteristics of Barclays Capital's involvement in RMBS or other esoteric derivatives. The business was mentioned in the accounts but it was impossible to work out its size from the data given. Board members could see the growth in Barclays Capital's balance sheet but its activities were so complicated and the investment bank appeared to be going so well that no detailed questions about the nature of its business seemed necessary. Broadbent apart, most non-executives still had no idea what Barclays Capital was really doing.

After HSBC's disclosure, hearing market rumours that some US lenders were in trouble and reading the Risk Committee's report, Barclays renegotiated the terms of the EquiFirst deal. On 2 April 2007, the acquisition was completed at a price of $76 million, a third of the original price.[13] The same day, New Century Financial, a US mortgage lender specializing in the sub-prime sector, filed for bankruptcy, and a few days later Countrywide Financial, the largest US mortgage lender, reported a slump in sub-prime profits. In June, the investment bank Bear Stearns suspended investors' right to redeem their money from two of its hedge funds that had invested heavily in sub-prime. In July, the chairman of the US Federal Reserve, Ben Bernanke, in evidence to the US Congress, warned that the crisis in sub-prime could cost financial institutions up to $100 billion, a figure he described as 'fairly significant'.

As the crisis developed over the second half of the summer, the Barclays board discussed its implications for the ABN bid. Was the downturn a buying opportunity or a warning to call off the whole venture? In public, it remained committed. Barclays announced half-yearly profits growth of 12 per cent on 2 August, referring to a strong performance in the very businesses where sub-prime mortgage problems would surface. A week later the dam broke. On Tuesday 7 August, afterwards widely acknowledged to be the start of the 2007 credit crunch, West LB Asset Management suspended investor redemptions from one of its asset backed securities funds and two days later BNP Paribas froze three of its hedge funds, indicating that they had no way of valuing the complex mortgage related derivatives in them. On 22 August, the credit agency S&P cut the rating on two mortgage backed funds arranged by Barclays and managed by Solent Capital Partners and Avendis Group, after investors refused to buy their debt.[14] The funds were wound down and the securities that comprised them sold at a loss. Sachsen LB, a state-owned German bank, collapsed after one of its US mortgage funds failed; Barclays had structured the fund, marketed it to investors and bought and sold shares in it for clients. The day after returning from his summer holiday, Edward Cahill, who ran Barclays Capital's collaterized debt obligation division, part of its US mortgage business, departed abruptly.

On 28 August, the *Financial Times* reported that Barclays had been left with hundreds of millions of dollars' worth of exposure to failed debt vehicles arranged by Barclays Capital.[15] A Barclays Capital spokesman said the report was untrue, adding that the bank had not provided any funding to the Sachsen vehicle. Barclays Capital merely structured and marketed investment vehicles, he said, and was not responsible for running them though it did have 'a handful' more SIVs.[16]

Diamond tried to put the crisis in context. 'We are weathering the storm. Everyone is getting some pain in July and August, but I've already said that our July results were better this year than last year. We'll manage our way through August as well,' he told the *Sunday Telegraph*.[17] In an interview with the *Sunday Times*, he estimated potential SIV losses to amount to a maximum of £75 million.[18] At a Lehman Brothers banking conference on 10 September he said: 'Barclays Capital traded profitably in August 2007, after full allocation of costs and the mark to market of all positions. This was on the back of a profitable July. Year to date profits are well ahead of 2006.'[19]

By now, however, the problems in the US mortgage market were threatening to disrupt the global banking infrastructure. All banks funded the long-term loans they made to customers by borrowing short term in the money markets. As nerves about the US sub-prime mortgage markets spread, financial institutions charged more to lend to each other, demanded more collateral for doing so and reduced the period over which they would lend. In August, central banks stepped in to ease the strain. The European Central Bank made €94.8 billion of credit available to banks and the US Federal Reserve Bank extended the term and cut the rates on its short-term loans to banks from 6.25 to 5.75 per cent.

Problems in the money markets did not seem to bother RBS's shareholders when they voted on the proposed acquisition of ABN AMRO on 10 August: 94.5 per cent of the votes cast were in favour of the deal. But bank share prices were beginning to show signs of nerves. Barclays' had gone through 700p when Leigh Pemberton called Varley on 24 July but it never stayed there long enough to secure victory. Instead, it dribbled down to 614p on Tuesday 4 September, putting the value of its offer £3 billion short of the Dutch bank's market value and

£10.5 billion below the consortium's bid. As the month continued and inter-bank liquidity problems multiplied, opinion on Barclays' board shifted. Having resisted the temptation to bid up, now the principal concern was not that they would lose out to RBS but what they would do if RBS called *force majeure* and pulled out.

The Bank of England did not join in the central bank interventions of August despite lobbying from the British banks, attracting pointed criticism from Diamond. In his interview with the *Sunday Telegraph* the head of Barclays Capital said: 'For the recovery to continue we need to find more ways to get liquidity into the short end of the curve. That's down to confidence, and that's down to the central banks. We've seen thoughtful moves by the Fed and the ECB.'[20] He meant that the Bank of England should lend more short term funds to the banks. Such public criticism of the Bank by a senior banker was rare. Diamond's remarks were widely reported and were noted in Threadneedle Street as a black mark against him.

On 12 September Bank of England Governor King wrote to the Treasury Select Committee with his own analysis. He was an academic economist of high standards – a Fellow of the British Academy, the UK's top club for humanities scholars – and tax expert who had joined the Bank of England as chief economist in 1991 and become deputy governor in 1998. Reflecting widely held economic theory, he believed that the banking sector was strong enough to withstand the impact of taking mortgage backed securities on to balance sheets; that the private sector would re-establish valuations; and that to step in prematurely would encourage 'moral hazard', the perception among financial institutions that they would be protected from the consequences of their actions by a government safety net.[21] It was the direct opposite of the view Diamond had put forward but the careful reader would have noted the penultimate paragraph of the governor's letter: 'lender of last resort operations remain in the armoury of all central banks.'[22]

THE RUN ON THE ROCK

The lender of last resort's role is to provide loans to institutions on the verge of collapse and when King wrote that letter he had already agreed with the Treasury and the FSA that the Bank of England would if necessary stand behind Northern Rock. He had also intimated as much to the company itself.

Northern Rock's June profits warning had been a sign of fundamental problems with its business model. It had been one of the most aggressive players in the residential mortgage market, raising its share from 6 to 20 per cent in a decade.[23] The money it lent came from securitizing and selling on its loans and from borrowing in the short term inter-bank money markets; by 2007, only a quarter of Northern Rock's £101 billion loan book was covered by retail deposits. When money markets dried up in August 2007, Northern Rock was unable to renew wholesale debt as it matured or lend to new borrowers – or even repay depositors. On 16 August, King had told Northern Rock's chairman Dr Matt Ridley that the Bank of England would, if necessary, act as a lender of last resort but that his strong advice was to find an alternative. No such alternative was forthcoming and on 10 September it had to seek emergency funds from the Bank of England, in secret. Nevertheless, on Thursday 13 September what had happened was reported on the BBC by Robert Peston, the broadcaster's business editor.

It was the most dramatic business story in living memory. The following day thousands of depositors rushed to Northern Rock branches anxious to withdraw their money before the bank went bust. The images were flashed round the world, spreading disbelief wherever they were shown. This was the UK, not a banana republic! Northern Rock's website crashed and staff in the branches did not have enough notes to fill the plastic bags that customers brought in for their cash.[24] Queues wound round street corners, pensioners were in tears, depositors with other British banks nervously wondered if their money was safe.

In the midst of all this angst, in his office in Portcullis House next to the House of Commons, Treasury Committee chairman John McFall MP studied the letter he had just received from Governor King. The governor's confidence in the ability of the banking system to withstand shocks and his concerns about moral hazard already looked out of date; King's 'steady as we go' position was not one the government could hold. On Monday 17 September Chancellor Alistair Darling announced the guarantee of all existing deposits with Northern Rock.[25] Two days later, to alleviate strain in longer-term money markets, the Bank of England announced it would provide three-month funds against a wide range of collateral. The following day King gave evidence to the Treasury Select Committee, defended the 'U-turn' to provide additional liquidity and said the British banking system 'is very well capitalized, it is very strong . . . I cannot believe and I do not believe that there is any lasting damage to the reputation of the British banking system.'[26] It was perhaps what he had to say at that moment. The run on the Rock, however, was the beginning of the end, not just of the banks' glory years but of the City's twenty-year grip on the nation's psyche.

It did not happen immediately. Northern Rock and the problems in the US mortgage and inter-bank borrowing markets killed Barclays' interest in ABN. By the end of September, Barclays' share price was 550p and Barclays withdrew its offer having received acceptances from just 0.2 per cent of ABN shareholders. The RBS consortium completed the acquisition a fortnight later. Like Goodwin, Varley had put his personal imprimatur on the deal and he had been soundly beaten on price by his rival. If RBS and its partners made a success of the acquisition, a feat that would require the banking market to stabilize, Barclays and its chief executive would have been publicly outsmarted. Varley was in Dubai at the time Barclays withdrew and honourably rang his chairman with an offer to resign. Agius' reply was noncommittal: 'Let's see what the next few weeks bring.'

KARL IS COLLARED

October 2007: Karl Edwards had at long last found a warehouse that fitted his needs; it was time to discuss a new mortgage. He phoned his relationship manager at Barclays, who he now regarded as a friend. He trusted the bank to look after his interests and Barclays evidently considered him a good customer. The relationship manager was pleased to help with the mortgage and agreed to come round to Edwards' office to discuss the details.

Edwards was surprised to find not one but two visitors from Barclays turning up at his door. The relationship manager introduced

Carol, a smartly dressed woman in a dark suit who he described as part of the team. That was only partly true. Carol worked for Barclays Capital in the Birmingham regional office with the title of corporate risk manager. It sounded reassuring but there was a hard commercial edge to the role. As she later disclosed on her CV, it involved actively managing people such as Edwards' relationship manager 'to achieve their team's financial objectives in the sale of derivative products.'[27]

After Edwards' relationship manager had taken down a few details about the new loan, Carol asked Edwards if he had considered what would happen if, as many economists were predicting, interest rates rose from their current level of 5 per cent. Would his business be able to meet increased interest repayments on the loan he wanted to take out?

Edwards said that he was confident about his business, that he never believed in overstretching and that the sum he wanted to borrow was well within his means. Carol turned on her laptop and clicked on a file. It was a presentation headed 'Interest Rate Risk Management, Corporate Risk Advisory, Barclays Capital'. She worked through it, talking about derivatives and hedges, things she said financial institutions were doing all the time but which were new to Edwards. She showed him graphs and used terms he had never heard of like 'structured collar cap with a double floor', 'mark-to-market', 'upward sloping yield curve' and 'forward rates'.

The presentation included a page which showed the corporate logos of companies which used such products, for example Citigroup, Goldman Sachs and HBOS, and Carol said that Barclays Capital had produced a simplified version for smaller companies. The pack included a page asking 'Which should I choose? Interest rate cap? Interest rate collar? Structured collar?' Each option was followed by a step-by-step guide: 'Choose this strategy if you think . . .' and then a series of interest rate scenarios. One of the later slides was headed 'Sounds a bit complicated? Why do it this way?'

She concluded: 'It's a great way to limit the risk. Lots of businesses are doing it. In fact, some banks make it a condition of taking out loans.' Among all the jargon, it was the only plain language she had used and Edwards took it to mean that the mortgage was conditional on buying this product. Edwards had barely understood a word but did not like to admit his ignorance. He was used to spending all his waking hours thinking about the day-to-day worries of running what had become a multi-million-pound business. He just sold records and left the money side to his accountant and the bank. But he agreed to think things over.

It was December before Edwards exchanged contracts on the new warehouse and it would be April 2008 before he got the keys. He had agreed a mortgage of £925,000 with Barclays but just before completion he received another visit from his relationship manager and Carol. She had clearly done well and now described herself as 'manager, corporate risk advisory'. She told Edwards that Barclays expected interest rates to go up and suggested that he look at a structured collar as a way of protecting himself against rising mortgage interest payments.

She showed him a chart illustrating how the cash flows on a structured collar would work, but to Edwards it looked like a complicated wiring diagram for an electrical installation. He did not understand it and asked Carol: 'Why would I do all that? I can buy the warehouse for cash and cut out the risk that way.' Carol could see her sales target receding and quickly countered: 'Of course, you could do that. But this way you could actually make money out of your mortgage. Other businesses do this all the time. I know about this kind of thing and your relationship manager does too.'

Edwards looked for guidance at the relationship manager, who nodded approvingly. If he said it was fine, that was good enough for Karl. He had been with Barclays since 1993 and trusted them. So he agreed to buy what he came to know as an Interest Rate Hedging Product [IRHP], and thought nothing more of it. He would not have been so carefree had he known that he had just been a victim of what Barrett several years before had called cross-selling and up-selling. Karl's basic banking business was not profitable enough for Barclays; they wanted to sell him financial products made in other parts of the bank, in this case interest rate derivatives invented by Barclays Capital. When Varley grouped retail and corporate banking together under Seegers he removed any organizational barriers to cross-selling and Barclays went at it with a will, organizing presentation evenings for people like Carol with titles such as 'Financial Products for

Derivatives Virgins' and loading on extra high sales credits for those who could sell them.

No one appeared to have thought through the consequences of incentivizing people like Carol. She was a school-leaver entrant to banking who had worked her way up and was now at one of the UK's most prestigious financial institutions, where she was given targets to meet and financial incentives to do so. If she did well, she could earn sums of money that paid for the lifestyle she craved, and she knew what happened to colleagues who failed to deliver. Her response was at least understandable; the failure of more senior management to anticipate the impact of the incentive structures they put in place was not.

GO FOR BROKE

Varley was phlegmatic as he waited to see how shareholders would react to Barclays' defeat by RBS. If the crisis passed, Barclays' caution in not paying up for ABN would have left its chief executive and indeed the bank itself open to attack; if it persisted or got worse, Barclays' prudence would look smart and its chief executive would be safe. A devout Roman Catholic, Varley drew comfort from his faith and resolved to do his best for the bank, whatever the outcome.

He did not have long to wait. Within weeks of Barclays' bid for ABN lapsing in September 2007, several of its role models were in trouble. Among many examples, Merrill Lynch revealed a $7.9 billion write-down for bad debts and on 30 October Stan O'Neal resigned as chief executive and chairman. A few days later, Citigroup, an inspiration for Barclays' universal banking ambitions, reported another $10 billion round of mortgage-related losses and Chuck Prince resigned as chief executive.[28] Citigroup's problems intensified in 2008. In January they took $18 billion in sub-prime write-downs and raised $12.5 billion in new equity capital from shareholders; the same day, Merrill Lynch raised $6.6 billion.

British financial institutions were also facing the consequences of the US sub-prime crisis. In February 2008 Northern Rock was nationalized, a victim of its own sub-prime adventures and a business model that depended on funding from other financial institutions.

In March HSBC announced $17 billion in impairment charges – write-downs to reflect the likelihood of borrowers defaulting – following a disastrous $16 billion acquisition in 2002 of Household International, a US bank that specialized in second mortgage lending. The same month, in a US government-sponsored deal, J. P. Morgan Chase bought the failed investment bank Bear Stearns for a song after it sustained huge losses in the mortgage markets.

Any semblance of order in the global financial system had gone. Central bank intervention, including a $200 billion Fed injection into markets in March 2008 and a Bank of England special liquidity scheme in the following month that enabled banks to swap securities for bonds issued by the government, was required to keep the system functioning. Central bankers and regulators worked round the clock, seven days a week: weekends, birthdays, anniversaries, school sports days were forgotten as they fought to restrain the beast. Banks dominated the news, rumours swept the markets and share prices plunged. Anxious executives and directors worried whether the next maturing debt would leave them with enough cash to open for business.

Far from facing criticism for losing ABN, Barclays was now applauded for not pursuing it and Varley was safe. Barclays survived the early days of the sub-prime meltdown comfortably, maintaining profits for 2007 at the previous year's high level despite US mortgage charges of £782 million, ten times Diamond's estimate six months before. Their total exposure was £15 billion, which had largely originated in 2005 and the first half of 2006, less than 2 per cent of Barclays Capital's total assets. Broadbent and Le Blanc's caution had saved them from further problems.

With the crisis deepening during the opening months of 2008, the board faced a vital decision about whether to carry on with its universal banking strategy. The financial world was clearly in trouble, but there was no sense yet that this would spread to the wider economy according to most economists. Global growth for 2008 was still expected to be 4 per cent, competitors such as Lloyds were looking to expand in the UK mortgage market and RBS, even as it digested ABN, was still bullish. Was this the time to lock down and wait for the storm to pass or was it an opportunity to push for the summit?

It could have been a turning point but the board, by now joined by

Sir Mike Rake, a former senior partner of the auditors KPMG, David Booth, a senior fixed income expert from Morgan Stanley, and Patience Wheatcroft, an influential conservative journalist, revealed its true colours. Despite the Risk Committee's report on the US mortgage market and three extra Audit Committee meetings to discuss it, they concluded that the problems in the banking sector would be short-lived and therefore for Barclays there would be no retreat. They had just enjoyed two stupendous years, and they weren't going to change course now.

It was the green light for Seegers and Diamond, set up by Varley to counter-balance each other in a fight for group capital. Seegers dashed on, buying businesses in Russia and Indonesia and expanding into India and Pakistan. Diamond played a cooler hand and began to look for an opportunity to buy a major US investment bank. The right deal would seal Barclays' status as a global investment bank and give Diamond the victory he desired on his home turf.

The deal maker in the chair, the ambitious chief executive, the hard-charging business heads, the growth merchants on the board: none of them was for turning. What value shareholders would have had from a contra-thinker rather than the corporate establishment represented on the board. Where were you, Martin Taylor, when Barclays so needed you?

PART III

Coronation, 2008–11

14
Twilight of the Gods, 2008

DIAMOND AND STEEL

In April 2008 Diamond was preparing for a flight to Zurich when he was interrupted by a call from an old friend.[1] Bob Steel had been building Goldman Sachs' business in London when Diamond was doing the same for Morgan Stanley in the late 1980s and early 90s. Steel had briefly served on the Barclays board and Diamond had once hoped that he would succeed Barrett as chairman, but instead in 2006 he became under-secretary at the US Treasury, reporting to his old Goldman Sachs boss, Hank Paulson.

Diamond and Steel spoke regularly during the crisis, updating each other on what was happening in the markets. During one of those conversations, in late March, Diamond had asked Steel whether there had been any other interest in Bear Stearns at the time it was rescued by J. P. Morgan. It was a calculated question, because talk was that, with an emergency loan from the New York Federal Reserve Bank to Bear Stearns and background help from the Treasury, J. P. Morgan had got a bargain. It was a polite way of saying: 'Look, if that happens again, don't forget us.'

Like most other bankers at the time, Diamond was still working on the assumption that the pre-crisis investment banking model – highly leveraged on a thin capital base – would remain the way forward. Barclays needed a stronger Wall Street presence if it was to become a top five bank and he had identified UBS's investment bank, a heavy loser in the sub-prime crisis, as a possible target. There had been two phone calls and two meetings between Diamond and the UBS chief executive, Marcel Rhoner, and he was preparing to meet him again when Steel called.

The under-secretary was a polished performer, and he was careful in what he said: 'If there were another shoe to fall, such as Lehman Brothers, would Barclays have an interest and if so what could we at the Treasury do to help?'[2] He stressed that this was not an official call but a background conversation to help his thinking.

Diamond was equally cautious in his answer. Lehman would be an interesting proposition. It was a long-standing member of Wall Street's bulge bracket of leading investment banks and, after an unhappy decade between 1984 and 1994 under the ownership of American Express, had re-established itself as a separate publicly listed company led by a tough bond trader named Dick Fuld.[3] Diamond knew that Lehman was highly leveraged and its hard-nosed management team would be difficult to penetrate. As a going concern, Lehman would be expensive and its balance sheet would be hard to value and complicated to unravel. At this stage, however, there was only one answer to give Steel: 'Yes. It would definitely be something to think about.'[4] Diamond reported the call to the board, obtained permission to do some analysis and phoned Steel occasionally over the next three months to update him.

DESERT SANDS

Barclays had always maintained good relations with the sovereign wealth funds of the Gulf States, especially Qatar. Former chairman Andrew Buxton had spent a lot of time there, and Barclays was careful to keep its network fresh, acquiring a banking licence from the Qatar Financial Centre's Regulatory Authority in 2006, opening an office in the Financial Centre's Tower in Doha in 2007 and in May the following year arranging for Varley and Roger Jenkins, head of Barclays Capital's Middle Eastern business, to meet Qatar's prime minister, Sheikh Hamad bin Jassim bin Jabr al Thani, known as HBJ.

The meeting in London at the Intercontinental Hotel on Park Lane went well. Qatar welcomed an opportunity to build a relationship with a prestigious and, they believed, undervalued institution and

Barclays was pleased to strengthen its connections in the region. On 25 June it announced a share issue to raise £4.5 billion from new and existing investors; the former included the Qatar Investment Authority and Challenger, a company representing HBJ's beneficial interests, which between them agreed to take up half the issue at a price of 282 pence, a discount of 9.3 per cent to the previous night's closing share price. The issue raised Barclays' tier one capital ratio – pure capital expressed as a percentage of risk weighted assets – to 8.8 per cent, comfortably ahead of its internal target of 7.25 per cent, and would enable it 'to take advantage of the current market circumstances which have created for Barclays an unusual competitive opportunity'. Scarcely noticed at the time, but later highly controversial, Barclays said that it was 'also pleased to have entered into an agreement for the provision of advisory services by Qatar Investment Authority to Barclays in the Middle East'.[5]

'PROJECT LONG ISLAND'

With the June capital subscribed for and, by the standards of the time, a strong balance sheet, acquisitions were now a serious possibility and Barclays Capital's interest in Lehman stepped up. Following Steel's call, a Barclays Capital team had been working on Lehman over the spring and early summer and presented 'Project Long Island', its code name for Lehman, to Barclays' July board.

Lehman's position had deteriorated over that period. Following second quarter losses of $2.8 billion announced on 16 June, the Lehman share price dropped to below $20, a fall of 70 per cent in the year. The Barclays Capital presentation said that Long Island had been 'a prime victim of recent market turmoil' and consequently 'might be on the block' giving Baltimore, its own code name, an 'opportunity to acquire Long Island at a substantial discount to the current valuation'. The combined business would rival Wall Street's dominant players and, with synergies of £1.1 billion by 2010, 'would generate £24 billion income and £8 billion profit before tax'.[6] Those figures were greater than Barclays' entire group results for 2007.

Diamond was enthusiastic but Varley was more cautious in the light of clear signs of distress in the US mortgage market.[7] President Bush had just asked Congress to give the US Treasury unlimited investment authority in Fannie Mae and Freddie Mac, the largest mortgage finance companies in the US, which between them owned or guaranteed $5.2 trillion of the nation's home loans – nearly half the total.[8] Varley thought Lehman was likely to get cheaper and wanted to be sure that the board had a proper strategic conversation before making a move. He described a bid for Lehman as 'a big call', adding: 'It is important that we are not hustled into a decision before we are ready.' The board decided that the opportunity was indeed interesting but only at a knock-down price. Diamond said: 'I want you to remember that if Lehman becomes available at a distressed price it is going to mean that there is a nasty world out there. Bear that in mind if we come back with a decision to take.'

Over the next few weeks the Lehman share price continued to slide, credit agencies downgraded its rating, the cost of insuring against its failure through credit default swaps rose sharply,[9] and Lehman's management frantically tried to sell bits of its business to raise cash. In August Diamond wanted to register interest, reporting to Varley: 'We do not want to be on the outside as there may be pieces here that would be of interest.' Varley fired back: 'You're right though to be choosy about what we might want.'[10]

9–10 SEPTEMBER – NEW YORK AND LONDON

Diamond was in New York on Tuesday 9 September presenting at a conference for investors. During the day Lehman's share price collapsed by 45 per cent to below $8 and the price of its credit default swaps rose by 50 per cent; its third quarter results were due the next day.

The following morning Diamond headed to Philadelphia on a recruiting mission at Wharton, one of America's leading business schools. While he was in the car, at 05.54 New York time, knowing that the Lehman results were imminent and that they would probably be dreadful, Diamond sent an email to Steel: 'Can u call me, rather important.' Steel had just left the Treasury to become chief executive of Wachovia, another troubled financial services business, but nevertheless Diamond wanted him to tell Treasury Secretary Paulson that Barclays could be interested in Lehman.

An hour later Lehman's third quarter results proved every bit as bad as Diamond expected. After a $5.6 billion write-down on its residential and commercial real estate portfolio, most of which was now put up for sale, as was its investment management business, the latest quarter's loss was $3.9 billion. The share price fell again to $6, taking the yearly drop to 90 per cent and the cost of its credit default swaps jumped another 20 per cent.

Diamond would be on stage at Wharton when Lehman's management updated investors and analysts later that morning but he asked Varley to listen in on their presentation from London. As the call progressed, Varley decided that the whole of Lehman would soon be available at a bargain price. This might be the opportunity they had been waiting for. If they were going to put such a big question to the board, he and Diamond should do so together. He summoned Diamond back to a board meeting in London scheduled for Thursday 11 September.

While this was going on, Steel made the call Diamond had requested. Paulson, a seasoned investment banker who had made a career advising chief executives on mergers and acquisitions, listened politely but was not impressed. He doubted that the British bank was agile or big enough to be seriously involved in the rescue. He had no time to waste. Three days previously, using the powers granted in July, he had nationalized Fannie Mae and Freddie Mac. AIG, the world's biggest insurer, with a large exposure to mortgages, was also in trouble; its shares had dropped 19 per cent the previous day.[11] With cracks appearing all around him, and so many pressing issues to deal with, he needed to focus on the potential Lehman buyers he regarded as serious, principally Bank of America. Still, he promised to phone Diamond later. At 14.01 Steel told Diamond: 'I spoke with HMP [Paulson], he will call you.'[12]

In fact it was Timothy Geithner, president of the Fed, and Anthony Ryan, an assistant secretary at the US Department of the Treasury, who called Diamond. He reported in an email to Steel at 18.06:

> Had substantive and interesting calls with Tim G and Tony
> R. Would be good to catch up in the morning if you can call. Did
> not hear from Hank, disappointing but probably understand-
> able. Will fill you in then. Bob, yr help has been perfect, thanks!!
> There may be a way forward, we will know very soon. Bob.[13]

Steel replied to Diamond at 23.09: 'Call me now if you wish,' and reported his Paulson conversation to Diamond. Diamond then told his lieutenants del Missier and chief operating officer Ricci: 'Learned a lot on this call. Steel is an ace.'[14]

While Diamond flew back, Varley worked out his next steps. If the board agreed, they would have to move quickly and that would require regulatory approval. To prepare the way, he decided to call Hector Sants, chief executive of Barclays' regulator, the FSA. It was a classic Varley call: quiet, understated and well judged. He told Sants that Barclays was taking a preliminary look at Lehman and that although he was personally sceptical that a deal would get done, he wanted to advise the regulator immediately of the board's interest. [15]

Sants had started his working life in 1977 with a leading British equi-ties broker, Phillips & Drew, leaving after twenty years only when a series of mergers broke the bloodline. After a few years with the US investment bank CSFB, he joined the FSA in 2004 as the managing director for Wholesale and Institutional Markets. Those were the days of 'light touch' regulation when the mandate from government to the regulator was to promote the City's international competitiveness as well as to keep it clean, but right now he had other concerns. Sants said he understood Barclays' strategic interest in Lehman but he was spending a lot of time resolving problems at other banks and had no wish to see Barclays overstretch itself. He told Varley that the FSA had no objection in principle but it was important for them to see the detail of any emerg-ing proposal. He asked to be kept closely informed of developments.

11 SEPTEMBER – NEW YORK AND LONDON

Varley took him at his word and phoned him again first thing in the morning to explain that a board meeting had now been formally convened at which a bid would be discussed. Progress would depend on the Fed's support and on agreeing a price a long way below Lehman's stated asset values. Sants thanked him and again reminded him that the FSA would be watching how any transaction impacted on Barclays' capital position and liquidity. Varley assured Sants that he would not put in place any structure that would reduce these positions unacceptably.[16]

A Barclays' car met Diamond at Heathrow on the morning of the 11th and whisked him straight to the board meeting. The board confirmed that they would be interested in Lehman at the right price but insisted that before sending a team to the US to start due diligence, Varley should check that the US authorities would take them seriously. In addition to Paulson, the attitude of the Fed's Geithner would be crucial.

Before Varley could take matters further, Diamond received an unexpected call from Paulson. Bank of America, the universal bank that the US Treasury considered the most suitable buyer of Lehman, was dragging its feet. Ken Wilson, another former Goldman Sachs man now working in government, had suggested to Paulson that he should keep Barclays warm in case Bank of America dropped out of the running. Remembering Steel's call but still doubtful of Barclays' capabilities, Paulson agreed to call Diamond, telling him: 'You'll need to move quickly. I also want you to know that we are unable to put public money in.'

Diamond said he understood but Paulson wondered whether he was speaking with authority and urged him to make sure the Barclays board was supportive. When the call ended, Paulson felt more positive about Barclays' intentions but was still doubtful about their ability to complete such a major deal.[17]

Later in the day, as instructed by the board, Diamond and Varley arranged to speak to Geithner and Paulson. They did so from a conference room in Barclays' office at 43 Brook Street, next door to Claridge's in Mayfair. Varley confirmed Barclays' interest and Paulson, knowing that Lehman was on the brink and that the collapse of a firm with $600 billion of gross assets – 50 per cent bigger than Bear Stearns when it was rescued – would be a disaster, said that any purchaser of

Lehman would need to make a bid before the end of the weekend. If none could be found, Lehman would be put into orderly run off.[18]

Then Tim Geithner spoke. He had spent all his career in public policy and had been president of the New York Fed since 2003; he was the technocrat to Paulson's practitioner. He suggested that Diamond call Lehman's chief executive, Fuld, to start discussions. Diamond immediately objected: 'I am not going to negotiate with Dick Fuld. We would not buy Lehman with him as chief executive and nor would you allow us to keep him there even if we did. He is the wrong man to negotiate with. We are not looking to do a deal at the market price.' The issue of who would call Fuld was not resolved, but Paulson once again emphasized that any buyer of Lehman would need to make a bid before the end of the weekend.[19]

The call was encouraging enough for Diamond and his team to head over to New York. To avoid attracting attention, they took separate British Airways flights, Diamond and his chief operating officer Rich Ricci on one and del Missier on the other with another member of Diamond's inner circle, the military strategy enthusiast Tom Kalaris. Ricci had actually joined Barclays in 1994, two years before Diamond, having held senior finance and technology positions at the Bank of Boston and the Bank of New England. He had a degree in finance, knew the nuts and bolts of investment banking infrastructure and had a capacity to chase things down relentlessly. Barclays' insiders said: 'We don't know what he does but he gets shit done', which was exactly what he did over the next few days. They arrived late at night on 11 September and two Barclays' cars took them into Manhattan to the midtown offices of Lehman's lawyers, Simpson Thacher and Bartlett on Lexington Avenue.

They took the lift to a large reception area and then climbed a staircase to the law firm's meeting rooms. There they discovered that there was no data room, no one of any seniority to guide them through the documents and no kind of welcome at all. Something was wrong. They believed they had come to do a deal, but the seller didn't seem to be taking them seriously. They checked into the Carlyle Hotel and grabbed a few hours' sleep before the following morning heading over to Barclays' office at 200 Park Avenue to join a Barclays' board meeting by video link.

12 SEPTEMBER – LONDON AND NICE

The second presentation to the full board noted that Long Island had become available at a distressed price and outlined an exit price of $5 per share, a total consideration of $3.8 billion, to be financed in Barclays' shares. On projected numbers, Lehman would reduce Barclays' dependence on the UK from 55 to 45 per cent of revenues, increase the US proportion from 10 to 23 per cent and lift Investment Banking and Investment Management to 52 per cent of Barclays' total profits, 'well within our long-term goal'. The board gave 'consent to conduct due diligence leading to a potential offer'. A Transaction Committee was set up and an indicative timetable was outlined with an announce date of Monday 15 September. The Barclays Capital report listed several potential risks to a successful deal – including legal action from Lehman's shareholders, a rival bid, counterparties refusing to do business with Lehman, a run on Barclays' share price and the loss of key personnel – with mitigating actions listed alongside.[20]

Varley knew that the regulators would have to be satisfied that Barclays' balance sheet could absorb a deal of this magnitude and after the board meeting contacted Sants for the second time that day, having already reported the previous evening's conversation with Paulson. He told him that he had been given authority by the board to go further but that Barclays would not buy Lehman's book of mortgages or real estate assets and would require the US authorities to provide Barclays with sufficient liquidity to meet Lehman's trading obligations. Sants understood the business logic but reminded Varley that Barclays would need to demonstrate that it had sufficient capital and liquidity to satisfy the FSA stress tests after any acquisition.[21]

In fact the FSA was one of three public bodies keeping an eye on Barclays. During the afternoon Sants liaised with Tom Scholar, director general of financial services at the Treasury, and Sir John Gieve, one of the deputy governors at the Bank of England. He told them that he had just spoken to Geithner who had said the Fed was exploring the possibility of Lehman being taken over by Barclays or Bank of America, with discussions with Bank of America being at the more advanced stage; he expected Bank of America would probably buy Lehman over the weekend. Sants also reported his conversations with Varley, describing his own tone as 'not encouraging to Barclays', and confirmed Varley's undertaking that Barclays would proceed only after FSA approval.[22] Sants was cautious but the Treasury and Bank of England were even more so. Their view was: 'They can't possibly be serious about taking on this amount of risk.'

Sants' boss at the FSA was a former civil servant, Sir Callum McCarthy, who at one time had been in charge of Barclays Bank North America. Soon after Diamond arrived he went back to the public sector in the role of UK's energy regulator and then became chairman of the FSA in 2003. He was not a natural risk taker, temperamentally more suited to regulation than banking. At four in the afternoon he briefed the chancellor of the exchequer, Alistair Darling, a calm Scotsman and former lawyer, about Barclays' interest in Lehman.[23] Darling and Gieve were in Nice for a meeting of European finance ministers to discuss how the European Union should respond to what was fast becoming a crisis. An adventurous move by Barclays was the last thing they needed and Darling asked his officials to set up a call with Paulson.

This took place late in the afternoon from Darling's hotel on the rue des Anglais. The gruff American who had made a fortune on Wall Street and the career politician who had never earned more in a year than a Goldman Sachs associate were a contrasting pair: Paulson said it all up front in a thick American accent; Darling played everything down in a gentle Scots burr. The scenario was set for a 'you say tomarto, we say tomayto' misunderstanding.[24]

Paulson outlined three options for Lehman: wind-down, takeover or purchase by an industry consortium. Darling explained that he was in principle not against a takeover or investment by Barclays but he needed to be certain that Barclays was not taking on more risk than it could manage. He said he 'did not want the British taxpayer to end up standing behind an American bank that was on the verge of collapse'.[25]

Darling was quietly warning Paulson that he did not want Barclays to be involved but Paulson pressed on, holding out the promise of Barclays becoming a major global bank with all the power of Wall Street.[26]

He said that the Fed might be prepared to offer some help in the shape of guarantees but at that stage was not in a position to do so.[27]

The idea of Barclays becoming a big player on Wall Street horrified Darling. He understood the linkages in the global financial system and the instability of highly leveraged financial institutions and had no wish to see a thinly capitalized British bank take itself deeper into this quagmire. He wondered what help Paulson had in mind. Before he went into dinner, he asked Sants to establish what this might be and to remind them of the British authorities' reservations.[28]

At nine that evening McCarthy contacted Geithner and told him that Barclays was still working out the possible impact of an acquisition on its balance sheet but that in any case the FSA would need to be satisfied that Barclays had the funding and capital to proceed. McCarthy intended to convey the British authorities' opposition to Barclays' involvement but Geithner appears to have taken this as conditional approval.[29]

While this conversation was going on, Darling, Gieve and their EU colleagues were in the grounds of the Villa Ephrussi de Rothschild in Saint-Jean-Cap-Ferrat, one of the French Riviera's most exquisite settings, where Darling's French counterpart, Christine Lagarde, was hosting a gala dinner. Beautifully sung operatic arias wafted over the moonlit Mediterranean but were wasted on the audience, most of whom were preoccupied with the turmoil in global financial markets, including Darling and Gieve who were hoping that by now the US authorities were fully aware of their reservations about Barclays' interest in Lehman.

THE SAME DAY – NEW YORK AND WASHINGTON

Geithner had continued to press Diamond to meet Fuld. Although Diamond knew that the Lehman boss still had in mind a merger of equals, which wasn't his idea at all, Geithner was insistent and so that morning at nine-thirty, soon after turning off the video link to Barclays' board meeting, Diamond suggested to Fuld that they meet on neutral ground, within walking distance from each other's offices at that favourite Diamond venue, the New York Racquet and Tennis Club. Fuld said 'There's too much buzz about the city to take that risk, come to us.' His office emailed Diamond's with the arrangements: 'Mr Fuld's driver Kevin will come and collect you and take you to their offices via the back entrance and private lift. Could you please advise if you would like to be picked up at 200 Park Avenue.'[30]

Diamond was driven to Lehman's head office at 745 Seventh Avenue and whisked up in the goods lift to Club 31, as the executive floor was known on Lehman's trading floors. Diamond was surprised to learn that the US government's preferred buyer, Bank of America, were also in the building. He felt slighted, cut short the brief meeting with Fuld and went back to the offices of Simpson Thacher, Lehman's lawyers, where del Missier, Ricci, Kalaris and a team of senior traders, trading managers, risk officers and compliance staff were now working on the files.

The mood was flat. They had discovered two major problems. The first was a $32 billion book of commercial property, a quarter of which lacked proper documentation. The second was a portfolio of unsaleable investments in private equity funds, taken in better times. Gloomily they sent a file note to head office in London:

> In the previous report to the Board, we estimated a total of $7.5 billion in further write-downs to Long Island assets based on a high level analysis of the risks of the valuation of key assets ... Based upon due diligence undertaken in the last 24 hours, this estimate of the further immediate write-downs to Long Island's book has increased significantly to $23–27 bn.

Of this, $16 billion related to real estate, $3–5 billion to residential mortgage-backed securities and $4–6 billion to the private equity portfolio.[31] The news was received with alarm in London. The write-downs revealed by the New York team would have jeopardized Barclays' future if they had not been discovered. What else was lurking in Lehman's dark corners?[32]

The Barclays Capital team were losing heart. Their boss had been sent on a wild goose chase to see the man who to all intents and purposes had lost control of the business, they were being fobbed off with juniors and probably being manipulated by the US authorities too.

Diamond was equally fed up. Ever the optimist, though, he dug deep into his reserves and geed up his team. 'You never know what is going to happen,' he told them. 'We have to be ready for every eventuality.'

In the afternoon they got their break. The large conference room they had been allocated at Simpson, Thacher had two doors, one of which had previously been kept closed. Suddenly it opened and Bart McDade and Jerry Donini appeared unannounced, Lehman's president and head of equities respectively. All of a sudden Barclays were in the presence of people actually running the business day to day and whose commitment they would need.

McDade and Donini presented to the Barclays team into the small hours, business by business, equities, fixed income, mergers and acquisitions. It was a polished performance that they had obviously put on a few times before. But behind the decks and the show reels was an enticing story of deep client relationships and a roster of professionally skilled staff, particularly in equities and mergers and acquisitions, the areas that Taylor had got out of ten years before but which Barclays Capital now needed if it was to join the bulge bracket.

THE SAME DAY – HAMPSHIRE, ENGLAND, AND AT 30,000 FEET

Diamond reported this positive development back to Varley, who was in his Hampshire home where he and his wife were welcoming Marcus and Kate Agius for dinner. Varley told Diamond that he would try to brief Paulson. Just before ten o'clock, after fish pie and white Burgundy, the couples were having coffee when the phone rang. Varley and Agius went upstairs to Varley's study to speak to Paulson, who was flying back to New York from Washington through a thunderstorm. With the noise of the storm crashing round the plane coming through on the speakerphone, Varley told Paulson what he had told Sants: Barclays could be interested in Lehman but the toxic assets had to be excluded and the US authorities would have to provide Barclays with access to short-term liquidity to complete the deal. Paulson replied: 'The first should be possible, the second might be harder.'[33] They arranged to have a longer conversation the following morning US time and the Barclays men rejoined their wives.

There was now a new problem to consider: if, as Paulson had implied, the US authorities would not provide temporary funding, or at least a guarantee, to Lehman's trading counterparties while a deal was being completed, Barclays would have to do it or find someone else to help.

13 SEPTEMBER – NEW YORK AND LONDON

After McDade and Donini left, Diamond had returned to his hotel to freshen up, dozed for a couple of hours and then woke up with a raging toothache. There would be no time to get it fixed and the throbbing pain was made worse by lack of sleep. The conference call at eight o'clock in the morning New York time (one in the afternoon UK time) was both important and well attended. Varley's team included general counsel Mark Harding, a bearded former Clifford Chance partner who had joined the bank in 2003. He ran a large department of in-house lawyers and managed the external law firms that advised the bank. Varley and company were at Barclays' head office at Churchill Place; Diamond and team were at the Barclays Capital office on Park Avenue, New York; Paulson, Geithner and their officials were at 33 Liberty Street, the Federal Reserve building in New York's financial district.

Barclays outlined a possible deal at between $3–5 per share, with the proviso that hard-to-value commercial real estate and private equity assets which were in the books at approximately $50 billion be ringfenced and excluded. Diamond suggested that the Wall Street banks be asked jointly to acquire these assets and manage them down. It would be risky for them but perhaps less risky than the alternative of letting Lehman go under and facing a market meltdown. Paulson, who was in fact already working on such a plan, shot back: 'Bob, you had better start calling your peers and get that done.' Diamond replied: 'Secretary Paulson, with all due respect, chief executives around Wall Street are not going to be taking my call today, but if you call they will listen. We are going to need your help on this. I think this is something you have to propose as an option.'

When the call was over, Barclays' New York team made their way across town to the Federal Reserve building, a grim fortress of fourteen floors of offices sitting on top of the world's biggest gold vault, and were shown to a small windowless room. Elsewhere in the building, Paulson went to meet the chief executives of Wall Street's largest banks, including Lloyd Blankfein (Goldman Sachs), Jamie Dimon (J. P. Morgan), John Mack (Morgan Stanley), Vikram Pandit (Citigroup), John Thain (Merrill Lynch), Brady Dougan (Credit Suisse) and Robert Kelly (Bank of New York Mellon). The previous evening, he and Geithner had briefed them on Lehman's plight and urged them to work together to resolve the situation. During the day, Bank of America's interest in Lehman declined as they zeroed in on Merrill Lynch instead. Now he told them that Barclays was the most likely buyer and that, despite having just snapped at Diamond for suggesting such a thing, they would need help. Barclays were rapidly becoming Paulson's best hope. He said: 'We're working hard on a transaction and we need to know where you guys stand. If there's a capital hole, the government can't fill it. So how do we get this done?'[34]

The Barclays team at the Fed were unexpectedly moved to a much larger but still windowless conference room. Taped to the door was a piece of paper marked 'Buyer'. Diamond turned to del Missier and Ricci and said: 'Whoever was in here is out. I think we're now in the right place.'

At half-past nine that night London time (four-thirty in the afternoon New York time), Varley and Diamond spoke again with Paulson and Geithner to impart some unwelcome news: Barclays' general counsel Harding had advised that if the US authorities were unwilling to guarantee Lehman's trading liabilities during completion, Barclays would need shareholder approval to do so itself, a process that could take several weeks. Such a delay would kill the deal. Without a guarantee, Lehman would be unable to trade and its business would dribble away. Varley told Paulson and Geithner that Barclays would not approach the FSA for consent unless the Federal Reserve guaranteed the trades over the completion period. Geithner pushed back and asked why Barclays could not provide the guarantee, as J. P. Morgan had done for Bear Stearns. Varley explained: 'Under UK listing rules, a guarantee of that size could not be provided without shareholder approval and that would take weeks.'[35]

Paulson was cross. He needed to get a deal done that weekend and couldn't take the risk of Barclays' shareholders voting it down. He concluded the meeting abruptly stating that there was no deal and that if Barclays wanted to stay in the game, it had better keep working on alternatives to guarantee the funding. He could only have meant the British authorities. Despite his conversation with Darling, and Geithner's with McCarthy, he evidently still did not understand their opposition to Barclays' involvement. 'See you around' were his parting words.[36]

By the evening, the Wall Street chiefs had agreed in principle to support a deal that would see them fund a special purpose vehicle to buy up the contentious real estate and private equity investments. Their analysis showed them to be worth $27 billion rather than the book price of $50 billion, but they were prepared to buy them for $37 billion, therefore standing to lose $10 billion as the assets were worked out. These were not the kinds of deals that they were used to, but the alternative – a market implosion following an unmanaged collapse of Lehman – was worse.

Paulson left the Fed and returned to his hotel, the Waldorf Astoria, feeling optimistic about the prospects for a deal and still believing that somehow a solution would be found to Barclays' problem of the shareholders' vote.[37]

While the Barclays New York team waited, they brainstormed what to do if a US government liquidity guarantee was really not available. The previous day Hans-Joerg Rudloff, a famous veteran of the European bond markets hired by Diamond to become chairman of Barclays Capital, had emailed him the suggestion that they engage Michael Klein, a brilliant corporate financier, who had recently left Citigroup to work on his own. 'Dear Bob,' Rudloff's email ran, 'I informed Klein that you will talk in an hour. I asked him whether he had any engagements in this affair, to which he said no.'[38] Klein agreed to advise Barclays but needed Citigroup to waive a 'no compete' clause to do so. Early that afternoon, Diamond received an email from Ricci. 'Subject: Klein cleared to work with us. 1. As long as there is no public announcement 2. They [Citigroup] would also like the banking business but not a condition.'[39]

Klein worked with Diamond solidly over the following twenty-four hours and that evening he suggested approaching Warren Buffett, the legendary US investor, with whom he had done business in the past, to see whether Buffett would fund the trading liabilities guarantees. Diamond, Klein and del Missier tracked Buffett down to a hotel in Canada, where he was just going out to dinner. He listened politely and told them to fax something over for him to look at when he got back. They left him a long voicemail explaining the documents they were sending over. They never heard back from him, but a few months later Buffett was driving with his daughter, who was playing with his phone. She said: 'Dad, you have a voicemail.' He replied: 'I don't think I have,' but she insisted: 'Oh yes, you do. Just listen to it.'

During the evening, the Barclays team discovered where in the Fed the Lehman team were waiting. They walked over, knocked on the door and asked: 'What are you guys doing for food tonight?' Someone on the Lehman team replied: 'We've been here before. We know what to do'. A pile of sandwiches was ordered and the two teams ate together before Barclays headed back to their own room.

Throughout the day Barclays and FSA executives had stayed in touch. Everyone understood that no deal would go ahead unless the regulator was satisfied with Barclays' post-transaction balance sheet and liquidity. Barclays' London team still hoped that in the end the Fed would provide the crucial liquidity guarantee without which no deal would be possible. The Barclays board said they would need written confirmation of that.[40]

During the evening the Fed effectively declined to give such a guarantee, stating that in spite of the earlier conversation in which Harding had explained the London Stock Exchange rules and Varley had told them about shareholder approval, they expected Barclays to guarantee Lehman's trading liabilities prior to closing in the way that J. P. Morgan had done for Bear Sterns. It was a killer blow. Barclays would either have to get shareholder approval, which would take too long or there would need to be a waiver from the London Stock Exchange, which was unprecedented. Varley phoned Sants, who was enjoying a long-planned weekend at his family cottage in Cornwall, to tell him that in view of the US government's intransigence, the deal could not go ahead.[41]

At about the same time, McCarthy again spoke to Geithner. He said that the FSA would have significant issues to resolve before approving any deal but that since no request for consent had been put forward, it was impossible to be definitive.[42] It was a similar misunderstanding to that which had occurred between them the previous day. McCarthy meant to convey that there would be no help from the UK, Geithner understood it to mean that the FSA were merely reserving their position pending more information.

During the evening, Varley emailed Diamond to say that the UK authorities could not waive the shareholder vote requirement and that the British government support was looking unlikely. But Diamond believed in doing everything possible to keep going. Paulson had just persuaded the Wall Street investment banks that although they hated the idea of keeping a rival alive, a disorderly collapse of Lehman would be worse. They were on the verge of agreeing to underwrite Lehman's toxic assets, thus removing one of the major obstacles. If Paulson could do that, Diamond was not going to give up easily. He asked Varley: 'Is there anything we can do? It looks like Hank has done the impossible here. Let's talk in the morning.'

Meanwhile, Diamond had been trying to speak to Geithner all day. When Geithner eventually walked into the 'buyer' room at midnight they went back to Geithner's office and sat across the coffee table in two easy chairs. As a result of his misunderstanding of the conversation with McCarthy and hunch that at the last minute Paulson would sanction a guarantee of the trading liabilities, Geithner still expected Barclays to move on Lehman and went home feeling hopeful.[43] Diamond knew that for this to happen, either the US or the UK government would have to yield. With his toothache still raging, he returned to the Carlyle and slept for a couple of hours.

14 SEPTEMBER – NEW YORK AND LONDON

At four o'clock on Sunday morning New York time (nine o'clock London time), Diamond dialled into a Barclays board meeting to tell them that Paulson had in all probability persuaded an industry consortium to guarantee the toxic assets but the US government were still not budging on the liquidity guarantee.[44] Varley, who had spoken directly to Darling to keep him informed, confirmed that no help would be coming from the UK side and the deal was off as a result. Diamond's tooth was still throbbing, his head ached and his eyes were prickly from lack of sleep. But despite all this and the cards stacked against him, he was still typically Bobtimistic. He had seen many deals come back from the dead. Geithner had seemed more positive last night and Diamond was not yet ruling out a concession from the US government.

Four hours later Varley and Diamond briefed Paulson, Geithner and Christopher Cox – chairman of the US Securities and Exchange Commission, the FSA's counterpart – that the FSA had no authority to waive the requirement for a shareholder vote. Again they repeated that to secure such a vote would take weeks, no one would trade with Lehman if the trades were not guaranteed, and as far as Barclays was concerned the deal was off. It was the first plain piece of speaking yet, and the US officials finally understood. They were furious and decided to make their own enquiries. Once again it was McCarthy and Geithner who spoke.[45] McCarthy explained that he still didn't know the details of any deal being considered. He repeated what he had said on earlier calls, namely that the FSA would need to decide if Barclays had enough capital to carry out an acquisition. He confirmed that Barclays would be unable to guarantee Lehman's trades without shareholder approval, a process that would take time unless the London Stock Exchange waived that requirement.[46]

Geithner pressed McCarthy: 'Are you saying that you won't approve this?'[47] The Scotsman was careful with his words but Geithner felt that he was talking in circles and asked Cox to pin him down.[48] Cox outlined a number of options but none dealt with the question of open-ended liability. The last words McCarthy said to Cox were: 'I am not hostile. I am just telling you the facts of life.'

Cox returned to Paulson's office ashen faced and told Paulson and Geithner: 'They are not going to do it.' Paulson decided to phone Darling. As he waited to be put through, he replayed in his mind the call of the previous Friday. It finally dawned on him that he had not grasped Darling's true meaning when he had expressed concern about a British bank buying Lehman. What he had taken to be caution had in fact been a clear warning.[49]

They spoke at half-past eleven New York time, when Paulson explained that it was close to the end of the line for Lehman, that the Wall Street banks were ready to make a grand gesture and now needed the UK to waive the shareholder vote. Darling made it clear that he was not willing to have the Americans unload their problem on to the British.[50] Darling pressed him to say what the US government would be doing to help and then moved the conversation on to plans for Lehman's bankruptcy.

Diamond had realized the game was probably up after the morning conference call. He spent the afternoon with his team trying to brainstorm but finally had to admit defeat. He felt foolish and angry that he had lost face with peers and his own country's government. He called Paulson to apologize and emailed Steel: 'Couldn't have gone more poorly, very frustrating. Little England.' He was asked to join the other chief executives to work out how to wind down Lehman's trades in the market on the Monday morning. His old rival Mack would be down there and every single leader of the elite banks he had hoped to join. Through fatigue, toothache and embarrassment he could not look them in the eye, and sent one of his lieutenants instead.

He returned to the Carlyle to find unexpectedly his wife and daughter waiting for him. They had heard the news and had taken the train in to the city to console him. Diamond had a dinner date with Ricci and del Missier at Smith & Wollensky, a macho steak house in midtown Manhattan. He said he would join them for drinks but would eat at a separate table with his family.

On the way to the restaurant, his phone rang. It was Lehman's McDade, wanting to know if Lehman went into bankruptcy, whether Barclays would be interested in the US broker-dealer. This was the equities, bond trading and corporate finance businesses without the toxic assets and was the piece of Lehman that Diamond had most wanted. Diamond agreed that he and McDade would get their teams together at the Lehman offices at five o'clock the next morning. By the time he arrived back at his hotel, there was a voicemail from Varley suggesting the very same thing.

15 AND 16 SEPTEMBER – NEW YORK AND LONDON

The teams gathered, bleary eyed, on the thirty-first and thirty-second floors of 745 Seventh Avenue to see if they could make it happen. They split into two groups, Barclays America's chairman, Archie Cox, leading one to carry out due diligence over Lehman and Diamond leading the other to meet the senior Lehman executives. They worked for over twenty-four hours with teams of lawyers, investment bankers, restructuring experts and analysts.

This time there would be no mistake with the regulators. Diamond asked Varley to speak to them and at 13.49 GMT Varley emailed:

> Spoke with Sants [FSA] and Gieve [Bank of England] to give them the rough shape. Seems ok, at the moment anyway. All clear for you to speak with Tucker [Bank of England]. Cox [Barclays] has telephoned McCarthy [FSA]. Hector [Sants, FSA] told me McCarthy said they (FSA) had no in principle objection but (I expect) that we had to stick to our capital plan. If so, that's ok. Note to board follows in draft shortly.[51]

At 18.32 Diamond emailed Varley and Barclays' finance director Lucas:

> High level numbers. 10,000 people (of 26000), maybe some separately from Europe and Asia, say 2,000 related to US businesses. 100 billion dollar balance sheet (of 600). Need US business, broker/dealer capitalized at $5 billion, we have 2 in barcap [Barclays Capital]. So need 3 to 5 billion equity raising I think. Price minimal we think.[52]

Lehman filed for bankruptcy soon after midnight, and when the news broke in the early hours of Monday morning, markets everywhere tumbled. The major Asian markets were closed for a holiday so European markets were the first to respond, the FTSE 100 in London falling by 3.9 per cent. After US markets opened at seven in the morning New York time, the Dow Jones index dropped 504 points, the bank-to-bank lending rate soared, panic selling hit the other investment banks, including Morgan Stanley and Goldman Sachs, and Bank of America declared it would buy Merrill Lynch for $50 billion. The panic in the markets meant that the US government could not risk another big firm failing and it announced an $85 billion bail-out of AIG which was on the brink of folding. By the following morning, Tuesday 16, a deal for Barclays to buy the Lehman broker-dealer was in place.

Diamond spoke to Varley and the Barclays board, telling them the FSA had indicated they were happy with the arrangement and there was no need for a shareholder vote on this smaller deal. Early that Tuesday afternoon, Diamond went back to the Carlyle, showered, changed and returned to Lehman with McDade. He visited all seven trading floors with the same message: they had been bought, they would get paid and he would try to save their jobs. There was a moment's cheering and a snatch of 'God Save the Queen' was played over the tannoy, but the Lehman people were still shocked. It was all too much to take in and they didn't quite believe it.

There was one last hurdle to jump. On Friday 19 September a New York bankruptcy judge approved the sale of Lehman to Barclays. Lawyers for Lehman's creditors claimed that Barclays were paying far too little but after eight hours of evidence and discussion the judge was resolute: 'This is not approving the transaction because I know it's the best available transaction. I have to approve this transaction because it's the only available transaction.'[53]

A week after it had proposed a deal at $3.8 billion, Barclays Capital had walked off with Lehman's US equities and corporate finance business, the part they had wanted all along, for $1.75 billion, a price that included the Lehman building north of Times Square and two data centres in New Jersey. Barclays was finally in the investment banking big league, completing the process that had begun with Camoys and Bevan back in 1983. Varley and Diamond had pulled it off and Barclays could at last rejoice in being a top five universal bank. After a weekend of agony, Diamond could now get his tooth fixed. He was not the only one feeling better: Michael Klein received $10 million for his weekend's work.[54]

15
Night Falls,
16 September – 13 October 2008

THE MOOD DARKENS

Gordon Brown had finally taken over from his long-standing partner and bitter rival Tony Blair on 27 June 2007. Within weeks, however, he found himself dealing with the failure of Northern Rock. To begin with, Brown himself escaped criticism. The public blamed Northern Rock's management for its fall and the government won praise for cleaning up the mess quickly. That first autumn in 10 Downing Street his personal ratings with the electorate soared. Speculation that Brown would call a general election to secure a personal mandate built up sharply in September but then, on 5 October 2007, confronted with private polling data that showed Labour's lead to be less commanding than public polls suggested, Brown decided that he would not be going to the country.[1]

Over the next few months the financial crisis worsened and the economy slowed down, draining consumer confidence. Being the world's global financial services capital was all very well in the good times, but it was a notoriously volatile industry; in the bad times its problems would affect the rest of the economy. When Tom Camoys started BZW, the City was an inward-looking community of fewer than 100,000 people quietly getting on with their business. It was comfortable and predictable and although the wider public probably paid a bit too much for banking, insurance and pension fund management services, the City posed no risk to the country at large.

Globalization, Big Bang and financial deregulation in the US changed all that. By 2007, the City was no longer the self-contained Square Mile around the Bank of England but a dispersed community with global reach. Eighty-seven thousand people worked in the towers of Canary Wharf with its underground shopping malls, glitzy bars and crowded gyms. To the west in Mayfair, hedge funds, private equity funds and family offices went about their business behind discreet nameplates.

The number of City jobs in London had more than trebled to 338,000 in a quarter of a century. If support functions were included, over a million people were employed in financial services in the UK and many more depended on them. Financial services accounted for 7 per cent of national output, making it the single most important industry in the UK – but its influence was even greater than that. Its high wages sustained consumer spending, property prices and jobs in thousands of supporting businesses in London and the south-east. If the sector collapsed, so would the economy – and so would the government.

The British banks were the key. Big Bang had propelled them into a rarified atmosphere. Barclays, HSBC and RBS were competing with the global banking giants, and the smaller banks, encouraged by shareholders, consultants and the investment banks, tried to match their growth rates. The banks' total assets had grown from £2 trillion in 2001 to £6 trillion in 2007 and they were now four times larger than the economy they were meant to be sustaining: that year UK GDP was £1.5 trillion. This growth had come in large part from borrowing over thirty times their equity capital in the inter-bank market, often from overseas institutions. A once safe banking model in which in 2000 loans to borrowers were matched by deposits from savers had become so reliant on wholesale funding that by 2007 the gap between loans and deposits was a staggering £700 billion.[2] If the inter-bank lending market seized up, most of the British banks would go bust. The sector became so large that it might destroy the economy and so unstable that it was quite likely to do so. And the man leading the country had been its cheerleader.

AUGUST 2008 – SOUTHWOLD

As the political temperature rose, Brown's reputation sank. His awkward, brooding style and ferocious temper were much written about by political commentators. Urbane David Cameron's Conservatives caught up in the polls and, by the summer of 2008, David Miliband and other members of Brown's own cabinet started to plan a leadership challenge for September. It never happened.

Brown's wife, Sarah, had spent her career in public relations and had a better instinct for the public mood than her husband. She realized that the venue for their family summer holiday that August would be closely scrutinized by the British media and insisted that the time be spread between Scotland and somewhere that would resonate with voters in middle England, lighting upon the family-friendly Suffolk seaside town of Southwold. Brown, however, did not look happy there.[3] He wanted to be in Scotland or at his desk in Downing Street. Instead he was in a place that was not big enough for a recognizable public figure to go unnoticed and not small enough to give him solitude.[4] The beaches, pier and town green provided good photo opportunities but Brown looked uncomfortable in his linen sports jacket, open-necked blue shirt and slacks. 'Stiff and frumpy' was one fashion expert's verdict.[5] What kind of person wears smart casual clothes for a walk on the beach, people wondered, as they looked at the staged photo shoots in their morning papers? Even his locally hired personal trainer attracted press attention.[6]

With his mind on the gathering financial crisis, Brown was never really on holiday that fortnight. Before going away he had had breakfast at Number 10 with Bank of England Governor King, their first private meeting since Brown had become prime minister. King's attitude to the banks had hardened since the Northern Rock crisis of 2007. He now believed that a sector-wide recapitalization of the banks would be necessary and he told Brown so over tea and toast that morning.

Brown's holiday reading included essays on the Great Depression of the 1930s by Ben Bernanke, chairman of the Fed, and he later admitted that 'the collapse of credit and its consequences for Britain's and the global economy was the question that obsessed me throughout our summer holiday in Suffolk.'[7] He came to the sickening conclusion that the world was on the verge of another catastrophic recession and that the UK would be at the sharp end of it.

Brown started planning for the resolution of what he was certain would be an economic disaster. On a lovely sunny terrace behind the Browns' rented Southwold holiday home, just a few yards from the families taking their buckets and spades down to the beach, the prime minister sat with his closest advisers. Most came for the day, one at a time. It was an awkward journey from London to the Suffolk seaside town: some took the train to Ipswich followed by a fifty-minute cab ride, others faced a two-and-a-half-hour slog down the A12 in anonymous government cars. Visitors included Jeremy Heywood, the most senior civil servant in Number 10, and a government minister, Baroness Vadera. She had spent fourteen years at the investment bank Warburg, leaving in 1999 to become a Treasury adviser to Brown when he was chancellor. Soon after he became prime minister he gave her a ministerial job, first of all at the Department for International Development, an area of personal interest to the former Ugandan Asian refugee, and then in 2008 a role straddling the Department for Business and the Cabinet Office. She was tough, took no prisoners and was Brown's most trustworthy troubleshooter. When she went to Southwold she was given the honour of an overnight stay. After she returned to London she forwarded under the heading 'Is it capital?' a long set of email exchanges outlining options she had been exploring with trusted City contacts.[8]

16–29 SEPTEMBER – EVERYWHERE

Soon after Brown, Sarah and their children returned to London, Lehman collapsed, the financial world fell apart and the cabinet plotters had other things to worry about. The two weeks following the demise of Lehman and AIG were the most traumatic fortnight in financial markets since the Great Crash of 1929. Regulators steered Washington Mutual, America's largest savings and loan bank, into the safe hands of J. P. Morgan.[9] Former Barclays director Steel organized a rescue of Wachovia by its former rival Wells Fargo. America had its Northern Rock moment when Reserve Primary, a cast-iron money market fund where risk-averse savers put their money, announced it could repay only 97 cents of each dollar, an event known as 'breaking the buck'. The public suddenly realized what this meant for them and the US government rushed through an insurance scheme to prevent mass withdrawals.

Iconic American financial institutions were falling like dominoes and the effects were felt instantly in the UK. Major British banks found it difficult to renew maturing debt for anything other than very short periods and the sterling Libor rate – the inter-bank lending rate – jumped from 5 to 6.8 per cent during the month. One bank in particular, HBOS, was finding it hard to fund itself, having reported a halving of profits and a one-third increase in bad debts at the end of July. The Bank of England was covertly providing it with funds but customers were withdrawing deposits at an alarming rate, and the British government had to facilitate its rescue by Lloyds on 17 September. There were similar bank runs and rescues across Europe: Glitnir bank in Iceland, Fortis Group in Belgium, Luxembourg and Holland, and Dexia in Belgium. In a futile attempt to stabilize markets, the British, American, Canadian and French authorities banned the short selling of bank shares.

Brown led other world leaders in thinking through the crisis, and he was the first to see where it might lead. In the last week of September he used the annual meeting of the UN General Assembly in New York to sound out other government heads, senior figures on Wall Street and the Fed's Geithner. Following these meetings, on Friday 26 he flew to Washington with Vadera to meet President Bush at the White House.

The president and the prime minister had built up a good relationship during several meetings and phone calls to discuss the crisis and other matters. That day Brown found Bush in remarkably good spirits, solicitously enquiring about the bandage Vadera was wearing on an injured hand. Brown told Bush that the banking crisis had moved from being a short-term liquidity problem to a more serious issue of long-term solvency and that in his opinion the solution was for governments to take direct equity stakes in the banks. Bush agreed he would raise the matter with Paulson but for now his administration was going down a different route. The previous week the US Treasury had announced its intention to seek congressional approval for a $700 billion fund to buy impaired assets from the banks, the Troubled Assets Relief Program (TARP). This plan was already meeting resistance on Capitol Hill and Bush doubted that Brown's more radical proposal would be acceptable to Congress. Brown thought that the US plan did not get to the heart of the matter but at least there was some common ground – both approaches had the same objective of strengthening the banks' balance sheets to get them lending again.[10]

As the meeting in the Oval Office finished in the early evening, Brown was told that he needed to speak to his chancellor urgently and went to an ante-room to take the call. Darling informed him that another large British mortgage bank, Bradford & Bingley, was in difficulty and that there was no alternative to nationalization. Jeremy Heywood was also in on the call from London and asked Brown to stand by to receive two confidential faxes, one from the Treasury, the other from Governor King.

The prime minister didn't get to read either until he was on the chartered BA plane flying him, his party and accompanying journalists back to London but when he did so, he was shocked. The first fax set out the Treasury's view of the capital that would be needed to stabilize the British banks; they put this at £50 billion. The second fax was even more startling: Governor King's estimate of the banks' capital requirements was no less than £100 billion.[11] At least they now had a range, and on the flight home Brown and Vadera talked through the options. Brown took out one of the thick black felt tip pens he always used and wrote on a piece of paper the words: RECAPITALISE NOW. For good measure, he underlined it twice.

29 SEPTEMBER – 8 OCTOBER – LONDON

On Monday 29 September Congress rejected Bush and Paulson's TARP plan and on Wall Street the Dow Jones index fell a record 778 points, a drop of 7 per cent. No one, least of all Barclays' board, knew where the carnage would end as its own share price, 438 pence on the day the Lehman deal was cleared in the US courts, fell to 300 pence.

If ever there was a time Barclays needed leadership this was it. And they got it. Diamond stayed in New York to grip the Lehman business, while in London Varley ordered finance director Lucas and chief risk officer Le Blanc to pull apart the balance sheet. The executive commit-tee met three times a day, Agius held daily board conference calls, big shareholders were offered meetings and there were continuous conver-sations with worried regulators.

Varley was very cool under this pressure. By the end of September he was confident that all positions were conservatively marked and that with access to the Bank of England's short-term borrowing fa-cility, Barclays had enough cash to keep going. His major problem was convincing shareholders and regulators that this was so. On Tuesday 30 September Varley was summoned with the chief executives of the other banks to a meeting at the Treasury, the most senior gathering of British ministers, officials and bankers that had ever been assembled.[12] The authorities had been through a nerve-wracking weekend nation-alizing Bradford & Bingley. The US government appeared powerless to act following Congress's rejection of the TARP plan. That morning, without international consultation, the Irish government guaranteed all deposits and loans to its banks, putting pressure on other countries, especially the UK, to do the same. The British banks were drawing heavily on the Bank of England's emergency cash window, the short-term facility that enabled them to refinance debt as it matured. HBOS, whose takeover by Lloyds was not yet complete, was unable to borrow in the market for more than a day.

The meeting was chaired by Chancellor Darling, who had been overshadowed by the prime minister during the early days of the crisis. Brown had been quicker to understand that this was a systemic problem requiring coordinated global action, but now the chancellor's calm, methodical approach came to the fore. That evening he was flanked by Mervyn King, Governor of the Bank of England, and Lord (Adair) Turner, a former McKinsey consultant who had impressed as director general of the CBI and was recently installed as chairman of the FSA. Others present included Paul Myners, a former fund man-ager who was about to be appointed to the government as a financial services minister through membership of the House of Lords; some senior Treasury civil servants, including its two permanent secretar-ies, Nicholas Macpherson and John Kingman; and Darling's special adviser Geoffrey Spence. They were there to meet the chief executives of the UK's largest banks, including those whom the government believed to be most in difficulty: Varley, Eric Daniels of Lloyds TSB (and soon HBOS), Fred 'the Shred' Goodwin, the usually bullish chief executive of RBS. Representing the banks believed to be relatively safe were Santander's António Horta Osório, Peter Sands from Standard Chartered, Graham Beale from the Nationwide building society and Dyfrig John from HSBC.[13]

The meeting did not go well. Their work over the summer had convinced ministers, officials and the governor that meltdown was imminent and that the banks would need extra capital and would have to ask either shareholders or the government for funds. The latter would be an admission of defeat that the chief executives were not yet prepared to make. Goodwin, looking shaken, insisted that the problem was not a lack of capital but just a temporary lack of liquidity. Confidence would be restored if the Bank of England increased its offer of short-term funds. Seated next to him, Varley could see that the authorities were not impressed. He tried to be as constructive as possible while agreeing in measured tones with Goodwin that a little more oil from the Bank of England would keep the wheels turning. To the authorities' amazement, other bankers took a similar line and it fell to Governor King to set out the alternative case. His intellectual prowess was second to none and he was coldly forensic. His preference for a market solution to Northern Rock had been criticized in the early days of the crisis and events had forced him to take a more pragmatic line. He now assured the chiefs that there was short-term money available to help inter-bank lending but that the lack of permanent capital was unquestionably a much bigger problem. Although he did not disclose to those present that in his fax to the prime minister a few days earlier he had given £100 billion as the sum he believed was required to bolster the banks' balance sheets, he made it clear that the banks would have to raise a lot of capital if they were to survive.

It was a powerful analysis, key words being emphasized with a slightly raised voice and a short pause to let them sink in. Despite an owlish appearance and a measured tone on camera, in person the governor didn't suffer fools – or many others – gladly. City lore attributed to him the statement that 'one good economist is equal to all the investment bankers in London', and there was no doubting his irritation at the blank faces across the table.

The Bank of England's standing from the days when a governor only had to 'raise an eyebrow' to bring the banks into line had been diminished in 1997 when the Labour government gave responsibility for regulating the banks to the FSA, stating that 'The Treasury has no operational responsibilities for the activities of the FSA and the Bank of England shall not be involved in them.'[14] The Bank of England's power over the banks had been diluted and with it the governor's authority. Consequently, the bankers listened politely to King but when the meeting broke up after only an hour, rather than immediately falling into line, they left muttering about his unwarranted pessimism and poor judgement.

While the chief executives returned to their chauffeur-driven Mercedes, BMWs and Jaguars in the Treasury courtyard, the authorities remained at Darling's table. They were exasperated by the bankers' refusal to face reality. Extensive work over the previous weeks, led by Vadera, Scholar and Kingman, left them in no doubt that a government bail-out would be required. Planning now resumed with added urgency with the help of advisers from the investment banks UBS and later Credit Suisse. The City's messenger in the night, David Mayhew, was also brought in.[15] His blue-blood firm Cazenove was now partly owned by J. P. Morgan, where Mayhew worked closely with Bill Winters, the head of the American firm's investment bank and one of the original architects of mortgage backed derivatives, the magic pill that worked wonders for risk management when taken as prescribed but that was fatal if overdosed.

Mayhew had grown up in the world of stocks and shares, brokers and jobbers and who you know being more important than what you know, but he had adapted quickly to the new world and learned a lot from Winters. Not only was he now familiar with modern investment banking products, he was still regarded as the City's best judge of investors' mood, and his presence completed Vadera's roster of those advising how to force, cajole or otherwise induce the banks to strengthen their balance sheets.

The chaos in the markets continued all week. On 1 October, the Bank of England stepped up covert support for HBOS – Lloyds did not complete the takeover until January 2009 – which had finally run out of institutions prepared to lend to it. In the US, Congress had to pass a revised version of Paulson's $700 billion TARP plan to put a floor under the rapidly disintegrating banking sector. There were more bank rescues in Europe, including in Germany where the government guaranteed all private bank accounts and agreed a €50 billion package to save the country's second-biggest property lender, Hypo Real Estate.

An outline plan to recapitalize the British banks was shown to the prime minister on Thursday 2 October and on Sunday evening, and it was decided to implement it that week.[16] Varley and the other bank chiefs were called back to the Treasury for another exchange of views on Monday, an inaccurate account of which was leaked to the BBC's Robert Peston. The following day he reported on the early morning *Today* programme that RBS, Lloyds and Barclays had all requested government help sooner rather than later.[17] The mild-mannered Varley was furious at being included in this list. The weaker banks were anxious to divert attention from themselves by getting as many rivals as possible to accept government money and Varley suspected them of trying to drag him down with them. He dismissed the stories at a seminar for investors later that morning and in a conference call with the other chief executives at six o'clock the same evening pointedly identified RBS and HBOS as the banks with the real problems.[18]

After that call, the chief executives made their way over to the Treasury for a seven-thirty meeting, again chaired by Chancellor Darling. While at a gathering of European finance ministers in Luxembourg earlier that day, he had received gut-wrenching news in a call from Sir Tom McKillop, chairman of RBS, who told him that the bank, swallower of ABN just a year before, would run out of cash that evening. The RBS share price halved during the day, and cautious corporate customers quietly moved billions to other banks but the gravity of the bank's situation was not known to the general public. Darling knew that if it got out or if RBS really was unable to fund itself, there would be a run on the bank and panic in the country. Prime Minister Brown was reported to have said:

> if the banks are shutting their doors, and the cashpoints aren't working and people go to Tesco and their cards aren't being accepted, the whole thing will just explode. If you can't buy food or petrol or

medicine for your kids, people will just start breaking the windows and helping themselves . . . it'll be anarchy. I'm serious . . . we'd have to think: do we have curfews, do we put the Army on the streets, how do we get order back?[19]

There could be no more debate and no more posturing from the banks. The chief executives were told that a government rescue plan would be announced the following day. The package would address both of the issues raised at the previous week's meeting – long-term capital and short-term liquidity. Inter-bank lending would be encouraged by a £250 billion Bank of England guarantee of the larger banks' credit and an extension from £100 billion to £200 billion of the special liquidity scheme, the short-term emergency facility which helped the banks to fund themselves day-to-day. This was what the bankers wanted to hear. But there was a sting in the tail. The government was going to insist that they raised more capital and it would be the FSA, not the banks themselves, that would decide how much each bank needed. Those banks that fell short would then have a choice: they could raise extra capital themselves in the markets or accept government money in return for a shareholding. Up to £50 billion of state capital would be available for them to draw on.[20]

Some of the bankers were furious at the idea of the FSA rather than their own boards deciding whether or not they should raise capital but Varley listened calmly. It could have been worse. There was to be no compulsory government capital provided that Barclays could satisfy the regulators. He had spent four years building a universal bank and had just succeeded in bagging a bulge bracket investment bank more or less for free. Nothing he had heard round the table suggested to him that the authorities would be supportive of a British bank with universal banking ambitions and he thought that keeping them off the shareholders' register was essential to the realization of his vision.

Over the next few hours, the bankers met at the Treasury discussing the details of the government plan, occasionally consulting with ministers and officials who were waiting in other rooms. Long after midnight, the new minister Myners was sitting in his office waiting for news from along the corridor. The lights were controlled by movement sensors and the room was dark. He began to doze. His mobile rang. Waving his arms wildly to activate the lights, he saw that the call was indeed from the chairman of one of the banks. 'Paul, could we just check one thing. This is entirely hypothetical but if the government was to take a stake in us, could we assume that we would still be able to pay the chief executive his bonus?'* Myners' reply was 'robust'.

It was half-past two in the morning before news finally came through that the bankers had no further objections to the government deal; in reality, they had no choice. Most of them then departed for a few hours' sleep leaving ministers, officials and their advisers to finalize the morning's announcement.

Varley briefed his board in a pre-dawn conference call on Wednesday 8 October and the government package was announced as the sun rose at seven. He was confident about the bank's position but much would depend on persuading the regulators to accept the valuations of assets in their books. He considered it fortunate that Barclays' key contact at the FSA was the former investment banker Sants. Sants understood the industry and was a reasonable man. He explained to Varley that over the following few days the regulator would model the banks' capital and liquidity under a variety of scenarios such as a 50 per cent fall in the housing market and a freeze in inter-bank lending. The outcome would reveal how much extra capital the banks needed to hold and the authorities would then consider each bank's proposals for raising the money.

8 OCTOBER – BIRMINGHAM

Driving along the M6 in his Mercedes convertible, Karl Edwards listened with amazement to news of the government's bank rescue plan. Callers to Radio 5 Live's morning show were enraged. People had thought Northern Rock was a one-off caused by bad management; now there was evidently a system-wide problem. The bankers were accused of incompetence, greed and worse. And what on earth had the authorities been doing while all this was building up?

---

* Myners has not disclosed the identity of the caller other than to say 'It's not who you might think.'

Edwards was not unduly worried about his own business. The new warehouse was finally up and running and he now had space to do things properly. His customers seemed unconcerned by the banking crisis and were still buying records and DJ equipment. According to 5 Live, the Bank of England had just cut interest rates by half a percentage point to 4.5 per cent and the US Federal Reserve and other central banks in Europe and Canada were expected to do the same. He was having no trouble meeting his mortgage payments and if that news was anything to go by, his monthly repayments might even go down. He turned on some music and accelerated past a line of slow-moving traffic.

9 AND 10 OCTOBER – LONDON

An FSA team had moved into Barclays' head office in Churchill Place on Wednesday 8th as soon as the outline of the rescue plan was announced and the results of their work arrived on Friday 10th. After years of lax regulation, the FSA finally got tough. Barclays' assets had nearly doubled to £2 trillion as a result of the Lehman deal and included a portfolio of mortgage-related derivatives and other property-related assets which were very hard to value. The FSA challenged Barclays' valuations, ran their own models and worked out what they regarded as safe capital ratios for Barclays to achieve by June 2009.

Sants broke the news to Varley. It was worse than he had expected, but at least Barclays had almost nine months in which to comply. A quick calculation converted the FSA's ratio into a money equivalent: Barclays would have to find £12 billion. Varley told Sants that he believed that they would be able to do so by raising private capital, suspending dividend payments to shareholders and reducing assets.

Sants, however, was less amenable than Varley had hoped. Sants wanted a safety net and suggested that this might have to include the disposal of businesses. They both knew that Barclays had only two discrete entities big enough to raise that sort of money: Barclaycard and its fund management firm, Barclays Global Investors (BGI).

Barclaycard was integral to the universal bank but a sale of BGI was an interesting idea. Its business was to invest other people's money.* It was a by-product of Big Bang, when Barclays' small Investment Management office looking after a pooled investment fund, Barclays' own pension fund and a few other pension funds, was merged with de Zoete's similar operation.[21] After a certain amount of jostling between the Barclays and de Zoete people, Donald Brydon, a fund manager Barclays had recruited in 1977, had been put in charge.

Brydon, who later rose to become deputy chief executive and briefly acting chief executive of BZW, and who gave a reading at David Band's memorial service, had no intention of whiling away time in an obscure corner of Barclays. A solid figure, trained in economics, with an educated Scots accent and a sometimes sharp turn of phrase, he planned to grow asset management into a substantial business. Growth would come from a new form of fund management in which computers were used to build portfolios that tracked the performance of markets. With no expensive fund managers to pay, these passive quantitative funds – also called index funds – could charge investors less than funds actively managed.[†]

By the mid-1990s, BZW Investment Management had £50 billion under management and was the European leader in passive quantitative funds. In 1995 it became the global leader with funds under management of £160 billion when it bought the West Coast-based firm Wells Fargo Nikko Investment Advisers for £275 million. It was then renamed Barclays Global Investors.[22]

A feisty American, Pattie Dunn, became chief executive in 1998 and soon decided that BGI would be better off without the bureaucratic constraints of a big bank. She secured backing from a US private equity firm and spent two years negotiating with Barclays for a buy-out of a majority interest. Before signing off on the proposed

* The money can come directly from high net worth individuals (HNWIs) but more usually comes from pooled investment vehicles such as pension funds, insurance companies or the various types of investment companies in which investors can buy units or make contributions.
† Most asset management firms at the time employed fund managers to weigh up investment decisions based on advice and analysis and invest in stocks and markets accordingly. It was a method called 'active fund management'. Academic research showed that after this differential in expenses, the passive funds often performed better as a group than the active funds.

$1.4 billion deal, Matt Barrett, the then finance director, Varley and Diamond appointed Barclays Capital's head of investment banking, Naguib Kheraj, to look at it.

Kheraj relinquished his investment banking role and temporarily became deputy chairman of BGI. After looking at the business, he and Diamond reported that the long period of building BGI was about to pay off, while Barclays' retention of a minority interest would leave it as the lender of last resort if things went wrong. In their view, the price was too low – especially given the ongoing liabilities as a minority holder – and in any case, the business should not be sold; what it needed was an injection of strong management under Barclays' continued ownership.

Barrett pulled the sale and made Diamond chairman of BGI in August 2002, giving him full participation in BGI's executive share plan. That plan, which had been set up by Dunn in 2000 and approved by Barclays' shareholders, gave senior management options to buy shares in BGI at a price that would reflect its value if it was an independent company. Three years after being given the options, the recipient could buy shares in BGI at the original price and after a further year sell them back to Barclays during two short annual windows. The maximum that employees could ever own was capped at 20 per cent and Barclays' financial position had to meet certain criteria before the window could be opened. Independent auditors were hired to set the figure for BGI shares and in 2000 calculated this at 611 pence.[23] Barclays management thought little of it because in the early years, profits were so low that they had to set up additional bonus schemes in 2002 and 2003 to keep employees happy.

Kheraj went on to run Barclays' Private Clients business and later became group finance director, while Diamond moved Ricci over to California to become BGI's chief operating officer. Ricci was a very good hands-on manager. Dunn left, they put in Andrew Skirton and Blake Grossmann as co-chief executives and motivated, nagged, put pressure on people, got them excited and made them feel part of a winning team. They took cost out of the business and tapered down development work. Revenues were already on a rising trend after the years of investment and with tight cost control, profits soared. In 2002 when Diamond and Ricci took over, profits were £110 million and assets under management were £460 billion; by 2008 it was one of the world's biggest fund managers with over £1 trillion under management, making a profit of £595 million, over 10 per cent of the group total. The agreed valuation of BGI shares on 31 March 2008 was £87.22, fourteen times the original.[24]

In October 2008 Varley and Sants both knew that if there was one business that had to be sold, it should be BGI. There would be plenty of buyers and although it generated cash and used little capital, it was not an essential part of Barclays' universal banking portfolio. Barclays still had a lot of work to do – raise fresh capital from investors, sell a business in a chaotic market and prepare shareholders and staff for bad news – but at last Varley could see a way forward and his master plan was still intact.

At Heathrow Terminal 5 the grey sofas, fresh fruit and flowers of British Airways' First Class lounge offered Barclays' elegant silver-haired chairman, Marcus Agius, a brief respite from reality as he waited on 10 October for his early evening flight to Washington. Then his phone rang and the initials 'JV' flashed on the screen. Varley carefully summarized Sants' message, telling him that the FSA had come up with some demanding capital ratios. Barclays were still working out exactly how much money they would have to raise but it could be £12 billion. Agius was absolutely stunned by the quantum but at least they had until 30 June 2009 to comply. He was now being paged to join the flight. Still anxious but at least now knowing what the bank had to do, he got on the plane and turned left to the front cabin.

11 AND 12 OCTOBER – WASHINGTON AND NEW YORK

The autumn meeting of the IMF and World Bank was due to take place in Washington on the weekend of 11 and 12 October. It was normally a routine affair at which the finance ministers and central bankers of the G7 group of industrialized nations networked with each other over discussions about the world economy, but this, however, was no ordinary meeting. The day before, the 10th, had been another black day in the world stock markets as investors realized that problems in the banking sector would soon tip over into the rest of the economy.

The G7 ministers and central bankers were of the same view and Chancellor Darling and Governor King spent the weekend trying to coordinate a global response to the crisis. It was Sunday afternoon before they were ready to say anything in public but the final G7 communiqué was decisive enough. It committed them to helping the banks 'raise capital from public as well as private sources', in effect endorsing the British conviction that banks needed more capital and that governments should be ready to provide it. For Britain's bank chiefs there could now be no doubt that the government's capital restoration programme outlined the previous Wednesday would indeed be going ahead.

The weekend was also scheduled to be an important one in Barclays' corporate calendar. On the Sunday, it was to hold a lunch party in the garden of a beautiful private house it rented for the week in Georgetown on the banks of the Potomac. Many of its most important clients and Washington contacts would be present and it was an opportunity for the bank to demonstrate its connections and show that no matter what problems other banks were having, it was business as usual at Barclays. Agius was to be the principal host, a role at which he excelled, and Diamond would be there to back him up. When on Wednesday 8 October the British government announced plans to bail out the banks, all bank chairmen and chief executives were asked to remain in London while the FSA ran its stress tests. Agius had flown to Washington only for fear of starting rumours if he pulled out.

11 OCTOBER – NEW YORK AND LONDON

In New York Diamond had a rare morning off. He had been working non-stop for a month, buying and then bedding in the Lehman business, often without sleep, and he needed some family time. He took his sons to play golf at the Liberty National Club, a recently constructed

$250 million course alongside the Hudson River in New Jersey. The views of Manhattan across the river were spectacular but Diamond never got to enjoy the vista or to play a single hole. Instead, he walked alongside his two boys while discussing with Varley on his mobile how to interpret the FSA ratios and working out what to do. They decided to leave the Georgetown lunch to Agius and that he should fly back to London and then head off again on another important mission.

In London, Black Friday in the markets and the continuing demands for liquidity from RBS and HBOS convinced the authorities that they would need to unveil the details of their plan to the markets on Monday 13. They summoned the top management of RBS, Lloyds and HBOS to the Treasury and invited the chief executives of the other banks to come along too. The subject would be whether or not public funds would be required to provide each bank with the capital they needed; Varley declined to attend until he had discussed the matter with his board, which he did in a conference call that afternoon. Some of the non-executives asked: 'What are the downsides of taking public money? Why not take the safe option, accept British government money and be done with it?' Varley explained that with the government as a shareholder Barclays would no longer be in full control of its strategy and he doubted whether the government would support their international ambitions. The Lehman deal had enabled Barclays to achieve its global investment banking ambition, competitors were wounded and this was not the moment to turn back.

There was no push back from a board which had spent years pursuing the universal banking vision. There was no notion that the credit excesses of the early 2000s would take years to work off and drag the world into recession, no sense yet that regulators would require banks to hold so much more capital that their business model would have to change. They were still thinking that after markets calmed down it would be business as usual. Having spent twenty-five years getting Barclays into a position to join the elite, Seegers and Diamond were building twin towers and Barclays would be able to go for the kill when other banks stumbled. Varley's plan to raise capital privately was considered far preferable to the repugnant idea of a government representative sitting on the board. They asked their advisers J. P. Morgan Cazenove and CSFB to explore over the weekend shareholders' willingness to contribute to a rapid fund raising to be announced on the Monday. After the meeting closed, Varley called Vadera and Myners at the Treasury, with Permanent Secretary John Kingman listening in, and claimed: 'We are fine. We can do this on our own' and – a calculated dash of braggadocio – casually enquired whether the authorities would object should Barclays ever consider mounting a bid for the stricken RBS. Their reply left him in no doubt that it was not an issue worth raising with his board.[25]

12 OCTOBER – QATAR

Diamond's flight from New York landed at Heathrow at seven in the morning. With a tail wind, it had been a short Atlantic crossing but Diamond had still managed to get a few hours' sleep. He showered in the First Class arrivals lounge and made his way to the private aviation building next to Terminal 4. Waiting for him were Roger Jenkins, chairman of Barclays Capital's Middle East operations, and Stephen Jones, the investment bank's expert in debt and equity capital markets. Passport and security checks were a formality for private jet passengers and a people carrier with tinted windows took them out to a waiting Gulfstream G550 jet on the tarmac. They were heading for Qatar and a meeting with investors who, on 25 June, had taken over half of the £4.5 billion Barclays' fund raising. They had paid 282 pence for their Barclays shares; now, four months later, the price was over 100 pence lower.

While Diamond's G550 was in the air, Varley called from London. Diamond put Varley on the satellite phone's speaker so that Jenkins and Jones, seated with Diamond round the plane's conference table in the middle of the cabin, could hear the conversation. As Varley outlined the capital ratios the FSA expected them to reach, Jones switched on the HP12 bond calculator he carried everywhere. Punching in the numbers as Varley read them out and making a few assumptions about the year-end balance sheet, he came up with a figure of £13 billion, close to the number that the Churchill Place team had calculated. Barclays' mission was to enlist the Qataris' help in reaching that target.

The plane landed in Doha and a limousine took them the short distance to the Four Seasons Hotel overlooking the Arabian Gulf. The heat of the desert hit them as they crossed the few yards from the car to the air-conditioned building and they took the lifts straight to the top floor. When they outlined their case that evening, and their Qatari hosts periodically disappeared along the corridor to another conference suite for longish periods, they had the feeling that they were not alone.

THE SAME DAY – LONDON AND WASHINGTON

Barclays held another board meeting on the Sunday afternoon, a dress-down affair in the boardroom at Churchill Place with advisers again present, including David Mayhew, back on the bank's side of the table. Over the previous months, he had developed a weekend routine of making calls to senior fund managers to test out their reaction to whatever drama was currently gripping markets. The latest was Barclays. He now reported that unless market conditions stabilized, his weekend conversations with the institutions indicated that the market would be closed for normal funding. That might change if calm returned but at the moment Barclays could not rely on traditional shareholders and the money would have to come from elsewhere.

Varley then reported to the board that he was under pressure from officials to meet them that day at the Treasury. Treasury ministers and officials were themselves being lobbied by Lloyds: 'You asked us to buy HBOS. Why don't you tell Barclays to accept government money?' Varley's view was that if he went to the Treasury it would give a signal of weakness and encourage the authorities to force Barclays to take state capital. Mindful of the competitive advantage of remaining private at a time when Lloyds, HBOS and RBS would be partly state-owned, the board decided to back their chief executive's decision to keep away from Whitehall.

But the Treasury were persistent. Barclays was not in the emergency room with Lloyds and RBS but officials feared it soon would be. Its leverage had now risen to over forty times, appreciably above the sector average of thirty, and customer deposits formed only a quarter of its total funding requirements, meaning that it was dependent on wholesale markets. Over half of its total assets were in the hard-to-value books of the investment bank.[26] Whichever way they looked at it, they saw Barclays flashing red lights.

The Treasury's most persuasive figure was the new minister Paul Myners, the self-taught son of a Cornish butcher, who had been a successful fund manager and risen to be chairman of Marks & Spencer. Myners was an avuncular tough guy who had been through many boardroom battles in his City days. He phoned Varley at five o'clock to make one last attempt to talk him round. 'Come over,' he urged Varley. 'This capital will not be available for ever. This is cheap money. Why take a risk? Come in and see us.' Varley was his usual polite self, replying that Barclays had shown the FSA its plans and they had been accepted. 'It's a matter of principle. I am confident we can raise the capital and reach the required ratios using private investors. We are grateful for the offer but we do not want state capital. My board is in total agreement about this.'

In the end the Treasury ran out of time. Barclays could open for business on the Monday, Lloyds and RBS would not, so the Treasury people decided to let Barclays show what they could do. At the Bank of England, however, the feeling remained that it was underwriting Barclays on the cheap. The bank was getting the benefit of state support through the special liquidity and credit guarantee schemes without paying a fair price or accepting that as a systemically important British institution, it had a duty to play safe. This feeling lingered for several years.

While Varley was telling Myners that he would not be coming over to the Treasury that day, Agius was preparing to receive guests at the Barclays lunch in Washington. At the house by the Potomac the turquoise Barclays flag flew from the flagpole, there were marquees on the lawns and liveried servants stood with silver trays to offer cocktails to the arriving guests.

It was an idyllic scene on a pleasant autumn afternoon but no one was talking about the perennials or the weather. French President

Sarkozy had already ordered his country's delegation to the IMF meeting back to Paris. The previous day Sir Nigel Sheinwald, the wavy-haired British ambassador to Washington, had been entertaining the British party at his residence. He was heard to mutter: 'I've no idea what's going on but the governor of the Bank of England and the chancellor of the exchequer have just left early, white as sheets and shaking like jellies.' Sheinwald probably knew quite a lot of what was going on and Darling and King were certainly not jellies, but the metaphors were plain enough.

At Barclays' garden party, all appeared calm. As the guests sat down for lunch at one o'clock, Agius made a short speech, touching on the crisis and assuring them all of Barclays' commitment, but giving nothing away. He sat down to polite applause, a reassuring figure in an uncertain world.

13 OCTOBER – LONDON

Early on the morning of the 13th, Chancellor Darling announced that the government was taking significant stakes in HBOS, Lloyds TSB and RBS. RBS would receive £20 billion, giving the government a holding of 58 per cent, later rising to 84.4 per cent. HBOS received £11.5 billion and Lloyds received £5.5 billion, giving a government holding of 43 per cent in the enlarged bank once the merger was completed in January 2009. The total investment of £37 billion in effect nationalized three major banks.[27] Prime Minister Brown explained why: 'In extraordinary times, with financial markets ceasing to work, the government cannot just leave people on their own to be buffeted about.'[28] The London stock market leapt nearly 10 per cent in relief.

RBS announced that Fred Goodwin would retire and there was at last a sense of things moving on. Barclays issued its own statement, announcing that following detailed discussions with the FSA and Treasury 'additional capital will be raised from investors without calling on the Government funding which has been offered to UK banks. Accordingly a plan has been agreed with and approved by the FSA.' It would raise £6.5 billion of new capital and release £1.5 billion in equity capital through balance sheet management and operational efficiencies.

The final dividend for 2008 would not be paid, saving £2 billion, and an existing shareholder had agreed to contribute £1 billion towards these commitments.[29] Barclays' trip to the Gulf had evidently not been in vain. A few days later, news that Credit Suisse had also raised money from Qatar confirmed suspicions that the Qataris had been talking to another supplicant that evening in the Doha Four Seasons.

The authorities had prevented a banking meltdown but for Barclays the immediate question was whether it could deliver on its promise to raise private capital on the scale and timeframe agreed. Later, the question would be exactly how that was done.*

TWO WEEKS LATER

Paul Tucker's full face was now pale and drawn. It was 29 October and the Bank of England's markets director had been working seven days a week for over a year. In the fortnight since Darling had announced the part nationalization of RBS and Lloyds-HBOS, the fifty-year-old Cambridge mathematics and philosophy graduate had been in the thick of the action, spending much of his time talking to Prime Minister Brown's office and the Treasury, where ministers and officials worried whether their intervention had been enough to stabilize markets.

A couple of weeks previously the US government had finally accepted the need to put capital into financial institutions, taking stakes in nine large banks. To Brown's frustration – given the coolness with which his advocacy of such a course had been met when he was in Washington – the US government's direct support for all the major banks now seemed to be working better than the UK government's programme of selective capital injections, liquidity support and credit guarantees. Market chatter was that Barclays was still in trouble, and it was damaging confidence in the UK's entire banking system. Tucker needed to do something about it and prepared to make an important call.

In the autumn of 2008 the money markets were being studied closely as a sign of the industry's health and nowhere more so than in

---

* At the time of writing the matter is *sub judice* and will not be discussed here.

10 Downing Street. As the financial world fell apart after Lehman's bankruptcy, the leadership Brown gave saw him emerge as a figure of global stature. But his reputation abroad was not matched in the UK. He trusted very few people, took too much on himself and treated his officials badly. He would lose his temper, change his mind and call them in the middle of the night if the mood took him. He was an office tyrant and few people enjoyed working for him.

The man expected to make order out of this situation was Jeremy Heywood, permanent secretary in the prime minister's office. This formal civil service title completely underplayed the importance of the role, particularly when it was in the hands of a person such as Heywood. He was methodical, unflappable and, crucially in the present crisis, he knew about markets, having spent a couple of years as the Treasury's head of Securities and Markets Policy and three as a managing director at Morgan Stanley. He returned to the civil service in 2007 and had been at Brown's right hand for nearly all of his premiership. He had a deadly ability to identify the issue that matters most and in the middle of October that was international confidence in the British banking system.

One closely watched indicator of this was Libor, the London Inter-Bank Offer Rate, the price banks had to pay to borrow funds. It was calculated in five different currencies and over seven different time frames from information provided by individual banks about what each was having to pay in the market and was therefore the reference point on which trillions of dollars of financial contracts were based. But it was also an indication of what financial institutions thought of each other's credit because each contributing bank's price was visible to the others. Banks that had to pay a high price to borrow were being judged by lenders as less healthy than those that could borrow cheaply. On Tuesday 21 October just before lunch, Heywood sent an email to Tucker asking: 'Why are UK LIBOR spreads not falling as fast as US?'[30] US banks were apparently being judged as less risky than their European counterparts. Why was the US government's rescue plan being better received than the UK bail-outs?

Tucker, however, knew that Libor was only an approximate guide to reality. There was actually little business going on in the money markets because the banks did not trust each other's liquidity and were cautious in what they would lend. Libor was, therefore, as Mervyn King later said, 'in many ways the rate at which banks do *not* lend to each other'.[31] Dealers had reported surprise at some submissions in the Libor fix since the banking crisis began in 2007, and well informed press reports during the winter and spring of 2007–8 also said that Libor did not reflect the real rate at which money was available.[32] Even the Bank of International Settlements, an organization in Basel which acted as a counterparty for sixty central banks including the Bank of England and the US Federal Reserve, published an article in March 2008 pointing out that banks had a reason to misquote during funding crises for fear of revealing weakness.[33]

The New York Fed looked into it, and in May 2008 Tim Geithner raised the matter with King, who in turn discussed it with Tucker. The daily calculation of Libor was overseen by the British Banking Association (BBA), a trade body, which had already been prodded into a review by the noise from across the Atlantic. Tucker encouraged them to make sure that their investigation was carried out thoroughly, but (as usual when an organization is asked to review itself) the resultant report was a whitewash. The BBA introduced a few minor changes to the procedure but retained its role as Libor gatekeeper.[34]

Tucker replied to Heywood that evening: 'I think (think) that may have something to do with the fact that a number of US money centre banks have been enjoying flight to quality flows, whereas (no doubt overstating it a bit) that's been true of only hsbc in sterling.'[35] Tucker was saying that of the British banks only HSBC was considered as strong as the big US retail banks.

Heywood remained concerned. The following day, Wednesday 22, at 14.47 he emailed Tucker again, this time heading his message: 'Might be scuttle butt [*sic*] – are u hearing this rumour.' He quoted market sources as follows:

> Sterling 3m Libor is high because Barclays are bidding it they are bidding 2bps ABOVE Libor. This has been going on for three weeks. The day BoE cut fifty Barclays continued to bid the old level (as tho rates had never been cut). A lot of speculation in the market over what they are up to.[36]

Heywood was asking why Barclays was having to pay more than Libor to borrow money and why its Libor postings had not reflected the Bank of England's cut of 50 basis points from 5 to 4.5 per cent in the official bank rate on Wednesday 8 October.

Tucker replied at 22.17: 'We are trying to monitor what's going on.'[37] Heywood came back immediately: 'Thanks. Obviously we are v concerned that US rates are tumbling but we remain stuck!'[38] A swift reply so late in the evening was a clear sign that Downing Street regarded it as an important matter.

A few days later Heywood emailed Tucker at 09.56 on Sunday 26 October, this time copying Tom Scholar. He quoted a report from UBS, one of the investment banks brought in to advise the government on the crisis:

> In the last 3 weeks the market has noticed that both Barclays and RBS have bid, after the 1030 fixing, at levels up to 5bps above the fixing throughout the rest of the day ... The market has been speculating over what these two banks might be doing and have interpreted these actions as a deliberate signal that they are prepared to borrow unsecured at 6.0%.[39]

In other words, the market believed they were desperate for cash and would pay above market to get it.

Every day during October, Barclays' Libor submissions in some currencies and maturities were the highest or the second highest of the panel of contributing banks. Although Barclays had just confidently declined government capital, these numbers suggested that it was still a bad risk and to the government's annoyance the numbers were giving a negative signal about the weakness of the UK banking system. Tucker decided to make sure that the top management at Barclays were aware of the impression their money market dealings were creating. That was the important call he had to make on Wednesday 29 October.

Tucker was an unusually gregarious central banker to whom having a good relationship with senior people in the City was part of the job. He had known Diamond for many years and had developed a good rapport with him during their regular discussions about the state of money markets. After exchanging pleasantries, he told Diamond that he was receiving calls from a number of senior figures within

Whitehall asking why Barclays was always towards the top end of the Libor pricing.[40] Diamond was careful in his reply. He knew about the Libor problem from his risk managers, who had told him that they didn't believe the rates being submitted by competitors. At times RBS and Lloyds, the recently nationalized banks, had scarcely been able to borrow at all, yet they were posting rates below Barclays', and several other banks were also suspected of posting fictitious Libor rates. He believed that Barclays was one of the few banks telling the truth.

Diamond did not want to name names but asked Tucker to 'relay the reality that not all banks were providing quotes at the levels that represented real transactions'. Tucker repeated that the level of calls he had received from Whitehall were 'senior' and that while he was certain Barclays did not need advice, Barclays did not always need to appear as high as it had recently.[41]

After the call ended, Diamond reflected. Two days later Barclays hoped to announce the £7.3 billion fund raising from the Middle East and he was concerned that misconceptions in Whitehall would spread to the potential investors. He discussed the call with Varley and wrote a file note to him, copied to del Missier to whom the money markets team ultimately reported.[42]

Six weeks later, on 10 December, it was announced that Tucker would become a deputy governor of the Bank of England. The following day Diamond sent him an email: 'Paul, Congratulations. Well done, man. I am really, really proud of you. Talk soon. Bob.' Tucker replied: 'Thank you so much. You've been an absolute brick through this. Paul.'[43]

16

When Amanda Met Roger, 2008

AMANDA'S STORY

St Catharine's College sits snugly at one end of Trumpington Street, Cambridge, its ancient redbrick court and manicured lawns forming a calm refuge from the passing traffic and tourists. Catz men and women sometimes modestly describe it as famous mostly for being next door to the unsurpassed architecture of King's College, though it actually has a proud sporting tradition and a roster of eminent academics. It attracts very many well-qualified applicants, and for those lucky enough to get a place, it is a passport to a successful career.

Amanda Staveley was classic Cambridge material. She grew up on a 175-acre North Yorkshire estate given by Thomas Wolsey to her sixteenth-century ancestors. Privately educated, she had been a promising schoolgirl athlete, had worked as a waitress at the Yorkshire theme park run by her parents and had the academic grades that St Catharine's demanded. The college liked her achievements and her spirit and in 1990 she was awarded a place to study modern languages. A conventional path to success beckoned. But unexpectedly she fell ill and left her academic life after a year.

Eight miles east of St Catharine's College is Bottisham, an East Anglian village with a mixture of traditional whitewashed cottages and newer bungalows in its High Street. Dickie Jeeps, a former England rugby star and then Cambridgeshire farmer, had run Stocks restaurant there for many years, drawing a crowd from Cambridge and the nearby racing town of Newmarket. It had been a successful venture, but in 1996 he was sixty-five years old and decided to sell it.

After leaving St Catharine's, Staveley spent time with her grand-father, a bookmaker in the South Yorkshire town of Doncaster and *habitué* of the local dog track. He taught her to fight back from adversity, weigh up odds, back her own judgement and be prepared to bet against the crowd. She had a good head for figures, knew the catering trade and looked for somewhere to apply her skills. She moved back to Cambridge, working as a bookkeeper and waitress in local restaurants. At the age of twenty-two, with a loan of £180,000 from the National Westminster Bank and remembering her grandfather's advice, she bought the restaurant in Bottisham. It was her first business.

Stocks was hard work. With the bank loan to pay off, she would get up at four in the morning to begin preparing food and work front of house in the evening. She spent the afternoons studying finance, occasionally going off to a dingy building on London Wall for classroom sessions. Bemused trainee bankers would enquire: 'Who do you work for?' and when she told them, asked, 'Why are you here?' The answer was simple: 'Because I am going to start my own financial firm.'

She ran Stocks for four years, while always keeping an eye on what was going on to the west in Cambridge and east to events in Newmarket. The restaurant was still popular with members of Newmarket's racing community, in particular those associated with Godolphin Racing, owned by the al Maktoum family of Dubai. Staveley was a strikingly attractive woman with big green eyes, blond hair and an engaging manner and the racing crowd liked her. The restaurant was also increasingly popular with people from Cambridge's high-tech businesses booming on the Science Park midway between Cambridge and Bottisham. Through the late 1990s she started dealing in shares and became a seed investor in some of the hundreds of technology and biotech firms springing up around Cambridge.

What the Science Park needed, she decided, was a focal point. She pitched the idea to Jeremy Fairbrother, the bursar of Trinity College, the immensely wealthy institution that had set up the park. Staveley got his and others' backing, put in some of her own money, closed Stocks and in 2000 opened Q.ton, a conference centre and ideas hub on Cambridge Science Park. She appeared on reality television and in 2000 won an award as 'Businesswoman of the Year'.

Cambridge was a hotbed of technology innovation but the academics needed help to commercialize their ideas and Staveley stepped in. She got to know the university and was involved in planning a visit there by King Abdullah of Jordan and Prince Andrew in November 2001. It was decided that they would visit the Science Park and Staveley offered to host them at Q.ton.

On the day of the visit, one of the university's deputy vice-chancellors facilitated a discussion with the royal visitors in the morning before their cavalcade moved out of the old city to the Science Park. Staveley swept down the stairs at Q.ton to greet her guests. She was smart, clever and fun and she captivated them. That visit led to a trip to Jordan as King Abdullah's guest and a romantic relationship with Prince Andrew.

The next few years were a roller coaster. In 2000 Staveley had sold a 49 per cent share in Q.ton to an Irish company, which later failed in the dot.com crash of 2001. Using money borrowed from Barclays and other banks she repurchased her shares, but paid too much for them. At the time she was also helping her parents' struggling business, and she ended up having to file an individual voluntary arrangement, an alternative to bankruptcy. It was a terrifying experience and it took her several years to work off her debts. In 2005 she set up a London-based private equity company, PCP Partners, developed her contacts in the Middle East, learned about Islamic finance, did a number of small private equity deals and moved to Dubai two years later.

Staveley absorbed the culture, worked her contacts book and had an eye for a deal. She gained access to the inner circles of the Gulf ruling families and became well known as a financier, advising and liaising between companies and investors. Her landmark deal was the £210 million purchase of Manchester City football club in September 2008 by Sheikh Mansour bin Zayed al Nahyan of Abu Dhabi. It was by far the biggest acquisition that she had advised on and was headline news in football-obsessed Britain.

Staveley had been discussing the possibility of investing in a UK bank with Sheikh Mansour since June 2008, the month when the Qataris invested in Barclays. Sheikh Mansour had been wondering whether to follow his Qatari neighbours into banking. Lloyds in particular interested him as a well-capitalized, well-managed UK bank.

Staveley believed things would get worse for the UK banks and advised him to wait until the British government had shown its hand. The two waited patiently all summer as the banking sector deteriorated and financial markets went into meltdown.

Staveley watched all this carefully and thought again about her grandfather's advice: do your sums, back your own judgement and if the odds are right, bet against the crowd. In the financial mayhem, shares were being marked down indiscriminately. After the reaction to Lehman and the US government's panicky rescue of AIG, Staveley considered it unlikely that governments would allow big financial institutions to fail, particularly in Britain where the banks had leveraged so much that their assets were several times larger than the whole economy.

She looked for a British bank where investors were mistakenly assuming the worst. Lloyds was about to take on the troubled HBOS and would need a long time to recover, and RBS was grappling with the ABN AMRO acquisition, which would probably take even longer. Barclays, by contrast, had made a smart acquisition at a knock-down price but despite that had been savaged by investors along with the other banks. She decided that it was the one to go for. She discussed the idea with Sheikh Mansour during September and early October and sounded out other potential members of a syndicate.

Staveley's business partner was an Oxford graduate named Craig Eadie who had trained as an articled clerk at Frere Cholmeley in the early 1980s, where John Varley was also completing his legal training. He had just finished working on the Manchester City deal when Staveley asked him to send an email to his old colleague. On Friday 10 October 2008 the Barclays share price had closed at 192 pence, the June shareholders' £4.5 billion investment was now worth only £3 billion and a state-led recapitalization of the British banking system was expected any day. Eadie's email on Sunday 12 October asked Varley whether he would be interested in speaking to a senior member of the Abu Dhabi ruling family about a possible investment in Barclays.

Staveley waited for Varley to respond to Eadie's message. She knew from her contacts elsewhere in the Middle East and Asia that it would not be easy for Barclays to raise money. Several days went by during which she had meetings in Abu Dhabi with Sheikh Mansour's advisers and International Petroleum Investment Company (IPIC), an Abu Dhabi state investment company, to work out a possible structure for a Barclays deal.

An arrangement struck three weeks earlier in America particularly interested her. The world's leading investment bank, Goldman Sachs, had itself fallen victim to the turmoil and needed to raise capital. On 23 September it borrowed $5 billion from Warren Buffett but the 'Sage of Omaha' struck a hard bargain. In addition to negotiating a high rate of interest on the loan, he also secured warrants – securities issued by the company – giving him the right (but not the obligation) to buy at any point over the next five years $5 billion of equity shares in Goldman at an 8 per cent discount to the already depressed share price. If, as he expected, Goldman Sachs survived the crisis and the share price recovered before the expiry of the warrants, he stood to make another fortune.

Staveley thought that Barclays was in a similar position to Goldman Sachs – a sound institution suffering temporary problems. Warrants would give Staveley and her investors a piece of the action if the Barclays price recovered. She hired none other than Goldman Sachs to advise her and had a long meeting with them in Abu Dhabi on 13 October at which they studied that day's announcement from Barclays.

The week passed agonizingly slowly. Every day brought fresh drama in the markets but nothing from Barclays. The US government announced that it would spend $250 billion of Paulson's $700 billion Troubled Assets Relief Program taking stakes in nine leading banks. The Dow Jones index fell 7.9 per cent on 15 October, its worst fall since the crash of 1987. Bank rescues were being carried out all over the world: Switzerland, France, South Korea, Holland, Iceland. Staveley wondered whether in this mess Barclays would have to go back to the UK government and accept their money after all.

Then on Saturday 18 October she received the message she had been waiting for. It came from Tom Kalaris: please contact Roger Jenkins, the man leading the capital raising exercise for the bank. His office number was attached.

ROGER'S STORY

The appointment of Roger Jenkins in early 2008 to chair Barclays Capital's Middle East business was a surprise. He was head of Barclays' Structured Capital Markets in London, a tax-planning business rescued by Diamond from the break-up of BZW. Though profits for the unit were not reported separately, with only around 100 employees and revenues in 2007 of £1.2 billion, at peak profits probably exceeded £500 million, easily half of the investment bank's total.[1] Barclays' gossips speculated: why would the bank risk disrupting such a cash machine? Was Jenkins bored? Was this some kind of retirement job? Had HMRC tightened the rules under which businesses like SCM operated? Whatever the truth, the tax business evidently no longer needed Jenkins' full-time involvement and there were other ways he could be useful to Barclays.

Jenkins was born in Edinburgh in 1955, the son of an oil refinery manager at nearby Grangemouth. He and his brother David both excelled at the Edinburgh Academy, an upmarket school in the city. David concentrated on athletics and went on to win Olympic silver. Roger's sport was rugby and he was a record try-scorer for the school's first fifteen. He was not a bad sprinter either, representing Scotland and Great Britain. He studied economics at Heriot-Watt University, followed his father into BP and then joined Barclays in 1978 as a graduate trainee. He stayed until 1987, then left for Kleinwort, before rejoining Bardays in 1994.

It was at this point that his career took off. Jenkins built the Structured Capital Markets team for BZW, arranging tax deals for large companies – a big business for all the investment banks and one in which Barclays now became a leading player. It required a detailed analysis of tax legislation in many countries, a deep understanding of clients' tax position, access to Barclays' balance sheet and use of the bank's own tax position. The bank itself was a client and part of any money Structured Capital Markets saved off the bank's tax bill was credited to their profit and bonus pool.

Jenkins was an imposing figure with a sprinter's powerful physique, a pale complexion and shaved hair. He lived in Mayfair, flew in a Gulfstream jet and relaxed on a big yacht. He said in one of his rare interviews: 'I don't want to be out and about. I guard my privacy,' but his then wife, a glamorous Bosnian called Sanela Diana Catic, associated with the famous, dressed in style and was frequently on the society pages. According to some reports it was she who introduced her husband to HBJ, Sheikh Hamad bin Jassim bin Jabr Al Thani, foreign minister and then prime minister of Qatar.[2] As Jenkins got to know HBJ, he introduced Varley to the Qataris and the relationship grew, finally leading to the June 2008 investment in Barclays.

Jenkins had to work hard in the summer of 2008 as the fall in the Barclays share price eroded the value of the Qataris' investment. As we have seen, the Qataris had committed a further £1 billion after Jenkins' and Diamond's dash to Qatar on 12 October but had also hedged their bet, investing an equal amount with Credit Suisse. Jenkins would have to find other investors if Barclays was to meet the FSA's fund raising target.

Staveley called Jenkins as soon as she heard from Tom Kalaris but had to leave a message with his assistant. Though she was wary of his reputation, when they finally spoke it was easy enough. Jenkins said that Barclays was looking for £3 billion and she outlined her plan, mentioning Sheikh Mansour. Jenkins invited her to meet him in London later that week and on Tuesday 21 sent an email confirming the meeting for the following Thursday. With all the commotion, Staveley was having to work hard to keep her potential investors interested, and on Wednesday 22 received an email in red. It came from the Abu Dhabi government's investment company IPIC and read simply: 'Barclays is beyond saving!'

If taken literally that message would mean the end of the deal and so she kept it to herself. Following further conversations with Jenkins, she took off from Abu Dhabi international airport in the early hours of the morning of Thursday 23 October on an Emirates flight to London. She landed at Heathrow just after six in the morning, was driven to her London home on Park Lane, had a swim in her pool and walked round the corner to the PCP offices in Hays Mews. She worked there all day and then, just before five o'clock took another short walk to Jenkins' house in Farm Street.

They greeted each other as if they were old friends, which they were not. Staveley noticed the gallery of framed photographs showing Jenkins and his wife with famous couples and reminded him of a brief encounter with them the previous summer at a party in St Tropez. Jenkins then introduced her to Stephen Jones and the three of them sat round the huge table in the kitchen, the espresso machine keeping them fuelled as they pored over piles of paper and spreadsheets entitled 'Project Mandolin'.[3]

Jenkins and Jones took Staveley through a document marked 'Presentation to HH Sheikh Mansour bin Zayed al-Nahyan', which included a page headed 'Summary of Investment Proposal'. It was dated that day, 23 October, and named £3 billion as the sum Barclays wanted. Staveley recalled (though Barclays did not subsequently agree)[4] that in conversation Jenkins increased that sum to £3.5 billion. It would be a private placement offered to a limited number of investors rather than a public issue available to all shareholders. This required less documentation and could be agreed quickly among investors, a vital consideration given the panicky state of markets. Staveley understood Jenkins to be confident of securing a similar-sized investment from Qatar, despite her concern that the Qataris' recent investment in Credit Suisse and in Barclays would leave them with little appetite for more exposure.

Staveley outlined how she planned to fund the proposed investment with Sheikh Mansour as the cornerstone. To enable any investment to take place, PCP would need £3 billion in five-year warrants at an exercise price to be settled later.[5] After a few days' discussion, Staveley settled for £1.5 billion of warrants and went off to reassure her potential investors, including the once doubtful IPIC, that Barclays was a viable investment.

That was something Staveley needed to be sure of herself. Barclays was a complex business carrying a myriad of derivatives and other assets and liabilities. The annual report was 292 pages long, assets held for trading totalled £194 billion and the balance sheet was full of opaque assets and liabilities that would be hard to value. A due diligence meeting was arranged at the offices of Barclays' lawyers, Clifford Chance, on 28 October and Staveley got to work briefing her advisers.

One of her team recommended that she speak to John Aitken, a brilliant and abrasive City banking analyst, who had followed the sector for years and knew the numbers inside out. She arranged to meet him in a quiet corner of one of her favoured venues, the Blue Bar at the Berkeley hotel, whose plush interiors and gentle background music added a sense of quiet sophistication to meetings and whose location on the edge of Knightsbridge straddled the moneyed worlds of Mayfair and Chelsea. After their discussion, they agreed he would be her forensic expert.

On the 28th, enough people to stage a rugby match trooped into Clifford Chance's boardroom at 10 Upper Bank Street, Canary Wharf. Staveley's advisers included Glenn Earle, the Goldman partner who was helping her through the deal; Mark Horrocks, a City fund manager who had just started his own advisory firm; and Aitken. Aitken was working freelance at the time and liked to wear jeans, T-shirt and a leather coat, as well as sunglasses, but Staveley was paying him well for this job and had told him to put on a suit and tie and to leave the shades in his pocket.

Staveley's team lined up along one side of the Clifford Chance boardroom, a revolving cast from Barclays faced them across the table and representatives of Barclays' Qatari investors sat to Staveley's right at one end. Robert Le Blanc, Barclays' chief risk officer, was on hand to help with detailed risk questions and the Barclays' business heads walked in one by one to present.

Diamond was clearly the main man. The room came to attention when he entered. He oozed power and was the master of the silent attack. If he was asked an unwanted question, his first response was a pause just long enough to make the questioner shift nervously in their chair, before making eye contact. People called it the death stare (though never to his face). As Aitken probed and pushed, he got the full Diamond treatment – and gave some back.

They worked through Barclays' business under four headings. Financial performance covering balance sheet, profit and loss, target financial ratios, liquidity; risk, with a particular focus on the Lehman assets, commercial real estate, mortgage related securities and leveraged loans; legal and regulatory issues, including questions such as 'have there been requests for information in relation to market abuse, insider dealing, control of information or conflicts of interest'; and the strategy for each business segment and the group as a whole.

Varley and Roger Jenkins appeared for the final part of the meeting. Later Staveley would recall telling them that in addition to Sheikh Mansour, she had a number of other potential investors, now including IPIC, whose concerns had been settled.[6] After the meeting Staveley's team gathered to review their findings. They decided that Barclays would survive but that large parts of the balance sheet were so hard to value that they should be marked down to zero when calculating asset values. At the right price a deal was still on and Staveley immediately flew to Egypt to meet another potential investor.

Barclays were still confident of securing further Qatari investment and were now planning an announcement for 31 October in which they wanted to say that a book had been built for the capital raising. The day after due diligence, in the evening of 29 October, Varley and Jenkins telephoned Staveley to ask how her side of the funding was progressing. They sounded pretty concerned.

She had just got back from Egypt, tired and worried. Nothing was firm, everyone's commitment was dependent on everyone else's and the only money she could definitely count on was the relatively modest amount that PCP itself could put in. Jenkins pushed hard. Staveley could see herself on the front page of the *Financial Times* being blamed for the demise of a great bank and the collapse of the British economy. She did her best to be reassuring but after the call ended she burst into tears. She had not had a full night's sleep for longer than she cared to remember and the flights and long days meant she was completely exhausted. She phoned her father, still crying, and said: 'I can't cope. This is just too tough.'

In fact, her investing group came together over the next twenty-four hours but neither side fully trusted the other. Varley worried about Staveley. She seemed responsive and reliable but personally owed Barclays £800,000 from the failure of Q.ton and there was a lot riding on this young and inexperienced woman. Barclays decided to seek assurances and on 30 October requested a written commitment from Sheikh Mansour. They received a statement from Ali Jassim, one of the sheikh's close advisers, confirming that Sheikh Mansour 'has authorized and instructed me to confirm to you' that the PCP investment companies 'will be fully funded in order to meet their obligations'.[7] Varley was still nervous and decided he needed to speak to Sheikh Mansour direct, so a call was set up for six fifteen the following morning.

For their part, Staveley and Ali Jassim were still fretting that Barclays would need to issue more equity shares at some future point. This would water down the share price and make their warrants less valuable or even worthless if enough shares were issued. The evening of 30 October was spent at the City offices of Allen & Overy, PCP's lawyers, in tense negotiations with Barclays and their lawyers at the other end of the phone.[8] After several hours of arguing, a clause to protect the warrants from dilution was agreed and the meeting finished at two in the morning. Staveley had a car coming to pick her up at five to take her to Canary Wharf for the call between Varley and Sheikh Mansour; it hardly seemed worth going to bed. Staveley, Ali Jassim and their advisers went back to her house and spent the next couple of hours checking drafts, reading emails and waiting for the morning.

When Staveley and Ali Jassim arrived at Barclays' offices in Canary Wharf at half-past five in the morning of Friday 31 October, press photographers were already waiting on the steps. At six fifteen UK time Sheikh Mansour was in a helicopter returning from a hunting trip. Reception was poor as his helicopter swooped over the desert. Varley opened the conversation in typically courteous style: 'Your excellency, it is an honour to speak to you. I look forward to welcoming you as an investor in Barclays.' The sheikh thanked him and confirmed he had authorized Ali Jassim to provide a comfort letter. The call was over in sixty seconds and a quarter of an hour later, the proposed deal to raise £7.3 billion from Qatar and Abu Dhabi was announced. When the market opened Barclays' share price jumped 4 per cent to 210 pence.

It appeared as though Barclays' board had defied the Treasury and pulled off a private fund raising but Staveley was nervous. In addition to fees of £110 million, she and her Abu Dhabi investors had obtained warrants on £1.5 billion shares at the previous day's closing price of 198 pence. If the share price rose at any time during the next five years, they would be able to sell the shares and make a gigantic profit. As recently as January, the shares had been at 400 pence; if they regained that level, the investors would make £1.5 billion and Staveley, who had negotiated a 10 per cent interest in the deal, would make £150 million. She would also be entitled to the benefits of her share of £4.2 billion of mandatory convertible notes paying interest of 9.75 per cent and £3 billion of other debt instruments paying interest of 14 per cent; base rates at the time were 4.5 per cent. The mandatory convertible notes were convertible into Barclays shares on or before 30 June 2009 at a price of 153 pence – a 22.5 per cent discount to the previous night's share price – thus offering the potential for further profits. It all added up to the deal of a lifetime. There was one problem: the final terms with her investors had yet to be agreed.

1–24 NOVEMBER – LONDON, NEW YORK AND THE GULF

The market's delight when the deal was announced did not last long. Once they knew the bank was safe, investor mood changed from nervous anxiety to outrage. There was criticism about the terms of the deal, the limited opportunities for Barclays' existing investors to participate and the fees paid. Vince Cable, Treasury spokesman for the Liberal Democrats, one of the UK opposition parties, described it as a 'scandal of mammoth proportions' and accused Barclays of avoiding British government money to ensure it could keep paying bonuses.[9] One of the bodies representing institutional investors, the Association of British Insurers, issued one of its 'red top' warnings, reserved for 'issues of grave concern', citing 'the preferential terms available to some investors and the overall cost of the issue to existing shareholders'.[10] The share price slid alarmingly over the next few days, ending the week after the deal was announced at 179 pence, a drop of 15 per cent.

Barclays were exasperated. Commissions, fees and expenses totalled £300 million, 4 per cent of the amount raised, a rich sum but that was the price of risk capital in the circumstances. From Varley's standpoint, the criticism from institutional investors was out of order. When sounded out by CSFB and J. P. Morgan Cazenove over the weekend of 11–12 October they had rejected putting any more money into Barclays; now they were complaining about being left out.

What they objected to was Barclays paying 14 per cent for £3 billion of debt at a time when government money was available to the banks at 12 per cent, as well as giving investors warrants to buy shares at a depressed price. The interest rate of 9.75 per cent on the £4.2 billion convertible notes was more acceptable but the institutions objected to this too because it potentially gave creditors shares at a discount and was not available to the main body of existing shareholders. Barclays were giving far too much of the bank away, the critics said. In return for cash up front, Barclays had agreed to a potential 51.6 per cent increase in the number of shares in issue, nearly all of which could be bought by the Middle Eastern investors at rock bottom prices. Barclays' existing investors, who thought they owned the whole of the bank, might soon own only two-thirds of it. Admittedly Barclays looked safer than it was before the issue, but angry shareholders said that Staveley and the Middle East investors had exploited its weakness.

The dissident institutions' case was clearly put by Peter Chambers, chief executive of Legal & General Investment Management, the British insurer that owned 3.9 per cent of Barclays shares: 'We regret that Barclays decided to raise capital from a small group of strategic investors without due consideration of its impact on existing shareholders and on terms that we consider to be expensive.' At this rate, there was every risk that shareholders would vote down the proposal.

As criticism mounted, Staveley also became concerned. The legal agreement was between PCP's shell companies with no capital of their own, and Barclays. The investment would be largely funded by Sheikh Mansour and IPIC with a debt element. The terms upon which they would do so had not been agreed and there was still room for them to withdraw or squeeze her out of the deal. As a precaution she contacted other potential investors, including the China Investment Corporation, the big US fund manager BlackRock and the private equity firm Vasari Global. She also spoke to half a dozen banks, including the British government-owned RBS, about funding the investment through debt.

On 7 November Barclays announced that an extraordinary general meeting (EGM) of shareholders to approve the proposal would be held on the 24th. Barclays, however, had not yet won over investors and Staveley's side was still not firm. She was terrified: she was not sleeping well and kept remembering her call with Jenkins and Varley on the evening of 29 October. Then on 12 November she received a text from Jenkins telling her they needed to talk.

Jenkins evidently knew exactly when to strike. He called her from New York and explained that the market hated the deal. As things stood, the institutions would vote it down at the EGM. It was too much for them. The investors needed to offer something to keep the existing shareholders happy. He proposed that Staveley's investors give up some or all of the warrants and the Qatari investors would do the same. Jenkins' proposal would have wiped out too much of their upside and she refused. After a few days' discussion, each side agreed to offer £250 million of the 14 per cent debt instruments to existing institutional investors but keep the warrants and the fees. They hoped this would secure the vote at the EGM and in addition create a traded market, enabling a fair price to be set for the debt from which to price any future issues.

Agius and Varley worked hard to sell the new deal, touring the leading institutional shareholders and drawing on the good relation- ship they had built up with them. A Barclays' letter to shareholders dated 7 November explained that a conventional rights issue would have needed to be at a 35–40 per cent discount to the share price and would have taken two months to complete, too long at a time of such uncertainty. The key meeting was with Peter Chambers at Legal & General, who now realized that their opposition could drive Barclays into government hands. Reluctantly, Chambers said that because these were 'exceptional circumstances, a failure to secure this capital could lead to a material detriment in shareholder value', Legal & General would vote its shares in favour.[11]

Staveley still had to keep her side solid. On 18 November, with the share price down a quarter since the capital raising had been announced on 31 October, she met her investors in Abu Dhabi, with Sheikh Mansour joining in by telephone. The meeting was to decide where the money was coming from and the key terms between Stave- ley and her investors. They agreed that the syndicate would fund most of the £3.5 billion required as debt and that Sheikh Mansour and IPIC would provide the balance as an equity investment, while Staveley would retain a free interest in a portion of the securities. The £110 million in fees and commissions paid by Barclays on the £3.5 billion investment would be split between the various participants.

Staveley had secured indicative offers of debt from Goldman Sachs,

Deutsche Bank and other investment banks who were willing to fund part of an investment in Barclays. But following the meeting in Abu Dhabi, Barclays' share price went further into freefall – from 146 pence to 118 pence in just two days. On 20 November Staveley received a call from Khadem Al-Qubaisi, the head of IPIC. Now it was her investors playing hardball. He indicated that IPIC and the sheikh had lost confidence in the deal and foresaw major difficulty raising the debt given the collapsing share price, which would mean Abu Dhabi would have to contribute vastly increased equity. The share price was now well below the exercise price of the warrants or the price at which the convertible notes would be redeemed.

Barclays, its future at stake, had become a chip in a poker game in which the players bluffed and counter-bluffed to get the most for their side. If the deal failed, the bank would have to turn to the government for help, would almost certainly be part nationalized and would have to give up its universal banking strategy. It was also a critical moment for Staveley. If she failed to raise the money to complete on the £3.5 billion investment, while there would be no recourse against her personally (the contracting parties were special purpose vehicles with no assets at the time of committing), her reputation would suffer. The Abu Dhabi investors were in a similar quandary. The deal was clearly no longer as good as it looked when they had agreed to take part. Yet Barclays had used Sheikh Mansour's name in its press announcement on 31 October 2008 and the market would have understood from that that he had committed personally. If they pulled out, it would look as if he had failed to deliver on a commitment.

Staveley continued in discussions with her Abu Dhabi investors for two days, but with the bank's EGM just a couple of days away and no time to bring in others, she could not maintain her position. She agreed to hand the whole deal over to Abu Dhabi and give up her own stake with nothing more than a verbal promise that she would be paid a fee for her time, to be discussed at some future point. It would be her investors who received the benefit of the high yielding financial instruments, convertibles and warrants for which she had fought so hard.

The bank's extraordinary general meeting was held the next day, 24 November. There was strong criticism from the floor, some describing the issue as 'morally indefensible' and 'a game of Russian roulette with all the chambers loaded'. The usually composed Agius looked uncomfortable. He said he naturally regretted the 70 per cent fall in the share price during 2008 but defended the deal: 'The need for speed and certainty overrode our desire to do right by our shareholders. I feel the full force of your unhappiness.' He described discussions over the fund raising as 'the devil's dilemma' but concluded that 'we had no alternative'.[12]

The questioning persisted: why had Barclays declined government money? Agius explained that the British bail-out could have required Barclays to allocate extra money to the British market even though its interests were more international. The bank, he said, could get a higher return on investment without government assistance.[13] Over 85 per cent of the votes were in favour of the issues, and completion took place on 27 November. In January 2009 Staveley agreed a fee of £30 million with her side, which she received in April that year. It was not what she had hoped for – or indeed what she believed she was entitled to when the terms offered to the Qataris were later revealed – but she would not be going back to washing dishes at Stocks any time soon.

17

Antiques Roadshow, 2009

'THE THINKER' THINKS AGAIN

William went back to work after the long Christmas break on Monday 5 January. He had spent the holiday at his parents' home in Oxford having just been told about his bonus for 2008. He was careful not to demean his academic parents' modest lifestyle by talking about money but it was an incredible sum: half a million dollars. Following his own analysis in 2007 and several weeks of further analysis and debate, the fund had carefully sold down its holding in Barclays, timing its activity to avoid depressing the price. While this was going on, the fund's technical experts were working out how to put on a sizeable short position, which would involve borrowing – in effect renting – Barclays shares from other institutions to settle the trade. Meanwhile, the fund's derivatives specialists worked out how to hedge some of the risk involved. It had been a painstaking process but in the end the hedge fund had gone short in Barclays for a full year as the share price fell from 700 pence to 300 pence and had made record returns for its investors and partners. They closed out the position just before the FSA ban on short selling in September 2008 and banked all the profits. William was the originator of the idea, and although they didn't do praise or formal year-end appraisals, he knew that he was now being listened to every time he spoke.

William had learned a lot from watching the trade being put on and taken off. He had a restless mind and he was now thinking about Barclays again. The news was dreadful. The British and American economies were shrinking, interest rates were being cut, governments were trying everything they could to stimulate business and consumer spending but investors were convinced a recession was imminent. The FTSE 100 index closed 2008 31 per cent down over the year, its biggest ever annual fall.

But 'the Thinker' believed that the markdown had been indiscriminate and that some good companies had been overlooked – Barclays, for example. The share price was trading at a third of book value, half the level of other UK banks, and even below the US banks, which he thought included some real basket cases. Was Barclays really the worst bank in its peer group? William did not think so and that meant that either Barclays was underpriced or the rest were overvalued. He switched on his computer and began to work out which.

UNHAPPY NEW YEAR

Over in Barclays' headquarters, Agius and Varley were exasperated. Their share price had become a roulette ball. Speculators cared only whether it landed on red or on black, whereas for them the survival of a three-centuries-old institution with 48 million customers and 156,000 employees was at stake. Agius took to pacing the long corridor outside the boardroom, which was lined with portraits of his predecessors. Nearest his office was the man with the film star looks, Barrett; then came Middleton, peering over his spectacles; then Buxton, with what looked like a hunting knife on a side table;* then Quinton, Bevan and Tuke. Round the corner, men in waistcoats and wing collars sporting whiskers on stern faces seemed to be saying: 'Mr Chairman, it didn't go down on my watch, make sure it doesn't go down on yours.'

Other shareholders were a long way behind William and were still worried about the issue he had identified in July 2007. Barclays was the most highly leveraged of the British banks and investors were punishing it. Leverage was standard banking practice – particularly after the rules were changed in 2004 by the Basel 2 international banking regulation, which allowed large banks to use their own models in applying risk weights to capital – but Barclays was at the extreme end. Its leverage rose to more than thirty-seven in 2007 and a peak of

---

* The object was a Khanjar, a ceremonial short curved sword from Oman – acknowledgment of the good business Buxton had built with Middle East institutions.

forty-three in 2008 while the board chased the universal banking vision despite the warning signs from the sub-prime mortgage market, Northern Rock, Lehman, Bear Stearns, the failed hedge funds, Wachovia, Merrill Lynch and the banking bail-outs. Investors were punishing Barclays.[1] The shares opened 2009 at 142 pence, far below the 198 pence at which the October investors could exercise their warrants, and plunged to 90 pence on Friday 16 January, the day of a second US government rescue of Bank of America and more heavy losses at Citigroup. At this rate the falling share price would become a self-fulfilling prophecy: nervous customers would withdraw their deposits and other banks would be just too scared to lend to it.

They hoped that a statement to the Stock Exchange would help and after trading closed on Friday 16 announced that the results for 2008 would be ahead of consensus estimates and that the capital position was strong. The *Financial Times Alphaville* column described it as 'a panic move' but added: 'Barclays had to do something – it simply cannot afford to have another session like Friday, when its market value plunged by a quarter.'[2] The board spent an anxious weekend wondering how investors would react when the markets reopened.

MINISTERS TAKE A LOOK

Monday 19 January 2009 was a wet and miserable winter morning in London, fitting the mood in Parliament as Chancellor Darling announced the government's second rescue package for the banks. The Bank of England was given £50 billion to buy assets such as corporate bonds, commercial paper and some asset backed securities to strengthen the banks' balance sheets. When this operation began in March 2009 it became known as 'quantitative easing'. In addition, various credit guarantees to encourage inter-bank lending were extended and access to the Bank's short-term liquid funds was facilitated. An Asset Protection Scheme was announced by which, in return for a fee, the government offered future protection against credit losses to banks lending to business and private customers.[3] It was a powerful package designed to improve confidence, liquidity and capital ratios and to encourage lending to the real economy.

Barclays' share price briefly rallied in response to its trading update but within hours resumed its downward path and on Friday 23 January closed the week at a miserly 47 pence. The days of a 720 pence target were a distant dream as was any thought of buying RBS. This was the kind of share price collapse that says 'the market expects you to go bust'.

Varley was deeply frustrated. The business was fine and he had told the analysts so in a formal announcement. But no one was listening. Once the final results and detailed annual report and accounts were released, he was confident that investors would be reassured but it was nearly a month until results day. If the share price kept falling during that time the money markets would close ranks on Barclays and it would be forced to go to the government.

In Westminster, ministers and officials were still deeply suspicious of Barclays, a suspicion that was shared by the Bank of England. Far from reassuring the authorities, the October fund raising had only alarmed them further. If Barclays could not complete the fund raising it promised, for example by selling BGI, or if, as competitors alleged, it had been mis-marking its books, there would be serious conse-quences. It was vital to the government's credibility that the October 2008 nationalizations cleaned up all the mess but it was not clear whether the Barclays' capital raising did that and the involvement of sovereign wealth funds added a diplomatic dimension. It was all very well for Barclays to say 'under no circumstances will we take govern-ment money' but to government eyes its ability to deliver had become a public interest issue as well as one for the company's shareholders. If Barclays was going to need a bail-out, the authorities were determined that it would be on their terms and at a time of their choosing.

Late one afternoon that week Varley received a worrying call from Myners' office. 'The minister would like to see you before the week-end. Please come to see him this afternoon,' was the message. As his car crawled along the Embankment from Canary Wharf to White-hall, Varley thought about his catastrophic share price and wondered what Myners was going to say.

It was always difficult to read Myners since he was genial even when delivering bad news. 'Thanks for coming over, John. So tell me. How bad is it?' he asked.

Varley replied: 'Despite the share price, it is actually fine. We have had a good year. We can fund ourselves on a day-to-day basis. There is really no cause for alarm.'

Myners' officials were deeply involved in running Lloyds and RBS and were telling him how difficult those banks were finding it. 'There is chatter in the market, John, that Barclays is in trouble.' Myners was typically low key: he never was one to create panic.

'Paul, we have no difficulty in funding ourselves, you know our results from last year are good, we are only two weeks into the New Year but that looks fine too. We are OK.'

Myners probed a little more, took what comfort he could from Varley's statements and wished him as pleasant a weekend as was possible under the circumstances.

Varley doubted that he had persuaded Myners and knew that if the share price kept falling, he would be back in the Treasury again very soon. He needed to convince two separate audiences, the authorities and the shareholders, that there was no crisis. He would address shareholders himself and would ask Diamond to tackle the authorities about Barclays Capital, which was still the business that they most doubted.

His finance team and auditors had told him it would be possible to bring the results forward by ten days to 9 February but that was still a fortnight away. Then he made a decision. He emailed Agius early on the evening of Friday 23, proposing that they simply write an open letter to shareholders; there seemed little to lose after nine consecutive days in which the share price had fallen.

Agius was due at a reopening ceremony of a Barclays branch in Piccadilly on the Saturday morning – a commitment he had to keep. Much as he enjoyed drafting, he asked Varley to make a start on the letter. While Agius glad-handed customers and staff amid turquoise balloons and actors dressed as Tower of London Beefeaters in Barclays' colours, Varley tapped away. Through frequent emails and phone calls, they put together a working draft. They met at Barclays' headquarters on the Sunday afternoon to agree the final version, arranged a conference call at forty minutes' notice for board approval, informed the FSA and by six o'clock were ready to brief the *Financial Times*.

The open letter was released the next day, Monday 26 January. It began:

> In view of the events in the banking sector last week, we have decided to communicate now with employees, customers, clients and share-holders in this open letter to address the principal causes of concern which we are hearing. Writing in this way ahead of the release of results is unusual, of course, but the turn of events is also unusual.

The letter assured them that 'we are well funded and we are profit-able.' The results would be brought forward to 9 February and would be 'well ahead of the consensus estimate of £5.3 billion'. Write-downs on credit market exposures at Barclays Capital would be £8 billion but income generation was strong and capital exceeded the FSA requirements by £17 billion.

> This scale of loss absorption capability, when looked at in the context both of the solid and diversified profitability of the Group during the stress test of 2008, and of the substantial write-downs that we have taken, gives us confidence that our capital resources are sufficient to manage Barclays safely and prudently even in these difficult markets. For these reasons we confirm in this letter that we are not seeking sub-scription for further capital – either from the private sector or from the UK government.

It was early days but 'we have had a good start to 2009'.[4] It was a brave decision for Agius and Varley to sign it and it put their reputa-tions on the line. If it went wrong, their careers were finished. They had judged it well: the share price rose from 68 pence to 84 pence during the day and opened at 94 pence on results day, 9 February.

The second part of Varley's plan was to win over government, where he was personally well regarded despite their concern over the bank's position. He was one of the few senior bankers to realize that the public mood demanded humility, telling the Treasury Committee in February 2009: 'If you look at the failure in the banking system over the course of the last two years, it is clear that the banks have contributed to that failure and it is clear that part of that problem has been the issue of compensation.'[5] Such statements were welcomed, but he also needed to speak directly to Downing Street, a task which was complicated by the frayed relations between the prime minister's circle at Number 10 and the chancellor's team next door. Varley could have an open dialogue with Chancellor Darling's minister Myners but Prime Minister Brown still relied heavily on Vadera, who had played a major part in the October 2008 banking sector recapitalization. She had accompanied Brown on his visits to New York and Washington in September of that year, brought in investment banking advisers to help the Treasury plan the recapitalization and (with Tom Scholar at the Treasury) provided a lot of the brainpower and expert knowledge herself in working out the bank bail-out. If Barclays wanted to convince the prime minister, she was the key. Varley asked Diamond, who had Barclays' prime relationship with Vadera, to contact her. It would not be easy. She was clever, demanding and no one was going to pull the wool over her eyes.

Diamond phoned Vadera and asked: 'Minister, can you give me some advice? We hear that the government still isn't comfortable with Barclays. How can we resolve this?'

Vadera replied: 'The market says your assets are overvalued and we can't see what's in them from the accounts. It's a matter of transparency. We just don't understand your numbers. How is it that every other bank has taken a bigger hit than Barclays?'

Diamond replied: 'I understand the concern but Barclays is proud of its risk management capabilities. I want to bring my team over to show you that the numbers in the balance sheet are real.'

Vadera agreed and added: 'If we're to have a meeting, there's no point in just convincing me. I will bring the right people from the Treasury too, including Paul Myners.'

Vadera had two offices in Westminster, one at the Department for Business at the bottom of Victoria Street, the other in the Cabinet Office at 70 Whitehall, a rambling rabbit warren of gloomy corridors with a direct passageway to 10 Downing Street. She spent most of her time in her 70 Whitehall office, up a short flight of stairs from the link door to Number 10, which she used to get to her frequent meetings with the prime minister.

Diamond arrived with his head of risk, Le Blanc, and some detailed schedules on oversized A3 paper. They sat down at Vadera's large oval table with splendid views over Horseguards Parade and St James's

Park and took the ministers and their officials through the spread-sheets. It was an excruciatingly slow session.

The discussion turned on Barclays' approach to the loans it parcelled up and then sold on to other institutions. Like all banks, Barclays kept slices of this packaged debt for itself, sometimes by choice, sometimes out of necessity if there was insufficient market demand.

It was like a property developer selling apartments in a block and buying the last one itself in order to say 'All Sold'. In such cases, some developers would take a profit immediately on the last unit and carry it in the balance sheet at the sale price. It was legitimate accounting but if the apartment had to be sold below that price, the loss would have to be recognized. A more prudent method would be to buy the apartment, mark it to zero in the balance sheet, take the loss imme-diately and take a profit only when it was sold.

Naguib Kheraj, who had progressed from Barclays Capital's chief operating officer to become finance director for the whole bank in 2004, ordered that Barclays would follow the latter method. This conservative approach meant that Barclays had been well protected from the crisis and was the reason, Diamond and Le Blanc told Vadera and Myners, that their valuations were holding up better than their competitors'.

Myners had interrogated many corporate executives during his time as a fund manager and did so again now. Le Blanc was clearly on top of the facts. If he did not have the answer to a question, he knew exactly where to look in his big ringbound folder. With the FSA soon to be testing the banks' balance sheets against a range of scenarios, Myners regarded their case as being just about on the right side of credibility but Vadera appeared more sceptical. As the meeting broke up, she said: 'Bob, by the way, the best of luck in passing the stress tests.'

It sounded like a thoroughly leading question. 'That's interesting,' Diamond shot back. 'We didn't know the criteria have been set.'

'They haven't,' replied Vadera.

LATE JANUARY – BIRMINGHAM

'Karl, have you seen this?'

The office manager pointed to a line on Edwards' bank statement for the final quarter of 2008: 'Debit, £4300, Derivatives'. It was totally unexpected. The Bank of England had cut interest rates from 4.5 in October to 3 per cent in November and 2 per cent in December, and October House Records had been expecting to benefit. They looked closely at the rest of the statement. 'Surely our mortgage payments should be going down? They look just the same as before,' said the office manager.

'I'll call the bank, I'm sure they can sort this out,' Edwards replied.

STRESS

Varley's presentation to investors on 9 February gave him another chance to be reassuring. The strapline was 'Reshaping Barclays from a UK clearing bank into a diversified global universal bank'. The message was very clear: despite the problems that other banks were having, Barclays was in good shape and was poised to take advantage of competitors' weakness. The strategy was intact and Barclays would press on.

The accompanying statement picked off the points that had been worrying investors. The business was 'solidly profitable', 'our marks are appropriate' and the Lehman deal 'accelerated our strategy and created a top tier global franchise' in investment banking. Leverage had already fallen as the capital base was rebuilt and would soon fall to twenty-four times – well below the extreme levels of forty-three times seen in the middle months of 2008. Short-term funding was not a problem because with low volumes of debt maturing in 2009 Barclays was well placed to meet its financing needs in 2010.[6] The share price rose from 94 pence to 107 pence on the day and the immediate heat was off.

But the Northern Rock debacle in 2007 had been a wake-up call to regulators, and Sants had used the new mood to change the FSA's approach from 'principles based' to 'proportionate' and from 'not enforcement led' to offering 'credible deterrence'. In March 2009 he made an important speech redefining the FSA's approach still further. He announced:

In the future, we will seek to make judgements on the judgements of senior management and take actions if in our view those actions will lead to risks to our statutory objectives. This is a fundamental change. It is moving from regulation based only on observable facts to regulation based on judgements about the future.'[7]

Barclays was one of the first banks to feel the force of this when, following the lead of Bernanke and Geithner's Fed, the FSA decided to put the major banks through new tests in the opening months of 2009 – the tests Vadera had referred to at the end of her meeting with Diamond. Any bank that failed would be forced into another government-led recapitalization, and Barclays was top of their list. FSA officials spent several weeks with Barclays in February and March running simulations.

It was an opportunity for the FSA to reassert itself following a reform of regulation announced in the previous June 2008. The danger signals from Northern Rock and the credit markets persuaded the government that the tripartite system it had designed in 1997 wasn't working. Legislation would be introduced to overhaul the system, giving the Bank of England statutory responsibility for financial stability and redefining its relationship with the FSA.[8] Although nominally an independent agency, the FSA was now in effect the junior partner to both the Bank of England, which was responsible for the stability of the banking system, and the Treasury.[9]

Treasury ministers and officials, therefore, expected to sign off the stress test results before they were agreed. Sants was nevertheless protective of his agency's independence. On the morning of Thursday 26 March he rang Varley and said: 'I have seen the first cut of the results. They look OK but we need to run them again. I'll call you later tonight.' Varley was relieved but there was a logistical issue: 'I am at a private dinner party tonight, it may be difficult to speak.' Sants replied: 'That's not a problem. I'll call between six and six-thirty.'

Varley went home to change. By the time his car came to collect him at half-past seven there was still no call. He set off to the Holland Park dinner party uneasily. Sants had told him that the final run-through would be done by six – had something gone wrong? When he arrived, he explained to his host that he was expecting a phone call and might have to leave early. At nine-thirty Varley's phone vibrated in his pocket, he excused himself and went to another room. It was indeed Sants.

'John, this is OK. There are certain further actions we will want you to take but you can assume we have agreed in principle.' Varley thanked him, and said: 'Of course, we can move more quickly. We'll discuss the detail when you wish,' and went back to the dinner table feeling happier.

But while Varley was feeling happier, his corporate affairs team were not. They had just seen the front-page headline of the first edition of the *Financial Times*: 'Fears rise Barclays will need injection'.[10] The article had been written by George Parker and Jane Croft. Howell James, director of Barclays Group Corporate Affairs, had joined the bank six months earlier from the civil service, where he had been permanent secretary, Government Communications. In that role he had witnessed plenty of crises, but was still feeling his way into banking. He sought advice from Alan Parker, doyen of the public relations industry and founder and chairman of one of its leading firms, Brunswick, who told him to ring Varley immediately.[11]

Varley had barely got home when James called. He was shocked by what his Corporate Affairs director had to say, having just been told the direct opposite by the chief executive of the FSA. Had Sants got it wrong? Had he been overruled by government? If the story was correct, Barclays would be in government hands within the hour. Even if it was wrong, counterparties would reduce Barclays' credit and force the bank out of business. They needed to find out the truth and if possible get the story corrected immediately. They decided that James would tackle the *Financial Times* and Varley would speak to the authorities. The latter proved difficult. Varley tried to contact Myners and Vadera but could not get through. Sants' phone was going to voicemail. He couldn't get anyone to explain what was happening. He called a meeting of senior executives at Churchill Place for six o'clock the next morning.

Varley spent a sleepless night, was collected at five and taken to Churchill Place. He need not have worried. Barclays' press office had tracked down Peter Thal Larsen, the *Financial Times*' banking editor, who was at a conference in Switzerland. The second edition of the newspaper carried a revised story with Thal Larsen's name added to the byline. The headline now was: 'Barclays stress test signals no new funds' and the article stated: 'The *Financial Times* has learnt that the Financial Services Authority will conclude its detailed trawl through the bank's books in the next few days and it has indicated that Barclays does not need any fresh capital.'[12]

Treasury ministers and officials were surprised to read the second *Financial Times* story. They knew that Barclays' core tier one capital had come in just above the minimum acceptable threshold of 4 per cent but this was below the 5 per cent level required of the nationalized banks Lloyds and RBS, and it was by no means clear to them that Barclays had passed. Although the FSA was in charge of the stress tests, the arrangement was that the results would be discussed by the tripartite authorities, following which the FSA's decision would be made public. Tom Scholar at the Treasury called Sants, who confirmed that he had indeed spoken to Varley, as he was entitled to do.

Further enquiries revealed a game of briefing and counter-briefing that was too late to unpack. Sants had perhaps run ahead of the game in exerting his agency's independence but both the Treasury and Barclays' spin doctors had been at work. The *Financial Times* articles had been co-written by George Parker, the paper's political correspondent, a man with contacts deep in Westminster and Whitehall. Coming soon after the BBC had misreported Barclays' involvement in the October nationalizations, this was the second time within a year that respected media organizations had misreported Barclays' results in government tests. The Treasury was evidently as leaky as the Barclays board, and Barclays believed that the Treasury was trying deliberately to undermine it.

The three authorities eventually held their meeting but it was too late. Barclays had forced their hand. It only added to the authorities' growing distrust of the bank and the way it operated.

SPRING – BIRMINGHAM

It had taken a few days for Karl Edwards to find time to call Barclays about the unexpected derivatives charge and a few days more for the relationship manager to get back to him. That in itself was a surprise for his calls were usually returned very quickly. When they spoke, the relationship manager was apologetic. 'I'm very sorry, Karl, life has suddenly got tough here. We are writing no new business, consumer confidence is shot and some of our customers are struggling. It's as though someone has flicked a switch and turned the economy off. I hear it's the same in other regions. How can I help?'

Edwards outlined the problem with his monthly repayments. There was a long pause at the other end of the phone. Then: 'You remember the structured collar you took out last year? The protection against interest rates rising. Well, that didn't happen and instead interest rates have fallen. We have to charge you for that.'

Edwards' stomach turned. He had never understood the 'structured collar' and was expecting to be the beneficiary, not a victim, of falling interest rates. The unexpected £4,300 meant his business was in loss for that month. Edwards was beginning to understand how the bank he had once trusted really worked and gloomily reflected on his own naivety. Then at midnight on 31 March, as he was enjoying a nightcap in his study, his fax machine began whirring. A scarcely legible sheet of paper from a Barclays office in Asia glided out. Edwards read with bemusement. It was a statement of derivatives charges for the quarter, this time for £11,000. The scarcely legible fax would become a three-monthly event for the next two years. Something would have to be done. He called Barclays the next morning – it was April Fools' Day.

He asked to speak to Carol, the woman who had sold him the product, but she had apparently done well and had been promoted. 'You had better speak to someone in London,' the relationship manager told him. 'I will get them to call you.'

It took a lot more time and much prompting for anyone from London to call Edwards but he finally got to speak to someone working in Barclays Capital's Risk Solutions Group in Canary Wharf. It was a very cold conversation. The Barclays man explained that Edwards had bought a form of interest rate hedging product sold by Barclays and other banks which protected the buyer against an increase in interest rates but entitled the bank to charge if interest rates went down. 'All of this was explained to you at the time and is made clear in the documents you signed,' he added.

Edwards said that he had not understood this and had relied on Barclays not to sell him a risky product. His relationship manager knew that he was a cautious businessman and Edwards had assumed after fifteen years with Barclays, that he could trust them to look after him. The voice on the phone turned hard: 'We explained how it worked, you signed up, now you are complaining. You made the bet, you lost.'

'I made the bet? I didn't even know I was in the betting shop,' Edwards replied. 'Risk Solutions Group?' he thought. 'The only risk they are solving is their own, not mine.'

SALE!

For millions of Britons and one family in particular, the weekend often finishes on a happy note. *Antiques Roadshow* is shown early on a Sunday evening on BBC television and is a gentle way to ease out of the weekend into the working week. Members of the public bring in bric-à-brac to have it valued by experts and the final item usually stuns the owner as a previously unconsidered family heirloom is revealed to have a value far in excess of expectations. So it was with Barclays Global Investors.

The week after Barclays announced that it had passed the FSA stress tests, Sants made the short walk from North Colonnade to Churchill Place to see Varley. When Barclays had outlined their plans to recapitalize the bank back in October 2008, Sants had got them to agree additionally to sell BGI. Now he wanted to hear what progress had been made.

There was much to report. Chairman Agius' old firm, Lazards, had been put in charge of the sale and approached CVC Capital Partners, a private equity firm that did a lot of business with Barclays. Lazards were expecting a bid any day but when it came in April, it was not for the whole of BGI. CVC bid £3 billion for I-shares, a business originally developed in Pattie Dunn's time for small investors who wanted a low-cost, easy-to-trade way to replicate the stock market's performance.

CVC and Barclays reached an agreement for I-shares but Barclays continued to explore other options. Back in 2002, soon after Diamond has become chairman, he and Varley had discussed a possible sale of the whole of BGI with Larry Fink and Ralph Schlosstein, who ran BlackRock, one of the world's biggest fund managers. There was no deal to be done then but Diamond wanted to sound them out again.

He saw from his schedule that the Barclays Capital team covering BlackRock were taking their client to an early season baseball fixture at the new Yankee Stadium up in the Bronx. Diamond was a diehard fan of the Boston Red Sox and didn't like going to either of the New York baseball grounds unless his team were playing there, but this was too good an opportunity to miss. In the carpeted comfort of the Barclays Capital suite, he made small talk with the guests, then towards the end of the game suggested to Robert Kapito, the senior BlackRock man present, that they take a walk round the concourse. As they strolled past the beer, popcorn and hot dog vendors, Diamond outlined the idea of a deal and asked Kapito to set up a meeting with Fink.

Diamond and Ricci met Fink in his New York office a few days later and offered him an exclusive for the whole business. They shook hands on a deal, kept it quiet for a few weeks and, in June 2009, announced the sale of BGI to BlackRock for a stupendous $13.5 billion, made up of £4.2 billion in cash and a 19.9 per cent stake for Barclays in BlackRock.[13] When the deal closed on 1 December, the subsequent rise in the BlackRock share price took the value of the deal up to $15.2 billion, giving Barclays a profit of £6.3 billion and adding 185 precious basis points to the all-important capital ratios.[14]

The sale dramatically rewarded many of BGI's employees, who at that stage owned or had options over 9 per cent of the firm. The final price per BGI share was determined to be £109.45 and the sale made them a profit estimated to be $500 million. Diamond, who because of his conflict of interest, took no part in board discussions of the transaction, received $36 million for shares he had acquired for $10 million.[15] It was a transformational deal for Barclays as well as for the individuals, taking its capital position well above the regulators' requirements and putting an end to speculation about imminent nationalization. When the deal closed, the share price was 280 pence and Barclays was safe.

18

Crown of Thorns, 2010

SOCIALLY USELESS

Before Northern Rock, the public considered banks (if they considered them at all) to be boring places. The queues in the streets changed all that. People learned from bitter experience what academic economists and the Bank of England knew intellectually: those boring places where they left their savings, took out mortgages and got cash are in fact the pumps that circulate blood round the economy. By 2010, no one was taking them for granted any more.

After the scare of 2008, enforced nationalizations, regulators' stress tests and shareholders' focus on capital ratios brought the decade-long leverage fest to an end. Banks cut back on credit, squeezing businesses and consumers and putting the brakes on the economy. Falling tax receipts caused the government to cut public spending to try to balance its books. The British economy entered the longest recession on record and 2009 was its worst single year since the Second World War. Conventional monetary policy was ineffective. Despite interest rates of only 0.5 per cent, the economy remained stubbornly unresponsive.

Only one group of people seemed unaffected by this crisis: the very people who had caused it. The principal beneficiaries of the coordinated bank rescues and quantitative easing were the banks themselves. The flood of government money stimulated market activity and the investment banks made hay. Profits in market-related businesses bounced back from the credit write-offs of 2008 and the bankers expected to get paid. But they had misjudged public opinion. The boring safe industry moved off the City pages of the newspapers into the headlines and the mood turned ugly when people read about their bonuses.[1]

The country was paying the price for their recklessness but the culprits appeared immune. The public wanted to shake them until the money dropped out of their Savile Row suits. Studio audiences at television and radio programmes such as *Question Time* and *Any Questions* booed whenever bankers were mentioned and applauded panelists who denounced them. As middle England vented, phone-ins were jammed with members of the public wanting to rant. Banks' annual general metings, usually dignified affairs offering small shareholders a day out and a free buffet, turned stormy.

A general election had to be held by June 2010, and politicians joined in the bank bashing. The Mansion House speeches in which Chancellor Brown had praised the City were now an embarrassment, and the prime minister tried to distance himself from the sector. He had influenced the Americans and led the European banking rescue but his own and his party's reputation for economic management was ruined. The opposition parties piled on the pressure. The Liberal Democrats' Treasury spokesman, Vince Cable, who had been chief economist at Shell before entering politics, captured the public mood: 'These people never learn. The bonus culture generated excessive and dangerous risk for the taxpayer and there is a real danger of this happening all over again.'[2]

The Treasury Select Committee became the court of public opinion. The Labour MP John McFall, a witty Scotsman, and former chemistry teacher with an eye for the mood of the man and woman in the street, had become its chairman in 2001. After the banking rescue package of October 2008 McFall decided to hold an enquiry and set up a website to publicize it, inviting the public to submit questions by email. Within a few days, over 5,000 questions had been received, an indication of the unprecedented strength of public feeling. Politicians, regulators and senior bankers squirmed under the committee's attack, dithering before questions such as 'Where has all the money gone?' and 'If you take the credit for the boom, why will you not accept some responsibility for the bust?'

The government needed to take a grip and had chosen Lord Turner to become FSA chairman when Callum McCarthy retired in

September 2008. Turner was known as an eloquent and trusted public figure, radical without being revolutionary, independent but never indiscreet. Then in August 2009 he surprised everyone when he was interviewed by *Prospect*, an intellectual magazine of modest circulation. In an unplanned answer to one question, Turner said: 'It is hard to distinguish between valuable financial innovation and non-valuable. Clearly, not all innovation should be treated in the same category as the innovation of either a new pharmaceutical drug or a new retail format. I think that some of it is socially useless activity.'[3] It was by far the most headline-catching thing he had ever uttered and the approval it received said much about public opinion.

BLOWING A RASPBERRY

One bank in particular should have been listening carefully to Turner. Barclays had enemies everywhere. The authorities believed that it had got off the hook by taking advantage of public backing in the form of liquidity support and use of the credit guarantee scheme. The Bank of England disapproved of its investment banking strategy. The FSA regarded it with suspicion. The public hated the compensation it paid its investment bankers. Now, the government faced an election in less than a year and needed to look tough. The Treasury Committee was on the prowl and the media had the banks in their sights. The disgraced managements of RBS and HBOS had departed, leaving Diamond and Varley next in the firing line. This was a time when Barclays needed to avoid antagonizing those gunning for it, but on 16 September, just a few days after Turner's *Prospect* interview, Barclays blew a raspberry at them.

In a very odd transaction, it sold a package of $12.3 billion of mortgage-backed securities from its own balance sheet to a newly formed Cayman-registered company named Protium. Forty-five Barclays employees, headed by Stephen King – who had once led Barclays' principal mortgage trading group – and Michael Keeley – a member of Barclays Capital's management committee – would leave the bank to run the fund.[4] They, a few colleagues and two hedge funds owned the business and borrowed $12.6 billion from Barclays to fund it.[5]

Barclays' intention was to reduce the size and volatility of its balance sheet. The $12.3 billion of mortgage-backed securities were held in the trading book which had to be marked to market value every day according to accounting rules. However if they could be reclassified as loans and moved to another part of the balance sheet, they would not have to be revalued daily and would carry a lower regulatory capital charge. At a time when every basis point of regulatory capital mattered, this would be a useful boost.

The deal was designed in Structured Capital Markets (SCM), the tax unit built up by Roger Jenkins and a clever lawyer named Iain Abrahams before Jenkins took over relationship management for Barclays in the Middle East. SCM was notorious, following the Guardian's publication on Monday 16 March 2009 of alleged internal memos sent by an anonymous whistleblower to Vince Cable. The documents revealed a number of elaborate international tax avoidance schemes in which SCM systematically assisted clients to avoid huge amounts of tax. Barclays immediately won an injunction to get them removed but the story was out. Cable told the Sunday Times: 'The documents suggest a deeply ingrained culture of tax avoidance. The Barclays team looks like the spider at the centre of a highly artificial web of non-transparent transactions through tax havens.'[6]

The Protium deal drew further attention to SCM and needed regulatory approval. Barclays' August board meeting was told that the FSA was approaching Protium cautiously. The board, however, gave more weight to management's arguments that Protium would provide a positive message to the market about Barclays' risk management capabilities. It was an extraordinary misjudgement.

Barclays' board at the time included the chairman of the National Audit Office, Sir Andrew Likierman, and former chairmen, of one of the UK's big four auditors, Sir Mike Rake, and HM Customs & Excise, Sir Richard Broadbent. Other board members had considerable public and private sector experience. They might have been struggling when it came to understanding the intricacies of derivatives, but they were politically experienced establishment figures who read the papers, watched the news and might reasonably be expected to pick up the signs the authorities were giving out.

Instead, they allowed Protium to proceed, contracting responsibility for oversight to a subcommittee, the Board Finance Committee, who considered it again on 14 September. It was informed by the management that although the regulator would not formally object: 'The FSA had found it difficult to get comfortable with the proposal. They were concerned that it would set a precedent and that the market would have difficulty in understanding the transaction.'[7] This should have been a warning sign, but with the approval of the Audit Committee, which had taken legal and accounting advice, on 16 September Barclays wrote to the FSA summarizing its plans before announcing the transaction later that day. There was no written reply. Barclays took this to mean that although the FSA had reservations regarding the complexity of the transaction and reserved its position on its capital treatment, it did not formally object.

In fact, the FSA's disapproval, which had been reinforced by a phone call between a very senior FSA official and a very senior executive at Barclays, was evident from the hard line it took on the capital treatment of Protium. The FSA insisted that Barclays include the portfolio when calculating its regulatory capital, effectively neutralizing the regulatory advantages of the trade. It was a deliberate act of retaliation by a regulator which was becoming increasingly concerned at Barclays' approach. The bank had just driven straight through an amber signal without even slowing down. Given the mood in Westminster, Fleet Street and the country at large, and coming just a few weeks after Adair Turner's 'socially useless' remarks, it was foolhardy. The authorities were starting to wonder what kind of parallel universe Barclays was inhabiting.

The bank's long-running attitude to Payment Protection Insurance (PPI) was another irritant. PPI was an insurance policy to cover debts in the event of illness, accident or unemployment. It had been a lucrative business for banks for over a decade, earning the twelve largest distributors of PPI products premiums of £3.8 billion and profits after tax and cost of equity of £1.4 billion; return on equity was an extraordinarily high 490 per cent.[8] If ever there was a case of something being too good to be true, this was it, and exactly the kind of signal the board should have picked up. Instead of asking why returns were so high, though, the banks loaded on sales credits for PPI sales;

by 2009, Barclays sales people could earn two and a half times more commission for selling a loan with PPI attached than for selling a straight loan.[9] Not surprisingly, they went at it with a will. But for some, profit overcame principles. Some borrowers were given the misleading impression that they had to buy PPI to get a loan. This was not true nor even relevant when customers were self-employed and hence not eligible to claim. In other cases there were legal exclusions which meant claims could not be made for common causes of absence from work such as back pain and stress.

Such tactics should not have been news to senior management. *Which?* magazine, the *Daily Telegraph, Sunday Telegraph* and others all campaigned on the issue. In November 2005, the FSA wrote to bank chief executives including Varley, identifying poor selling practices and lack of compliance controls in PPI. In public, Barclays appeared to be taking this warning seriously. In July 2006, Firstplus, a part of Barclaycard that sold PPI, had told visitors to its website:

> Of course, as a responsible lender FIRSTPLUS will never encourage you to borrow more than you can afford, and we'll help you choose a loan and repayment level that will fit easily with your lifestyle. However, sometimes the worst happens – people fall ill, have accidents, or are suddenly made redundant when they're least expecting it. And if anything like that happens to you, the last thing you'll want to worry about is meeting your loan repayments. That's why we suggest all our FIRSTPLUS customers take out our Payment Protection Plan.'[10]

The product was advertised with an eminently reasonable explanation from the television personality Carol Vorderman, well known as a mathematics expert.

But *Which?* magazine later exposed the case of one couple who in autumn 2006 took out a loan of £91,500 secured against their home, to be paid over twenty-five years. They borrowed a further £22,500 to pay for a Firstplus PPI policy that, by the time interest payments were included increased to £52,500. The insurance provided by the Firstplus policy lasted only five years and was capped at £28,500 for unemployment and £43,000 for disability; a life insurance policy could have been bought for a tiny fraction of the £52,500 paid for Firstplus.[11] This policy was sold less than a year after the warning letter from the FSA to chief executives, the year during which the Vorderman advertisements had run.

It was in 2009, however that Barclays' attitude to PPI really confounded the regulators. In January, the FSA banned the sale of PPI as part of loan and credit card packages but in May Barclays and Lloyds challenged aspects of this decision in the courts.[12] Taking on the regulator at such a moment ignored public opinion, the already clear evidence that PPI was a rip-off and the authorities' hardening attitude. Barclays had just squeezed through the stress tests, annoyed the Treasury and was on watch with the FSA. If ever there was a time to keep a low profile, this should have been it.

CORRECTING A MISTAKE

At ten-thirty in the morning of Monday 3 August, John Varley stood up at the Barclays auditorium at 1 Churchill Place. Behind him a large display screen in Barclays' blue showed the words 'Interim results presentation, 2009'. Before him sat dozens of journalists and he knew that hundreds more were listening online. But Varley was calm. He had been presenting the bank's results as chief executive or finance director four times a year since 2000, and for the first time since 2007 he believed he could really answer the bank's critics.

After a run of difficult quarters in which the journalists had pressed him about the bank's future, he now had an opportunity to push back. The recently announced sale of BGI had eased the balance sheet, Lehman was bedding in and fixed income markets were flying. He said: 'The investments we have made, particularly in our international businesses, are driving very strong income performance and allowing us to absorb the consequences of the economic downturn. Our capital base is stronger and we have significantly reduced leverage.'[13]

Leverage had fallen back in line with the industry norm of twenty times equity capital, Barclays was no longer under pressure to accept state capital and the share price was finally starting to show some life. That morning it stood at 276 pence. Varley believed he was within touching distance of delivering the bank's long-standing ambitions, an achievement summed up in the following morning's headline in the *Daily Telegraph*: 'Barclays makes the case for universal banking'.[14]

However, digging deeper there was a striking contrast in the two parts of the business. Barclays Capital was indeed flying, doubling its profits in the six months but Global Retail and Commercial Banking was struggling. Profits were down in UK retail, commercial banking and Western Europe and there were losses in emerging markets. The plan that Seegers should be a counterpart dynamo to Diamond wasn't working.

It was not for lack of trying. Seegers had embarked on an ambitious expansion plan in 2007 and 2008, trebling Barclays' branch network in Portugal, launching or expanding retail banking operations in India, Pakistan and the Middle East, buying Expobank in Russia and Akita Bank in Indonesia. By the end of 2008 there were over 3,000 outlets handling £80 billion of loans, a doubling of the business in two years.

Seegers had a deep knowledge of retail banking but his abrupt manner and impatience – identified before his appointment – made him unpopular. Staff lived in fear of him, going to extraordinary lengths to please him. He liked a certain type of coffee but it had to be hot. When he was expected on a branch visit, as the time of his arrival approached, junior bankers were sent down to the local Starbucks every ten minutes to bring in a fresh cup so that it would be piping hot when he arrived. Staff were afraid to bring him bad news, let alone to tell him that the data on the much admired screen in his office, apparently showing him in real time how the business was performing, was always badly out of date.

He brought an entourage from Citigroup and paid them richly. He was contemptuous of Barclays' lifers and showed them a bar chart comparing their lack of global experience with the experience of others – for example, his own. For senior managers, monthly performance meetings with him were a nightmare in which they were asked for quantities of information they believed to be unreasonable. Banking relationships take time to mature but Seegers demanded results very quickly. People felt under permanent threat: the message they took away was 'achieve results fast or get the sack'. It was all too pushy and flash. Offsite meetings were held in exotic overseas locations even when the majority of attendees was from London. Investment banking-style pay packages were handed out to people who neither expected nor needed them.

Seegers' style had worked at Citigroup in a bull market but he arrived at Barclays just as the banking cycle turned. His aggressive approach would have been tolerated if the financial results were good but his business was struggling and his acquisitions looked mistimed and overpriced. Barclays did not fully understand the new markets he took them into. They did not really know what was on the books of the banks they bought or what customers in Russian towns and teeming subcontinental cities needed. It was a round-the-world trip with a Barclays cheque book. Varley accepted his share of the blame: he had recruited Seegers and signed off on the acquisitions. He had to face up to his mistake.

In October 2009 he called Seegers into his office and was unusually blunt: 'I need a behavioural role model and a potential chief executive. You fail on both counts.' Seegers' contract was paid off and he left immediately. His empire was broken up and the cost of bad acquisitions and overexpansion of the global retail banking division eventually totalled several billion pounds.*

Varley's annual report for 2009 delivered in February the following year was impersonal but firm: in emerging markets 'we have been too aggressive in our approach to business expansion here over the past two years. This business must now convert investments made in the last three years (in terms of people, customer recruitment and sales outlets) into sustainable profits.'[15]

Varley had a successor to Seegers already in mind. Antony Jenkins had spent three years miserably keeping Seegers at arm's length. He had frequently considered leaving but Barclaycard was performing well and he could see the Seegers experiment unravelling. Thanks to Varley's largesse, he was well paid, so he decided to be patient. In October 2009, at one of their weekly meetings Varley told Jenkins:

---

* Retrenchment, closures or disposals over several years occurred in Italy, Russia, Indonesia, Uganda, India, the UAE, Spain and Portugal.

'Seegers will be leaving and I would like you to be his successor. You will be joining the executive committee immediately.'

CHRISTMAS COMES AGAIN

For William 2009 had been another good year. When he had run his numbers after the 2008 year-end holiday, he had decided that the stock market undervalued Barclays and other banks. In March 2009 the Bank of England began its quantitative easing programme – buying up financial assets – pumping billions into the markets. The Bank hoped that quantitative easing would trickle back into the real economy, but William believed that the influx of so much new money into markets would mostly serve to put a floor under asset prices and help investment banks such as Barclays Capital. As he did his sums, he realized that having caused the crisis in the first place, the banks would now be the first to benefit from the cure. Having originated the idea to sell, he had the full attention of the managing partner when he requested a slot at the weekly meeting. More analysis followed. Step-by-step they poured over the possibilities before they decided that there was indeed another opportunity. Over the spring and summer the hedge fund had rebuilt the position, watched the share price treble and taken profits in the autumn. At the end of 2009 they again rewarded William handsomely; he spent Christmas 2009 on a singles holiday in the Seychelles.

But in January 2010, the Thinker was still thinking. He came to the conclusion that BGI was a tactical sale forced on the board by outside factors that had far-reaching strategic consequences. It was taking Barclays away from a stable cash-generating business down the dangerous route of relying on the capital-intensive, unpredictable business of investment banking – and it would not take long for other investors to appreciate that. At the first weekly ideas meeting of 2010 he explained why Barclays had done it. BGI was easily saleable because it was a cash-generating business but was it wise to sell cash flow when capital was king?

The managing partner ran his fingers through his long black hair. He had seen this situation before: distressed companies selling prize assets to sustain a pet project when the pet project was really the cause of the problem. He knew that under pressure, strategic thinking goes out of the window. 'What on earth are they doing?' he asked. 'Wouldn't it have been better to pare back the capital-consuming investment bank? Have they become so obsessed with investment banking that they're no longer thinking strategically?' The studious figures around the glass table nodded agreement.

Emboldened, William described 'the sale of a cash-generating business to sustain a volatile capital-hungry monster as the worst trade ever'. The managing partner, who never liked emotion to get in the way of reason, narrowed his eyes in disapproval. Barclays had sold BGI partly because they had been told to, and this was no time for extreme language. But the men in their Boggi sweaters and ponytails had heard enough. The relaxation of the FSA's ban on short selling in January 2009 reopened possibilities and they spent the next few weeks checking the analysis, calculating portfolio risk, locating the stock to borrow and putting on hedges. William's big short was soon back on.

HANDING OVER

The light cut through the top windows of the Brompton Oratory, illuminating the high altar in early morning spring sunshine. John Varley felt at peace. Barclays had just been through global banking's most turbulent times. It had survived and was on the verge of becoming a fully diversified leading international bank. With Seegers gone, the twin towers were back under control. For six years there had been little time in his life for anything other than Barclays but now he was about to fulfil a long-standing promise to himself.

When he arrived at Churchill Place, he dropped in to see his chairman. It was an easy relationship and Agius was not surprised to see his chief executive. Varley's first words, however, were totally unexpected: 'If I were you, Marcus, I would have the next chief executive in place and ready to take over from 1 January 2011.' He explained that, in 2003, before he had formally taken over as chief executive he had told the then chairman, Peter Middleton, that he intended to retire when he was fifty-five years old on 1 April 2011; a note to that effect had remained on his file, largely forgotten. Agius probed a little, wanting to check if this was just a passing whim, but Varley had obviously thought matters through and was determined to do other things while he was still young enough to enjoy them.

If it occurred to Agius that this would be an appropriate moment to reconsider Varley's universal banking strategy, he did nothing about it. The Nominations Committee he chaired included two other investment bankers, Booth and Broadbent, and two other non-executives, Rake and Sunderland, known for their commitment to the grand plan. It could have been an opportunity to review the size of the investment bank in the light of steepening regulatory requirements. But the bank seemed to be recovering well, so they pressed on with the strategy.

Agius engaged a search firm to advise on Varley's successor. As he explained to shareholders: 'Given the size of our investment banking business following the Lehmans acquisition, we felt that knowledge and experience of investment banking would be essential.'[16] Once that decision was taken, Diamond was the only real candidate. They followed due process, produced a long list of possible names, chose one other investment banker to run against Diamond but the outcome was a foregone conclusion. He was one of a very few individuals in the world with the charisma, product knowledge and technical skills to manage the investment bank. The Barclays Capital franchise was Diamond's as much as Barclays'; now that it was back in profit after the write-offs of 2008, he was unstoppable and pretty much irreplaceable.

Diamond had built the UK's first globally competitive investment bank without spending a cent on acquisitions. Then the integration of Lehman had been successful, thanks to a 100-day plan led by Ricci: 10,000 Lehman and 16,000 Barclays Capital employees were put together, leadership roles were decided and 4,000 employees were laid off from overlapping businesses. There were clients to be spoken to, many of whom were upset at losing money in the Lehman bankruptcy, and claims to be dealt with totalling $10 billion from Lehman's creditors. But by September 2009 Diamond was able to say credibly: 'Today there is no European, no non-US institution stronger in the US than Barclays Capital. And there are no US institutions stronger outside the US than Barclays Capital. And that's a very interesting and a very good position to be in.'[17] By 2010 the investment bank made up over half of Barclays' profits and risk weighted assets and earned 16 per cent on equity, well above its cost of capital.

However, Diamond would need managing. Although he had been president of Barclays since 2005, he and Varley had slightly different agendas. Diamond's mission was to compete with the biggest players in investment banking – which he was doing; Varley's had been to build a universal bank of which the investment bank would be part. The chairman and board needed to sort this out with Diamond and he would have to change his lens as he stepped up to the role.

To British eyes, he came with baggage. He was American and there were real cultural differences. He was photographed playing golf with Phil Mickelson and socializing with some of the Chelsea players at Stamford Bridge where he had a box. The Bank of England did not like his style or his business model and his implicit criticism of the governor in September 2007 had not been forgotten in Threadneedle Street.

He also had an American attitude to pay in which the bigger the number, the bigger the success; this contrasted with the British, who liked to keep their pay quiet and resented ostentatious success. Diamond saw his peer group as the leaders of Goldman Sachs and J. P. Morgan and measured his pay against theirs; to ordinary British people, these were telephone numbers for faraway countries. Diamond's pay had indeed become a lightning rod for the industry. When he had joined the board in 2005 his total pay package was £6.5 million and had passed without comment, as did the £18.9 million he received the following year. These were the glory days of banking, the chancellor was bragging about the financial services industry and it was unfashionable to question bankers' pay.

But 2007, 2008 and 2009 were different. Pay became political in the years of the crash and as the general election loomed. In February 2009 a spokesman for Gordon Brown said the prime minister was 'very angry' about proposed bank bonuses and wanted bankers to waive them. The following month, a review written for the government by Turner linked compensation with risk taking.[18] In May, McFall's Treasury Committee report said Turner had not gone far enough, accused the FSA of giving insufficient priority to tackling pay and lambasted remuneration committees and non-executives for the 'ratcheting up of remuneration levels for senior managers whilst setting relatively undemanding performance targets'.[19] In December, the pre-Budget report introduced a 50 per cent payroll tax on bank bonuses above £25,000, a gesture the Liberal Democrats (soon to be in government) described as 'pathetic'.

Diamond's total package in 2007, 2008 and 2009 was £23 million, £16 million and £27 million respectively, including compensation deferred from previous years and profit on shares he had acquired in Barclays Global Investors. Although Diamond and Varley declined performance bonuses for 2009 (as they had in 2008), when these figures were revealed in February 2010, there was outrage. Peter Mandelson, no longer intensely relaxed about people getting filthy rich, described Diamond as 'the unacceptable face of banking'. 'He's taken £63 million not by building business or adding value or creating long-term economic strength, he has done so by deal-making and shuffling paper around.'[20] Vince Cable said: 'The issue the Liberal Democrats have been raising is why it's possible for extremely generous remuneration packages to be paid in a bank that has been taking such high risks and which relies on the taxpayers' guarantee.'[21]

Diamond met the members of the board in small groups at three board dinners and then had to see the regulators. By the Financial Services and Markets Act of 2000, senior managers in financial institutions carrying out 'controlled functions' needed regulatory approval and Diamond was interviewed by Sants at the FSA for three hours. At that meeting he asked about an enquiry into alleged manipulation of Libor by Barclays and other banks. US regulators had been investigating the issue for two years but the FSA had only become involved in May 2010, even though much of the alleged activity occurred in the UK. Diamond was told: 'We're aware of it. It is not currently a problem.' The regulator intended to imply that if circumstances were to change they might have to revisit the question, but Diamond didn't pick up any such signal.

Diamond's accession was a formality and the one other candidate to have a formal interview knew it. The appointment was announced on Tuesday 7 September 2010 and he would start on 1 April the following year. At Varley's request this was brought forward to 1 January.

The share price fell 3 per cent on the day of the announcement. The *Independent* noted: 'Mr Diamond had become the lightning rod for critics of the banking industry and "casino capitalism".'[22] According to the *Daily Telegraph*:

His assumption of the chief executive role is likely to be seen by observers as a defining moment in the institution's transformation from one that has for much of its history been focused on retail banking in Britain to an investment banking powerhouse that has ambition to rival its peers in New York.[23]

Investors warned that Diamond would need a strong chairman and careful preparation for one of the top jobs in Britain. The change from being the chief executive's deputy to being the man himself was a very big one and he needed help. That would not be simple, for Diamond was not an easy man to guide or to challenge. His aura of hostility to those with different views from his own was intimidating. In his new role he needed to lighten up.

These reservations were well known within Barclays, and Diamond should have been told explicitly about them. He needed public relations advice to keep a lower profile and a board that understood Turner's message about the social purpose of banking. He needed people around him with the courage to say that, for however long he was in office, personal pay should be the last thing on his mind. He was an American in a foreign land, a trader who had smashed through the wall of tradition into the heart of the British establishment. He needed firm and statesmanlike advice from the board, but instead he was left to work it out for himself.

HOW THE CITY DID FOR GORDON BROWN

Gordon Brown's reputation as the man who had led the world out of the financial meltdown of 2008 did not last long. Five successive quarters of declining output from the second quarter of 2008, a collapse in consumer confidence, banks cutting back on lending to bolster their own reserves and the bursting of the housing bubble ruined Labour's reputation for sound economic management. The City had been the making of Brown between 1997 and 2007 but the recession it brought about was his downfall.

After declining the opportunity to secure a personal mandate from the electorate in 2007, Brown was stuck and delayed calling a general election until 6 May 2010, the last possible moment. The campaign was a disaster for Brown who looked uncomfortable in live televised debates with the other leaders and was caught on a live microphone describing a Labour voter he had just visited as a 'bigoted woman'. He had to go back and apologize to her, despite which she unsurprisingly declined to endorse him.

The election produced a hung Parliament and again Brown clung on too long, trying to do a deal with the Liberal Democrats, who eventually formed a coalition with the Conservatives. David Cameron became prime minister, with the Liberal Democrat Nick Clegg as his deputy. Getting tough with the banks was one of the things Conservatives and Liberal Democrats could agree upon, at least in public.

STANDARD PRACTICE?

In June 2010 the new chancellor, George Osborne, announced that the FSA would be split up.[24] The Bank of England would once again have the lead in banking supervision through a new Prudential Regulatory Authority, and a new Financial Conduct Authority would take over the rest of the old FSA remit. An Independent Banking Commission was set up to investigate the industry headed by Sir John Vickers, professor of political economy and Warden of All Souls College, Oxford. The other members were Clare Spottiswoode, a former gas regulator; Bill Winters, a former J. P. Morgan banker; Martin Wolf, chief economics commentator at the *Financial Times*; and one Martin Taylor. The 'tough on banks' theme was continued with the introduction of a special tax on banks' balance sheets.

Cable, by now business secretary in the coalition government, expressed his concerns about Diamond's appointment, and at the soon to be dismembered FSA, Sants and Turner pondered how to reflect the new mood in government. Barclays had a long record of missing the regulator's drumbeat and they doubted that Diamond, now residing in New York, would be any more attentive. They resolved to make Agius aware of their concerns. Eight days after Diamond's appointment was announced, Sants called Barclays' chairman in.

Agius was handed a letter that approved Diamond's appointment but with some unusually strong recommendations:

> The FSA expects Bob Diamond to continue to develop a close, open and transparent relationship with his regulators both here in the UK and globally. It has already been identified that this will require an increased level of engagement from Bob Diamond and we have made our expectation known to him . . . As you would expect, we place considerable emphasis on the CEO setting the right culture, risk appetite and control framework across the entire organization.[25]

Agius read the letter carefully and thanked Sants without comment. To ensure the Barclays chairman had understood this was a very pointed, clear warning that the FSA had concerns about Diamond, Sants then talked him through it paragraph by paragraph, fleshing it out with examples of what had worried the regulator. He told Agius that the FSA expected him to explain all this to Diamond and emphasized the importance of taking Diamond carefully through the letter: 'It's what chairmen have to do, Marcus', he said. Agius replied 'OK, I've got it.' When he discussed the letter with Diamond though, the new chief executive simply interpreted it as standard regulatory practice and confirmed that he would be moving back to London.

'GOOD LUCK!'

The Christmas of 2010 was a white one in much of the UK. Snow began falling on 17 December and stayed on the ground until the middle of January 2011. It was the coldest December in over a hundred years, and families hunkered down for the long festive holiday.

In the late afternoon of New Year's Eve, as dusk fell over Hampshire, snow still covering the fields around his country home, John Varley – whose achievements would be marked at a board dinner in the 1 Churchill Place boardroom hosted by Agius – had one last job to do as chief executive of Barclays. He turned on his laptop and sent a message to Bob Diamond: 'Over to you! Good luck!'

Varley had been a great conundrum in the long line of Barclays chief executives. With his gentle manner, precise diction and good works he looked like a throwback to an earlier era of Barclays leaders. Although regulators regarded Barclays as being seriously out of line in many respects and distrusted the business strategy, Varley himself was well thought of. In contrast to Diamond, he had carried the authorities with him and was not perceived as the driver of a dangerous strategy. Chancellor Darling considered him 'one of the comparatively few bankers who could see the bigger picture' and regarded his support during the darkest days of the banking crisis as 'invaluable'[26] and even after he left, Varley continued to lead 'Project Merlin', an industry-wide initiative to encourage the banks to stimulate the economy by lending more.

The results for 2010 would show that he had seen Barclays safely through the crisis. He had taken risks – as we have seen, at its 2008 peak Barclays' leverage was over forty times its equity capital, the highest of any British bank – but it had worked. He had given Diamond the freedom to build a globally significant investment bank. He had avoided buying ABN AMRO at the wrong time and Lehman at the wrong price. He would be leaving a bank that had been restored to financial health and that was at last fulfilling his ambition for it as an important global bank.

Appearances, however, were not quite what they seemed. Becoming a top five universal bank was a strategy that was more suited to the previous boom and bust, shareholder value age than the post-crisis world of capital conservation. It would need attention from his successors. So too would the rising tide of reputational issues that were threatening to engulf the industry and to which Barclays was fully exposed.

Global regulators had worked out that there was systemic cheating going on in the banking industry and clamped down. The FSA's

18. Gordon Brown uneasily meets the people as the world starts to wobble, Southwold, August 2008.

19–20. Gordon's trouble-shooters: Lord Myners, Treasury Minister 2008–10, and Baroness Vadera, Minister for International Development 2007–8 and for Economic Competitiveness 2008–9.

21–2. First we take Manhattan: the Lehman building before and after the Barclays takeover, 17 September 2008.

23–4. Amanda Staveley in deal-making mode and the hard-charging Roger Jenkins, protagonists in the Barclays fund raising of October 2008.

25. The headline turns: the first and second editions of the *Financial Times*, 27 March 2009.

26. Happy days: John Varley, Bob Diamond (just announced as his successor) and Marcus Agius, chairman 2007–10.

27. Alison Carnwath, Super-NED: non-executive director 2010–12 and chairman of Remuneration Committee 2011–12.

28. Lord Turner, FSA chairman 2008–13, famously called some financial activities 'socially useless'.

29–30. The public stirs: demonstrations at Canary Wharf, London, 5 April 2011, and at the Barclays AGM, 27 April 2012.

31. Trying to deliver stability in very unstable times: Hector Sants, FSA chief executive 2007–12, Paul Tucker, deputy Governor, Bank of England, 2009–13, and Mervyn King, Governor, Bank of England, 2003–13, at the Bank, 24 June 2011.

32–3. Bob Diamond's wingmen: Rich Ricci, owner of the racehorse Fatcatinthehat, enjoying himself at Ascot, 23 November 2013; and Jerry del Missier, after giving Libor evidence to the Treasury Committee on 4 July 2012, the day after he and Diamond resigned.

34–6. Trial by television: Bob Diamond's grilling by the Treasury Committee on 4 July 2012 stopped work across the City.

37.

38.

39.

40.

41.

Sir David Walker (37), chairman 2012–15, appointed Antony Jenkins (38), chief executive 2012–15. Jenkins was summarily removed after a board meeting at Lucknam Park (39). The news was delivered by John McFarlane (40), chairman since 2015; Jenkins was replaced by Jes Staley (41), chief executive since 2015.

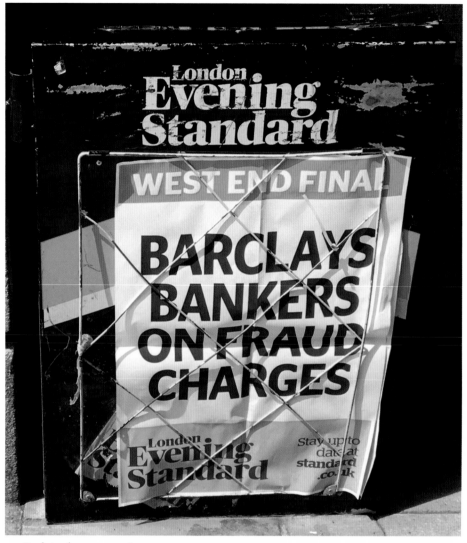

42. Back in the news, 21 June 2017.

43. Intensely relaxed: Lord Mandelson and Bob Diamond at dinner in New York, February 2018.

responses to Protium and PPI were examples of this tougher approach, which was matched in other countries. In 2010 Barclays paid $298 million, half in the form of a deferred prosecution agreement with the New York district attorney, to settle charges of breaching the International Emergency Economic Powers and Trading with the Enemy Acts in dealings with Cuba, Iran, Libya, Sudan and Burma between 1995 and 2006. It was a sign of things to come.

Although he didn't know it, Diamond had won a crown of thorns. A business model that was more suited to a past world, a hostile regulator, a business secretary keen to blame the banks for a sluggish economy and unaddressed reputational issues going back decades sat uneasily on the new chief executive's head. The swashbuckling American who had built an investment bank from scratch, got rich along the way and seen off all the internal competition would not have long to enjoy his prize.

PART IV

Humiliation, 2011–17

19

Thin Ice, 2011

1934 AND 2010 – LONDON

At the Grosvenor House on Park Lane, guests and visitors chatted and joked as they glided round the hotel's ice rink. The eight-year-old Princess Elizabeth had just finished a skating lesson and a group of expatriate Canadians were about to start an ice hockey match. It was a welcome diversion from events in the wider world, where the Wall Street Crash of 1929 had triggered the steadily deepening Great Depression, by now leaving one in five British workers unemployed.

A year afterwards a floor was laid over the ice-making machinery and the rink was converted into a banqueting hall, a vast subterranean space, lit by enormous chandeliers. It was named 'the Great Room', and it has been a place of celebration and congratulation ever since, no matter what was happening in the world outside.

Three-quarters of a century later, on a warm September evening, above the rusting and long-forgotten ice equipment, more than a hundred circular tables were laid to seat the 1,100 managing directors of Barclays Capital at the close of their annual strategy meeting. They had flown in from New York and other parts of America and from the financial capital cities of Europe, the Middle East, Africa and Asia to join their Canary Wharf colleagues for two days of briefing. This was the final night.

There were a few power-dressed women flashing the red soles of their Louboutins and a broader ethnic mix than Diamond had seen on the trading floors when he had started at Barclays in 1996, but most of those present were still white males. There were high-living

traders, introverted derivatives geeks, wily tax experts, studious analysts, extrovert salespeople, suave corporate financiers, sombre risk
managers and browbeaten operations chiefs; Barclays Capital needed
them all.

Very few had worked at Barclays when Diamond had formed Barclays Capital twelve years before. Half had come from Lehman, the
rest from the likes of Goldman, Morgan Stanley and CSFB, and they
had been shaped by wildly different corporate cultures. Many of
them were the mobile ones who scented the excitement, the challenge
and of course the personal opportunity, for money always came into
a decision to move firm. The early recruits had been through a minimum of ten hours of interviews and found a copy of Brad Smart's
book *Topgrading: How to Hire, Coach and Keep A Players* on their
desk on their first day.

Diamond's mentor, Bill Cook, drilled new arrivals on doing things
the right way, but alas he had become ill in 2007 and died the following year. The pace of growth was fast, standards slipped and the old
camaraderie had weakened. 'No jerks? It looks more like a jerk convention to me,' said one of the first recruits. Nonetheless, that evening
there was a victory buzz in the room. Diamond's promotion to group
chief executive had been announced only a few days before. Their
man had won and the managing directors had no doubt that he would
be strongly committed to the investment bank.

Barclays Capital now had two co-heads, the Canadian derivatives
expert del Missier and the American Ricci. Ricci had become Diamond's enforcer, growing wealthy along the way, particularly after
he cashed in his BGI shares when the asset management firm was
sold in 2009. He was a straight-from-the shoulder Wall Streeter. The
British considered him brash, wisecracking and overbearing. He liked
to gamble, and was sometimes seen at Walthamstow dog track in
East London. He was even photographed buying a lottery ticket in
Canary Wharf at a stage of life where he hardly needed more money.
He developed a passion for racing and in 2005 set up Double R
Stables to look after his racing interests.[1] One of his first jobs as co-
chief executive of Barclays Capital after Diamond's promotion was
to organize the dinner at the Grosvenor House.

Ricci had prepared a surprise for his boss: a five-minute video send-off entitled 'The Wonder Years'. He introduced it by ribbing Diamond: 'I'd like to say that he's too humble to recount what we are about to show in this video but you'll probably just have to hear it twice.'[2] A trumpet fanfare introduced a video scrapbook of Barclays Capital, beginning in 1997 with a youthful-looking Diamond talking about his plans to build a bond market leader. The film included a pastiche of the children's cartoon character Bob the Builder with Diamond's head superimposed, a clip from his first talk to Lehman employees and snaps of him with various celebrities, including the Rolling Stone Mick Jagger. It closed with a cartoon of Diamond dressed as Superman, heading for the stars.

To some of the British present it smacked of organizational hubris. A few of the old Barclays hands wondered whether Ricci was aware of a recent survey by *Which?* magazine that showed 81 per cent of the public believed that senior bankers had managed to avoid paying the price for their mistakes,[3] or that elements in the media regarded Diamond as the demon banker.

The one man who had tried to give Diamond a steer was unfortunately not present. Hans-Joerg Rudloff, a jowly seventy-year-old German, was an elder statesman of the bond markets. After Rudloff's distinguished career at CSFB and other banks, Diamond had made him chairman of the Barclays Capital Executive Committee in 1998, which impressed influential clients and brought wise counsel into the firm. Rudloff had long experience as a foreigner working in London, and when he joined Barclays he warned Diamond to be careful: 'Never underestimate the British establishment. They like to do business with foreigners to demonstrate their openness but my advice is to stay out of their affairs. Enjoy the welcome, keep out of the social scene, do your business. They are just waiting for a slip.'

Diamond had not heeded that advice. When he was running the investment bank, his public profile had been written off as Wall Street exuberance, but now that Diamond was running the whole of Barclays, Rudloff knew things would be different. Barclays was part of the country's economic and political fabric, a vehicle for transmitting the government's economic policy; the role of Barclays' chief executive was a position of symbolic importance and the establishment would be watching. Rudloff wondered whether Diamond understood the need to observe British traditions, to consult the authorities, to make courtesy visits to the governor of the Bank of England even when there was nothing much to say, to be respectful towards those in public life. Ricci's presentation would have worried Rudloff but most of the managing directors present loved it and gave their hero a standing ovation.

Diamond had achieved what he had been striving for since 2003 but now he had a difficult transition to make. It was a big step up from president to chief executive. After the Lehman acquisition, he had moved his family back to New York, where he needed to spend a lot of time to keep an eye on the US business. Now it was an awkward stage in the children's education and this time they did not buy in London but rented a house in Lygon Place, Belgravia. Heidi Smith, his assistant since 2008, moved him into head office at Churchill Place. He decided not to use Varley's corner office and instead set up a glass-walled office right in front of the lifts, where he could see and be seen. He left Varley's senior officers – finance director Lucas, risk officer Le Blanc and general counsel Harding – in place, trusting them to look after his own reputation as well as Barclays' interests.

Diamond decided straight away that he would continue with Varley's strategy, indeed that he would 'be focused squarely on increasing the pace and intensity of execution of that strategy'.[4] He was characteristically confident. Banking was changing fast as the regulators got tougher. Capital requirements were being increased, the Independent Commission on Banking – including, of course, Martin Taylor as a member – was discussing the separation of investment and retail banking, and a ban on proprietary trading was in the air. The US banks were recapitalizing and changing their business models. European banks such as UBS, Credit Suisse and Deutsche Bank were already cutting their balance sheets and withdrawing from some businesses. But Diamond maintained Varley's 13 per cent as the medium-term target for return on equity – it was currently making 7.2 per cent – noting that 'the difference in performance between winners and losers by this vital measure will be stark. Our priority is to ensure we are a winner.'[5]

This was typical Diamond: winner takes all, and I'm a winner. There was no serious board discussion of whether the Varley plan was still appropriate: that opportunity had gone when they chose as Varley's successor a man who had been in on the strategy from the beginning. A chief executive from the outside, even another invest-ment banker, would have carried out a strategic review, if only to check that everything was still in place. A more forceful and intel-lectually diverse board might have insisted that Diamond pause before saying publicly that he 'had no intention of materially altering the strategy'.

REMORSE

One of Diamond's first engagements as chief executive of Barclays was to appear before the Treasury Committee on 11 January 2011.[6] The Conservative Andrew Tyrie had taken over as chair from McFall after the 2010 general election. This public school and Oxford-educated economist – a former special adviser to Chancellor Nigel Lawson and John Major – was very different from the streetwise McFall but he was an equally persistent chairman. The bankers called him 'Andrew Tiresome'.

It was the kind of occasion at which the pedantic Varley had excelled and Diamond prepared carefully for his appearance. Initially he did well, setting out the case for Barclays' model: 'We have revenue pools that come from around the world; we have funding sources – both equity and debt – that come from around the world, so the financial stability of Barclays is stronger as a result of the integrated universal banking model.'[7]

Diamond described Barclays Capital as London's last shot at the global investment banking business:

> Having a UK-based investment bank in Barclays Capital, competing
> for the best talent in the world, doing business with our UK compa-
> nies and our UK corporates and being located here, is an advantage to

the UK. It's not a disadvantage. I don't know how the system would be better if these people were just located offshore.[8]

But then he ventured into more dangerous ground, warning of a consequence that the public would not like: 'Barclays Capital doesn't compete with Lloyds or Northern Rock. It competes with J. P. Morgan, Deutsche Bank, Credit Suisse, Morgan Stanley and Goldman Sachs. So we can't isolate bonuses and say, "Let's leave everything else in the business the same and just take out bonuses." '[9]

One of the committee members, Andrea Leadsom (later, briefly, a candidate to lead the Conservative Party and then Leader of the House of Commons) pressed Diamond, telling him that she had 'worked for Barclays and BZW for ten years'. She asked: 'What are we to say to our constituents who write to us in rage and absolute frustration that they will almost certainly lose their £20,000 to £30,000 per year jobs, and yet the chief executives who effectively, as far as they're concerned, got us into this mess, are carrying on business as usual and about to take home very generous bonuses.'[10] Diamond was dismissive:

> From big bang in 1986 until 1996, the investment bank of Barclays was BZW. I'll be frank; it didn't pay very big bonuses. I'll also be frank: it never earned its cost of equity. It was a business that had a weak client base, a weak international position and had a lot of push-back from shareholders who said, 'We don't want you to be in that business.' I am so proud of Barclays Capital. It's the only global investment bank that's been successful that's been built from scratch.'[11]

It was a robust performance and contained a measure of understandable pride. However, the lines that were remembered came in an unguarded answer to a question about lending. The banks were blamed by the public for causing the recession and then blamed again for not doing enough lending to restart the economy. Diamond said: 'How do we put some of the blame game behind us? There's been apologies and remorse from bankers. Today, how do we get banks into the private sector?'[12] What he meant was that the banks needed to stop retrenching and instead play their part in economic recovery by lending more to businesses, but the following day every paper had a similar headline.

'Bob Diamond: no apologies. No restraint. No shame,' said the *Independent*. The *Daily Telegraph* led with: 'Bob Diamond: "Time for banker remorse is over."' The bankers' bible, the *Financial Times*, was equally direct: 'Diamond says time for remorse is over. Barclays chief says bonuses vital to banking sector.'[13] Britain's trade union leader, TUC General Secretary Brendan Barber, later denounced Diamond as 'the poster boy for everything that is wrong about Britain today'.[14] It was an unfortunate start for the new chief executive.

Barclays earned some kudos for leading an industry commitment to increase lending and curb bonuses in February 2011 but the credit went to Varley, who had led the initiative, and the respite was brief. Later that year, the Financial Services Authority revealed that Barclays was the most complained about finance brand in Britain in the first half of the year[15] and the bank attracted further criticism when it unwound the controversial Protium transaction. It provided £532 million for impairments against its loan to the management company and paid a break fee of $83 million to the managers. The *Financial Times* reported:

> Some analysts see the Protium escapade as another example of Barclays' unnecessary complexity that has fuelled distrust among shareholders, holding back the bank's share price and rating the stock at barely 80 per cent of the group's asset value, a discount to many peers.[16]

The results weren't going to plan either. The global economy deteriorated and trading conditions in markets got tougher as the central banks' emergency stimulus eased. Barclays' profits for 2011 declined slightly and return on equity fell from 7.2 to 5.8 per cent.[17] Jenkins' retail bank performed strongly despite the costs of unwinding Seegers' expansion and the first provision against PPI claims (£1 billion) but there was a one-third drop at Barclays Capital in difficult fixed income markets. It was only one of many distractions for Diamond. He spent a lot of time in New York, where the Fed had raised a red flag over regulatory issues, and the transition to del Missier and Ricci was not going smoothly either.

The board now included two former Wall Street investment bankers, David Booth, formerly of Morgan Stanley, and an ex-Goldman banker, Reuben Jeffery the Third. The non-executives were pressing Diamond to replace Ricci and del Missier, believing that they were partly responsible for the poor results and a deterioration in the culture. Feelers were put out to former J. P. Morgan investment banker Bill Winters to see if he was interested in becoming chief executive of Barclays Capital, but nothing came of it.

26 MAY – BIRMINGHAM

The fax machine in Karl Edwards' study was chattering at exactly midnight at the end of every quarter spewing out the latest derivatives charge. Interest rates were falling steadily and Edwards, by now an avid reader of the financial pages, feared that his quarterly payment would rise still further from the latest figure of £12,000. On 26 May he had another conversation with the Risk Solutions Group at Barclays Capital which was once again failing to live up to its name.

Edwards proposed paying off the entire Barclays mortgage as a way of saving money for his by now hard-pressed business. He was told that this wouldn't be possible while the interest rate hedge was in place and that the break fee for the hedge would be £200,000. Edwards could see the fruits of his entire working life dribbling away into their grasping hands. He could not afford to give up and called the Risk Solutions Group weekly throughout the summer. Finally, in October the men in Canary Wharf allowed him to pay off his mortgage. It was a partial victory – but still left the outstanding matter of the interest rate hedge.

TODAY

On 3 November at his cramped desk at the BBC, John Humphrys stifled a yawn. The star interrogator of *Today*, Radio 4's iconic early morning news and current affairs programme, had finished his three hours in the studio and wanted to be home in Hammersmith catching up on sleep. Instead he was hunched over a banking brief prepared by other BBC journalists, and was struggling to find an angle. He had interviewed many bankers since the crisis and knew them to be slippery, well prepared and quick on their feet. That evening he was to record a long interview with Bob Diamond. Humphrys knew that the public would expect him to nail the Barclays chief executive, but he had not been given long to prepare and was worried that he would let the opportunity slip. In the dozen questions he had asked bankers before, Humphrys could see nothing that might tempt the American into an indiscretion. He pulled on an old green sweater he kept by his desk and settled down to study the brief.

Over in his office at Churchill Place, Diamond was also uneasy. He was to deliver the inaugural BBC Today Business Lecture that day before an audience of 200 invited guests at the new BBC Broadcasting House just behind Oxford Street – the prompt for the Humphrys interview. Diamond was media trained and had learned his script. He knew he would be facing a man whose job was to skewer public figures on live radio, who was quick witted, intelligent and always well briefed. He had a cross voice that rose with indignation if his subject did not give the answer Humphrys thought the public wanted to hear. Diamond had been through several practice sessions with his media team but none were as sharp as the BBC veteran and he would need to be on his guard.

Diamond's head was spinning as he practised answers to possible questions; he had been over it all so many times that he was getting confused. His car would arrive in a few minutes and he needed to clear his mind. He stood up from his desk, picked up a putter he kept in the corner and rolled a few golf balls along the carpet. He looked for inspiration at his favourite photograph of Jennifer and the children. Then Heidi Smith told him it was time to go and he made his way to the lift.

In the car heading into London, Diamond reread his speech. The theme was being a better citizen. A key passage ran:

> It's a very personal thing, but throughout my career – from my time as
> a teacher, to my time as a banker – I have seen just how important
> culture is to successful organizations. Culture is difficult to define, I
> think it's even more difficult to mandate – but for me the evidence of
> culture is how people behave when no one is watching. Our culture

must be one where the interests of customers and clients are at the very heart of every decision we make; where we all act with trust and integrity.[18]

It was what Diamond believed and he was happy with it. He stared out of the window and composed his thoughts.

Humphrys watched from the back of the theatre as Diamond delivered his speech. The banker was plausible and seemed like a nice man. Humphrys wanted to believe him. But to find out if what he was saying was true, he would press him as hard as he could on the issues that bothered the public to see if Barclays' story of being a reformed bank held up.

The two men made their separate ways to Barclays' headquarters, where one of the board meeting rooms at Churchill Place had been set up chat show-style for the interview. Humphrys planned to start with some general banking themes and then narrow the conversation onto more personal issues. He began by asking whether the banks were now safe. That was an easy one for Diamond and he patted it away: 'We do believe, in Barclays, that we are running the bank in a way that if there is event risk across Europe, that we can manage through that – because of higher levels of capital, because we have less borrowing.'

Humphrys picked up on risk as a theme. 'I take a risk,' he said, 'if I cross my High Street without looking carefully at the traffic but I would take a different sort of risk if I tried crossing the M1 wearing a blindfold. What I am suggesting to you is that that is precisely what you the bankers collectively have been doing and there is precious little evidence yet to suggest that you have mended your ways.' Pressed further, Diamond replied: 'I recognize none of what you describe when I look at Barclays.'

Thirteen minutes in, Humphrys turned up the heat. He quoted Mervyn King's view that the way banks pay out bonuses 'is a form of compensation which rewards gamblers if they win but with no loss if they lose and there is no doubting the rewards at the top for bankers'.[19] Diamond disagreed, arguing: 'There were definitely examples of pay for failure, there were definitely examples of banks having to take taxpayer money when things went wrong. We feel very strongly that that shouldn't happen, hence Barclays had better aligned compensation with risk through claw back and deferral.'

It was a set-up and Humphrys moved in for the kill: 'So Mervyn King has got it wrong?'

It was time to get personal. 'So you were overpaid. Just remind us how much you were paid during those good years. What was the best year you had?' Humphrys of course knew what the answer was – £27 million in 2009 – but he wanted him to say it.

Diamond felt his anger rising but remembered his training and told himself to keep calm. This was not the moment for one of his death stares. 'It is really nice of you to turn this on to my compensation but this is not about me . . .'

'But it is about banking and you are symbolic for many people of the kind of banker and – obviously you won't accept this – but bankers are lumped together into a group who are regarded as public enemy, that's the image we now have of bankers and you, Bob Diamond, were pre-eminent. So it's not irrelevant to ask how much you got at that time at the peak of your earnings.'

Diamond tried to swing from himself onto trust but Humphrys would not go away: 'You talked in your speech about being a good citizen but can you be a good citizen if you are earning maybe a thousand times as much as the average annual income?'

Diamond protested that there was only so much he could influence but Humphrys would not let up: 'To listen to you one might think you, Barclays, the banks, were everyone's favourite uncle, cuddly old banks doing just what we want. The reality is that you, Barclays, have had a vast number of complaints over the past year. People no longer think of the banks as somewhere they can go to have a chat with a friendly bank manager and sort out their problems. They regard them as the enemy.'

Diamond had one last shot: 'We can win that back. We can be cuddly.'

The microphones were switched off, they shook hands and went their separate ways. Diamond's team congratulated him but he had been beaten up and they all knew it. They talked about damage limitation in the media but they did not even consider whether any of Humphrys' points were valid. It was just another job done, it might have gone better, it could have been worse, but it was really only a presentational matter. There was no need to change anything in the way they did business.

Back in Hammersmith, Humphrys stopped off on the way home for a pint of London Pride at his local pub, cross with himself for, as it felt to him, letting Diamond off the hook. He knew he had not laid a finger on the banker's inner beliefs and that it was indeed just another job done. He had wanted it to be so much more.

20

A Boardroom Row, 2012

SUPER-NED

It was the perfect City CV: boarding school, good university, accountancy and seventeen years in investment banking, ten of them at Schroders, then retirement from executive duties leaving more time for opera and skiing and a late-stage career as a multiple non-executive director. But with her short grey hair and brisk manner, a casual observer could have mistaken her for a stern headmistress. Alison Carnwath was the only female chair of a FTSE 100 company, Land Securities. Marcus Agius had wanted her on the Barclays board for some time but in addition to chairing Land Securities, she already had board positions or advised an impressive list of companies: Evercore, an investment bank; Isis Private Equity, another investment firm; Paccar Inc, a Fortune 500 manufacturing business and Man Group, one of the UK's leading hedge funds. It was a busy life but she had the nous to know when to intervene and when to step back. When Agius approached her in 2010, she was aware that although Barclays had escaped nationalization, there was still interesting work to be done there. The executive directors were Varley, Diamond and chief financial officer Chris Lucas. Varley would be leaving soon, Lucas was relatively new and Diamond, the heir apparent, held all the cards. She wondered whether the rest of the board would stand up to him and looked carefully at their backgrounds.

A group of overseas non-executives reflected the breadth of the universal bank. These were Jeffery, the former Goldman Sachs investment banker who had been chairman of the US regulator, the Commodity Futures Trading Commission (CFTC), before serving in the administration of George W. Bush; David Booth, the former Morgan Stanley man with a reputation for tackling any subject; Dambisa Moyo, another Goldman Sachs alumnus, well regarded as a development economist; and Fulvio Conti, a senior Italian businessman.

She knew the British non-executives much better, led by chairman Agius. Richard Broadbent, an old colleague from Schroders, would be standing down soon. Simon Fraser had been a leading investment manager with the prestigious US firm Fidelity. She was pleased to see the name of Andrew Likierman, dean of the London Business School, who had previously been professor of accounting and financial control there. He had sat on the Cadbury Committee, been managing director of Financial Management, Reporting and Audit at the Treasury and was still chair of the government's auditor, the National Audit Office. John Sunderland was a respected former chairman and chief executive of the FTSE 100 company Cadbury Schweppes; and Sir Michael Rake, chairman of the crucial Audit Committee, would take over from Broadbent as the senior independent director.

They were her crowd. She knew most of them personally and had been shooting with a couple of them. They met at City dinners, the Chelsea Flower Show and the opera at Garsington and Glyndebourne. It was the Club. If you couldn't trust this lot, who could you trust?

Rake's presence was especially reassuring. His executive career had been spent with the accountants KPMG, where he had risen to become chairman. After leaving there, he joined the board of its British regulator, the Financial Reporting Council, and became chairman of the UK Commission for Employment and Skills and the charity Business in the Community. He chaired BT from 2007 and easyJet from 2010. When Prime Minister David Cameron invited a small group of business leaders to form his Business Advisory Group, Rake was one of them. There were few more prominent members of the British corporate establishment, and Carnwath felt confident that with him as senior independent director, the board would present a robust challenge to the executives. She met Varley, they liked each other, Agius was charming as ever and she agreed to join Barclays on 1 August 2010.

Just before she started, Agius called her with the news that a successor to Varley had been agreed upon. 'There is no one in the market who matches up to Bob Diamond. The job is going to him,' he said.

Carnwath had met Diamond and knew of his excellent reputation as a leader. She probed a little about the selection process, though. Agius said there had been a thorough search, but it was obvious that they had actually assembled a very small field, in effect a field of one. Diamond was undoubtedly talented and important to the business but she felt that more could have been done to explore serious alternatives. However, she was not yet a board member and was in no position to argue, so she thanked him for the call and said that she looked forward to working with them all. She was in for a shock.

Carnwath had never sat on a board quite like the Barclays board. The agenda was so full that there was no time for proper debate and there were too many people round the table, some of whom clearly had ambitions to succeed Agius. Board members asked polite questions but rarely followed them up with sustained challenge. In a fully functioning board, by her lights, management presents, the non-executives challenge, management responds, non-executives re-challenge and management re-responds. Then the fun starts. Other non-executives pile in and there is a vigorous debate. It was the latter stages that were missing at Barclays: the discussion never got down and dirty. When, as Carnwath believed she was paid to do, she asked more direct questions, she was taken aside and reproached for being difficult. 'That's not the way we do things here,' she was told. With a different board and in very different circumstances, it was just what Tom Camoys had been told twenty-five years earlier,

It soon became obvious that the board was in Diamond's thrall. In private, members would say: 'He is too headstrong, we can't hold him to account,' but there was rarely any sustained challenge. Agius was having chats with the chief executive in private but Diamond had them over a barrel. In contrast to the leading American investment banks, which were so well established that the corporate franchise was bigger than that of any individual, Barclays Capital was Diamond's bank. If he went, it did too. It was like unstable gelignite: with proper care, it could be used to blast Barclays to the top; carelessly handled, it could blow up in their faces.

With an ineffective board, the role of the board committees was crucial. In a small forum, without the executives present, Carnwath hoped that there would be full debate. Agius appointed her to Rake's

Audit Committee, a key body in the governance machinery. Share-holders were told that this committee's remit included ensuring that 'our control environment is robust and maintained'[1] and with a senior accountant at the helm, Carnwath felt confident it would be effective. She herself would chair another important committee, the Remuneration Committee when Broadbent left in 2011. In the latter at least, she would ensure that detailed discussions occurred.

THE RETURN OF 'LONG TALL SALLY'

After leaving Barclays in 2000, Sally Bott took a job at another financial services company and then five years later became global HR director for BP plc but had stayed in touch with Diamond. In November 2010 he called her and came straight to the point. 'I have an idea for you,' he said. 'I wonder whether you'd like to come back to work with me when I take over as chief executive?' It was a good offer from a man she respected. Sally and Diamond discussed it over a game pie supper at Wilton's, a traditional British restaurant in Jermyn Street, London, and she began work in March 2011.

The previous month, on 9 February, Chancellor George Osborne had made an important announcement. Now that the banks were no longer in danger of going bust, they needed to face up to their responsibilities. Osborne extended a special bank tax he had introduced soon after taking office and the major High Street banks agreed to lend up to £190 billion to business during 2011, including £76 billion to the struggling small and medium-sized enterprises (SME) sector. The Bank of England would monitor whether this commitment was kept. The banks also agreed to provide £200 million of capital for the Big Society Bank, a pet project of Prime Minister David Cameron to help socially oriented enterprises, and to chip in £1 billion of capital over three years to the Business Growth Fund, targeted at small firms in the most depressed parts of the country. The recently departed Varley had brokered the agreement on behalf of the banks and his role was praised by the chancellor: 'I want to thank John Varley, the former chief executive of Barclays, for the huge amount of time and personal commitment he has given to this project.'[2]

In addition to these lending commitments, the top four banks agreed that the aggregate 2010 bonus pool of UK-based staff would be lower than in 2009, Remuneration Committees would sign-off the ten highest-paid staff in each business area and the pay of the five highest-paid senior executive officers would be published annually (though they would not be named) as would the number and aggregate remuneration of 'code staff'– people whose professional activities could have a material impact on a bank's risk profile.

Barclays published its first remuneration report under these rules on Monday 7 March just as Sally Bott was starting back there. The five highest senior executives below board level received £38 million in compensation and would be entitled to £10 million more under a long-term incentive plan if certain targets were met. The 231 code staff received £504 million and stood to gain a further £50 million under the long-term incentive plan; in addition, they had £608 million in unvested deferred compensation.[3] Under the headline 'Barclays hands five bankers £110 million', the *Guardian* described these figures as 'astonishing'.[4] Bott too felt she needed to understand how such sums had been earned.

The problem, she found, lay in the incentive plans. The Barclays schemes paid out earlier than those at other banks. Targets looked easy. Market data showed that although compensation for most Barclays people was in line with the industry norm, in 2010 the top seventy executives were paid 35 per cent above the market benchmark for comparable roles.[5] There were too many side deals. Incentive pay of £3.4 billion was over six times higher than shareholders' dividends of £543 million and the closely watched ratio of compensation as a proportion of revenues was rising again.[6] For whose benefit was this business being run? The problem needed to be addressed as soon as possible or next year's report would be another embarrassment.

'SHOW ME THE REAL NUMBERS'

Diamond would have to be confronted. It would be a tricky conversation. Bott wondered if he would be surprised: had his top people been open with him? She knew that he had a Wall Street attitude to compensation and believed in rewarding high performance with high pay. When she told him that his people were being seriously overpaid, he would have nothing of it. He didn't believe the comparisons with other firms, who, he said, didn't disclose all they paid out. He had deliberately recruited good people at the top and top people were expensive. He had built a global investment bank without paying a single penny for an acquisition. It had not been done by magic and of course he had to pay people a premium to join. He added: 'When they joined, they performed. That is why Barclays Capital is top of the league tables and that is why the incentive plan is paying out.'

Diamond was busy being group chief executive and she was not connecting well with Ricci, who was both one of the architects of the incentive plan and one of the main beneficiaries. After a few months Bott contemplated leaving but decided to stick at it and engage with Carnwath when she took over as chair of the Remuneration Committee in July 2011.

The straight-talking American and the sensible Englishwoman met at head office. Carnwath came straight to the point: 'I want five years of data and I want to go through this name-by-name. I am going to hold you accountable. Show me the real numbers.'

Bott's story was one of greed gone mad: 'We are the highest payer on the street. The competitors all say we are driving up pay rates. We are Barclays Capital, not Morgan Stanley. No other bank has a scheme quite like our long-term plan.' Between 2002 and 2009, Barclays Capital's long-term incentive plans had paid on average £170 million each year to sixty people on top of their salary and bonus. Over the same period, the Barclays Capital LTIPs paid 80 per cent of the possible maximum, which was set at eight times average earnings. Bott said that the targets were clearly too easy and the cap was too high. That was why Barclays' top people were getting a 35 per cent premium over their already lavishly paid competitors.

Carnwath was not amused. Various remuneration committees over the years had agreed easy targets for executive management and had failed to take the precaution of properly capping the schemes' maximum payout. Her predecessor, Broadbent, had grown increasingly frustrated at the complexity and opacity of the plans and had simply refused to sanction the most egregious sums. Nevertheless, Carnwath heard of a senior executive below board level who had just received an annual award of £40 million and there were other payouts 'on the runway' that would also deliver extraordinary amounts. The board must be told at the next meeting and Carnwath insisted that Sally brief the non-executives beforehand.

That meeting took place in the Lehman building, the scene of many breathtaking pay awards during Fuld's time. Sally took the non-executives through the remuneration plans, setting out the special deals that various business units had negotiated over the years and the long-term incentive plan. She handed out a spreadsheet listing details of the top twenty-five earners going back five years. She laid out the total amounts that had been paid and the sums that individual executives had earned, name-by-name, year-by-year, just as Carnwath had asked. There was silence when she finished. It had all gone too far. 'We should all be fired,' one senior non-executive observed.

THE FULL ENGLISH

Carnwath now knew that by joining Barclays she had taken on the full English breakfast. During 2011 she attended thirty-one board and committee meetings and spent many hours unravelling the intricacies of the compensation plans. For this she received £158,000; senior independent director Rake, at £188,000, was the only non-executive to receive more. It was a proper job with proper pay but paled beside the £751,000 received by Agius and Diamond's £6.3 million. She was on a mission to bring compensation back under control and there was one signal she was determined to give immediately.

Diamond's pay was already an issue when her predecessor, Broadbent, had cut his bonus for 2010 from £8.75 million to £6.5 million after pressure from institutional shareholders; even Diamond's chief supporters evidently felt there should be some restraint. In view of Diamond's profile and the fall in Barclays' profits in 2011 due to difficult market conditions amid investors' concerns about global economic growth prospects, his remuneration would be of great public interest. The chief executive's pay was a matter for the full board but the group chairman always made the initial proposal and, as chair of the Remuneration Committee, Carnwath would be the first to hear it.

In January 2012 she and her husband were on a skiing holiday in Vail, Colorado, one of America's top resorts. Early one morning, before setting out for the slopes, she took a prearranged call with Agius to hear his proposals. 'Alison, good morning. I hope you are having a pleasant vacation and I'm sorry to interrupt you. As you know, this is about Bob's pay. Let me remind you that the maximum bonus executive directors can earn is two and a half times annual salary which in Bob's case is £1.35 million.[7] Bearing in mind previous promises made to him, his agreement to follow Varley's lead in waiving his bonuses for 2008 and 2009 and to defer other payments and the fact that he has achieved seven of the eight objectives set for him for the year, my proposal is that he be given a discretionary bonus of £2.7 million which is 80 per cent of the maximum he could have earned.'

Diamond's pay would therefore be £4 million with a further £2.3 million of deferred payment due to vest from the long-term incentive plan in a year when profits had fallen. Carnwath remained calm. She understood the mathematics but not the reasoning. 'Chairman, let me reflect on that. My initial reaction is that the number is too high. The political environment is wrong, the bank's returns are not good enough, shareholders are getting a poor deal. Surely the chief executive should be setting a leadership example? In my opinion, he shouldn't be getting a bonus for the year.'

Carnwath left for her day's skiing wondering if she was on a different planet, as well as a different continent, from Agius. Not only was the size of the award certain to be highly inflammatory but the accounts which followed would throw fuel on the fire. When Diamond was appointed chief executive, he was resident in the US. Coming back to the UK meant that under US tax rules, he would be taxed twice on some income. Barclays had agreed to pick up the cost of this under a tax equalization agreement, the first payment of which had been £5.7 million in 2011 and this was bound to be controversial.

Back in Britain, Carnwath put these views across in a number of further calls with Agius, and it was agreed that there would be a full discussion at the next meeting of the Remuneration Committee. The other committee members were Fraser and Sunderland. Fraser's old firm, Fidelity, had taken a stand against executive pay and he himself was prominent in the corporate governance debate. Sunderland had spent his executive career at Cadbury Schweppes, once a role model for responsible capitalism. Surely, she thought, there would be some recognition from such people of the need for restraint.

She was to be disappointed. The Remuneration Committee had asked Diamond to set an example when he was appointed in 2010 but his attitude to pay was well known in Barclays and in the market. Her predecessor, Broadbent, had grown weary of arguing with him and the committee had not pressed the matter. They were no more inclined to confront Diamond in 2012.

When the committee met at the end of January, Carnwath described Diamond as a talented banker who had done a great job in building Barclays Capital but he was being judged now on his performance as chief executive and the results for the year were poor. Profits and return on equity were down. The share price had collapsed again. These were not the right circumstances to shell out millions of pounds more to a chief executive who was already very well paid. She proposed that Diamond be given a zero bonus for the previous year. Agius, on the other hand, argued that Diamond had shown energy, skill and enthusiasm as chief executive and met most of his objectives. The dip in profits and low return on equity were due to external events and Diamond deserved his bonus. Fraser tried to find some middle ground but Sunderland supported Agius' proposal.[8]

Carnwath was outnumbered, but there would be an opportunity to put her case to the full board in a few days' time. At the start of February she held private discussions with individual board members to explain her position and try to garner support. The American investment banker David Booth saw how Agius' plan would be received in the British press. He suggested setting up a transatlantic phone call with her one evening. They agreed that he would represent her views at the meeting.

CROSSED LINES

On 9 February, the day of the Barclays board meeting, Carnwath had a prior engagement she couldn't get out of, a strategy meeting in Harrogate for Land Securities. SuperNED could not be everywhere, but it was a bad meeting to miss: as well as the discussion about Diamond's pay, the board would hear the bank's annual review from the FSA. This would be delivered by Andrew Bailey, an executive director of the Bank of England, who in 2011 had become deputy head of the FSA's Prudential Business Unit monitoring the big banks.*

With Lloyds and RBS safely in state ownership and the much bigger and well-capitalized HSBC popular in official circles, Barclays remained a worry. It was evident from Bailey's time at the Bank of England that the governor did not like its business model and that the Treasury still believed it was free riding off cheap government money. Soon after joining the FSA he was told of concerns about repeated gaming of regulators, Protium and PPI being prime examples, and discussed this with his bosses, Turner and Sants. They had had enough. Barclays did not understand that the world had changed. There were various investigations in the background in which Barclays and other banks stood accused of manipulating markets in virtually every financial instrument that could be traded: interest rates, foreign exchange, energy prices, gold, mortgages – you name it, and somewhere in some part of the world a regulator was taking a look at what the investment banks had been up to. Following Protium and PPI, the FSA (which was now actively involved in the Libor investigation) decided to use the next annual review to tell the board what the regulator expected and where Barclays was falling short.

Bailey is not by nature confrontational but it was time to give Barclays a strong message and he set out the regulator's concerns to the board. Barclays' minutes of the meeting record that Bailey reported:

> a perception in the market and amongst some regulators that Barclays was not all that it should be. Barclays is seen as relatively aggressive sometimes and Protium would be an example of being on the wrong side of the line. Mr Bailey emphasised that the [FSA's] relationship with senior management was good. However, at lower levels in the organization there was a desire to engineer solutions rather than find real answers to regulatory issues. An improvement in attitudes at lower levels would help the relationship with the FSA. Mr Bailey also noted that it was important that external attitudes to Barclays improved.[9]

* Bailey became managing director of the unit in July 2012.

The drift of the words was clear enough but Bailey had not quite nailed it, as his own later account of the meeting made clear: 'Had I gone into the board and levelled an allegation about Bob Diamond personally, then I think the board would have reacted very negatively. They would have challenged me on the evidence and I did not have the evidence.'[10]

He had backed away from confronting Diamond and by implication the other senior executives, the people regulators believed were really responsible for setting the tone. Barclays board members present at that meeting were remarkably consistent in their recollection that Bailey endorsed senior management that morning.

The board minutes recorded:

> Barclays was generally perceived as being too aggressive for a number of historical reasons. The senior leadership team took responsibility for the interactions with the FSA at a more junior level and the frustration that that was causing for the FSA. The board discussed the need to get the tone from the top right so that all interactions with regulators are appropriate at all levels. The issue could and would be addressed. The Group needed to be consistently on the right side of the line to rid itself of the perception of being too aggressive. Resolving this was critical to the future of the Group.[11]

It should have been an absolute wake-up call that should have framed the discussion that followed about the chief executive's bonus. But no one made the connection between the discussion they had just had with Bailey and a pay award that would be bound to annoy regulators, politicians, and the public.

After Bailey left, Agius explained that there was a difference of opinion on the Remuneration Committee, set out both views in a fair and balanced way and invited Carnwath's comments. She was listening in over the phone and said: 'As you all know by now, the chairman and I disagree on this matter. I hold the strong conviction that the bonus should be zero,' and she summarized the points she had made to the Remuneration Committee. She concluded: 'If we go ahead with this plan, there will be problems with the institutions. This will be highly contentious and the media are bound to pick up on it.'

The board members carried on the discussion and Booth put the case for a compromise, but in the end the other directors agreed to support Agius: Diamond's bonus for 2011 would be £2.7 million. They were, at root, frightened that their chief executive would leave and unwilling to risk that by reining him in. The board's diffidence meant that in effect he was controlling them.

If corporate governance at Barclays had lived up to the statements in the annual report about challenge and independence, shareholders would have been told that the chair of the Remuneration Committee had been outvoted on an important matter. But that was not how the upper echelons of the corporate world worked. Carnwath would not resign before shareholders voted at the annual general meeting. She believed in cabinet responsibility and would not dissent publicly.

While the board were discussing Diamond's pay, Bailey took the three-minute walk from Barclays' head office to the FSA building at 25 North Colonnade. He told Turner and Sants that he was not sure whether the message had really sunk in. The board seemed ready to blame middle management whereas in his view 'you really could not escape the fact that the culture of this institution was coming from the top.'[12] The right time to have made that point was at the board meeting but the regulators realized that Bailey had perhaps not made it sufficiently clear and Turner decided to take the unusual step of writing to Agius. Agius would know that chief executive to chief executive letters were quite common in the world of regulation but that chairman to chairman letters were almost unknown. A letter from Turner should guarantee that Agius would have no option but to inform the board and then the chief executive of the regulator's concerns. Bailey went away to prepare a list of the points Turner should make, Turner added a few of his own and the draft went to and fro. The letter would be sent in early April after the Easter break.

'DEAR MARCUS . . .'

As Carnwath had predicted, the publication of the annual report in March provoked uproar. Incentive awards at the investment bank had been brought down 35 per cent and across the whole bank by 26 per cent but Diamond's £2.7 million bonus and the tax equalization package stood out. Agius and Diamond toured the institutional shareholders ahead of the meeting explaining the board's thinking. The one thing they did not mention was the piece of information shareholders most needed: the opposition of the chair of the Remuneration Committee to the proposals. Even so, a number of investors, including Fraser's old firm, Fidelity, were vocal in their opposition. One analyst told the *Sunday Telegraph*: 'the fact that the share price is down 70 per cent in the past ten years and bankers still believe they're incredibly talented and need to be rewarded with all sorts of special bonus plans is just laughable.'[13] Business Secretary Cable said: 'This is a company that paid out three times as much in bonuses to its top executives as it paid out to its own shareholders and I think shareholders are drawing their own conclusions from that.' He suggested Diamond should 'listen to his shareholders'.[14] That opportunity would come at the AGM at the end of April.

Ahead of the AGM, Agius received a formal invitation to a meeting with Turner in the first week of April. It was a meeting of two of the City's most handsome figures. Turner was perfectly but unobtrusively groomed from his full head of grey hair down to his black laced shoes. Agius' tasselled loafers, signet ring and beautifully tailored suit spoke of a well-bred banker of a certain age. Like wary peacocks, they greeted each other politely in the waiting area outside Agius' L-shaped office.

Agius had no doubt that this was going to be an important conversation. He and Turner had met many times during their business careers, but they were not friends. Turner's set was the metropolitan intelligentsia, Agius' the corporate and country crowd, but they came across each other where the two circles crossed. Other than that they never socialized and there was no question that this was anything but a serious business meeting.

Turner set out the regulator's concerns and gave specific examples of the kind of behaviour which worried them. This included Protium, which was described as 'a convoluted attempt to portray a favourable accounting result', and Barclays' approach to marking-to-market, the valuations issue that Diamond and Le Blanc had explained to Myners and Vadera but which the FSA still thought was 'clearly at the aggressive end of the acceptable spectrum'. Other examples alleged that Barclays had gamed its calculation of the risk weightings regulators required it to put on its assets and had attempted to 'spin' the results of some European stress tests in 2011. Agius acknowledged that these had been controversial but added that everything should be considered in the context of the times. He said that the marks-to-market used by Barclays had in fact proved to be appropriate. However, he assured Turner that the board was aware of the regulators' perception and had adopted a more conservative approach. Turner returned to his office, checked and signed the letter to Agius and wondered whether anything would really change.

The letter, dated 10 April, laid everything on the line. It referred to the FSA's

> concerns about the cumulative impression created by a pattern of behaviour over the last few years, in which Barclays often seems to be seeking to gain advantage through the use of complex structures, or through arguing for regulatory approaches which are at the aggressive end of interpretation of the relevant rules and regulations.[15]

It finished by saying that

> the cumulative effect of the examples set out above has been to leave us with an impression that Barclays has a tendency continually to seek advantage from complex structures or favourable regulatory interpretations. These concerns are sufficiently great that I felt it was appropriate to communicate them directly to you, and to urge you and the Board to encourage a tone of full co-operation and transparency between all levels of your Executive and the FSA.

A TORRID AGM

Agius scarcely had time to do anything about Turner's letter before the AGM on Friday 27 April at the Royal Festival Hall on the South Bank of the river Thames. Most boards regarded AGMs as a chore, a chance for small shareholders to have their say. Long before the meeting began a queue of mainly elderly individual shareholders, huddled into their raincoats and anoraks and sheltering from the pouring rain beneath umbrellas, formed outside.

This time their wait was enlivened by agitators from the Robin Hood Tax Campaign dressed as the Sherwood Forest outlaw and pretending to fight a man in a dark suit and bowler hat for a cheque for £420,000. They claimed it was what the state subsidy was worth to every single Barclays investment banker 'because Barclays is able to borrow money more cheaply as creditors expect it to be bailed out by taxpayers if it gets into financial trouble'.[16] Another group, the World Development Movement, campaigning against global poverty, came on London's Barclays-sponsored bikes, wearing Barclays' eagle face masks and carrying placards saying: 'Barclays banks on hunger'.[17] It was a line that would have been particularly sensitive for non-executive director Dambisa Moyo who had written a book about how to make aid to Africa more effective.[18]

At 10.30 the doors opened and shareholders trooped into the hall to the sound of soothing music. Half an hour later the Barclays board filed on to the stage and sat behind their place names. Agius opened proceedings by welcoming everyone, then introduced a short video of the year with the statement that '2011 was a pretty tricky year'. He apologized for not doing a better job of communicating about executive pay and introduced the chief executive. At 11.20 as Diamond got to his feet, there were a few boos but he gave a bullish message, claiming that 'in the face of economic and regulatory uncertainty, we did not flinch'; he sat down to loud applause.

Carnwath had just flown in from Seattle and spoke at 11.40. There was lots of heckling as she tried to explain the Remuneration Committee's work. She said: 'Managing remuneration is a critical element of delivering returns to shareholders' – admitting, in response to an interruption from the floor: 'We realize that not all our shareholders agree.' She continued: 'The balance of rewards between employees and shareholders has to change.' A voice from the hall yelled: 'Why have you only just woken up to this?' She made no mention of her own opposition to the chief executive's pay.

At 11.45, it was time for questions. Despite Agius' request that these be framed in an 'adult and orderly fashion' it was a torrid session with several angry questions about Diamond's pay. A shareholder demanded: 'How can any bonus be justified when not long ago the shares were over three times what they are today?' Agius responded as best he could: 'We don't sit in a closed room and think about what we can get away with,' but he was already on the back foot. Questioners from the floor were relentless: 'Why are Barclays' assets worth 450 pence but the shares are 210 pence?' And the judgements were damning: 'You have brought the bank into disrepute.' It was 13.14 before the questions ended, a quarter of an hour later than planned. The private shareholders were then able to get to the drinks and canapés.[19]

The heavyweight institutional shareholders in big companies rarely attend the formal annual meetings, preferring to meet the board privately and to vote by post or online ahead of the meeting. Their silent vote would now determine the outcome of the two key Barclays resolutions: would the Remuneration Committee report be accepted and would Carnwath be re-elected? But because they had not been told about Carnwath's true position, just like the small shareholders, they were voting without knowledge of all the relevant facts. At 15.30 the results were announced. Both were comfortably passed by 73 and 79 per cent respectively. However, as they entered the summer of 2012, the fuss left the bank and its chief executive vulnerable to further criticism.

The storm over Diamond's pay did produce some changes. At the May Remuneration Committee, Carnwath reported that Diamond acknowledged the need for change and had given some ground. He had recognized that some of the historic long-term plans were rewarding staff too highly and had agreed to cut them. He also agreed to cap some investment bankers' annual total reward. Soon, though, he would have other things besides pay to worry about.[20]

21

Here Today, Gone Tomorrow, 2012

MAY 2010 – AN INVESTIGATION GOES GLOBAL

The feeble BBA inquiry of 2008 did not end regulators' interest in Libor.[1] A US futures and derivatives regulator, the Commodity Futures Trading Commission (CFTC), had been doing background work on it since April 2008 and that month asked the banks involved in setting the rate for information. The CFTC had no direct control over them and many ignored its request, but Barclays was one of the few banks to take it seriously. They hired McDermott Will & Emery, a Chicago law firm, to advise them and carried out a more thorough investigation than the overstretched CFTC, busy on an inquiry into suspected manipulation of oil price futures, could mount. The official Libor inquiry seemed to be going nowhere – in February 2009 the FSA endorsed a BBA request not to participate – until McDermott Will & Emery briefed the CFTC on Barclays' discoveries in January the following year.[2] Sensational emails, tapes of phone calls and chat room messages retrieved by Barclays convinced the CFTC that it had stumbled across an industry-wide scandal that trumped the problems in oil price futures.[3] It stepped up the inquiry, brought in the US Department of Justice and other regulators in America, Japan, Canada and Switzerland as well as the European Commission. On 6 May 2010, the slow-footed FSA finally joined the investigation.[4]

All the leading banks were now told to produce documents and emails and to make staff available for interviews, and this time they had no option but to comply. At Barclays, general counsel Harding and Agius decided to extend their inquiry and screen millions of emails and thousands of voice messages to discover the extent of the problem.[5]

The regulators' investigation ran for over three years and Harding played it by the book. He considered the matter to be sub judice and excluded Varley and Diamond from the briefings he gave to Agius and an informal board subcommittee. The other non-executive board members occasionally received updates in which they were told that the inquiry was industry-wide, that just fourteen Barclays Capital traders were involved and that Barclays was cooperating fully with the investigation. The inquiry rumbled on and Varley and Diamond got on with their jobs unaware of its emerging findings.

18–22 JUNE

In the middle of June, Agius and Harding received the global regulators' verdicts. The news was worse than expected. Ironically – given that it was Barclays' high Libor submissions that had interested Jeremy Heywood back in 2008 – it was the fact that its submissions had been suppressed on many occasions between January 2005 and May 2009 that upset the regulators. A serious control weakness was also revealed: Barclays Capital's compliance department had failed to respond to alerts about the manipulation three times during 2007–8.

In addition to sometimes posting artificially *low* Libor submissions during the crisis in order to make the bank appear strong, Barclays' derivatives traders had also pressed its Libor submitters to manipulate rates – higher or lower – to benefit their own and external traders' trading positions. As Libor was the benchmark for pricing trillions of dollars of derivatives and interest rate contracts, a small change in either direction could earn millions for the banks and their traders' bonus pots.

The combination of misrepresentation, manipulation and poor controls was bound to be damaging. It was only a few weeks since Turner, already aware of the Libor findings – as Agius now realized – had warned Barclays of the need to clean up its act. Barclays' response would be watched closely.

Agius took the matter to the board, who were shocked at the revelations. However, they were told that the small number of Barclays' people involved and the bank's cooperation with the authorities in disclosing events and settling early would earn it goodwill and a smaller penalty. Faced with a tactical dilemma, they agreed that it was pointless to string things along and decided to seek a prompt settlement, subject to the advice of Brunswick's Alan Parker. Parker's advice was indeed to settle early and get the bad news out of the way in the hope of putting the matter behind them as quickly as possible.

Barclays' legal advisers negotiated a settlement with the authorities, which was signed off by senior independent director Rake and Agius, and reported both to the board subcommittee and to the full board. Though the next week would be uncomfortable, by settling early they were saving shareholders a lot of money and other banks would have to follow. They had no idea of the strength of the storm that was about to break.

23 AND 24 JUNE

With his family still in the US, Diamond had the house in Belgravia to himself and plenty of time to catch up on work over the weekend. Top of the list was the regulators' final statement, which Barclays had just received. He had been briefed that Libor would be seen as an industry issue, that the regulators would praise Barclays for its cooperation and that shareholders would approve of the financial settlement. It would be embarrassing for the bank but not for him personally. The regulators had not raised his own involvement at his approval interview in August 2010 or during the investigation.

Diamond clicked on the attachment to an email from Barclays' legal department and waited for it to download. Nothing happened. He clicked again. Still nothing. The internet connection was slow and he was getting frustrated. Finally the technology worked and he started to read. As he worked through the documents he felt physically sick.

The FSA had not previously disclosed its intention to quote from chat room messages and emails between traders. A Barclays Capital derivatives trader had asked: *'If it's not too late low 1m and 3m would be nice, but please feel free to say "no" . . . Coffees will be coming your way either way, just to say thank you for your help in the past few weeks.'* The submitter responded: *'Done . . . for you big boy.'* An external trader thanked a Barclays' trader for arranging a fix: *'Dude. I owe you big time! Come over one day after work and I'm opening a bottle of Bollinger.'* Such revelations by the FSA were not the balanced judgement he had been led to expect. His traders had been manipulating an important global benchmark and regarding it as a bit of sport to be rewarded with free champagne. When the news broke, it was going to need very, very careful handling of shareholders and the media.

Diamond spent the first half of the next week working out a detailed plan with Barclays' corporate communications and investor relations people. He made a few calls to Barclays' bigger shareholders, telling them that the bank intended to get out in front with an early settlement of an industry-wide issue and that the news would break shortly. There would have to be media, employee and investor briefings; Diamond would need to lead them. In the second half of the week he was due to be in Maine to chair a meeting of the board of trustees of Colby College. He asked the vice-chair to stand in for him and started to rehearse his lines.

27 JUNE – THE VERDICT

At two o'clock in the afternoon London time (nine in the morning New York time) on Wednesday 27 June the FSA, the CFTC and the US Department of Justice announced their verdict. A settlement had been agreed with Barclays, respectively fining the bank £59.5 million, $200 million and $160 million. The FSA gave Barclays a 30 per cent discount for prompt payment and the US Department of Justice praised Barclays' 'extraordinary co-operation'. The FSA's fine was the largest ever imposed by the British regulator and its summary of the issues was brutal:

> Barclays' breaches of the FSA's requirements encompassed a number
> of issues, involved a significant number of employees and occurred
> over a number of years. Barclays' misconduct included:

- making submissions . . . that took into account requests from Barclays' interest rate derivatives traders. These traders were motivated by profit and sought to benefit Barclays' trading positions;
- seeking to influence the . . . submissions of other banks contributing to the rate setting process; and
- reducing its LIBOR submissions during the financial crisis as a result of senior management's concerns over negative media comment.

In addition, Barclays failed to have adequate systems and controls in place . . . until June 2010 and failed to review its systems and controls at a number of appropriate points. Barclays also failed to deal with issues relating to its LIBOR submissions when these were escalated to Barclays' Investment Banking compliance function in 2007 and 2008.[6]

Tracey McDermott, the FSA's acting director of enforcement and financial crime, said: 'Barclays' misconduct was serious, widespread and extended over a number of years.'[7]

Diamond announced that 'to reflect our collective responsibility as leaders, Chris Lucas, Jerry del Missier, Rich Ricci and I have voluntarily agreed with the Board to forgo any consideration for an annual bonus this year.'[8] Leading shareholders privately praised Barclays for negotiating a good settlement, the share price initially rose and the board's optimism that this would be a storm in a teacup appeared vindicated.

28 JUNE

The morning headlines told a different story and led with plenty of quotations from the most salacious of the traders' chat room messages. Investors realized that this was going to be a bigger deal than they had first thought and the Barclays share price fell 19 per cent that morning. The public was shocked by this insight into the City's dealing rooms, a world they had long suspected but had never been able to prove was bent. At this stage, no one could actually say what they had lost personally as a result of Libor being manipulated but it was a symbol of all that was wrong with banking.

The country was still suffering from the recession, public services were being squeezed by the government's austerity programme, yet the bankers had gone unpunished. This was the opportunity to hold them to account and Barclays became the focus of the public anger that had been building up since the crash.

The *Economist* noted:

> Barclays has tried its best to present these incidents as the actions of a few rogue traders. Yet the brazenness with which employees on various Barclays trading floors colluded, both with one another and with traders from other banks, suggests that this sort of behaviour was, if not widespread, at least widely tolerated.[9]

Nils Pratley at the *Guardian* wondered 'why no director of Barclays has offered his resignation – a voluntary waiving of boardroom bonuses is woefully inadequate'.[10]

A major shareholder said: 'Taking off a couple of million from Bob's bonus isn't enough. People should be considering resignations. This has happened under the board's nose. Where is the accountability?' Lord Oakeshott, an ally of Business Secretary Cable, said: 'If Bob Diamond had a scintilla of shame, he would resign.'[11] Even the prime minister, David Cameron, waded in, pointedly saying that Barclays' management has 'serious questions to answer'.[12]

29 JUNE – BIRMINGHAM

Karl Edwards had had enough. By 2012 he knew a lot about interest rate derivatives. He knew that every cut in interest rates increased the payments he had to make under the structured collar that Barclays had sold him. Now he read that Barclays had been suppressing Libor rates from 2005 to 2009, and the bank's behaviour took on a whole new dimension. He and thousands of other small businesses who had been persuaded to buy structured collars had been cheated, not just by the mis-selling at the point of sale but by the bank's deliberate falsification of interest rates. This was not a victimless crime: Libor did have victims, and he was one.

He read the regulators' description of Barclays' 'extraordinary co-operation' with astonishment. His experience and that of other structured collar victims he met through the pressure group Bully Banks was of obfuscation, delay and indifference. The supportive bank he had known since 1993 had been replaced by a cold-hearted monster. It refused to engage with him on anything, let alone the structured collar: 'we explained it to you, you signed up to it, it's your problem' summed up their attitude on the rare occasions he could get someone to talk to him.

And by 2012 quite some problem it was. With the British economy still flat on its back, consumer spending on discretionary items such as records and DJ equipment fell. The Bank of England cut interest rates to 0.5 per cent in March 2009 in an effort to stimulate spending but for Edwards and others who had bought interest rate hedging products, this made matters worse not better. With declining sales and penalty payments on its structured collar totalling £175,000, October House Records was in serious financial trouble.

Edwards heard from Bully Banks that there were many other small business owners who had been sold interest rate hedging products by their bank. The FSA was apparently looking into the issue and Edwards had heard that a settlement was expected shortly. He decided to get his own report from a derivatives expert. In June he and the expert met the latest relationship manager and Carol's successor as corporate risk manager. The expert's report alleged serious deficiencies in the sales process, so Edwards asked for a refund of all payments and immediate cancellation of the derivatives contract. The corporate risk manager argued that Barclays Capital had not given any advice, that Edwards was an experienced businessman and he denied Barclays' liability.

Edwards was stunned. He had documents coming from Barclays Capital's Corporate Risk *Advisory* team; on social media Carol had described her role as 'advising clients' and Edwards had no doubt that she had advised him. However, Barclays was clearly going to be difficult and he wanted to move his life forward. He decided to fold the business. He left the meeting and immediately phoned a liquid-ator, asking him to put October House Records into voluntary liquidation. In the West Midlands in the midst of a recession, the liquid-ator was busy. 'The first date I have is Friday 29 June.' Edwards said: 'Let's do it then.' First thing in the morning on 29 June, October House Records closed, making twenty-six people redundant.

That very day the FSA revealed the results of its inquiry. It agreed with Barclays, HSBC, Lloyds and RBS that the banks would review all sales of interest rate hedging products made to 'unsophisticated customers' since December 2001 and provide appropriate redress to those who were sold structured collars.[13] The banks involved agreed to stop marketing interest rate structured collars to retail and small business customers.[14]

That afternoon, as Edwards read the announcement on the FSA website, his anger mounted. He had no doubt that he was one of the cases identified by the FSA and that he would be entitled to compen-sation. But he had just wound up the fruits of over twenty years' work and put twenty-six young people out of work. If he had known that this was coming, the business would have survived. The banks' settle-ment with the FSA must have been on the cards for weeks; why hadn't Barclays mentioned it to him when they had met just a couple of weeks before? These people were disgusting.

THE SAME DAY – LONDON

Barclays' share price closed the week at 150 pence, a fall of 15 per cent since the Libor announcement, and a board meeting was held that evening to take stock. It was a sombre affair. The reputational damage was far greater than the board had anticipated, and there was clearly a requirement for further action. For the first time, there was discussion – in Diamond's absence – about whether he should be asked to resign. The external adviser present was James Leigh Pem-berton of Credit Suisse, who had spoken that week to Barclays' largest investors. He reported that: 'The one outcome that the share-holders did not want to see was the removal of Bob Diamond as they believed in him as a very effective Chief Executive.'[15] The board were relieved. Just as Varley had realized back in 2003, they couldn't exe-cute the strategy without the man. They decided that Diamond was responsible but not culpable and that the loss of his bonus was indeed the appropriate punishment. Then they just hoped that they would be able to ride out the storm.

As the meeting closed, Agius was given a note to call FSA chairman Turner as soon as possible. Turner had read the FSA's final notice a few days before it was released and knew that it was going to be a very big public issue. Sants was on leave and would not come back to the office before stepping down and Turner was now executive chairman. The previous day he and Andrew Bailey had sat down to talk through what their response should be to the press reaction to their announcement. Barclays' gesture in waiving the bonus payments of the four senior men was clearly insufficient. That afternoon they would be observing a rehearsal at the Bank of England for the next day's Financial Policy Committee press conference and they decided to discuss the matter with Governor King.

They were exasperated. Barclays was still not getting it. Despite Sants' letter after the appointment of Diamond, Bailey's address to the February board, Turner's letter and meeting with Agius, the uproar over Diamond's bonus and now a public shaming, Barclays was apparently still not willing to reform. This could not be allowed to continue. A bank that ignored its regulators was effectively out of control. They decided that in public they would say that the culture was for Barclays' board to deal with, but would work behind the scenes to get a tougher response.

Less than three months after the first chairman-to-chairman meeting, it was time for a further conversation. Now there was something else that Turner needed to tell Agius. The FSA had just heard from the Serious Fraud Office that it was investigating some of the commercial arrangements between Barclays and Qatar Holding LLC in relation to the fund raisings of 2008.[16] It would not be an easy discussion.

When Agius called him as requested, Turner said: 'You must have had a difficult week. I'm afraid I am calling with more bad news.' He told him about the SFO investigation, then turned to the subject of Libor:

> 'I'm sure you are considering whether you can continue with Bob Diamond as CEO. Let me be clear. We have not found anything against Bob Diamond, so we are not in a position to give, and we are not giving,

any instruction or direction that we don't consider him fit and proper or appropriate to do this job. But you have to think about whether he is the right person to lead the substantive change which is required in the culture, given his association with some of the things in the past.'[17]

Agius asked him to elaborate. Turner replied:

As a board, you need to think not just about whether Diamond is capable of leading that substantive change, but also about whether the external world would perceive that. I think perception is part of the reality in these circumstances and it is something you have to take into account. You have to think about whether that is something which Bob Diamond will find impossible, or simply too difficult to do. You also need to consider whether Bob the brand is now something which isn't going to work.[18]

Turner thought that Agius could not ignore this warning. He rang Bailey afterwards and said: 'I would be quite surprised if the net effect is not that Bob Diamond resigns.'[19]

Agius, however, felt differently. The regulators had found nothing concrete against Diamond and shareholders had made it clear that they wanted him to stay. So stay he would.

30 JUNE AND 1 JULY

Diamond and his executive team spent the weekend at Barclays' offices in Canary Wharf and Brook Street, Mayfair, crafting a 'business as usual' communications brief to staff, customers and shareholders, a letter to the media and booking television slots for Diamond. Over in Chelsea, Agius was doing some thinking of his own.

A few weeks before, in a series of badly handled conversations, the board had asked him to step down early as chairman. Agius had not seen this coming and was not happy. The board had the end of September in mind as the date for his departure but Agius had resisted leaving before the 2013 AGM, which would be in April. After some discussion with Mike Rake, a compromise had been reached that he would go at the end of December, by which time he would have been chairman for six years.

Agius now wondered whether he should go straight away. He would be off soon anyway and as the ultimate person responsible for the reputation of the bank, he felt that he should perhaps resign as a matter of principle. It might also draw some of the fire away from Diamond and make the chief executive more secure. He discussed the situation with his wife, Kate, and called David Mayhew, who was on a fishing holiday in Scotland. Mayhew advised that there was nothing Agius could do that would make Diamond's position any better. 'As far as the regulators are concerned, Bob is the critical person. Your resignation would make no difference.'

That evening, still musing, Agius cycled the twenty minutes from his house in Chelsea Square to Diamond's home in Lygon Place. They drank some wine and Diamond told him about his day's work, drafting an announcement planned for Monday, which would unveil a review of what had gone wrong and a new code of conduct for employees. Agius said nothing about his own position but he returned to Chelsea believing that Diamond was worth saving. That Saturday night he decided he should go, told Rake on the Sunday morning and conveyed it to the board on Sunday afternoon. By the Sunday night, the news had already leaked out and had been reported by the ever well-informed Robert Peston at the BBC.[20]

In Brook Street Diamond and his communications team cranked up their preparations. They rehearsed Diamond for his media interviews, filmed a video that would be released to staff the next day and finalized the open letter, now adding a tribute to Agius. Diamond briefed Bailey at the FSA, and went to bed believing that the board, investors and regulators were right behind him as chief executive.

THE GOVERNOR MOVES IN

On Monday morning 2 July, Agius released a statement he had drafted personally:

Last week's events – evidencing as they do unacceptable standards of behaviour within the bank – have dealt a devastating blow to Barclays' reputation. As Chairman, I am the ultimate guardian of the bank's reputation. Accordingly, the buck stops with me and I must acknowledge responsibility by standing aside.

The board had accepted Agius' resignation on the Sunday and confirmed their support for Diamond. Agius would 'remain in post until an orderly succession is assured'. Mike Rake was appointed deputy chairman and 'the search for a successor both from within existing board members and from outside ... will commence immediately', led not (as might have been expected) by the deputy chairman but by John Sunderland.[21]

Over at the Bank of England Sir Mervyn King – he had been knighted in 2011 – was entering the last year of his second five-year term as governor. His career in Threadneedle Street went back to 1991, and during those years he had come to distinguish between what he later described as 'the respectable activities of traditional banking, managing the deposits of and lending prudently to established customers and the "splendid financiering" of those who cross the boundary into more dubious practices'.[22] The last five years had convinced him that Barclays had moved from the former to the latter group, a move epitomized by its chief executive Bob Diamond.

King, a keen Aston Villa supporter, occasionally met Diamond in the directors' box at Chelsea or the Barclays' box at Arsenal when his team were playing in London. They both played tennis too, but although King invited Varley to play with him on the exclusive courts at Wimbledon where he was a committee member, there was no such invitation for Diamond. Both had originally trained as economists but their lifestyles changed radically after Diamond left academia for business. He sometimes earned more in a year than King had in his lifetime, and while Diamond flew in private jets, the governor booked economy class on a Bank of England ticket in austerity-hit Britain. Diamond had publicly implied that King's response to the banking crisis was slow, and he stood for a type of banking King mistrusted. Always polite to each other, philosophically and personally they were a long way apart.

As the weekend drew to a close with no news from Barclays, King was surprised to learn from the BBC website that in fact it was Agius not Diamond who had resigned.[23] Breaking the news in this way was typical of the industry's inability to respect the proper channels, let alone make the right decision. The Barclays problem had been building for a long time and he wanted it sorted. He called Turner and Bailey to enquire whether they had been informed of the decision and was astonished to learn that they had heard nothing from Barclays either. Nor, apparently, had Chancellor Osborne.

Turner and Bailey had been nonplussed by Agius' resignation. Before the weekend their plan had been to allow things to settle down and for Diamond to leave after due process, probably followed by Agius once a new chief executive was in place, but that had now been turned on its head. They could not countenance one of their biggest and most problematical regulated firms being without a chairman and a chief executive: Diamond would have to stay on. Turner and Bailey sat down together on the Monday morning and wondered: 'What should we do now?' They did not have long to wait before the governor took things out of their hands.

Although King thought Agius' intentions had been honurable, his resignation put his successor in a difficult position.[24] He doubted if the last had been heard of Barclays' reputational issues with further inquiries into matters such as PPI and possible criminal prosecutions over Libor. A new chairman would either have to buy into Diamond despite those worries or demand his removal as a condition for taking the job.

Polite chats, stiff communications and Turner's unambiguous letter had all been ignored. Barclays was in a state of denial and needed to be told that these concerns had been shared with the Bank. He did not consult his deputy governors, as would have been his normal practice before making an important decision, but spoke to the Bank's chief legal adviser, who outlined what he could and could not say.[25] He told Turner, Bailey and Osborne that he planned to call in Barclays' chairman and senior independent director that day, adding that he was not looking for the FSA's or the Treasury's advice or permission to do so and that he would not be speaking on their behalf. King later told the Treasury Committee that the point of the meeting, which was set up for six in the evening at the Bank of England, was to say to Agius and Rake: 'Look, you really need to understand the depths of the concerns that the regulators have about executive management. I want you to go away and reflect on that.'[26] But Turner and Bailey, as they discussed the call, were uneasy. King had not been specific about his intentions and this could all get very confusing. Turner decided to call the Bank and the Treasury to set out his concerns.

That morning Agius' office received a message from the governor's office saying that King wished to see Agius and Rake that evening. As he briefed colleagues on the reasons for his resignation, Agius had no sense that it would be a climactic meeting.

He and Rake arrived at the Bank just before six and were waiting in the governor's anteroom when King burst in, bristling. He said that although this was an informal meeting, the prime minister and the chancellor knew that it was taking place. He had spoken to the regulators who had no confidence in the executive management. Determining an institution's culture was a matter for the executive management, not the non-executive chairman. 'The wrong man has gone', he said. The governor also told them how upset he had been to learn through the media of Agius' resignation. Agius, referring to him formally as Mr Governor, apologized. He later recounted:

> It was made very plain to us that Bob Diamond no longer enjoyed the support of his regulators. The governor was very careful to say that he had no power to direct us, but he felt that this was sufficiently important, as indeed it was, for us to be told in absolute terms what the situation was.[27]

Rake said that the shareholders wanted Diamond to stay to which King shrugged his shoulders and replied that shareholders' opinions were not a concern for regulators. Rake added that the board had a fiduciary duty to shareholders and the FSA had endorsed Diamond as chief executive and cleared him of wrongdoing over Libor. The governor replied: 'I am afraid, gentlemen, that in this matter you have been let down by a weak regulator.'

He told Agius and Rake that when – as a result of the 2012 Financial Services Act – the Bank of England took over responsibility for banking regulation in a few months' time, there would be a 'fit and proper persons' review of the senior management at all banks. This could lead to great difficulties for Diamond, King said, adding that it would be wise to make any change before Diamond's scheduled appearance before the Treasury Committee the day after next to discuss Libor.

It was a stark warning. Rake told the governor: 'Until today, we had not, and I, as senior independent director, had not been fully aware of the loss of confidence of the regulators in the executive management.'[28] Rake said that he understood the governor was asking the board to remove Diamond immediately. King replied simply that was a matter for the board. He brought the meeting to a close with a request: 'I would like you to make clear to the board that the regulators have expressed these concerns. The board as a whole needs to know that they are very concerned and have lost confidence in the executive management.'[29]

Agius was shocked. Two working days previously the FSA had given Barclays a slap on the wrist and said nothing about the suitability of Diamond; now he was being told in no uncertain terms that Diamond did not have the support either of its regulator or of the Bank of England.[30] It seemed that Barclays' board was not the only body to have been shaken by the media reaction to the Libor revelations.

After leaving the Bank of England, Agius and Rake made their way to Brook Street for a hastily arranged conference call with the non-executives. Agius briefed them on the conversation with King, and there was a moment's silence. Some of the British non-executives began to say that under the circumstances they really had to follow King's lead, but others burst in, questioning the governor's authority. 'We have had enough of regulation on a handshake. What does it say about the financial system if the Bank of England – not even our regulator – can take out the chief executive of a major financial institution on a whim? What about the shareholders? Who were the witnesses to this conversation? Who has the Governor consulted?' After an emotional discussion the board decided that only when they had established that Osborne and Turner were in agreement would they call for Diamond's resignation.

2 JULY – WORMSLEY PARK

While Agius and Rake waited in the governor's anteroom, Turner mingled in the grounds of a Buckinghamshire country house with

600 other music lovers resplendent in evening dress. Garsington rivalled Glyndebourne as a place for the corporate crowd to enjoy summer evenings of opera over dinner, wine and gentle networking. Mozart's prelude to *Don Giovanni*, a dark tale of lust, deception, ambition and retribution soared across the newly built opera house in Wormsley Park and Turner settled down to enjoy the music.

At about seven-thirty he and other guests made their way to the Long Room restaurant overlooking Wormsley Park's cricket ground for the extended dinner interval. As Turner checked his phone, he saw a message to phone Alex Brazier, the governor's principal secretary. He made the call and Brazier told him what had just happened.

The usually unflappable Turner swallowed hard. If there was to be a change of chief executive, he wanted it to be done in an orderly fashion. But it was clearly too late for that now. Turner thanked Brazier for letting him know and made for his table, but was interrupted by a further call. This time it was Agius. He reported his and Rake's conversation with King and asked Turner: 'Is this what you want as well?'

Turner thought quickly. The governor had gone further than he was expecting but a complicated situation was developing, so he simply replied: 'I think we are in a situation where that has to occur.' Saying nothing of those exchanges, Turner rejoined the rest of his party in time for the second half of the opera and to see Don Giovanni being dragged down into hell.

THE SAME DAY – MAYFAIR AND BELGRAVIA

Having spoken to Turner, Agius phoned Chancellor George Osborne's office to confirm King's request. Meanwhile, the rest of the board agreed to ask Agius to stay on, now as executive chairman. Agius accepted their invitation and the whole board then agreed, reluctantly in some instances, to ask Diamond to resign. Agius reported this to King, also speaking to Bailey at the FSA to confirm that the regulator would approve his own return. It was time to tell Diamond.

Diamond was working at his kitchen table when Agius called him and asked if he and Rake could come over. It was late and these were abnormal times but Diamond's reaction was nevertheless chilly. He had not heard from anyone on the board since having breakfast with Rake that morning and the long silence had made him uneasy.

The doorbell rang and he greeted the visitors politely, ushering them into the kitchen. Agius came straight to the point: 'The governor has told us that he, the chancellor and the chairman of the FSA no longer have confidence in you. We've been left in no doubt that it would be in the best interests of the bank and the board for you to resign. We don't think we have any choice in the matter.'

For the second time in a week Diamond had a sick feeling in his stomach. He thought back to briefing conversations with Bailey over the weekend. He had picked up no signs that he was at risk personally. He briefly considered resisting but it was too late for that. The only words he said were: 'I must speak to my family.' He ushered his visitors out of the house quickly and called Jennifer in the US and the rest of the family before the news broke.

3 JULY

The next morning, Barclays announced Diamond's resignation along with that of del Missier. Agius would lead the search for a new chief executive before himself leaving Barclays. Diamond stated:

> My motivation has always been to do what I believed to be in the best interests of Barclays. No decision over that period was as hard as the one that I make now to stand down as Chief Executive. The external pressure has reached a level that risks damaging the franchise. I cannot let that happen.[31]

But he had one final duty for the bank from which even resignation could not release him.

4 JULY

Until a few days before, Diamond had been hoping to spend 4 July at the family home on Nantucket. Diamond's father had been principal of the local high school and several of his siblings had been educated there and had remained on the island. There would have been a party for family and friends with music and fireworks. Instead, he spent over three hours on a sunny London afternoon facing the Treasury Committee in Portcullis House. Never before had a parliamentary committee hearing gripped the public like the trial of Bob Diamond. Work stopped in Whitehall as civil servants followed proceedings on live television. The BBC's Radio 5 interrupted coverage of Andy Murray's Wimbledon quarter-final with summaries of events in Westminster. The public area in the committee room itself was full and people waited in the corridor outside to take the place of anyone who left early – but no one did.

The committee room was a bear pit that day, a semi-circle of questioners taunting a wounded beast. In a blue suit, pale blue shirt, cufflinks and green tie, Diamond looked tired. Things went wrong from his very first words:

> Wow. I love Barclays. That's where it starts. I love Barclays because of the people. It is sixteen years ago today, on 4 July 1996, that I began at Barclays, and it has been 16 years of tremendous enjoyment; and that enjoyment has been driven by the incredible 140,000 people in over 50 countries around the world.[32]

The tone was wrong and Diamond never got a rapport going with the committee, frequently using first names and getting a stony 'Mr Diamond' back in return.

MPs eager to score political points fired questions from all directions. One here on Barclays' culture, another one there on his span of control, from the chair his relationships with regulators, yet another on the recently disclosed file note which he had written about the conversations with Tucker in 2008. Old scores were raised again, including PPI, Protium and the interest rate hedging products such as those bought by Karl Edwards. Extensive questions were asked about what he knew about Libor and when. Chancellor Osborne's comment on Diamond's departure that 'I think it is the right decision for the country' was quoted to him.[33]

Diamond was apologetic: 'It was wrong. I am sorry. I am disappointed, and I am also angry. There is absolutely no excuse for the behaviour that was exhibited in those activities and the types of e-mails that were written.' But he also tried to preserve the good: 'This does not represent the Barclays that I know and I love and it does not represent the work of 140,000 people who are working day in and day out for their clients and customers.'[34]

Committee members such as the former BZW banker Andrea Leadsom with whom Diamond had crossed swords at previous sessions, took their revenge:

> 'Mr Diamond, you seem to be inhabiting a slightly parallel universe, because you talk about the culture of Barclays as if that is the thing that saved Barclays, but that is the thing that is the problem. Surely you must realize how enraged people are at the criminality. You talk about reprehensible behaviour, but it is actually criminality. There is certainly a lot of talk that you have been unapproachable and that that is part of the reason for this.'[35]

Andrew Tyrie, the committee chair closed the meeting by acknowledging that Diamond must have been through a difficult few days, but that was small comfort.[36]

LATER THAT MONTH

Diamond eventually got to the family home on Nantucket, but he hadn't been there long when he was called by Sally Bott. She wanted to give him a heads up about a board meeting at which the question of £20 million of deferred compensation due to him had been discussed. With nothing left to lose from offending a man who had already gone, the board had finally decided to stand up to him and said 'no'. She told him to expect a call from Agius sometime soon and that he should think carefully about how to respond. Diamond could have fought it but he too had now learned. If he wanted to rebuild his reputation in the UK, he would need to forgo that bonus. By the time Agius phoned the following day, he was ready to agree to the board's request.

The humiliation of Bob Diamond sent a message to the City of London. The hubris and greed which had been building in London since Big Bang, and which had left the country with the biggest hang-over in economic history, would no longer be tolerated. The people and the politicians had had enough and Diamond was the lightning rod. Where that left Barclays and investment banking was a conun-drum for his and indeed King's successors.

22

A Complete Mess, 2012

DOING THE RIGHT THING

A month after the Libor news broke, Carnwath resigned from the board on 24 July 2012. Before it became public, the company secretary, Lawrence Dickinson, a devoted Barclays' servant, and Rake, now deputy chairman, tried to change her mind. But Carnwath had decided that Barclays was ungovernable. The board was not asking the right questions or tackling the culture. It should have been possible for her distinguished colleagues to work out what was going on, but they had bottled it. She had had enough.

Nevertheless, she kept all this to herself, merely saying in her resignation statement: 'With regret I have concluded that I am no longer able to devote sufficient time to my role of Director of Barclays given my other commitments.' There was truth in that. She had not been able to attend the crucial board meeting of February 2012 in person and had flown in overnight for the annual general meeting. But even at this late stage she did not feel able to reveal the real reason she had decided to go, believing that she had acted correctly in maintaining collective responsibility for a decision she did not agree with. It was a very English way of doing things.

However, Nils Pratley of the *Guardian* newspaper had heard rumours that her resignation was really about Diamond's pay. 'If that's the tale, then the time to resign was February, when bonus matters were being settled by the board. At the annual meeting in April she gave a robust defence of Barclays' pay policies.'[1] Her failure to disclose her opposition to Diamond's bonus was a symptom of how corporate governance in the UK really worked. In the end, Carnwath came clean when she gave evidence to the Parliamentary Commission on Banking Standards in January 2013.

'GO AWAY AND THINK AGAIN'

Barclays was now in a complete mess. The once grand bank that had lorded it over Britain's high streets and shires had become a symbol of all that was wrong with banking. There were reports of branch customers verbally abusing staff, spitting on the floor and taking their business elsewhere. The chairman was on borrowed time, there was no chief executive and the board had apparently been asleep at the wheel. The universal banking business model looked out of date, the culture was rotten and the press appeared to hate the whole organization. If there had been any financial institution anywhere in the world strong enough to pounce, this would have been the moment, but there was none. Instead, the task of sorting out the mess fell to Barclays' discredited board.

Round the corner from Barclays' head office, the FSA was also under temporary management pending its imminent break-up. As the statement accompanying the Libor fines showed, though, it was in no mood to go quietly. After Diamond's sudden exit, Turner, chairman and de facto chief executive, held several one-on-one meetings with Barclays board members, including deputy chairman Rake. At those meetings some non-executives turned on Agius, criticizing him for supporting rather than challenging the chief executive for too long. Turner wondered what they imagined they themselves were meant to be doing if not challenging. He was equally unimpressed with the lack of support they gave Carnwath in the fight over Diamond's pay and he was not surprised when she decided to stand down. Barclays' board, he reckoned, needed shaking up.

At Barclays, there was still no sign that the board understood their strategic bind or their own culpability. The search for Agius' successor was led by Sunderland, and the FSA insisted on being kept in touch. Before making a recommendation, Sunderland decided to test the water. He told Turner in July that the board had compiled a long list of six candidates and that a clear favourite was emerging. 'If I said

the board's unanimous decision is Mike Rake, what would you say?'
An internal candidate chosen by a buck-passing board was not what
Turner had in mind. It would be perceived as a terrible appointment
and he was surprised that Barclays could not see that for themselves.
He told Sunderland that that was not a very good idea. 'You should
go away and think again.'

SAFE PAIR OF HANDS

Sunderland was not the kind of man who needed to be told twice. He
now realized that Barclays needed a chairman from outside who
would be acceptable to regulators and shareholders. Two names came
to mind: Sir David Walker and Glen Moreno.

Moreno was a senior American businessman who had spent
eighteen years at Citigroup before coming to the UK. To British eyes,
he was the right kind of American: capable, low key and attuned to
British ways. Investors liked him and so did government, which had
given him several part-time roles over the years. However, he already
had many other commitments, among them as chairman of another
FTSE 100 company, Pearson, and as a board member of the asset
management firm Fidelity International, and Barclays needed
someone in a position to make a substantial time commitment.

That left the 72-year-old Walker, the safest pair of hands in the
City. He had spent a distinguished career at the Treasury, the Bank of
England, a long-forgotten regulator, the Securities and Investments
Board, and had been a deputy chairman of Barclays' rival in the High
Street, Lloyds. He had joined Morgan Stanley as a senior adviser in
1997 and was still there facilitating the American investment bank's
relationships with government and regulators.

The authorities liked him. In 2009 Prime Minister Brown asked
him to report on corporate governance reforms in banking and he
produced a hard-hitting review. A key section read:

> The right sequence in board discussions on major issues should be:
> presentation by the executive, a disciplined process of challenge, decision
> on the policy to be adopted and then full empowerment of the executive

to implement. The essential 'challenge' step in the sequence appears to have been missed in many board situations.[2]

Nothing could have been plainer and it was there for all banks, including Barclays, to read from the autumn of 2009 onwards. It was a clear statement of what should have been happening and a blueprint for how things would be if Walker became chairman. He met Sunderland, Rake and the finance director, Christopher Lucas. The board knew that he was highly regarded in government, the Bank of England and the FSA and decided he would be just the man to help rehabilitate them and their deeply troubled bank.

The FSA was now taking a much closer interest in the qualifications of banking board members and Turner led a robust two-hour interview before approving Walker's appointment. Walker retreated to Wiltshire to prepare, Barclays' public relations team came down to visit him, he recorded a video message for staff and his appointment was announced on Thursday 9 August 2012.[3] He would take over as chairman on 1 November.

With the chairman in the bag, the next job was to find a chief executive. It needed to be someone to appease the regulators, satisfy the shareholders and, in the board's eyes, be fit to carry on the strategy. Spencer Stuart were set to work.

27 JUNE – PORTUGAL

The sun was shining over the graceful steel arches of the Estádio da Luz football stadium as Antony Jenkins looked out over Lisbon from Barclays' office. The chief executive of Retail and Business Banking had one call to make before going out for lunch with Barclays' local man. It was a routine matter but just as the call was ending, his compliance officer in London said: 'By the way, you should know that we have just received the Libor press release from the FSA.' 'How bad is it? asked Jenkins. As the statement was read out to him, he felt as though he had swallowed a lead weight.

Jenkins returned to London the next day and sensed an ugly atmosphere developing. On the evening of Sunday 1 July he and his wife were about to leave for a drinks party when Diamond called him and said: 'Marcus is going to go. Sorry, I've got to hang up, it's on television now.' The following evening, the Jenkinses were dining with finance director Lucas and his wife in Scott's, a glitzy restaurant in Mayfair. In the entrance lobby, Simon Fraser was standing on his own, ashen-faced, with his phone clamped to his ear, dialling in to the meeting at which Agius and Rake were briefing the non-executives about their discussion with King. Halfway through, his mobile went dead and he dashed off to Barclays' Brook Street office to attend the rest of the meeting in person.

Jenkins went to bed and turned his own phone off. When he switched it back on in the morning there was a message from Diamond asking him to call, but by then he had gone. Jenkins cancelled a planned visit to Barclaycard in Northampton and went into Churchill Place. Diamond was emotional, close to tears and simply said to him: 'Protect the legacy.' It was an enigmatic comment but it got Jenkins thinking. He decided to throw his hat into the ring.

Jenkins had got on well with Diamond and was sorry to see him go. Diamond had given him a lot of room. When Diamond had taken over as chief executive he had taken Jenkins to dinner at Mark's Club, a traditional private members club just off Berkeley Square much used by investment bankers. As they sat down, Jenkins' mobile rang and the screen flashed 'Amanda'. He apologized and made as if to decline the call, saying: 'It's my wife.' Diamond reached across and touched his arm. 'Answer it. You should always take a call from your wife.' Over smoked eel and Chablis, Jenkins spoke knowledgeably about the worlds of cards and branch banking. It was not a business Diamond knew well and for the moment he decided he wouldn't need to. Jenkins could be trusted to run it while he looked after the rest of the group.

Jenkins was no babe in the woods – the world of cards where he had made his name was not averse to high-pressure selling – but when he took over from Seegers in 2009, he saw an opportunity for Barclays to differentiate itself. In March 2010 he called a leadership conference for his top one hundred executives in the Langham Hotel, opposite the BBC in Portland Place. He made it a theatrical occasion with round tables, bright lighting and a stage. Harking back to his early days in banking – his first job in 1983 was at Barclays' South Kensington branch – the theme was 'Lives Made Much Easier'. He had a heavy cold that day but the message was strong: our business is about the social purpose of banking not 'how many mortgages can you shift today?' Formal sales targets would be replaced by customer satisfaction metrics and profit-related pay would be phased out.

It was a good call. Jenkins' business increased its return on equity from 10 to 11 per cent in 2010 with good profit growth in the UK, Barclaycard and Africa offsetting poor performance from some of Seegers' pet projects.[4] There was a similar pattern in 2011, when profits increased again despite a £400 million provision for PPI.[5] By then, non-PPI customer complaints in his business had dropped by 30 per cent.[6] Jenkins had a track record to show to the recruiting panel.

THE GHOST OF BOB DIAMOND

With Walker not taking over as chairman until 1 November, Agius and Rake were leading the search for a chief executive but neither was convinced that Jenkins was the ideal candidate. He had put in a good shift at the retail bank, deflecting some of the criticism that the banks were getting for not lending enough, improving customer service and coming across as a sober and responsible banker when he appeared alongside Diamond at Treasury Committee sessions. He would have been a solid enough candidate if Barclays was just a retail bank, but the board were still committed to broad scale universal banking. Barclays Capital was the key to achieving that and they needed an investment banker to take charge; almost inevitably that would mean another American.

After several meetings in New York and London, they had three names in mind: Bob Steel, Bill Winters and Jes Staley – all American. Former Barclays director Steel had recently become deputy mayor for economic development of New York City and said he was not ready to return to banking. That left Winters and Staley.

Winters was an American who moved to London in 1992. Until 2009 he was J. P. Morgan's boss Jamie Dimon's most trusted lieutenant, running its investment bank. He was regarded as one of the finest risk managers in the industry, was widely credited with helping the US bank avoid the worst of the credit crunch and received a standing ovation from the bank's London trading floor on the day his departure was announced after a rumoured disagreement with Dimon.[7] He was chosen by Chancellor Osborne to serve on the Independent Commission on Banking and would have been a popular choice with regulators and shareholders. However, he had recently set up an asset management business and would be difficult to move.

Staley was his successor as chief executive of J. P. Morgan's investment bank and was spoken of as a successor to Dimon. He had made his name running the firm's wealth management division and, like Diamond, was a Massachusetts-born, liberal arts college man. But following derivatives losses of $6.2 billion in the London arm of the chief investment office in the spring of 2012, Staley's career took a jolt. Dimon initially described the losses as 'a tempest in a teapot', but when their full extent emerged, he believed that Staley's risk management team had been slow to respond. He separated the roles of chairman and chief executive of the investment bank, giving Staley only the former, albeit with an office on the executive floor. There would now be no question of his succeeding Dimon; Staley was, in effect, on the market. He was a good fit for Barclays. Though he was less familiar with British banking than Winters and had never worked in London for an extended period, during the Olympic summer of 2012 he emerged as the board's choice.

While the board had been charging ahead, Walker had been doing what his new colleagues should have done long ago: thinking about Barclays' business model and taking soundings at the Bank of England and the FSA. His review of corporate governance in banks in 2009 had said: 'The role of the chairman is paramount, calling for both exceptional board leadership skills and ability to get confidently and competently to grips with major strategic issues.'[8] Now he would have to live up to his own words.

One strategic issue stood out. He believed that universal banking on the scale envisaged by the board was unsustainable given the ever increasing requirements from shareholders and regulators to preserve capital. The pinch point was likely to be the investment bank and he was picking up strong signals that the British authorities were uneasy with a full-blooded Barclays Capital.

He doubted that Barclays needed another chief executive with an investment banking background. Walker knew that the kind of person they chose would in effect determine the bank's strategic direction, and he was determined to prevent them careering down the universal banking path without due consideration. He had interviewed Jenkins in a meeting room at Spencer Stuart and had been surprised by his qualities. His background fitted Walker's ideas of the kind of bank Barclays should become.

It had been difficult to get the board together during the holiday month but on a Friday evening in mid-August, just after the Olympics had finished, a full board meeting was held, with most people dialling in. Walker would not be on the board until 1 September and would have no vote on the matter but he made it known at the meeting that he wanted to see Jenkins' name considered along with Staley's.

After the board confirmed Walker's appointment, the merits of the candidates for chief executive were discussed. It would cost £10 million to buy out Staley's deferred compensation but he was prepared to wait until retirement before he received that and he would work for a fraction of his annual salary at J. P. Morgan. Simon Fraser, the former Fidelity investment manager, and David Booth, the Morgan Stanley man, supported Jenkins, the other eight board members preferred Staley. Agius was deputed to keep Staley warm while the discussions continued. He phoned the American, a keen yachtsman, who was sailing in Scandinavia. Staley confirmed that he was still interested but was concerned that Dimon at J. P. Morgan might hear about it before things were finalized.

He was right to be anxious. Walker was not sure that the board was going in the right direction, and in a series of one-to-one phone calls and meetings sounded out the non-executives. He was concerned that Staley was still too expensive and might commit Barclays to an unmodified investment banking strategy before the issue had been debated. He floated the idea of Jenkins as chief executive and Winters as head of the investment bank. He also called the recently departed chief executive of the FSA, Sants, and asked if he would be interested in working with Jenkins in a senior support role. Sants said that this might be possible after the end of his six months' gardening leave but also indicated that he might be interested in being considered for the chief executive job itself.*

Staley's fears of a leak were justified. The top management at Barclays Capital got to hear of the plan to hire him, and the last thing they wanted was for a heavyweight investment banker to come in and challenge their autonomy. The *Sunday Telegraph*'s business editor, Kamal Ahmed, wrote an article putting Jenkins' case:

> Mr Jenkins is everything Mr Diamond is not. As far as I'm aware, Mr Jenkins has never met Beyoncé or Jay-Z. He does not support the Boston Red Sox nor have a row of pearly-white teeth that would find a happy home in any Hollywood A-lister's mouth. Mr Jenkins is from Manchester, likes running marathons and has never handed the Premier League trophy to John Terry. Mr Jenkins is not flash . . . But 'safety first' is now the guide for all in the financial sector. Mr Jenkins fits the mould.[9]

Senior Barclays Capital staff called Walker and other board members to lobby for Jenkins, who they thought would concentrate on areas he knew best and leave them alone. Jenkins himself made it clear to board members that he would go if he was not given the job.

The board meeting the next Monday evening was a tense affair. Sunderland and the former Goldman Sachs banker, Jeffery, argued strongly for Staley. The search firm Spencer Stuart, who had been told to put Jenkins on their short list, knew that he understood trading, credit and risk but had no direct experience of investment banking. Barclays Capital was in mourning for Diamond and the new chief executive would have to be capable of invigorating a demoralized team. Would Jenkins be able to do that?

Rake dialled in from his French holiday home and after a while said: 'I have to go to dinner. They are both good candidates. I will go along with the consensus.' Parker remained the board's principal public relations adviser and was asked to consider the likely external reaction to both Staley and Jenkins. He too was on holiday and joined the meeting

---

* Sants eventually worked for Barclays in 2013 as head of Compliance and Government and Regulatory Relations.

by phone. He outlined how various parties – shareholders, the media, government and the regulators – might react to each man's appointment. It was a balanced analysis in which he was careful not to comment on either man's merits. His crucial point was that so soon after Diamond's departure, the media would have focused hard on the payment of £10 million to another American investment banker.

It was the decisive intervention. Walker had played it just right. The original eight to two majority for Staley became an eight to two majority for Jenkins. Walker had grasped that the appointment of a chief executive was not just a choice between two candidates but a vote between two different strategies. He knew which way the authorities were leaning and cleverly brought home an acceptable business model. The safe pair of hands had delivered once again. Staley would be disappointed. As the meeting broke up, one of his admirers was heard to mutter: 'We were right the first time. They are afraid of the ghost of Bob Diamond.'

23

'Barclays is not the place for you', 2015

A GRUDGING SETTLEMENT

October House Records turned out to be one of 14,700 small businesses who were sold interest rate hedges without a clear explanation of the risks being run. The FSA forced the banks to pay compensation and victims received £2.2 billion in redress and £500 million to cover consequential losses – but only after a fight.

On Monday 2 July 2012, the first working day after the liquidation of his business and the FSA-brokered redress scheme, Edwards had spoken to his latest relationship manager at Barclays. 'Does this FSA announcement mean that I can stop paying the penalty charges?' 'We'll get back to you on that,' he was told. It was another six months before the bank released him from the collar and in the meantime they took another £20,000 from his account. Edwards was getting more and more agitated at the lack of response and threatened to stop making his derivatives payments. 'If you do that,' an impersonal voice from Barclays told him, 'we will call in the bailiffs.'

Eventually Barclays agreed that Edwards had been mis-sold a structured collar and he was offered full repayment of the penalty charges with the addition of 8 per cent for every year he had been out of pocket. It was a satisfactory offer but Edwards reckoned that the structured collar had cost him his business and that he was entitled to further compensation under the FCA's consequential loss scheme.

Barclays then offered what Edwards regarded as a token consequential loss settlement but added the condition that they would not pay back any of the interest until he accepted their new offer. Edwards therefore brought an application for Summary Judgment, which Barclays eventually offered to settle in 2015 after niggardly last-minute haggling on the day the case was due to be heard. They had done the bare minimum at the last possible moment.

IN THE DOGHOUSE

In the years after Libor, a blizzard of other scandals brought the banking industry into further disgrace. Already excoriated for reckless behaviour, its reputation sank even lower with evidence of corruption in nearly every line of business. The foreign exchange markets were evidently as crooked as Libor.[1] The gold market was rigged.[2] Traders in the energy markets were playing with prices to suit their own positions.[3] Private securities exchanges, known as 'dark pools', were being abused by the banks that ran them.[4] Client money was getting mixed up with the banks' own trading funds.[5] Low grade mortgage backed securities were being packaged up, falsely described and sold as if they were blue chip credits.[6] Breaking the rules had become so widespread that the only way to survive was to join in: the dilemma for those who thought they should play it straight was that if you stuck to the letter of the law, the opposition would eat you up or shareholders would complain about poor results. The extraordinary rewards for success had led to institutional cheating and the sports mad British did not have to look very far to find an analogy.

Football is a contact sport played at a high pace and a certain amount of foul play is always possible as the tackles fly in. The referee's job is to judge when players' commitment becomes dangerous or breaks the rules; the players naturally come up as close to that boundary as possible. Rule breaking is inevitable, punished by free kicks, penalties, dismissal from the field and suspension for regular offenders.

In the first century of professional football attempts to dupe the referee or to question his authority were rare, but in the 1960s that broke down. Sly play became widespread, players routinely argued with the referee and pretended to be fouled when contact had been fair. The abolition of the maximum wage for players and the arrival of big money – very big money – from television made the temptation to cheat irresistible. The game's governing bodies were weak and did not stamp it out. Diving, feigning injury and pressuring the referee became ubiquitous.

In 1986 England was knocked out of the World Cup by Diego Maradona's 'Hand of God' goal in which the Argentine player illegally used his hand. In 2009 Thierry Henry, a soccer idol previously considered to be a role model for sportsmanship, sent Ireland out of the World Cup by using his hand to set up a goal. Despite clear television evidence of what had happened on both occasions, Maradona was fêted in his home country and is regarded everywhere as one of the best footballers ever to have played the sport; Henry became a high-profile television pundit after he retired.

These and other exponents of 'gamesmanship' were tolerated because everyone was doing it. If there were any teams that committed no fouls and played strictly by the rules, they would be beaten and the managers would be fired by impatient owners. Professional football had become a business in which cheating and gaming were not just tolerated but expected of the players.

That was what happened to banking as an industry in the last quarter of the twentieth century too. Even before Big Bang, brokers and bankers sailed close to the wind, but a rap on the knuckles from the Stock Exchange and in extreme cases a raised eyebrow from the governor would be enough to restore good behaviour. After Big Bang, high rewards, weak regulation and the demands of short-term shareholders corrupted the business. You could not survive as a trader, salesperson, analyst or corporate financier if you told the truth, the whole truth and nothing but the truth when everyone else was lying. Regulators, boards, managers and sophisticated investors either knew about it and did nothing or did not look too hard to find out what was really going on.

The banking crisis alerted everyone to this, and a wave of public disgust finally persuaded the authorities to come down hard on all the banks, including Barclays. It was fined $2.4 billion for manipulating, along with other banks, foreign exchange markets.[7] The day after the Libor news broke, a Barclays Capital trader fiddled the gold price to a customer's disadvantage, which eventually incurred a £26 million fine for the bank in 2014.[8] The US energy regulator fined Barclays $453 million for manipulating the Californian energy markets.[9] Barclays and Credit Suisse were fined a combined total of $154 million for cheating users of their dark pools.[10] A damaging internal report on Barclays Wealth was shredded by managers.[11] US and other regulators included Barclays in their investigations into mis-selling mortgage backed securities.[12] By the end of 2015, Barclays had made total provisions of £10 billion against PPI and interest rate hedging cases, ranking it number five in the league table of total fines for the banking industry behind Bank of America, J. P. Morgan, Lloyds and Morgan Stanley. It was not the kind of top five universal bank the board had in mind when it signed up to that vision in 2006.*

Some of these issues dated back to the 1990s and occurred in all parts of the group – the retail, commercial and investment banks – at different times. Barclays Capital's success sucked in Wall Street's investment banking pay culture and Barrett spread it into the retail bank with his exhortations and incentives to cross-sell. Seegers, like Diamond, had an American attitude to pay, and the rewards for Barclays' top retail bankers joined those of their investment banking colleagues as the best in the market. In the super-confident early 2000s, when the benefits of the very free market were rarely questioned, no one at Barclays, or indeed at any other bank, looked too closely at the effect of lavish incentives on the behaviour of those receiving them.

Supremely confident in their business model and with an ideological conviction that business worked best if it was left to its own devices, management assumed that their job was done if they signed off on virtuous values and ethics statements. The UK's corporate governance reforms of the 1990s – professional boards, board committees, independent risk management and compliance – made no difference. It all looked fine on paper but was worthless if those at the top asked the wrong questions or failed to drill down into suspicious issues. Good governance required knowledge, persistence and an enquiring mind; instead shareholders, regulators and boards themselves took comfort from process and structures. No one reading the detailed descriptions in the Barclays annual reports would have reason

---

* This result is sensitive to the precise period used. Barclays' position varied between fifth, sixth and seventh.

to believe that the bank was anything other than a model of good corporate governance. But the procedures had no bite.

Not one of the chairmen and chief executives of the period made them stick and none of the boards noticed. All the committees and all the correct description of governance in the annual reports had counted for nothing. Barrett's Brand and Reputation Committee, successive Audit and Remuneration Committees had all failed to make the connection between 'take the money and run' incentives and the likely consequences on individual behaviour. The board that was meant to stand back and challenge had become a box ticker. It looked bad, it was bad and Jenkins and Walker were determined to fix it.

In March 2013 Jenkins received an audit of Barclays' business practices by Anthony Salz, a senior City lawyer. It had been commissioned by Agius in July 2012 after his brief extension as chairman and had been prepared with the help of consultants. It was a thorough piece of work that had left no stone unturned. It put to shame generations of those responsible for setting the bank's culture.

> There was no sense of common purpose in a group that had grown and diversified significantly in less than two decades. And across the whole bank, there were no clearly articulated and understood shared values – so there could hardly be much consensus among employees as to what the values were and what should guide everyday behaviours.[13]

The report set out the cultural issues facing Jenkins following Barclays' 'rapid journey from a primarily domestic retail bank to a global universal bank twenty or so years later'. Barclays was silo based, prioritized short-term financial gains above other business purposes and lacked an identifiable ethical core. These problems were most deeply entrenched in the investment bank. The review noted: 'Despite some attempts to establish Group-wide values, the culture that emerged tended to favour transactions over relationships, the short term over sustainability, and financial over other business purposes.'[14] The report confirmed Jenkins' doubts about Barclays Capital's influence on the rest of the group and hardened his resolve to clean everything up.

The gravity of the situation was underlined in September 2013 when Barclays received formal Warning Notices from its regulator, the FCA, relating to two advisory services agreements with Qatar

Holdings at the time of the June and October 2008 fund raisings. Barclays' annual report for 2013 said:

> The existence of the advisory services agreement entered into in June 2008 was disclosed but the entry into the advisory services agreements in October 2008 and the fees payable under both agreements, which amount to a total of £322m payable over a period of five years, were not disclosed in the announcements or public documents relating to the capital raisings in June and November 2008. While the Warning Notices consider that BPLC and BBPLC believed at the time that there should be at least some unspecified and undetermined value to be derived from the agreements, they state that the primary purpose of the agreements was not to obtain advisory services but to make additional payments, which would not be disclosed, for the Qatari participation in the capital raisings. The Warning Notices conclude that BPLC and BBPLC were in breach of certain disclosure-related listing rules and BPLC was also in breach of Listing Principle 3 (the requirement to act with integrity towards holders and potential holders of the company's shares). In this regard, the FCA considers that BPLC and BBPLC acted recklessly. The financial penalty in the Warning Notices against the group is £50m.[15]

Barclays contested the finding but by the time the annual report was written there had been a further development:

> The FCA proceedings are now subject to a stay pending progress in an investigation by the Serious Fraud Office into the same agreements. The SFO's investigation is at an earlier stage and the Group has received and has continued to respond to requests for further information.[16]

But the FCA and SFO were not the only parties interested in Barclays' arrangements with the Qataris. Amanda Staveley believed that her syndicate had been promised the same deal as other investors and began to consider legal action of her own.

THE FAT CAT IN THE HAT

'There might be some who don't feel they can fully buy in to an approach which so squarely links performance to the upholding of our values. My message to those people is simple: Barclays is not the place for you.'[17] Antony Jenkins' challenging New Year 2013 letter to Barclays' staff was born of the belief that he had the full backing of a board that was finally facing up to its responsibilities. But its forthright tone brought him into head-on conflict with the investment bankers, who were once again full of themselves.

There had been a brief moment of humility after the departure of Agius and Diamond. No one, not even the most brazen bond trader, liked working for a publicly disgraced bank, and they were shocked by the visceral public reaction to the Libor revelations. As the weeks passed, however, and other banks got dragged in to the scandal, they forgot their sackcloth and ashes and went back to focusing on what really interested them: making money.

With market activity boosted by quantitative easing, global governments' policy of buying up securities to reflate the economy, the investment bank had a big year in 2012, with profits up 37 per cent and a return on equity of 14 per cent, a result that fuelled the bankers' self-belief. They had no time for all this cultural crap. They thought they had got through the storm, that it was business as usual and that pre-crisis bonuses would soon be back on the table.

Jenkins flew to New York to tell the US managing directors they would all be sent to London for values training. After his address, a fiery trader, a rare woman in a male-dominated world, shot back: 'This is the fourth quarter. It makes or breaks my year. I'd rather be at my desk earning some dollars.' There were other less than respectful comments from the trading floor and the intentionally derogatory nickname of 'Saint Antony' took hold. Jenkins wondered whether the investment bank would ever be governable.

He believed in leading by example and decided to send a clear message throughout the bank. Although underlying profits were up by a quarter and total returns to shareholders were improving much faster than those of other banks,[18] declarable profits had drained away in a flood of provisions and accounting issues. Jenkins waived his bonus for 2012 but there was no sign of reciprocation from the investment bankers, who expected to get paid regardless. With contractual arrangements in place, previous years' deferred compensation vesting and some Wall Street banks hiring again, Jenkins had to pay up for now but the problem Carnwath had laid out for the board still needed to be solved.

Walker and Jenkins abolished revenue related pay in the retail bank and the Remuneration Committee, now chaired by Sunderland, began a line-by-line review of compensation in the investment bank. It took eighteen months to complete, and further infuriated the investment bankers who were already unsettled by the strategic plan Jenkins announced in February 2013, a month after his values statement.

That strategic plan in respect of the investment bank had been prepared by Ricci with the help of Deloitte. He code named the work 'Project Mango', reportedly after a box of the fruit sent by a client as a consoling gesture following the departure of Diamond. Project Mango looked at every single business in the investment bank, recommended closing some desks and cutting 2,000 jobs in Asia and Europe. But this was less than 10 per cent of the total and was not the radical downsizing Jenkins – who had already closed Structured Capital Markets, the controversial tax business – had in mind.

Ricci had done what he was told, but off the trading floor his other interests were becoming a problem for the bank's image. He had been snapped at a race meeting wearing a jaunty trilby and shades. The caption underneath the photograph read: 'Who's the fat cat in the hat? The rich world of Rich Ricci'. He then named one of his racehorses Fatcatinthehat, a gesture that showed no appreciation of the need to rebuild Barclays Capital's reputation. In March 2013, he cashed in his deferred shares as soon as they vested, a £17.6 million bonanza. It was no surprise when he and Kalaris left the following month. Jenkins thanked them for their service and paid them a year's salary in lieu of notice. Tom King, a mergers and acquisitions banker hired by Diamond from Citigroup, and Eric Bommensath, a former colleague of del Missier at Bankers Trust, were made the co-chief executives of the investment bank.

2013 – THE HONEYMOON ENDS

In contrast to the reaction of the investment bank, Jenkins' values, which were spelled out on tablets seven feet high in the lobby at head office, each engraved with a separate word – Respect, Integrity, Service, Excellence, Stewardship – and the strategic plan of January and February 2013 initially went down well with the stock market. Barclays' shares outperformed other banks' in the first months of the year, but markets were tough, regulators were demanding and the bank's capital position needed to be rebuilt. In July Barclays surprised investors with a £5.8 billion rights issue and Jenkins was criticized by shareholders who had understood him to have said that no such capital raising was imminent. The shares began to underperform those of other banks and there was a nasty reaction to the results for 2013 when they were released in February 2014. The good times of 2012 had not lasted. In 2013, profits at Barclays Capital were down 37 per cent as a result of poor market conditions in fixed income trading, the return on equity dropped to 8 per cent and the hubris of 2012 disappeared.

But, though profits were down a third, bonuses were up 10 per cent as the old schemes vested and contractual agreements with traders kicked in. Angry investors calculated that the staff were taking out 50 per cent more in bonuses than they, the owners of the business, were getting in dividends.[19] Jenkins waived his bonus again but the February 2013 cost-cutting plan was criticized outside the bank for not going far enough. As the April 2014 annual general meeting approached, the pressure on him increased. Little did investors know that behind the scenes Jenkins was developing a more radical plan.

2014 – 'PROJECT ELECTRA'

After Ricci and Kalaris had gone, Jenkins tried to engage with their successors. King was another New England liberal arts college man with an MBA. He was a smooth and personable corporate financier who understood the British, having worked with Schroders, the London investment bank bought by his previous firm, Citigroup. He had been courted by Diamond for a long time and joined Barclays Capital after the Lehman deal with the brief to build equity origination in London. Although he had no direct experience of trading, he would learn from the Frenchman Bommensath, an expert in fixed income derivatives. It was a good combination.

The world of investment banking had changed dramatically since Barclays had bought Lehman. The Dodd–Frank Act of 2010, which reformed banking regulation in the US, included a provision known as 'the Volcker Rule' which would ban banks from proprietary trading; internationally agreed banking regulations in 2011, Basel 3, proposed new global banking rules on capital, liquidity and stress; and new accounting regulations for derivatives made the old model obsolete. Investment banks were effectively required to hold 50 per cent more capital, depressing returns and forcing senior management to prioritize. The paradigm that drove the Varley–Diamond model of high octane investment banking needed re-examining. In the autumn of 2013, following Project Mango's quick fix, Jenkins ordered a long overdue full strategic review. Named 'Project Electra', it would redesign the investment bank for the new world in a difficult trading background. King and Bommensath led the review and Jenkins persuaded them to take advantage of the new mood of realism to make some radical changes.

The results of Electra were announced in May 2014 but insiders already knew what was coming. In the preceding weeks several senior investment bankers had left suddenly, including Skip McGee, head of Barclays Americas and the most senior survivor from the Lehman deal. Electra was a three-year plan to rebalance the business away from trading towards the less capital intensive business of advising companies and financial institutions. The balance sheet would be cut, some businesses would be closed and 7,000 jobs would go over the next three years. $90 billion of assets described as 'non-core', including a back book of derivatives with risk that stretched out for decades would be ringfenced and wound down.[20] The glory days were over. The bankers hated it and blamed Jenkins.

In contrast, in Threadneedle Street and on North Colonnade the regulators nodded approvingly: Barclays was finally coming to its senses. The ever reliable Walker had delivered yet again. Big investment banks, including Morgan Stanley, UBS and Credit Suisse, had already reoriented their businesses to wealth management, slashing the assets employed in their fixed income businesses. Even Goldman Sachs and J. P. Morgan, the only firms still pursuing grand investment banking strategies, had cut back on capital. Barclays had been alone among major institutions in having bigger assets on the balance sheet at the end of 2012 than it had had in 2009, and to Barclays' regulators, Project Electra was a welcome return to reality.

Walker had steered Electra through a hard core on the board who still resented being strong-armed into losing Diamond and having their grand plans curtailed. They were lying low for the moment, chastened by poor results from the investment bank and the watchful eye of the regulator but they would be back. Walker was due to retire at the annual general meeting in April 2015 when he would be seventy-five. Much would depend on who the board chose to follow him.

Deputy chairman Mike Rake was once more a candidate to take over from Walker and again handed over the search to the senior independent director Sunderland with the inevitable help of Spencer Stuart. It was a thorough process, by far the most rigorous Barclays had ever been through, involving the whole board and discussions with regulators. Rake got the regulators' green light 'in principle' this time, but with some on the board wanting a break with the past, he withdrew.

The man they chose was John McFarlane, whose appointment was announced in September 2014. He would join the board on 1 January 2015 and take over from Walker after the annual general meeting in April. McFarlane was a guitar-playing former chief executive of ANZ Bank in Australia (where he had been dubbed 'Jonny Cash') and had extensive commercial and investment banking experience, including a spell with Citigroup during which he had closed their London investment banking operations soon after Big Bang. He was a decisive, experienced banker and the regulators liked him. He would stand down as chairman of First Group and Aviva to do the Barclays' job. Aviva had sacked the chief executive when McFarlane was chairman-designate and the press now called him 'Mack the Knife'.

CUTS BY STEALTH

By the time McFarlane joined, the heat was off Jenkins: 2014's results would show underlying profits up and bonuses down. The balance sheet was in better shape, leverage had stayed within regulators' comfort levels at twenty-six times tier one equity capital[21] and the share price – now 243 pence – outperformed that of other banks in the second half of 2014. But McFarlane, who had been through several turn rounds in his career and was not the passive kind, knew that the job was not yet done.

The investment bank dominated his interviews and first board meetings. He had always been wary of a business with high fixed costs and unpredictable revenues and had been pleased to see them cut under Walker and Jenkins. Now he wondered whether Electra had gone too far or not far enough. He discussed the issue several times with Jenkins before he took over, including twice during dinner at Jenkins' South Kensington home, where he ended up sharing his host's view that further cuts were necessary. The question was, how deep? Too much would damage the investment bank's revenue potential, too little would leave Barclays over-invested in what was now a low return business.

Jenkins formed a small team in head office, the Stealth Group, to look at this question. Its conclusions were startling. They believed that the investment bank was the reason Barclays' shares were trading at less than half book value – the bank's assets minus the liabilities spread across the number of shares in issue – and that Barclays would never cover the cost of its equity while it retained an investment bank. In 2010, Barclays Capital used £200 billion of risk weighted assets; Project Electra had cut this to £120 billion, but the Stealth Group believed that a further cut to £60 billion was required to bring the risk weighted returns up to acceptable levels. Stealth examined how other banks had made similar cuts, set out how Barclays could do the same and argued that even with the costs of further downsizing, the resultant increase in the share price would leave investors better off.

Jenkins shared these findings with the investment bank's chief executive, King, who was disbelieving. 'Antony, we just can't do this,' King had protested. 'We have £30 billion tied up in operational risk, £30 billion with long term counterparties that we can't get out of and £25 billion in trading inventory. We might as well close the business if this is what you think.' Jenkins did not believe him. He told him to go away and work through a series of scenarios showing the costs and consequences of each option.

Disheartened, King set his team to work and considered his own future. The end of light touch regulation and public demands for more accountability had led to tighter controls over bankers. The Senior Managers Regime, a set of new rules to increase the accountability of banking managers in the UK, would come into force in March 2016 and at the time included a provision for 'reverse burden of proof'. If it had been implemented – it was dropped from later versions – this would have assumed that in enforcement cases those running banks were guilty unless they could prove otherwise. King did not relish taking such responsibility for a strategy with which he disagreed. At one of Jenkins' senior leadership group away days, he decided to have a quiet word with McFarlane.

He explained his concerns about the Senior Managers Regime and told the new chairman that it was not feasible for the bank to have a chief executive and a head of investment banking with different strategies. He would be fifty-five years old on Christmas Day and proposed to retire before then. 'That's not really what I want to hear just now,' said McFarlane. 'We have a series of strategy sessions at the April, May and June boards. Get us through those sessions and we will consider retirement then.'

The last of these meetings would be at a board away day to be held at the Lucknam Park Hotel and spa near Bath. It was a perfect place for a country retreat but its charms were wasted on the Barclays board. This was to be two days and a night of long knives.

COLONEL MUSTARD WITH A DAGGER IN THE LIBRARY

A couple of weeks before heading to Bath, McFarlane called a meeting of the senior non-executives with Jenkins and Tushar Morzaria, the finance director, who had joined from J. P. Morgan in 2013. Those present were the new Audit Committee chairman, Mike Ashley, a serious-minded accountant; Tim Breedon, a former chief executive of Legal & General, who chaired the Risk Committee; Crawford Gillies, a former management consultant, who chaired the Remuneration Committee; and Rake, the deputy chairman.

McFarlane had been trying to achieve an agreement between King and Jenkins for several weeks but they were a long way apart. He had been using a Barclays Capital investment banker, Ben Davey, a specialist in financial institutions to advise him, a job that tested Davey's abilities to manage conflict of interest to the full. Now McFarlane wanted to line up board support for the chief executive's plans in advance of the meeting.

Jenkins knew that he would have to justify every single step to win over that audience. Rake had always backed the investment bank and the Varley–Diamond vision. Ashley had worked with him for twenty years at KPMG. Gillies had spent much of his career at Bain, a management consultancy closely associated with investment banking. Breedon, who had run an institution with a long record of protecting shareholders' rights, he thought, might be more persuadable.

The meeting was held in McFarlane's office suite at 1 Churchill Place, laid out according to the instructions of his feng shui adviser, a Mr Wong. A picture moved here, oriental ornaments placed around the room and carefully arranged furniture created the positive energy McFarlane desired. He had told Jenkins and King: 'We are not going to the offsite with you guys having a difference of views. Get it resolved first.'

The premise of the plan Jenkins presented to the senior non-executives was that the changed regulations in investment banking would depress returns for the foreseeable future. Leverage, the old game in which investment banks played the market with borrowed money, had been killed by the new capital rules and the US regulators' ban on proprietary trading. The Independent Commission on Banking under John Vickers had recommended that retail banks within banking groups be separated from other businesses, and legislation effective from January 2019 required UK banks to place their retail banks in ringfenced subsidiaries.[22] Jenkins believed that this would deprive Barclays Capital of the benefit of the retail bank's credit rating, increase its cost of funds and pare back its already diminishing margins. Consequently, he said, the investment bank would never cover its cost of equity. Given the massive execution risk in the business, it should be shrunk still further.

Jenkins had gone some way to meet the concerns raised by King.

He proposed that risk weighted assets at Barclays Capital be reduced from £120 billion, not to the £60 billion he had originally suggested, but to £100 billion by the end of the first quarter of 2016, with a further cut to £80 billion by the end of 2017. Jenkins said that unless the investment bank could operate on these figures, Barclays would have to approach shareholders for extra capital.

It was a powerful analysis and Jenkins believed that he had won their support. He wrote a cover note summarizing the conclusions of the meeting and called each of those present to confirm that he had their approval. He then directed King to produce a plan that reflected these views: 'Show me a bank that works on £80 billion of risk weighted assets and how we could get there.'

As Jenkins prepared the board pack for the meeting, he looked over King's presentation. It was a seductive investment banker's pitch that worked through various scenarios. As instructed, King had included two slides on the chief executive's plan. But Jenkins was worried. The board had changed a lot from Agius' board of 2012 and only Rake and the former Goldman Sachs people Moyo and Jeffery remained. The new arrivals included two more former investment bankers: Steve Thieke, once head of fixed income at J. P. Morgan, and Diane Schueneman, who was attending her first Barclays meeting after thirty-seven years at Merrill Lynch.

Rake, Gillies and Ashley had seemed supportive at the pre-meeting but Jenkins knew he could not rely on them. That meant that seven of the eleven non-executives might be sympathetic to King, and although Jenkins thought that he had the support of McFarlane and hoped to get a fair hearing from Wendy Lucas Bull, a South African banker, Diane de Saint Victor, a former general counsel, and Breedon, he realized that he could take nothing for granted.

If King was given the floor with this presentation, he would carry the day. Jenkins called him and suggested that he dispense with the handouts and just talk through his strategy but the chief executive had been outmanoeuvred: 'I apologize, Antony, the material has already gone out. The board have seen the packs. I'm sorry if there has been a misunderstanding. I will present this in a balanced way and of course you will be in the room to see that I do.'

The meeting at Lucknam Park culminated in the deepest strategic discussion that Barclays' board had ever had. Participation in Big Bang had been rushed through a quiescent board, Martin Taylor's attempt to have a demerger debate in 1998 had been swept aside and subsequent reviews, including the offsite meetings of 2006, had been designed to enhance rather than challenge the status quo. Now, at last, there was a radically different, properly worked through alternative on the table.

The board pack was voluminous and Jenkins circulated a summary of the background and main issues ahead of the meeting. 'In common with many banks, from around 2000 onwards Barclays pursued a strategy of broad-based global growth, initially focusing on Investment Banking and later Retail and Commercial Banking.' It was the strategy associated with Varley, Diamond and Seegers, and as Jenkins admitted, made sense when the regulators' capital and leverage requirements were low. It had indeed 'provided significant returns to shareholders with returns on equity [ROE] in excess of 20 per cent'.

Then came the crisis. The world changed and Barclays didn't. The fund raisings of 2008 and the sale of BGI in 2009 enabled it to survive but Varley's vision had never been adjusted to meet changed business and regulatory conditions. It was only when the scandals broke in 2012 that the strategy was modified through Project Electra, the 2013 rights issue and Jenkins' cost-cutting programme. These actions, Jenkins said, produced a rise of 3 percentage points in Barclays' tier one equity ratio since 2012, significantly lower leverage, a more focused business model and an improving reputation.

Despite this progress, Jenkins' note continued, the bank's returns were not good enough to please shareholders. Barclays' return on equity was poor and remained below the cost of equity. As a result, the share price was far below the book value of each share. Many banks at the time experienced this same problem but Barclays' discount to book value was more than that of many of its peers.

Wherever the bank operated, Jenkins said, returns were being squeezed by the demands of regulators. In the UK, the ringfence between the retail and investment banks would increase costs from 2019 onwards. In the US, foreign banks such as Barclays with assets of over $50 billion would have to place all their US businesses into a separate intermediate holding company with tight regulation and strict capital rules. The pressure was equally high in every other jurisdiction and accordingly, Barclays now needed to prioritize its capital allocation and investment in favour of businesses showing higher returns and the best growth potential.

The detailed papers accompanying this note included proposals for ringfencing the UK retail bank as the legislation required and taking advantage of the technology revolution which was redefining banking at high speed. There were strategic reviews of two businesses in particular: Africa and the investment bank.

The board met on the first floor of the hotel's conference wing in a room that was slightly too small for comfort and much too warm for a pleasant June day. With the windows open and the board crowded round an oblong table, they went through a very full agenda. The plans to ringfence the retail bank, cut overheads at head office and accelerate the automation of the retail bank were endorsed and there was a long discussion about Africa.

Barclays had been in Africa since 1925. Barclays Africa had been formed in Diamond's time by the consolidation of its existing banking operations in eleven countries across eastern and southern Africa with Absa, one of South Africa's biggest banks, in which Varley had taken a 62.3 per cent stake in 2005. It employed 45,000 people and was quoted on the Johannesburg Stock Exchange.[23] Jenkins had taken the consolidation a stage further in 2013 and his paper was positive about Barclays' prospects in Africa, noting that 'while Africa has the challenges of an emerging market, it is likely to be a relatively high growth area of the world over the next decade.' To realize this potential, Jenkins proposed integration across the continent with other parts of Barclays' retail bank through the sharing of branding, technology and risk management to maximize synergies and to make more use of the Barclays brand name. His plans were roundly supported by the board.

The most contentious topic for discussion, as everyone expected, was the investment bank. King, a classy mergers and acquisitions banker, well used to presenting to boards, had been invited to attend. He worked logically through his pack. He called it 'Project Colours' and it was a description of how to take 'Project Electra' forward over the next few years. Under these plans, Barclays Capital would exit Brazil, Russia and most parts of Asia. European equities would be cut back, as would the capital allocated to the US business. The whole package would equate to £100 billion of risk weighted assets by the end of 2016. Jenkins' amendment was as shown to the senior non-executives and would accelerate the timetable for the cut to £100 billion by nine months to the end of the first quarter of 2016, with further cuts to £80 billion by the end of 2017.

King defended his business robustly. Investment banking, he argued, was not like a light-fitting where you could take out a 200-watt bulb and replace it with a smaller one. If the bank fell below critical mass, revenues would fall faster than costs. 'It is just not possible to shrink your way to greatness.' King understood that Barclays wanted the smallest investment bank possible that worked for clients and for the bank through the cycle but that would need to be bigger than Jenkins thought.

The crux of the matter was whether Barclays Capital would be viable under the Jenkins shrink plan or whether King was right that this would leave Barclays with a sub-scale investment bank. It was a very animated debate but it was not going Jenkins' way. The Wall Street crowd had a lot to say and Jenkins could see the support he had so carefully built up ebbing away. Reversing the position agreed a few days before, the board decided to back King's plan of a cut to £100 billion by the end of 2016 and to leave it at that. It was the most detailed discussion a Barclays board had ever had on the investment bank – and was thirty years late.

Jenkins decided to wait until King left the room before intervening and said nothing further. McFarlane thanked King for his input, and as the door closed behind him tried to move onto the rest of the agenda. Before he could do so, Jenkins spoke up: 'Chairman, before we move on, I really would like to continue the discussion. The cuts we have just agreed do not go far enough. We cannot let the matter rest here.'

McFarlane swore under his breath and looked cross. He was personally sympathetic to Jenkins' view but this subject had been rumbling on for months and it needed to stop. It was time to be decisive. 'No, Antony, there will be no further discussion. We have agreed this. The decision stands.' The meeting discussed a few other items until the conclusion of the formal part of the agenda. Jenkins and Morzaria then departed, leaving the chairman and his non-executives to a prearranged private session. It was to be an informal review of the chief executive's performance that year, something that McFarlane periodically did at all the companies he had chaired. From Jenkins' point of view the timing could not have been worse. There was a lot of anger in the room. It had been a long and tiring day and Jenkins' attempt to prolong the discussion had been badly judged. McFarlane said that he would go round the table one-by-one asking for feedback on Jenkins' performance over the previous months.

Antony Jenkins did not fit the corporate stereotype of a FTSE 100 chief executive. Quiet and serious, cerebral rather than instinctive, an introvert not an extrovert, he did not naturally light up a room when he walked in and was easy meat for investment bankers who might sometimes put style above substance. At every opportunity they had bent board members' ears whingeing about a chief executive who was not one of them and whose strategy threatened their very existence.

Now it was obvious that most of the board and the chief executive wanted to take completely different paths. As it happened, the most strident voices got to speak first, led by the deputy chairman, Rake. 'We have the wrong chief executive and he has to go.' As McFarlane worked his way round the table, more balanced voices were heard. 'Maybe so but he has a lot of strengths. Now is not the time.' The afternoon was drawing to a close and people needed a break, but the board was divided. There would be no resolution that day and McFarlane closed the session.

While the non-executives talked, Jenkins and King had tea in the hotel's grounds. The chief executive was unaware that inside, just a few yards away, the board were discussing his future. He was confident that he would be able to reopen the investment banking debate in due course; he would just have to be patient. Jenkins thanked King for his work and politely expressed regret that he would be leaving. King promised that he would remain fully committed up until his retirement, then returned to his room to pack for the journey home.

King was just putting his things together when he was surprised by a knock on his door. It was McFarlane and he suggested they take a walk together. As they strolled through Lucknam Park's 500 acres, McFarlane said: 'We are not going to let you retire just yet. You have just put a proposition to the board, they have approved it and you cannot just walk out. And why don't you join the board for dinner this evening?'

McFarlane had had a rough day. He was not in the mood for more work and the board needed to cool down. He decided to make the dinner a convivial affair, pouring a lot of wine and keeping the conversation away from the day's discussions. However, Jenkins noticed that Rake sat next to King and was obviously giving him a hard sell about something.

The following morning the board reconvened. McFarlane reminded everyone that the £100 billion target had been agreed and that he expected the investment bank and the chief executive to work to it together. There was a brief further discussion of the investment bank and the rest of the morning was spent working through other items, McFarlane closed the board meeting and left the room with Jenkins and Morzaria.

Now Rake chaired a meeting of the non-executives. He told them: 'We have two big questions to address. Is Antony our man and if not, what should we do about it and when?' and asked them to clarify their views about Jenkins. Overnight, opinion had hardened against Jenkins because of fears that a destabilized investment bank would jeopardize the whole bank. It was a relatively brief discussion – with a brutal conclusion.

After the meeting Rake met McFarlane in reception and they too took a walk in the grounds. Rake told him: 'The non-executives have come to the unanimous decision that Jenkins should go and he should go sooner rather than later. They would like you to become acting chief executive while we carry out a search.' This unanimity would have been a surprise to McFarlane bearing in mind that the previous day the board's opinion had been mixed. Over the next few days he spoke individually to Jenkins' original supporters on the board and asked them to confirm that this was now their view, which they did. Reluctantly, he prepared to deliver some bad news: he would be playing Mack the Knife, not Jonny Cash.

ANOTHER ONE BITES THE DUST

Friday 3 July was a beautiful English summer's day. Jenkins appeared on an editorial panel organized by the *Financial Times* and spoke expertly about 'fin tech', the potential of technology to transform banking. Late in the morning he returned to his office and was called in to see McFarlane. He was told that the board had been discussing his position for some time and that it had been decided that he must step down. 'In the end it was unanimous,' McFarlane told him.

Jenkins paused for a moment. 'I have to say that I am surprised. I received a very strong performance appraisal at the year end. There has never been any suggestion that I should do anything differently. If you fire the chief executive every time that the investment bank says so, this bank is going to have problems. I need to speak to my lawyer.'

McFarlane had been down this road before when Andrew Moss had been fired at Aviva, but now he looked uncomfortable. 'I understand. I have been very worried about this. I haven't been sleeping well. This is in no way personal.'

Jenkins cleared his diary for the rest of the day and went back to South Kensington. He needed time and space to think. He was bemused. And angry. He had been asked to come in to clean up the bank. Through a programme of deep cultural change, Barclays had rediscovered some of the real purpose of banking. Relations with the authorities had been rebuilt. The capital position had been restored and non-core assets run down. The investment bank had been tidied up and negotiations with global regulators over Barclays' past misdemeanours – well, these had gone as well as could be expected. Setting aside fines and provisions for the past, profits for the first half year when they came out would show growth of 11 per cent and a return on equity that at last covered the cost of capital. The share price had risen by 50 per cent during his time, comfortably ahead of the rise in the FTSE 100. This did not feel like failure, and yet his career at Barclays had just been brought to an abrupt end.

He suspected he was the victim of a well-planned coup that had been brewing ever since he had been appointed. The investment banking lobby on the board had kept their heads down while he did the hard work. But now Barclays was off the regulators' naughty step and the political environment had changed. King had been replaced as governor by the Canadian former Goldman Sachs man, Mark Carney, who had a less puritanical view of banking than his predecessor. There would be no instinctive opposition to investment banking from him. Business Secretary Cable was out of government and the authorities' opposition to Barclays' culture and business model had diminished. Chancellor George Osborne had called for a new settlement with banks and would shortly sack Martin Wheatley, a senior regulator thought to be too tough on them. Some of the more stringent aspects of the UK's banking reforms had been rolled back and reconciliation was in the air. Barclays' investment banking lobby had timed their strike to perfection.

Jenkins spoke to his lawyers and worked out Barclays' contractual obligations: he would be paid a year's compensation totalling £2.4 million and would collect £11 million in deferred bonuses and £15 million of shares that had been awarded to him over the previous nine years, including Varley's largesse. The announcement would be made on Wednesday 8 July. On the evening of the 7th Jenkins hosted the Business in the Community Awards, a charity of which he was chairman; it took a lot of fortitude to get through it.

A week after Jenkins' departure was made public, there was more drama from the Barclays boardroom. On 15 July, news was leaked that Rake planned to leave the bank before the end of the year to become chairman of Worldpay, a large payments processor about to be listed on the stock market. Down North Colonnade, a few hundred yards from 1 Churchill Place, Andrew Bailey, by now Barclays' regulator as head of the Bank of England's Prudential Regulation Authority, heard of Rake's intentions only a few hours before the leak. The prospect of the deputy chairman stepping down and leaving McFarlane as acting chief executive and chairman with no experienced deputy would simply not do. He called Barclays and said that Rake would have to stay on the board until a new chief executive and deputy chairman were in place, which he wanted to be as soon as possible. The following day Barclays issued a second statement: Rake would remain until a new chief executive was appointed.[24] He did not have long to wait.

24

The Second Coming of
Jes Staley, 2016

'CAPTAIN CREDIBLE'

Jes Staley was at his desk in an air-conditioned sanctuary in midtown Manhattan on a blistering August afternoon in 2015 when he got a call from Chris Hart, head of Spencer Stuart's financial services practice. Executive search had changed a lot since the intuitive days of Charles Bycroft's entry into the business over thirty years before. Hart was a brilliant academic, had won a fellowship in law at Queens' College, Cambridge and then worked as a derivatives journalist at *Risk* magazine before joining Spencer Stuart. He was quiet and cerebral and had planned this conversation carefully.

Staley was no longer working at J. P. Morgan. On a Saturday morning back in August 2012 he had taken calls from Agius and Walker while sailing his 90-foot boat *Bequia* off the Swedish coast and believed that, subject to the confirmation of a board meeting the following Monday, he would be the next chief executive of Barclays. He had spent that weekend enjoying the cool air of a Scandinavian summer and thinking about how his life would change.

But come Monday, his phone stayed quiet. By the evening he became concerned, and neither Hart nor his contacts at Barclays could tell him what was going on. The following day he heard that Jenkins had got the job. A few days later, newspaper reports identified Staley as the losing candidate and Jamie Dimon, the chief executive of J. P. Morgan, asked him to move off the executive floor.

Soon afterwards, he brought a thirty-year career at J. P. Morgan to a close, becoming a managing partner at Blue Mountain, a New York hedge fund founded by a former colleague. He had been there for three years when Hart called with the news that Barclays wanted to talk to him again. Staley was partly annoyed and partly intrigued. Barclays had embarrassed him three years earlier, but he was not the sulking kind and the possibility of becoming chief executive of a great bank was tempting. Hart told him there were other candidates but everything would be done properly this time. Staley doubted Barclays' ability to keep anything quiet, but it would be easier to talk from an informal hedge fund than it had been from strait-laced J. P. Morgan. He agreed to speak to Barclays, but told Hart: 'Let's not repeat what happened last time.'

There was a different political environment now, and following Jenkins' reforms Barclays itself was in better condition and now looked like a bank that was under control. Furthermore Staley himself had a personal and professional background that the Barclays board and regulators liked. His father had a good business pedigree as president and chief executive of a privately owned Philadelphia chemicals company, while his grandfather, James Rhyne Killian, had been the tenth president of the Massachusetts Institute of Technology and had known Churchill and Eisenhower.

Staley attended public high schools – the US equivalent of British state schools – and was a gifted classical trumpet player. His music helped him win a place at Bowdoin College, a New England liberal arts college, where he majored in economics. He realized that he wasn't going to make it as a professional musician and after graduating got a place on the J. P. Morgan graduate training programme. One of their case studies was the 1976 bankruptcy of the retail chain W. T. Grant, in its day one of the biggest losses in J. P. Morgan's history. The role of Staley's great grandfather Edward Staley, a past chairman and chief executive of W. T. Grant, caused much amusement to the class of 1979.

Once Staley had completed his training, J. P. Morgan sent him to São Paulo, Brazil, where he worked as a corporate and investment banker. It was there he met his future wife, Debora, who worked in her family's office furniture business, Aceco.[1] After returning to New York in 1989, he was taken aside by the firm's president, the Englishman Dennis Weatherstone – who gave the eulogy at David Band's memorial service – and was handed an interesting project. Weatherstone had been lobbying the Federal Reserve to waive parts of a cornerstone of

US banking legislation, the Glass–Steagall Act of 1933, which forbade deposit taking banks such as J. P. Morgan from underwriting securities. The Federal Reserve was about to soften its stance – it finally gave J. P. Morgan permission to trade and sell corporate securities in 1990 – and Staley was one of the three people deputed to build an equities business in preparation for this deregulation.

Staley's role was to set up and run equity capital markets, a vital bridge between corporate clients seeking funds and institutional investors who could provide them. In 2003 he was promoted to take charge of a different side of the business, asset management and private banking, where he took controversial but successful decisions to stay out of passive fund management and buy a majority stake in the hedge fund Highbridge Capital. He could be impulsive but the illness of his HIV-infected brother softened his attitudes, his easy manner and diplomatic skills were well liked, his contrarian decisions paid off, and in 2009 he was promoted again to become chief executive of J. P. Morgan's global investment bank.

He was a different kind of banker from the former bond trader Diamond. Diamond worked his way through college, Staley glided through, mixing holiday jobs with an internship in Washington. Diamond entered Wall Street via the back office, Staley walked straight in the front door. Diamond worked on the trading floor, Staley did corporate deals. British regulators liked his kind as much as they were suspicious of Diamond's.

The Barclays board too had liked Staley's style the first time round and they liked it again now. In sacking Jenkins they had made a strategic choice to stay with investment banking, and many reputations were on the line. Staley went through a long sequence of interviews in August and September with the board and regulators and had the last of several dinners with McFarlane at the London Hotel in New York City on 1 October. His appointment was announced later that month.

Staley's love of sailing was well known – after leaving J. P. Morgan in 2013, he had sailed his boat across the Atlantic – and not long after he joined Barclays, the *Financial Times* described him as 'Captain Credible'. It was a reflective piece which reported that the Jenkins era was already fading fast and quoted one insider as saying: 'When he left, it was as if he was instantly expunged from corporate history.' Referring to the division on the board at the time Jenkins was appointed, the article continued: ' "It has taken us three years to realise that this was a mistake," says a person involved in choosing Mr Jenkins and Mr Staley. "But at the time, there was such hysteria around Barclays, we felt we had no choice." '[2] In South Kensington, a still smarting Antony Jenkins read the piece over his morning coffee. 'I wonder who that could be?' he mused.

'FIRST CLASS BUSINESS IN A FIRST CLASS WAY'

Staley started work on 1 December. The first things he saw when he walked into 1 Churchill Place, were Jenkins' values tablets distributed sculpture-like around the lobby. They jarred with him. He wanted to move Barclays on from fixing the culture to getting the business model right. However, he knew the media would be watching carefully; the tablets would have to stay for a while.

He took the chief executive's corner suite on the thirty-first floor, put a model of his boat on the wall and kept on his desk a book signed by Winston Churchill for his grandfather. He framed a quote from St Augustine, 'Lay first the foundation of humility . . . the higher your structure is to be, the deeper must be its foundation', but otherwise kept the office bare. His glass box in the sky was a world away from Tim Bevan's fusty old study at 54 Lombard Street where Tom Camoys had outlined his plan, but thirty years on the principal issue remained the same. How should Barclays tackle investment banking? The board had chosen to stay in the business but there were different ways of doing it. The question facing Staley was whether universal banking was dead, as Jenkins believed, or whether the bigger ambitions of Varley and Diamond were still appropriate.

J. P. Morgan loomed over the solution. Barclays' finance director, Tushar Morzaria, had reported directly to Staley when they both worked there. He was soon joined by Paul Compton and C. S. Venkatakrishnan, heads of operations and operational risk at J. P. Morgan. By the time Tim Throsby, J. P. Morgan's head of equities, joined to replace the retiring King in January 2017, five of the top six executives at Barclays had come from the same institution.

Just as Camoys had done over thirty years earlier, the J. P. Morgan team looked to their old bank for inspiration. They found it not in the American bank's eponymous founder, sacked by Camoys' great-great-grandfather in the nineteenth century, but in the work of one of Camoys' mentors, Sir Dennis Weatherstone. In taking J. P. Morgan into securities trading, Weatherstone had been pursuing a carefully thought-out strategy. He believed that J. P. Morgan's commercial banking business operated on a different cycle from investment banking, so reckoned that a downturn in one would be offset by an upturn in the other, and he steadily built up its investment bank. After he retired, his successors took his idea of a balanced business a stage further. They decided that consumer banking offered a reliable counterweight to the volatile wholesale businesses of investment and commercial banking. They merged J. P. Morgan with the retail banks Chase in 2000, Bank One in 2004 and Washington Mutual in 2008 to form a full service universal bank.

Events after Weatherstone's death in 2008 seemed to prove the Englishman's counter-cyclical theory. Although J. P. Morgan had its share of problems – including the $6.2 billion derivatives loss in 2012, the response to which had seen Staley replaced as the investment bank's chief executive – the consumer bank got the investment bank through the crisis in 2008 and the roles were reversed in 2009 when investment banking bailed out consumer banking. Throughout the crisis, J. P. Morgan never posted an overall loss. Staley concluded that although there were plenty of examples of universal banks that had got into difficulties – including another early Barclays' role model, Citigroup – diversification worked provided that it was properly executed.

In contrast to Jenkins, Staley believed that the crisis had reinforced not discredited, the argument for universal banking. The US government had given credibility to the idea by engineering J. P. Morgan's takeover of Bear Stearns and that of Merrill Lynch by Bank of America in 2008. In his opinion, and despite structural change and tighter capital rules, there was still room to operate a universal banking model.

In the opening months of 2016, the J. P. Morgan boys carried out a strategic review, testing whether the cash flows from Barclays' consumer bank would be big enough to accommodate the volatility of an investment bank. They kept coming up with the same answer: an investment bank the size of J. P. Morgan's would be too big for Barclays but it could become the leading foreign investment bank on Wall Street provided that the retail bank and other consumer businesses were tightly run.

To learn how to do that, they took another look at their old firm. The merger with Chase in 2000 had taken J. P. Morgan into retail banking for the first time and the subsequent acquisitions of Bank One and Washington Mutual expanded it. Distinct names were preserved after the merger, whereas Barclays operated all its retail banks around the world under the Barclays name. If it was true that retail bank brands had distinct rather than global identities, Barclays' overseas retail banks could be sold or closed down without damaging their own or the group's business. This would conserve capital, improve focus and open up various strategic options.

They did a similar piece of work on investment banking. The business they inherited benefited from the work done by Jenkins and King. Jenkins had insisted on the closure of all proprietary trading businesses in anticipation of the Volcker Rule. Project Colours, King's follow-up to Project Elektra, had begun to refocus the investment bank, but they took the analysis further. They believed that because the biggest users and providers of capital operated out of London and New York, strong banks in those centres could compete globally without being everywhere. All this pointed to a transatlantic investment bank and retrenchment elsewhere, including Africa.

The board meeting at Lucknam Park had identified Africa as a high growth region and looked to create synergies with other parts of Barclays' retail bank but, as Jenkins had pointed out, staying committed to investment banking had capital implications. When Barclays had bought ABSA in 2005 and folded its other African businesses into it, the South African government capped Barclays' ownership at 62 per cent. Regulatory changes after the crisis of 2008, however, made it less attractive for big global banks to hold stakes in other banks because they had to stand behind the full risk of their associate companies while taking only a portion of the reward. This required Barclays to hold capital against 100 per cent of the Barclays Africa balance sheet while consolidating only 62 per cent of the profits. Staley decided that it was the right business with the wrong owner and he wanted to sell it.

Staley took the board through this in January and February 2016. They had taken a big gamble in rejecting Jenkins' focused business and would look foolish if the investment bank blew up. Staley's middle ground between Jenkins' slimmed down version and Diamond's full service global investment bank got them off the hook. The strategy was revealed to the stock market on 1 March. The dividend would be cut, the African business would be sold down to a minority interest and non-core assets would be sold by the end of the following year. Barclays would be positioned as a diversified transatlantic consumer and investment bank. Ahead of the UK's ringfencing regulations, which would come into effect on 1 January 2019, the business was divided into Barclays UK, the consumer bank, and Barclays International, the corporate and investment bank, within a holding company, Barclays PLC. According to early indications from the credit ratings agencies, both the operating companies would be given the coveted status of 'investment grade'.

OUT OF AFRICA

At half-past five in the afternoon of Monday 18 April 2016, Jes Staley knocked on the door of a first floor suite at Claridge's hotel in Brook Street, London. A fellow American, about the same age, opened the door and beckoned him in. Bob Diamond was in town and they had business to discuss.

After his brutal expulsion from Barclays, Diamond had spent the summer of 2012 at his family home on Nantucket. In the early mornings he sat on the front porch in his favourite chair watching the Cape Cod ferries coming in, having a first coffee and catching up with the news on his iPad. He liked to take a morning dip, swimming up and down the pool deep in thought. In the afternoons he would go over to his local golf club to practise his chipping and putting and sometimes play a round. In the evening, friends would often come round for wine on the porch. It looked idyllic, but inside Diamond was burning.

Thousands of supportive messages from employees, clients, friends, even competitors had helped, but the feeling that he had been hard done by would not go away. Friends told him he had been stitched up by the British establishment, but he knew the situation was more nuanced than that. He watched other banks get caught up in the Libor crisis, yet saw their chief executives escape the opprobrium dished out to him. Being the first bank to settle had not turned out well. Far from enabling the bank to put the matter behind it, Barclays and its chief executive had become synonymous with Libor, and in the public mind Libor had become synonymous with everything that was wrong with banking.

It wasn't as if he had failed. It turned out that the marks in Barclays' balance sheet had been no worse than anyone else's and the authorities' suspicions had been ill-founded. The amount it wrote off as a percentage of total loans and advances to customers was the lowest of the major UK banks following the credit crunch. Barclays Capital's £6.1 billion write-down on mortgage and other credit related exposures in 2009, the year the authorities were most worried about, was easily absorbed by a £7 billion increase in trading income that year.

Then there was BGI. He had stopped the board from selling it in 2002 for just over $1 billion and had become executive chair himself. In the following seven years the profitability of BGI grew from just over $100 million a year to nearly $1 billion a year. There were many people who made that happen and there had been a decade of patient investment to prepare the ground. But who had driven it hard and focused on execution? The sale of BGI to BlackRock in 2009 for $15.2 billion provided more capital relief for Barclays than all the equity issuance in 2007 and 2008 combined and, together with a £2.4 billion accounting gain on the acquisition of Lehman, had kept it independent.

He knew that he had been too trusting of the trading floor and had forgotten some of Bill Cook's teaching about culture and values but so had every other firm in the business. Between 2010 and 2016, Barclays paid £15.2 billion in misconduct costs and fines – less than Lloyds (£21.2 billion) and RBS (£17.9 billion) – three-quarters of which was in the retail bank and most of which stretched back to before his time. OK, it wasn't great, but why was he the bad guy? Maybe Rudloff had been right: the British would let an outsider go only so far.

As he swam, paced and putted, Diamond realized he had lost a shoot-out with Mervyn King, governor of the Bank of England. Perhaps it was personal, perhaps it was philosophical. Either way, he had misjudged the mood. King's apparent opposition to the universal banking model and those he saw as 'splendid financiers' put Diamond in his sights and Libor was the excuse to pull the trigger. Diamond thought it was a bit rich coming from an institution that in 2008 had allowed HBOS and RBS to post rates that implied they could borrow in the public markets when really they could fund only from the Bank of England.

On the universal banking model, Diamond read things differently. In 2008 those banks focused only on the UK and only on retail and commercial banking – Lloyds, HBOS, RBS, Northern Rock, Alliance & Leicester, and Bradford & Bingley – all needed to be bailed out or ultimately failed and were merged. The only UK-based banks that successfully navigated through the crisis – Barclays, HSBC, Standard Chartered – had an international footprint, taking deposits around the world and diversifying their income across multiple products and regions.

These thoughts went round and round Diamond's head, but he needed to move on. He had good offers from private equity firms and hedge funds but had no financial necessity to do another day's work in his life and could easily fill his days with the philanthropic Diamond Family Foundation, Colby College or the other charitable causes he supported. What he liked doing, though, was building businesses and he had a conviction that as the financial world settled down after the crisis, there would be potential to acquire financial services businesses that did not fit with existing owners' new strategies. So in 2013 he founded Atlas Merchant Capital with private equity funding, which would be his main vehicle in the search for such opportunities.

Barclays' decision to sell down its African business might be one. He knew the business from his Barclays days and he was attracted to the growth prospects of Africa, where still less than a third of adults had bank accounts. In 2013 he had set up and listed on the London Stock

Exchange Atlas Mara, raising $625 million to build a banking business across sub-Saharan Africa. By the beginning of 2016, he had made several acquisitions, but Barclays Africa was much bigger and was therefore of more interest to his master company, Atlas Merchant Capital. Under the code name 'Project Sesame', he secured commitments of $3–5 billion from American, Asian and Middle Eastern investors.

This was the idea that Staley had come to Diamond's suite in Claridge's to discuss over a glass of white wine. Barclays, however, intended to sell only enough of its African business to avoid consolidation and Diamond did not want to buy a minority interest. Barclays was thus spared the embarrassment of negotiating with its former chief executive.

As 2016 progressed, Staley became increasingly confident. Legacy issues persisted – in January Amanda Staveley lodged papers in the High Court claiming her firm was due £721 million from Barclays in connection with the 2008 fund raisings – but conditions in trading markets picked up and there was a good demand for shares in Barclays Africa when placings with institutional investors began. Analysts were talking up Staley and his vision of a more modest version of Varley's universal bank and Diamond's global investment bank. There were unresolved historical issues with the UK and US authorities, non-core assets to run down, the return on equity did not cover the cost of equity and the share price was trading at below book value, but for the first time in years, Barclays could look forward to a happy New Year and it would soon be safe to take down Jenkins' values tablets from 1 Churchill Place.

'THE THINKER' STILL THINKING

William had become a star. He was thirty-five years old and a partner in the firm. Although the goatee beard divided opinion, he looked the part of an established hedge fund manager. The industry's glory days had ended with the onset of the crisis but the rewards were still there for those who were good, and William and his colleagues were very good indeed. They had ridden the Barclays wave several times, shorting it in 2007–8, picking up a rebound in the share price from 100 pence to 300 pence in 2009, selling out close to the top and then shorting it again in 2010 at 300 pence. They closed the position only when the price had fallen to 200 pence two years later. Each manoeuvre had been the product of careful analysis and precise execution but William had often been the originator. The timing hadn't always been perfect but they had made a lot of money. In the summer of 2017, William once again had Barclays on his mind.

He and his wife had rented a villa in the hills above Grasse, high enough to escape the stifling heat of the Côte d'Azur in August but close enough to Cannes to attend the parties on their friends' yachts. In the early evening he would walk down the lane to the Bar du Senat to drink some beer and watch the world go by. He never completely switched off, though, keeping in touch with the market by day and doing some thinking by night.

Barclays was the stock that had made his name and his fortune and he followed it obsessively. It was still trading at a discount to its book value and William believed he understood why. Investors worried that the investment bank had an inbuilt capacity to self-destruct and would always pull down the value of the whole bank. The market believed it was so interwoven with the retail bank that it could never be detached and would be a permanent drag on the share price.

William, as he often did, thought differently. He believed that once the misconduct costs had been cleared up – and the worst was already past – the bank would have the capacity to increase the dividend. The consumer bank was a strong business and the now much reduced investment bank was capable of covering the cost of its equity. William for one was not writing off Staley's strategy.

However, Staley had faltered after a good start. His transatlantic banking strategy was initially well received. Staley performed well at a dinner hosted by Prime Minister Theresa May soon after she took office in the summer of 2016 and to the British he seemed to be the acceptable face of Wall Street. But then things started to go wrong. Eyebrows were raised at the influx of recruits from J. P. Morgan as outsiders wondered whether this risked creating an inner cabal at the top of Barclays.

Staley hired another former J. P. Morgan banker, Tim Main, to lead the financial services business within the investment bank. Main had left J. P. Morgan several years earlier and after taking a health-related sabbatical had resumed a successful career at a smaller investment bank. He was considered a good catch for Barclays but had not been long appointed before the bank received apparently whistleblowing letters complaining about his behaviour at J. P. Morgan. Staley regarded the allegations as false and malicious and the matter might have rested there except that he unwisely tried to find out who was responsible for sending them. Given the bank's long list of reputational issues and its commitment to rebuilding a better culture, it was a serious misjudgement. The board censured Staley and regulators carried out an inquiry.

McFarlane had to defend the decision not to dismiss Staley over the incident at the 2017 annual general meeting, but the chief executive's reputation sank further a few days later when he was duped by a hoax email he believed to have come from the chairman. The hoaxer purporting to be McFarlane – who had successfully duped other leading banking figures including Bank of England Governor Mark Carney – told Staley he was due a large Scotch for defending him at the annual meeting. Staley replied to the hoaxer: 'You are a unique man, Mr McFarlane. You came to my defence today with a courage not seen in many people. How do I thank you?' He continued: 'You have a sense of what is right, and you have a sense of theatre . . . You mix humour with grit. Thank you John. Never underestimate my recognition of your support. And my respect for your guile.' After more hoax messages which he still believed came from McFarlane he concluded: 'Thanks for sharing the foxhole.'[3]

This was perhaps merely embarrassing, but Staley's judgement was further questioned when he got involved in a dispute between the private equity firm KKR and Aceco, the Brazilian company founded by his father-in-law and for whom his wife Debora had once worked. Aceco had moved from office equipment into technology and Auckland, a private equity fund put together by KKR, had bought a majority stake in the firm from Debora, her brother Jorge Nitzan and others. The business floundered in 2015 when Brazil went into deep recession. Auckland wrote off its $475 million investment and Jorge Nitzan effectively bought back control from the Brazilian bank that funded Auckland. KKR were furious. Amid hotly contested allegations of fraud against his brother-in-law, Staley tried to intervene and in doing so gave KKR an opportunity to publicize his involvement and retaliate by diverting potential business from Barclays. These events and disappointing first half 2017 results led the *Lex* column in the *Financial Times* to liken Staley to the accident-prone children's entertainer Mr Tumble; others wondered whether he had been premature in sanctioning the removal of Jenkins' values tablets from the head office lobby early in 2017.

William decided that Staley's accidents were a side issue and he would probably recover from them. His plan for the business might succeed or it might not, but with the shares far below book value, there were other ways to create shareholder value even if it failed. Barclays' intention was to run the retail and investment banks within the same holding company and the new structure gave them some interesting options. They could float off the retail bank, listing it on the Stock Exchange as a separate company and return the proceeds to shareholders. Or they could try to sell the investment bank as a stand-alone entity and leave investors holding shares in a pure retail bank. Or they could bring in a partner to help grow the investment bank to the levels Diamond had once envisaged. Or they could shrink it, perhaps as a prelude to a full or partial buyout. In 1998 Martin Taylor had failed to carry the board with his plan to demerge retail and investment banking. Twenty years on, however, William reasoned that the new structure would reopen that debate should it become necessary.

There was a lot that could still go wrong. Demerger would be complicated and Staley's strategy would only work if market conditions were favourable. To please investors, Barclays would have to make more money than it had ever done before with a balance sheet only half the size of peak levels. Legal issues further clouded the picture. In June 2017 the Serious Fraud Office charged Barclays, John Varley, Roger Jenkins, Tom Kalaris and another senior executive, Richard Boath, with conspiracy to commit fraud by false representation and unlawful financial assistance over its arrangements with Qatari investors.[4] The trial would start in January 2019 and as a result Amanda Staveley's civil action – by now claiming £1,477 million – was stayed until October 2019.[5] There were plenty of unknowns but William was ready to take a chance. It was time to call another meeting.

On a foggy day in November 2017, Rodin's *Thinker* still occupied one end of the table and the traders and portfolio managers trooped in as before. The BlackBerries had given way to tablets and there were now more suits than T-shirts but it was still a pretty alternative crowd. William sat in the middle of the table; this would be a discussion not a presentation. He had long ago made his name and had no nerves.

At thirty-five minutes past four, the managing partner eased into his chair, an i-Watch on the right wrist, the Rolex on his left. There were a few streaks of grey in the swept-back dark hair and just a hint of receding at the temples. He had given a lot of money to philanthropic causes and was tipped for a knighthood. His eyes narrowed and fixed laser-like on his cleverest young partner. 'So, William, what do you have for us today?'

Epilogue:
And Then

'How do we put some of the blame game behind us? There's [sic] been apologies and remorse from bankers. Today, how do we get banks into the private sector?' Seven years later Bob Diamond's much derided and often misquoted questions to the 2011 Treasury Committee remained unanswered. The past continued to haunt Barclays and the other banks even as they rebuilt their balance sheets and tried to restore their reputations. But the problem was no longer for Diamond or his contemporaries to solve for there had been a generational change at the top of the global banking sector.

Most of those responsible for causing the crisis had left and so too had those who led the initial clean-up. Sometimes the clean-up crew had also been the perpetrators (it could only happen in banking). US Treasury Secretary and former Goldman Sachs banker Hank Paulson left Washington with President Bush in 2009, the year after his work resolving the crisis won him a runner-up award to Barack Obama as *Time* 'Person of the Year': the same magazine also named him one of the twenty-five people most to blame for causing it. The crash cost Gordon Brown the 2010 UK general election but he remained an MP until 2015. He wrote two books in which he positioned himself as a long-standing opponent of the free market, blamed everyone but himself for light-touch regulation and described – rather more convincingly – his subsequent role in stabilizing the financial system. Alistair Darling produced a typically balanced memoir before leaving the House of Commons in 2015 and entering the House of Lords. There he found former ministers Baroness Vadera and Lord Myners, although neither were any longer affiliated to Labour. Shriti Vadera took official leave of absence from the House of Lords after she left government in 2009 and became chair of the bank Santander UK in 2015. Paul Myners participates regularly in House of Lords business, and after leaving government, took up several non-executive positions in financial services and other sectors.

On the day in September 2008 when Brown and Vadera were seeing President Bush in the White House, Jeremy Heywood and Tom Scholar were at the other end of the fax line in London. As British civil servants do, they remained in post when the government changed. In 2012, Heywood was knighted and became cabinet secretary, later also head of the civil service; he remained a trusted adviser to Prime Minister David Cameron and, despite enduring a serious illness, to Cameron's successor, Theresa May. In 2016 Tom Scholar further enhanced his standing as one of Whitehall's most impressive officials, becoming permanent secretary at the Treasury.

The top central bankers of the time glided out of office. Mervyn King retired from the Bank of England in 2013 and was appointed to the House of Lords as a crossbench peer; he became a Knight of the Garter, Britain's highest chivalric order. More prosaically, he served briefly as a director of Aston Villa before discovering that it is even less fun running a struggling football club than it is supporting one. He became a senior adviser to Citigroup and wrote a highly acclaimed book. The Diamond file note of 2008 did not unduly damage the reputation of Bank of England deputy governor Paul Tucker. He left the Bank in 2013 after Mark Carney arrived, was knighted in that year's New Year Honours and went to Harvard to teach and write. Timothy Geithner, the US central banker most directly involved with Barclays during the Lehman acquisition, took over from Paulson as US treasury secretary in 2009 and served for four years before writing his memoirs and becoming president of the private equity firm Warburg Pincus.

The FSA was replaced by the Prudential Regulation Authority and the Financial Conduct Authority in 2013. Andrew Bailey headed them both in succession. Adair Turner remained chairman of the FSA until its abolition, then became chairman of the Institute for New Economic Thinking. He has written extensively and is now much interested in climate change and alternative energy. Turner's predecessor at the FSA, Callum McCarthy, keeps bees and became chairman of Promontory Financial Group, a consultancy that advises financial services firms on regulatory issues. Hector Sants was knighted in 2013 soon after leaving the FSA. He worked briefly for Barclays that year but left, suffering from stress and exhaustion, partly attributable to the strain of the crisis years. He later became vice chair of the consultancy Oliver Wyman and chair of the debt charity StepChange.

Many of the people in senior positions in Barclays during the period covered by this book also suffered stress-related illnesses. Tom Camoys recovered from his stroke and served as an executive director of Barclays until 1994. Stonor Park became a country estate in the modern idiom with gift shop, teas and tours, and its owner became a Permanent Lord in Waiting to the Queen in 2000. As noted in the text, Camoys' successor as chief executive of BZW, David Band, died of a heart attack in 1996, and Band's successor, Bill Harrison, stayed only a year. After leaving BZW, Harrison celebrated his fiftieth birthday with a party at Madame Tussaud's waxworks museum in London in 1998, formed his own investment banking firm and remained an influential adviser on the UK corporate finance scene until his death in 2005. Like many City people of that generation, he was happier as a deal maker than as a manager.

Four men held the top job at Barclays during BZW's history. The first, Sir Timothy Bevan, remained on the Barclays board for a further six years after he retired as chairman in 1987; such continuity would be frowned upon under modern corporate governance guidelines. He died at the age of eighty-eight in 2016. The second, Sir John Quinton, held several non-executive positions after he retired in 1992. He was the last Barclays chairman to have been knighted and died in 2012 at the age of eighty-two. His successor, Andrew Buxton, after serving on the Court of the Bank of England and holding board appointments in the UK and Far East, retired happily to live in Scotland; his wife, Jane, died in 2015. Martin Taylor became chairman of Syngenta AG, a leading agribusiness based in Switzerland, and held various non-executive and advisory appointments in the public and private sectors, including secretary general of the prestigious transatlantic discussion forum, the Bilderberg Group. As his work on the Parliamentary Commission on Banking Standards drew to a close in 2013 he was appointed to the Bank of England's Financial Policy Committee. He still writes occasionally in his old paper, the *Financial Times*.

As related in the book, BZW was succeeded as Barclays' investment bank by Barclays Capital, before it too was rebranded, this time as Barclays Corporate and Investment Bank in 2012. There were five Barclays chairmen and chief executives during the Barclays Capital years. The former Whitehall mandarin Sir Peter Middleton committed himself fully to his second career after he retired from the civil service. He left Barclays in 2004 at the age of seventy after thirteen years on the board; among other appointments, in 2009 he became the first chairman of the litigation finance company Burford Capital. The stock market valued that business at over £2 billion in 2018. Matthew Barrett returned to Canada and joined the Goldman Sachs and other boards after he left Barclays in 2006. John Varley's retirement was blighted by the fraud charges he and others face in January 2019. On being charged, he immediately resigned from his portfolio of corporate and not-for-profit non-executive roles. Bob Diamond took time to get over his ousting, gradually working his way back into the financial services industry through his acquisition vehicle Atlas Merchant Capital. His London office was across the lift lobby from that of Lord Mandelson, who, as business secretary, in 2010 accused him of getting rich 'by deal making and shuffling paper around'. There are no hard feelings. Marcus Agius, the chairman who appointed Diamond and then offered himself as a sacrifice, became chairman of PA Consulting Group and of the Royal Botanic Gardens at Kew: plants had always been a passion.

What of Bob's people? Rich Ricci, the 'fat cat in the hat', joined Barclays before Diamond but made his fortune under his fellow American. After leaving Barclays in Antony Jenkins' time, Ricci's jaunty trilby and the pink and green silks worn by his jockeys became well-known on the National Hunt racing scene. Always fascinated by betting, he became executive chairman of the internet bookmakers BetBright in 2015. His one-time co-chief executive of Barclays Capital, Jerry del Missier, took a lower profile after leaving Barclays, but in 2015 set up an investment firm on the outskirts of London. Tom Kalaris also set up an asset management business before being charged by the SFO.

Sally Bott left Barclays in 2000 during Matt Barrett's tenure. She became BP's global group HR director from 2005 to 2011, until Diamond rehired her to that role at Barclays. When he left, she worked briefly with Antony Jenkins, but after Diamond launched his new business, she went to work with him again. Diamond's assistant at Barclays, Heidi Smith, also joined Atlas Merchant Capital.

Sir David Walker retired as chairman of Barclays in 2015. Like Middleton, the veteran kept up with contemporary developments in the financial services industry and became chairman of Winton Capital, a computer-based hedge fund. It was run by David Harding, a Cambridge graduate who Walker had met while chairing the university's 800th anniversary campaign. After leaving Barclays, Antony Jenkins served out his term as chairman of the charity Business in the Community and took over as chair of the Institute for Apprenticeships. A strong believer in the potential of digital technology to increase competition in banking, he became a thought leader in 'fintech' and, among other things, founded 10x Future Technologies in order to become involved directly. Walker's and Jenkins' successors as chairman and chief executive respectively, John McFarlane and Jes Staley, remain in post at the time of writing. The regulators' inquiry into Staley's hunt for the whistleblower reported in April and May 2018: Staley was reprimanded and fined £642,430, but kept his job. The bank docked £500,000 from his bonus.

In February 2018, McFarlane wrote to shareholders with the results for 2017. His letter said that Barclays had been through

> one of the largest restructuring situations in bank history. While this was partly a consequence of the Global Financial Crisis, it was also partly a consequence of the doubling of the balance sheet and the seven-fold increase in derivatives across 2007 and 2008 immediately prior to the full onset of the Global Financial Crisis.

The effects were 'a sobering lesson':

> Over the past six years, reasonable underlying operating profits have been fully eroded in the process. Over this period we saw £15.1 billion in litigation and conduct charges, £2.4 billion in bank levies, £10.1 billion in losses from Non-Core, a £2.5 billion loss from the sell-down of Barclays Africa and £7.1 billion in taxes (at an average rate of 65%).

All of this, totaling £35.6 billion over the six years, resulted in an aggregate attributable loss of £1.0 billion over the same period. Imagine if all the underlying profits had gone to shareholders and to investment in growth.*[1]

At the time of going to print, the share price was a lacklustre 214 pence.

Most of the non-executive directors who were on the Barclays board after 2000 stayed on the corporate merry-go-round, many holding multiple board appointments, including at FTSE 100 companies. Neither shareholders, regulators nor the search industry held them accountable for what had happened at Barclays.

Of the advisers and other related parties, Charles Bycroft still works in the search industry but is also an active private equity and venture capital investor. David Mayhew stayed at J. P. Morgan Cazenove and also became chairman of Alzheimer's Research UK. Having advised Barclays as it strived to avoid a direct British government stake, James Leigh Pemberton switched sides in 2013 when he became executive chairman of UK Financial Investments, the body created to manage the assets the government acquired during the banking crisis. This included its holding in RBS and, if things had gone differently, might also have included one in Barclays. Chris Hart remained as head of Spencer Stuart's global financial services search business in Europe. Alan Parker was knighted in 2014 and continued to chair Brunswick, the corporate affairs firm he founded in 1987. Amanda Staveley remains an active deal maker; her civil action against Barclays is on hold until after the conclusion of the SFO case. Her 2008 adversary Roger Jenkins was one of the four men charged by the SFO.

William, the Thinker, remained a fund manager, and early in 2018 noted with interest reports of another hedge fund's $1 billion investment in Barclays and the subsequent acquisition of a 5 per cent stake in the bank by Edward Bramson, an activist investor.[2]

Karl Edwards founded a new business, October House Wines. He no longer banks with Barclays.

---

* Readers will note that the total losses identified here amount to £37.2 billion, not £35.6 billion.

Appendix i. Barclays Board Members, 1986–2017

(Shown in date order of retirement, most recent first)

CHAIRMEN

John McFarlane: 2015–ongoing
Sir David Walker: 2012–15
Marcus Agius: 2007–12
Matthew Barrett: 2004–6
Sir Peter Middleton: 1999–2004
Andrew Buxton: 1993–9
Sir John Quinton: 1987–92*
Sir Timothy Bevan: 1981–7*

*Executive chairman, in effect chief executive

CHIEF EXECUTIVES (from first appointed in 1992)

Jes Staley: 2015–ongoing
Antony Jenkins: 2012–15
Bob Diamond: 2011–12
John Varley: 2004–10
Matthew Barrett: 1999–2004
Michael O'Neill: 1999

Sir Peter Middleton: 1998–9
Martin Taylor: 1994–98
Andrew Buxton: 1992–3

DEPUTY CHAIRMEN

Sir Gerry Grimstone: 2016–ongoing
Sir Michael Rake: 2012–15
Sir Richard Broadbent: 2009–11
Sir Nigel Rudd: 2004–9
Sir Brian Jenkins: 2000–4
Sir Andrew Large: 1998–2002
Sir Peter Middleton: 1991–9
Sir Martin Jacomb: 1985–93
Andrew Buxton: 1991–3
Sir Peter Leslie: 1980–91
Sir john Quinton: 1985–7
Derek Pelly: 1986–8

SENIOR INDEPENDENT DIRECTORS
(position first created 2004)

Sir Gerry Grimstone: 2016–ongoing
Sir Michael Rake: 2011–15
Sir Richard Broadbent: 2004–11

NON-EXECUTIVE DIRECTORS

Mike Turner: 2018–ongoing
Matthew Lester: 2017–ongoing
Sir Ian Cheshire: 2017–ongoing
Mike Ashley: 2013–ongoing
Tim Breedon : 2012–ongoing

Mary Frances : 2016–ongoing
Crawford Gillies: 2014–ongoing
Sir Gerry Grimstone: 2016–ongoing
Reuben Jeffery III: 2009–ongoing
Dambisa Moyo: 2010–ongoing
Diane Schueneman: 2015–ongoing
Diane de Saint Victor: 2013–17
Steve Thieke: 2014–17
Wendy Lucas-Bull: 2013–16
Fritz van Paasschen: 2013–16
Sir John Sunderland: 2005–15
Fulvio Conti: 2006–14
Simon Fraser: 2009–14
David Booth: 2007–13
Sir Andrew Likierman: 2004–13
Sir Michael Rake: 2008–15
Alison Carnwath: 2010–12
Sir Richard Broadbent: 2003–11
Leigh Clifford: 2004–10
Professor Dame Sandra Dawson: 2003–9
Sir Nigel Rudd: 1996–2009
Stephen Russell: 2000–2009
Patience Wheatcroft: 2008–9
Dr Danie Cronje: 2005–8
Sir David Arculus: 1997–2006
Robert Steel: 2005–6
Dr Jurgen Zech: 2002–5
Dame Hilary Cropper: 1999–2004
Sir Brian Jenkins: 2000–2004
Sir Nigel Mobbs: 1979–2003
Graham Wallace: 2001–3
Sir Andrew Large: 1998–2002
Peter Jarvis: 1995–2001
Mary Baker: 1988–2000
Lord Nigel Lawson: 1990–98
Jan Peelen: 1991–98
Sir Denys Henderson: 1983–97

Lord Patrick Wright: 1991–6
Sir Derek Birkin: 1990–95
Shijuro Ogata: 1991–5
Sir James Spooner: 1983–94
Sir Timothy Bevan: 1966–93
Sir Michael Franklin: 1988–93
Dr David Atterton: 1984–92
Ian Butler: 1985–91
Henry Lambert: 1966–91
Sir Charles Tidbury: 1978–91
Sir Anthony Favill Tuke: 1965–90
Frederick Goodenough: 1979–89
Sir Richard Pease: 1965–89
Lord James Prior: 1984–9
Francis Dolling: 1976–88
Jason Henderson: 1983–8
Sir Christopher Laidlaw: 1981–8
Deryk Vander Weyer: 1973–88
Lord Ashton: 1969–87
Sir Douglas Wass: 1984–7
Julian Wathen: 1973–87
William Birkbeck: 1970–86
Simon Bolitho: 1959–86

EXECUTIVE DIRECTORS

Jes Staley: 2015–ongoing
Tushar Morzaria: 2013–ongoing
Antony Jenkins: 2012–15
Chris Lucas: 2007–13
Bob Diamond: 2005–12
John Varley: 1998–2010
Frits Seegers: 2006–9
Gary Hoffman: 2004–8
Naguib Kheraj: 2004–7

Matthew Barrett: 1999–2004
David Roberts: 2004–6
Roger Davis: 2004–5
Sir Peter Middleton: 1991–9
Chris Lendrum: 1998–2004
John Stewart: 2000–2003
David Allvey: 1999–2000
Oliver Stocken: 1993–9
Michael O'Neill: 1999 (nineteen days)
Sir Andrew Large: 1998–98
William Gordon: 1995–8
Martin Taylor: 1993–8
Bill Harrison: 1996–7
David Band: 1988–96
Alastair Robinson: 1990–96
Lord Camoys: 1984–94
Sir Martin Jacomb: 1985–93
Humphrey Norrington: 1985–93
Peter Wood: 1991–3
Andrew Buxton: 1984–92
Sir John Quinton: 1985–92
Kenneth Sinclair: 1988–92
Brian Pearse: 1987–91
Alan Tritton: 1974–91
Sir Peter Leslie: 1980–91
Anthony Rudge: 1972–91
Owen Rout: 1987–90
Peter Ardron: 1983–7
Anthony Barrett: 1982–7
Robert John Sayle: 1984–7
Derek Pelly: 1974–88

Appendix ii. Barclays Share Price, 2007–2017

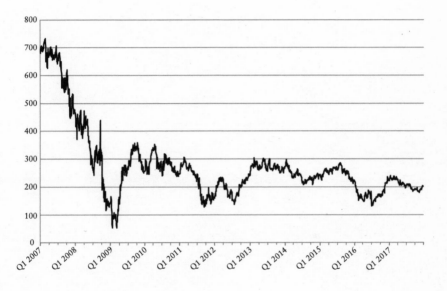

(Key events. Q = quarter)
1. Q2, 2007. Bid for ABN
2. September 2007. Northern Rock
3. Q1 and Q2 2008. The credit crunch
4. September and October 2008. Government recapitalizes Lloyds, HBOS and RBS. Barclays buys Lehman and raises funds.
5. January 2009. Agius–Varley letter to shareholders
6. January 2011. Diamond becomes CEO. Global economy and markets deteriorate.
7. Q2 and Q3 2012. Libor. Jenkins becomes CEO.
8. Q4 2015. Staley becomes CEO.

Notes

1. Lord Camoys' Dream, 1983

1. Philip Robinson and Jonathan Clare, 'Stock Exchange reforms may end legal action', *The Times*, 28 July 1983; Andrew Lorenz, *BZW: The First Ten Years*, BZW, London, 1996, p. 10
2. David Rogers, *The Big Four British Banks*, Macmillan Press, Basingstoke, 1999, p. 70
3. Margaret Ackrill and Leslie Hannah, *Barclays, the Business of Banking, 1690–1996*, Cambridge University Press, Cambridge, 2001, p. 219
4. Christopher Fildes, 'It's not a bad thing to tell it as it is', *Daily Telegraph,* 30 September 2002
5. Ackrill and Hannah, *Barclays*, p. 122
6. Barclays Annual Report 1978, p. 72
7. Ackrill and Hannah, *Barclays*, p. 101
8. Ibid., p. 83
9. Ibid., pp. 396, 399, 424
10. Ibid., p. 378. One measure of a company's performance is the return it makes on shareholders' funds, that is the money originally invested in the business plus the accumulation of subsequently retained profits. To compensate for the risk of investing in a private enterprise, shareholders expected returns to be higher than the rate of return on funds deposited with the government.
11. David Kynaston, *The City of London*, vol. 4: *A Club No More, 1945–2000*, Chatto & Windus, London, 2001, pp. 436–8; Ackrill and Hannah, *Barclays*, pp. 164–5; Rogers, *The Big Four*, p. 28
12. Ackrill and Hannah, *Barclays*, p. 249
13. The secondary banking crisis and the Bank of England's support operations, pp. 233–7, bankofengland.co.uk/archive
14. Ackrill and Hannah, *Barclays*, pp. 399, 402, 409

15. Ibid., p. 241
16. Ibid., p. 424
17. Ibid., pp. 219–221
18. Ranald Michie, *The London Stock Exchange, a History*, Oxford University Press, Oxford, 1999, p. 556; Philip Augar, *The Death of Gentlemanly Capitalism*, Penguin Books, London, 2001, p. 123; Kynaston, *A Club No More*, p. 514
19. Ackrill and Hannah, *Barclays*, p. 243
20. Obituary, Robert H. B. Baldwin, *New York Times*, 6 January 2016
21. Obituary, William Bernard Cook, *Greenwich Times*, 24 January 2008

2. The Golden Ticket: BZW, 1985–95

1. David Kynaston, *The City of London*, vol. 4: *A Club No More, 1945–2000*, Chatto & Windus, London, 2001, pp. 484–93; George G. Blakey, *The Post-war History of the London Stock Market*, Management Books 2000 Ltd, Chalford, 1997, pp. 147–83
2. Andrew Lorenz, *BZW: The First Ten Years*, BZW, London, 1966, pp. 26–7
3. Jehanne Wake, *Kleinwort Benson: The History of Two Families in Banking*, Oxford University Press, Oxford, 1997, pp. 413–24
4. Ibid; Lorenz, *BZW*, p. 29
5. Lorenz, *BZW*, p. 30; Margaret Ackrill and Leslie Hannah, *Barclays, the Business of Banking, 1690–1996*, Cambridge University Press, Cambridge, 2001, p. 243
6. Martin Vander Weyer, *Falling Eagle: The Decline of Barclays Bank*, Weidenfeld & Nicolson, London, 2000, pp. 207–10
7. Harry Enfield, *Harry Enfield and His Humorous Chums*, Penguin Books, London, 1997, p. 24
8. Philip Augar, *The Death of Gentlemanly Capitalism*, Penguin Books, London, 2001, pp. 181–2
9. Vander Weyer, *Falling Eagle*, p. 215. Shareholders compare return on capital to the rate of return on a risk-free investment such as the yield on government stock and to the cost of capital, a complex calculation based on interest rates and the company's share price. In 1993, the risk-free rate of return was 8 per cent and Barclays' cost of capital was a couple of percentage points higher.

3. The Scholar's Tale, 1986–1993

1. Geoffrey Owen, *The Rise and Fall of Great Companies: Courtaulds and the Reshaping of the Man-Made Fibres Industry*, Oxford University Press, Oxford, 2010, p. 119
2. Courtaulds Textiles Annual Report 1990, p. 5
3. Owen, *Rise and Fall of Great Companies*, p. 184
4. Milton Friedman, 'The social responsibility of business is to increase its profits', *New York Times Magazine*, 13 September 1970. Management's 'responsibility is to conduct business in accordance with their [shareholders] desires, which generally will be to make as much money as possible while conforming to the basic rules of society'. This idea was quickly picked up by other academics – notably Alfred Rappaport of the North Western University Business School – management consultants and investment bankers.
5. Barclays Annual Report 1983, p. 3
6. Martin Vander Weyer, *Falling Eagle: The Decline of Barclays Bank*, Weidenfeld & Nicolson, London, 2000, p. 149
7. Ibid., p. 152
8. Barclays Annual Report 1991, p. 29
9. Vander Weyer, *Falling Eagle*, pp. 137–8
10. Margaret Ackrill and Leslie Hannah, *Barclays, the Business of Banking, 1690–1996*, Cambridge University Press, Cambridge, 2001, pp. 222, 358–60
11. Produced by a working party set up by the London Stock Exchange, the Financial Reporting Council and the accountancy profession, recommendations of the Cadbury Committee were formalized into Stock Exchange Listing Rules in 1994. They required companies to comply with best practice or otherwise explain their deviation from it.
12. David Rogers, *The Big Four British Banks*, Macmillan Press, Basingstoke, 1999, p. 98; *Financial Times*, 25 April 1992

4. The Changing of the Guard, 1994

1. When Mercury was formed, private individuals owned 50 per cent of shares in public companies listed on the Stock Exchange, but by 1993 this was down to 25 per cent, institutional investors holding most of

the rest. John Plender, 'Snap and the 21st century governance vacuum', *Financial Times*, 22 February 2017

2. Martin Vander Weyer, *Falling Eagle: The Decline of Barclays Bank*, Weidenfeld & Nicolson, London, 2000, pp. 180–90

3. Geoffrey Owen, *The Rise and Fall of Great Companies: Courtaulds and the Reshaping of the Man-Made Fibres Industry*, Oxford University Press, Oxford, 2010, pp. 183–4; Barclays Annual Report 1993

4. John Jay, quoted in Vander Weyer, *Falling Eagle*, p. 193

5. Patrick Hosking, 'Change of style at Barclays', *Independent*, 21 August 1993

6. David Rogers, *The Big Four British Banks*, Macmillan Press, Basingstoke, 1999, p. 101

7. Ibid.

8. Vander Weyer, *Falling Eagle*, p. 193

9. Rogers, *Big Four*, p. 35

10. Vander Weyer, *Falling Eagle*, p. 197

11. Margaret Ackrill and Leslie Hannah, *Barclays, the Business of Banking, 1690–1996*, Cambridge University Press, Cambridge, 2001, pp. 358, 374. Barclays introduced compulsory redundancies in 1993 and changed employees' terms and conditions to facilitate a more flexible work force. The unions objected and there was a partial strike in 1995.

12. Ibid., p. 364. Disposals included American Mortgage and Business Credit in 1995, enabling Barclays to cut its US loan book from £9 billion to £3 billion.

13. 'New buy-back by Barclays after 15% profit rise', *Irish Times*, 7 August 1996

14. Kirstie Hamilton, 'Barclays chiefs called to account', *Sunday Times*, 4 October 1998

5. A Dark Night in Essex, 1995

1. Securities Industry Association, Securities Industry Fact Book 2006, p. 31

6. The Dumb Money, 1996

1. Tom Wolfe, *The Bonfire of the Vanities*, Pan Books, London, 1988, p. 19

7. In Memoriam BZW, 1997

1. Andrew Lorenz, *BZW: The First Ten Years*, BZW, London, 1996, p. 191
2. Barclays Annual Report 1996, p. 81
3. *Financial Times*, 4 October 1997
4. Barclays confirms sale agreement with CSFB, Barclays press release, 12 November 1997
5. Strategic reorganization of BZW: financial effect, Barclays press release, 2 February 1998; Barclays Annual Report 1997, p. 82

8. Diamond's Halo Slips, 1998

1. Barclays Annual Report 1997, p. 4. This figure excluded BZW's operating losses prior to completion, which took the total to £688 million.
2. Martin Taylor, 'I too fell for the Diamond myth', *Financial Times*, 8 July 2012
3. 'Consequences of Russia', 22 September 1998, board note
4. Roger Lowenstein, *When Genius Failed*, Fourth Estate, London, 2002, p. 198; Statement regarding Long Term Capital Management, 24 September 1998, Barclays press release
5. Martin Vander Weyer, *Falling Eagle: The Decline of Barclays Bank*, Weidenfeld & Nicolson, London, 2000, pp. 15–18
6. 'Consequences of Russia'
7. Barclays Annual Report 1999, p. 92. 'Andrew Large relinquished his duties as an Executive Director on 31 December 1998.' His total compensation fell from £303,000 in 1998 to £227,000 in 1999.

9. Middleton's Law, 1998

1. Quoted in Martin Vander Weyer, *Falling Eagle: The Decline of Barclays Bank*, Weidenfeld & Nicolson, London, 2000, p. 146
2. Lisa Buckingham, 'O'Neill could return to Barclays', *Guardian*, 19 June 1999; 'Is O'Neill for Barclays after all?', *Daily Mail*, 18 June 1999, quoted on This is Money website
3. Nathan Vardi, 'Meet the man who is really running Citigroup', *Forbes*, 17 October 2012

10. Matt Barrett's Master Class, 1999

1. 'Royal–Montreal bank merger', *McLean's*, 2 February 1998; The Andrew Davidson interview: Matt Barrett, *Management Today*, 1 June 2002; John H. Christy, 'Phoenix rising', *Forbes*, 23 July 2001

2. Sarah Hampson, 'For Anne-Marie Sten, it's about love – and money', *Globe and Mail*, 31 August 2013

3. Jon Ashworth, 'Man who banks on giving his best', *Bankwatch*, 29 August 2004

4. Martin Vander Weyer, *Falling Eagle: The Decline of Barclays Bank*, Weidenfeld & Nicolson, London, 2000, pp. 256–7

5. Helen Dunne, 'Cheerleader keeps his bank balanced', *Daily Telegraph*, 4 August 2001

6. Philip Augar, *Reckless: The Rise and Fall of the City*, Vintage, London, 2010, p. 39

7. Geoff Mulgan, quoted in ibid.

8. Peter Mandelson, Speech in California, October 1999, oxfordreference.com

9. Anthony Salz, 'Salz Review: an independent review of Barclays' business practices', Barclays, London, 2013, p. 215

10. 'Barclays would be better off in bits', *Guardian*, 23 March 1999

11. 'The world's most improved investment bank', *Euromoney*, July 2002

12. 'Barclays Capital raids bond teams at Deutsche Bank', *Wall Street Journal*, 15 May 2001; 'Barclays Capital on a headhunting mission', Reuters, 16 May 2001

13. 'Diamond comes up trumps', *Forbes*, 31 March 2003; 'The man who achieved the impossible', *Euromoney*, May 2003

14. 'Barrett's better way to a better Barclays', *Daily Telegraph*, 13 August 2000

15. Michael Becket, 'Not us mate – we're only doing our job', *Daily Telegraph*, 20 May 2002; http://www.publications.parliament.uk/pa/cm200102/cmselect/cmtreasy/818/2051404.htm

16. http://news.bbc.co.uk/1/hi/business/3199822.stm

17. Barclays Annual Report 2000, pp. 66–7

18. Barclays Annual Report 2001, pp. 5, 20

19. For example, Michael Jensen and Kevin Murphy, 'CEO incentives – it's not how much you pay, but how', *Harvard Business Review*, May –June 1990 edition

20. 'Phoenix rising', *Forbes*, 23 July 2001
21. Salz, 'Review', p. 56
22. Barclays Annual Report 2004, p. 12

11. Diamond or Varley?, 2003

1. 'Chairman is named at Barclays Global Investors', *New York Times*, 9 August 2002

12. The Big Vision, 2004

1. Patrick McGeehan and Andrew Ross Sorkin, 'Chase Manhattan to acquire J. P. Morgan for $30.9 billion', *New York Times*, 14 September 2000. In 1999 the US Congress had passed the Gramm-Leach-Bliley Act effectively repealing the Glass-Steagall Act of 1933. Congress. gov/106/plaws/publ102/PLAW-106publ102.pdf
2. Barclays Annual Report 2004, p. 8
3. Ibid., p. 111; Barclays Annual Report 2005, p. 104
4. Barclays Annual Report 2005, p. 33
5. 'Grown up stuff', *Financial Times*, 28 May 2005
6. Barclays Annual Report 2005, p. 41
7. Barclays Annual Report 2006, p. 133, £1.6m pay and bonus, £3.4m buy out, 802.208 shares. Price on 10 July 2006 was 580 pence
8. Calculated by taking the annual appreciation in share price and assuming that all dividends to shareholders were reinvested in shares, Barclays Annual Report 2006, p. 2; Anthony Salz, 'Salz Review: an independent review of Barclays' business practices', Barclays, London, 2013, p. 23
9. Barclays Annual Report 2006, p. 4
10. Speech by the Chancellor of the Exchequer, the Rt Hon Gordon Brown MP, at the Mansion House, London, 21 June 2006
11. Ibid.
12. Barclays Annual Report 2003, pp. 154–62
13. Barclays Annual Report 2006, p. 119; Barclays Annual Report 2007, p. 136; 'Corporate Governance in Barclays', Barclays Corporate Secretariat, March 2007, p. 6, voxmarkets.co.uk/static_files/governance/559e56d5e7498.pdf

13. Dutch Courage, 2007

1. Ian Fraser, *Shredded: Inside RBS, the Bank that Broke Britain*, Birlinn, Edinburgh, 2014, pp. 232–3; Iain Martin, *Making it Happen: Fred Goodwin, RBS and the Men who Blew Up the British Economy*, Simon & Schuster, London, 2014

2. ABN AMRO, Full Year Results 2006, abnamro.com/en/images/ 050_Investor_Relations/010_financial_Disclosures/010_Archives//010_ Results_Releases/ABN_AMRO/files/x/Presentation_full_year_results_ 2006_pdf

3. Speech by the Chancellor of the Exchequer, the Rt Hon Gordon Brown MP, at the Mansion House, London, 20 June 2007. Brown quoted some statistics to prove it: over 40 per cent of the world's foreign equities were traded in London, more than New York; the City's share of global currency trading was over 30 per cent, more than New York and Tokyo combined.

4. Jane Croft, 'Barclays back in the game for ABN', *Financial Times*, 23 July 2007

5. 'Barclays to acquire EquiFirst from Regions Financial Corporation', 19 January 2007, prnewswire.com/news-releases/barclays

6. Michael Lewis, *The Big Short*, Allen Lane, London, 2010, pp. 22–4

7. Anthony Salz, 'Salz Review: an independent review of Barclays' business practices', Barclays, London, 2013, p. 35

8. Ibid., p. 223

9. Ibid., 'Barclays to acquire EquiFirst'

10. Shawn Tully, 'How J. P. Morgan steered clear of the credit crunch', *Fortune*, 2 September 2008; Lewis, *Big Short*, p. xviii; Jenny Anderson, 'Winners amid gloom and doom', *New York Times*, 9 March 2007

11. Barclays Annual Report 2006, p. 68

12. Barclays Annual Report 2007, p. 140

13. 'Barclays buys EquiFirst but at lower price', Reuters, 2 April 2007

14. Reuters, 'S&P slashes SIV-lite ratings on mortgage woes', 22 August 2017, uk.reuters.com

15. Peter Thal Larsen and Paul J. Davies, ' "Hundreds of millions" of failed debt for Barclays', *Financial Times*, 28 August 2007

16. Richard Blackden, 'Barclays shares fall despite Sachsen denial', telegraph.co.uk, 28 August 2007

17. Iain Dey, 'Barclays comes out fighting', telegraph.co.uk, 2 September 2007

18. Reuters, 'Barclays boosts shares with charm offensive', 3 September 2007

19. Barclays plc, Speech at investor conference, investegate.co.uk
20. Iain Dey, 'Barclays urges BoE to bail out money markets', telegraph.co.uk, 2 September 2007
21. Mervyn King, 'Turmoil in financial markets: what can central banks do?' Paper submitted to Treasury Committee, 12 September 2007, especially pp. 3, 8
22. Ibid.
23. Philip Augar, *Reckless: The Rise and Fall of the City*, Vintage, London, 2010, pp. 152–3
24. Robert Peston, *Who Runs Britain?*, Hodder & Stoughton, London, 2008, pp. 169–70
25. Alistair Darling, *Back from the Brink: 1000 Days at Number 11*, Atlantic Books, London, 2011, pp. 28–30
26. House of Commons Treasury Committee, Fifth report, 24 January 2008, vol. 2, Minutes of evidence, 20 September 2007, Q114
27. Linkedin, Carol, Corporate Risk Manager
28. Darling, *Back from the Brink*, p. 326

14. Twilight of the Gods, 2008

1. Tom Junod, 'The deal of the century', *Esquire*, 11 September 2009
2. Andrew Ross Sorkin, *Too Big to Fail: Inside the Battle to Save Wall Street*, Penguin, London and New York, 2009, p. 127
3. Philip Augar, *The Greed Merchants*, Penguin, London, 2006, pp. 40–41
4. Sorkin, *Too Big to Fail*, p. 128
5. 'Barclays announces share issue to raise approximately £4.5 billion', 25 June 2008, barclays.com
6. Project Long Island Discussion Document, July 2008, Barclays Capital, jenner.com/lehman/docs/barclays
7. Statement of the Financial Services Authority [FSA], 20 January 2010, published 12 March 2010, para 4
8. Federal Reserve Bank of New York, Staff report number 719, March 2015, 'The rescue of Fannie Mae and Freddie Mac', p. 1. Stephen Labaton, 'Treasury acts to shore up Fannie Mae and Freddie Mac', *New York Times*, 14 July 2008
9. FSA Statement, 20 January 2010, para 4
10. Email correspondence between John Varley and Bob Diamond, jenner.com/lehman/docs 24 and 25 August 2008

11. Hank Paulson, *On the Brink*, Headline, London, 2010, p. 156
12. Emails between Bob Diamond, Rich Ricci, Jerry del Missier and Robert Steel, 10 September 2008, jenner.com/lehman/docs/Barclays
13. Ibid.
14. Ibid.
15. FSA Statement, 20 January 2010, para 7
16. Ibid., para 9
17. Hank Paulson, *On the Brink,* p. 158
18. FSA Statement,20 January 2010, para 12
19. Ibid., para 11; Timothy F. Geithner, *Stress Test: Reflections on Financial Crises*, Random House Business Books, London, 2014, p. 219; Paulson, *On the Brink,* p. 158
20. Barclays, Internal Presentation, Long Island – Transaction Overview, 12 September 2008, jeinner.com/lehman/docs/barclays
21. FSA Statement, 20 January 2010, paras 18, 19
22. Ibid., para 15
23. Ibid., para 20
24. Paulson, *On the Brink,* p. 162
25. Darling, *Back from the Brink*, p. 121
26. Sorkin, *Too Big to Fail*, p. 357
27. Darling, *Back from the Brink*, p. 121
28. Ibid.
29. FSA Statement, 20 January 2010, para 26
30. Email from Heidi Smith to Bob Diamond, 12 September 2008, jenner.com/lehman/docs/barclays
31. Barclays, Internal Presentation, Long Island key exposures – key due diligence findings, jenner.com/lehman/docs/barclays
32. Sorkin, *Too Big to Fail*, pp. 357–8
33. Paulson, *On the Brink*, p. 164
34. Ibid., p. 169
35. Ibid., p. 175
36. Ibid., pp. 169, 174
37. Ibid., p. 177
38. Email from Hans-Joerg Rudloff to Bob Diamond, 12 September 2008, jenner.com/lehman/docs/barclays
39. Email from Rich Ricci to Bob Diamond, 12 September 2008, jenner.com/lehman/docs/barclays
40. FSA Statement, 20 January 2010, para 33
41. Ibid., paras 39, 40
42. Ibid., para 42

43. Geithner, *Stress Test*, p. 228
44. Paulson, *On the Brink*, p. 178
45. Sorkin, *Too Big to Fail*, p. 420; Paulson, *On the Brink*, p. 178
46. FSA Statement, 20 January 2010, paras 46–9
47. Geithner, *Stress Test*, p. 229
48. FSA Statement, 20 January 2010, para 54
49. Paulson, *On the Brink*, p. 179
50. Ibid., p. 180; Darling, *Back from the Brink*, p. 123; Geithner, *Stress Test*, pp. 186–8
51. Email from Bob Diamond to Rich Ricci and Jerry del Missier, 15 September 2008, jenner.com/lehman/barclays
52. Email from Bob Diamond to John Varley and Chris Lucas, 15 September 2008, jenner.com/lehman/barclays
53. Sorkin, *Too Big to Fail*, p. 552; 'The deal of the century', *Esquire*, 11 September 2009
54. Peter Latman, 'Klein got $10 million advising Barclays on Lehman', *New York Times*, 30 August 2016

15. Night Falls, 16 September–13 October 2008

1. Gordon Brown, *My Life, Our Times*, Bodley Head, London, 2017, e-edition, p. 286. 'Gordon Brown and the 2007 election: why it never happened', Damian McBride, *Daily Telegraph*, 5 October 2012
2. Bank of England Financial Stability Report, October 2008, pp. 1–8
3. Andrew Rawnsley, *The End of the Party: The Rise and Fall of New Labour*, Penguin Books, London, 2010, pp. 560–61
4. Brown, *My Life*, p. 388
5. 'Was Gordon Brown's summer outfit at Southwold really that bad?', *Daily Telegraph*, 2 August 2008
6. Brown, *My Life*, p. 388
7. Gordon Brown, *Beyond the Crash*, Simon & Schuster, London 2011, pp. 43–59, quote from p. 58
8. Brown, *My Life*, p. 389
9. Federal Deposit Insurance Corporation, Information for Washington Mutual Bank, fdic.gov
10. Brown, *Beyond the Crash*, p. 64
11. Hugh Pym, *Inside the Banking Crisis: The Untold Story*, Bloomsbury Publishing, London, 2014, p. 70

12. Alistair Darling, *Back from the Brink: 1000 Days at Number 11*, Atlantic Books, London, 2011, p. 145

13. Ibid., p. 146

14. 2005 MOU, http:// hm-treasury.gov.uk/6210.htm; Philip Augar, *Reckless: The Rise and Fall of the City*, Vintage, London, 2010, p. 50

15. Brown, *Beyond the Crash*, p. 79

16. Ibid., pp. 76–9

17. Pym, *Inside the Banking Crisis*, p. 97; Darling, *Back from the Brink*, p. 150

18. Iain Martin, *Making it Happen: Fred Goodwin, RBS and the Men Who Blew up the British Economy*, Simon & Schuster, London, 2013, p. 30

19 . Damian McBride quoted in Pym, *Inside the Banking Crisis*, p. 109

20. Darling, *Back from the Brink*, p. 150; Pym, *Inside the Banking Crisis*, p. 109

21. Andrew Lorenz, *BZW: The First Ten Years*, BZW, London, 1996, pp. 47–50

22. Ibid., pp. 176, 182–3. It was initially renamed BZW Barclays Global Investors.

23. Barclays Annual Report 2000, p. 146

24. Barclays Global Investors Equity Ownership Plan, excerpt from Barclays plc Form 20F, filed 24 March 2009

25. Brown, *My Life,* p. 405

26. Anthony Salz, 'Salz Review: an independent review of Barclays' business practices', Barclays, London, 2013, pp. 215, 216, 223

27. Darling, *Back from the Brink,* p. 329; Brown, *Beyond the Crash*, p. 92

28. 'Bank shares fall despite bail-out', 13 October 2008, bbc.co.uk

29. 'Update on capital, dividend and current trading', 13 October 2008, newsroom.barclays.co.uk

30. Tucker-Heywood, bankofengland.co.uk/publications/Documents/other/treasury committee/financial stability/emailsbetweenptjh.pdf

31. House of Commons Treasury Committee, Minutes of Evidence, 25 November 2008, Mervyn King, Q34

32. Gillian Tett, 'Libor's value called into question', *Financial Times*, 25 September 2007; Carrick Mollenkamp, 'Libor fog: bankers cast doubt on key rate amid crisis', *Wall Street Journal*, 16 April 2008

33. Jacob Gyntelberg and Philip Wooldridge, 'Interbank fixings during the recent turmoil', *BIS Quarterly Review*, March 2008

34. David Enrich, *The Spider Network: The Wild Story of a Math Genius, a Gang of Backstabbing Bankers, and One of the Greatest Scams in Banking History,* W H Allen, London, 2017, pp. 200–202
35. Tucker-Heywood, ibid.
36. Ibid.
37. Ibid.
38. Ibid.
39. Ibid.
40. Treasury Committee, *Fixing Libor,* vol. 1, File note, Bob Diamond, 29 October 2008, para 72
41. Ibid.
42. Ibid.
43. bankofengland. co.uk/publications/Documents/for/disc 170712a.pdf

16. When Amanda Met Roger, 2008

1. Author estimate and Anthony Salz, 'Salz Review: an independent review of Barclays' business practices', Barclays, London, 2013, pp. 71–2
2. Caroline Binham, 'Qatari connection casts long shadow over Barclays', *Financial Times,* 23 March 2017. Other reports credit the wife of an Italian industrialist with the introduction.
3. Claim number CL-2016-000049, PCP Capital Partners and Barclays Bank plc
4. Ibid.
5. Ibid. Barclays later challenged her account.
6. Ibid. Barclays would dispute that there was any discussion of other investors.
7. Ibid.
8. Louise Armitstead, 'Amanda Staveley: the woman behind Abu Dhabi's capital injection into Barclays', *Daily Telegraph,* 1 November 2008
9. Harry Wallop, 'Barclays secures bankers' bonuses by turning to Middle East investors', 31 October 2008, telegraph.co.uk
10. Sam Jones, 'Chastising BARC: "an issue of grave concern"', 19 November 2008, ftaphaville.ft.com
11. 'Top Barclays investor will back fundraising plan', uk.reuters.com, 20 November 2008
12. Landon Thomas, 'Angry shareholders vent over Barclays' investment plan', *New York Times,* 24 November 2008
13. Ibid.

17. Antiques Roadshow, 2009

1. Anthony Salz, 'Salz Review: an independent review of Barclays' business practices', Barclays, London, 2013, p. 222
2. Neil Hume, 'That Barclays statement', *Financial Times*, 16 January 2009
3. 'Bank bail out: key points of the government statement, *Guardian,* 19 January 2009
4. Open letter from Marcus Agius and John Varley, 26 January 2009, newsroom.barclays.com
5. House of Commons Treasury Committee, 'Banking crisis: reforming corporate governance and pay in the City', 12 May 2009, p. 14
6. Investor presentation, spring 2009, Barclays.com/investorrelations
7. Hector Sants, 'Delivering intensive supervision and credible deterrence', 12 March 2009, fsa.gov.uk
8. Letter from Chancellor to Treasury Select Committee, 19 June 2008, parliament.uk/documents/upload/Chancellor08619F.pdf
9. Philip Augar, *Reckless, The Rise and Fall of the City*, Vintage, London, 2010, pp. 50, 195
10. George Parker and Jane Croft, *Financial Times*, 27 March 2009; Faisal Islam, *The Default Line*, Head of Zeus, London, 2013, e-edition, pp. 510–16
11. Ibid.
12. George Parker, Jane Croft, Peter Thal Larsen, 'Barclays' stress test signals no new funds', *Financial Times*, 27 March 2009
13. Barclays Annual Report 2009, p. 74
14. 'Barclays completes the sale of BGI to BlackRock', December 2009, newsroom.barclays.com
15. Barclays announces receipt of binding offer of $13.5 billion (£8.2 billion) by BlackRock for BGI, 12 June 2009, Securities and Exchange Commission Form 6-K, sec.gov

18. Crown of Thorns, 2010

1. Jill Treanor, 'Bonus time as banks pay out £40 billion', *Guardian*, 8 January 2010
2. Simon Duke and Olinka Koster, 'Sachs of gold', mailonline, 15 April 2009, dailymail.co.uk

3. 'How to tame global finance', *Prospect*, September 2009

4. Sam Jones, 'Barclays creates £12 billion credit vehicle', *Financial Times*, 16 September 2009

5. Anthony Salz, 'Salz Review: an independent review of Barclays' business practices', Barclays, London, 2013, p. 46

6. 'Barclays gags Guardian over tax', *Guardian*, 17 March 2009

7. Salz, 'Review', pp. 45–50

8. Market investigation into payment protection insurance, Competition Commission, 29 January 2009, webarchive.nationalarchives.gov.uk

9. Salz, 'Review', p. 57

10. Web.archive.org/web/20060705165338/http://www.firstplus.co.uk:80/01_aboutloan_protect.asp

11. publications.parliament.uk/pa/jt201213/jtselect/jtpcbs/writev/misselling/sj015.htm

12. Rebecca Atkinson, 'Banks challenge PPI ban', moneywise.co.uk, 5 May 2009

13. Barclays interim results statement, 3 August 2009

14. Philip Aldrick, 'Barclays makes the case for universal banking', *Daily Telegraph*, 4 August 2009

15. Barclays Annual Report 2009, p. 16

16. Barclays Annual Report 2010, p. 159

17. Barclays Capital Global Financial Services Conference, New York, 15 September 2009, Barclays.com

18. Adair Turner, 'The Turner review: a regulatory response to the global banking crisis', Mar 2009, fsa.gov.uk

19. House of Commons Treasury Committee, 'Banking crisis: reforming corporate governance and pay in the City', 12 May 2009, p. 3

20. Rachel Sylvester and Katherine Griffiths, 'Lord Mandelson gets personal over banker's pay', *The Times*, 3 April 2010

21. 'Lord Mandelson attacks Barclays head', 3 April 2010, news.bbc.co.uk

22. James Moore, 'Does Bob Diamond have polish for top job?', *Independent*, 7 September 2010

23. Harry Wilson and Richard Blackden, 'American Bob Diamond to take over as new chief executive of Barclays', *Daily Telegraph*, 7 September 2010

24. Eilis Ferran, 'The break-up of the Financial Services Authority', University of Cambridge, Faculty of Law Research Papers, series no. 10/4

25. Hector Sants, 'The application for Bob Diamond to perform controlled functions 3', Group Chief Executive for Barclays Bank plc, 15 September 2010, fsa.gov.uk
26. Alistair Darling, *Back from the Brink: 1000 Days at Number 11*, Atlantic Books, London, 2011, pp. 146, 162

PART IV

19. Thin Ice, 2011

1. James Moore, 'Rich Ricci', *Independent*, 22 March 2013
2. Stephanie Baker and Jon Menon, 'New boss at Barclays', Bloomberg, January 2011
3. 'Britain needs better banks', *Which?*, October 2009
4. Barclays Annual Report 2010, p. 16
5. Ibid.
6. House of Commons Treasury Committee, Competition and choice in the banking sector, 11 January 2011, Bob Diamond and Antony Jenkins, oral evidence, publications.parliament.uk
7. Ibid., Q532
8. Ibid., Q586
9. Ibid., Q564
10. Ibid., Q545
11. Ibid., Q564
12. Ibid., Q579
13. James Moore, 'Bob Diamond: no apologies, no restraint, no shame', *Independent*, 12 January 2011; Harry Wilson and Louise Armitstead, 'Bob Diamond: "Time for banker remorse is over"', *Daily Telegraph*, 12 January 2011; Sharlene Goff and George Parker, 'Diamond says time for remorse is over', *Financial Times*, 11 January 2011
14. 'Ministers have unconditionally surrendered to the banks', 11 January 2011, tuc.org.uk
15. Elaine Moore, 'Barclays tops FSA customer complaints', *Financial Times*, 28 September 2011
16. Patrick Jenkins and Megan Murphy, 'Protium assets return to haunt Barclays', *Financial Times*, 27 April 2011
17. Barclays Annual Report 2011, pp. 20, 175

18. Today Business Lecture 2011, news.bbc.co.uk

19. 'Financial crisis: the Bank of England's surprising bonus culture', *Prospect*, 11 August 2009

20. A Boardroom Row, 2012

1. Barclays Annual Report 2011, p. 14

2. Statement on banking by the Chancellor of the Exchequer, 9 February 2011, gov.uk

3. Barclays plc Remuneration Report 2010, p. 14, barclays.com

4. Jill Treanor, 'Barclays hands five bankers £110 million', *Guardian*, 7 March 2011

5. Anthony Salz, 'Salz Review: an independent review of Barclays' business practices', Barclays, London, 2013, p. 134

6. Barclays Annual Report 2010, p. 187. Salz, 'Review', p. 220 and for a general discussion of remuneration, pp. 130–50

7. Barclays Annual Report 2011, pp. 55, 58

8. Parliamentary Commission on Banking Standards – Minutes of Evidence HL Paper 27-III/HC 175-II, 30 January 2013, Sir John Sunderland, Q3322

9. House of Commons Treasury Committee, 'Fixing Libor: some preliminary findings', 9 August 2012, vol. 1, para 128

10. Ibid., para 133

11. Ibid., para 128

12. Ibid., para 133

13. James Quinn, 'Barclays pay row lifts the lid on the bank's closed culture', *Sunday Telegraph*, 14 April 2012

14. Laura Kuenssberg, itv.com, 26 April 2012

15. Adair Turner, Letter to Marcus Agius, 10 April 2012

16. robinhoodtax.org.uk/nurses-versus-bankers-barclays-agm

17. Jill Treanor, 'Barclays' investors vent anger on boardroom pay', *Guardian*, 27 April 2012

18. Dambisa Moyo, *Dead Aid: How Aid is not Working and How There is a Better Way for Africa*, Penguin Books, London, 2010

19. Harry Wilson, 'Barclays annual meeting as it happened', *Daily Telegraph*, 27 April 2012

20. Parliamentary Commission on banking standards, written evidence, Alison Carnwath, 21 January 2013

21. Here Today, Gone Tomorrow, 2012

1. Liam Vaughan and Gavin Finch, *The Fix: How Bankers Lied, Cheated and Colluded to Rig the World's Most Important Number*, Wiley and Bloomberg Press, Chichester, 2017, pp. 111–15
2. Ibid., p. 131
3. Ibid., pp. 111–14
4. Ibid., p. 162
5. 'Fixing Libor: Some preliminary findings', written evidence, vol. 1, p. 1. By the end of the investigation, Barclays spent £100 million screening 22 million emails and over 1 million audio files.
6. 'Barclays fined £59.5 million for significant failings', 27 June 2012, fsa.gov.uk
7. Ibid.
8. 'Barclays Bank plc settlement with the authorities', 27 June 2012, newsroom.barclays.com
9. 'The rotten heart of finance', *Economist*, 7 July 2012
10. Nils Pratley, 'Can Bob Diamond hang on after Barclays' Libor scandal?', *Guardian*, 27 June 2012
11. Harry Wilson, 'Barclays hit with £290m fine over Libor fixing', *Daily Telegraph*, 27 June 2012
12. 'Barclays: Cameron says bank faces "serious questions"', 28 June 2012, bbc.co.uk
13. Financial Conduct Authority, Interest Rate Hedging Products, background to review, fca.org.uk
14. 'FSA agrees settlement with four banks over interest rate hedging products', fsa.gov.uk/library/communication/pr/2012/071.shtml
15. 'Fixing Libor', evidence from Marcus Agius, vol. 2, Q541, 10 July 2012
16. 'Barclays confirms SFO investigation', 29 August 2012, newsroom.barclays.com. As this book goes to press, the matter is *sub judice* and cannot be discussed.
17. House of Commons Treasury Committee, Bank of England, June 2012, Financial Stability Report, Adair Turner, 17 July 2012, Q1
18. Ibid. and 'Fixing Libor', vol. 2, Q1, Q2 and Q1205
19. Treasury Committee, Financial Stability Report, Q3
20. 'Fixing Libor', vol. 2, Q541
21. 'Barclays board changes', 2 July 2012, barclays.com
22. Mervyn King, *The End of Alchemy*, Little, Brown, London, 2016, p. 141

23. Treasury Committee, Financial Stability Report, Evidence from Mervyn King, Q27
24. Ibid., Q88
25. Ibid., Q31
26. Ibid., Q28
27. 'Fixing Libor', vol. 2, Q635
28. Treasury Committee, Financial Stability Report, Qs 39–40
29. Ibid., Q36
30. 'Fixing Libor', vol. 2, Q635
31. Barclays press release, 'Board changes', 3 July 2012, newsroom.barclays.com
32. 'Fixing Libor', vol. 2, Evidence from Bob Diamond, Q1, 4 July 2012
33. Ibid., Q115; 'George Osborne: Bob Diamond resignation is "right decision", bbc.co.uk, 3 July 2012
34. 'Fixing Libor', vol. 2, Q114
35. Ibid., Q136
36. Ibid., Q319

22. A Complete Mess, 2012

1. Nils Pratley, 'Alison Carnwath quits Barclays: wrong time, wrong job', *Guardian*, 25 July 2012
2. HM Treasury, 'A review of corporate governance in UK banks and other financial industry entities', Final recommendations, 26 November 2009, p. 12
3. Sir David Walker appointed to succeed Marcus Agius as chairman, Barclays.com, 9 August 2012; Martin Vander Weyer, 'Barclays surprise choice of chairman is Old Father Time with his lyre', *The Spectator*, 18 August 2012
4. Barclays Annual Report 2010, p. 18
5. Barclays Annual Report 2011, p. 176
6. Ibid., p. 24
7. Ben Wright, 'Just who is Bill Winters, the new chief executive of Standard Chartered?', telegraph.co.uk, 28 February 2015
8. HM Treasury, 'A review of corporate governance in UK banks and other financial industry entities', p. 12
9. Kamal Ahmed, 'If Barclays' new chief needs to be "safety first" then Antony Jenkins fits the mould', telegraph.co.uk, 18 August 2012

23. 'Barclays is not the place for you', 2015

1. 'Forex rigging settlement', *Financial Times*, 15 May 2015
2. Financial Conduct Authority [FCA], 'Barclays fined £26 million for failings surrounding the London Gold Fixing', 25 May 2014, fca.org.uk
3. Javier Blas, 'Barclays case shocks the energy market', *Financial Times*, 1 November 2012
4. Matthew Coupe, 'Dark pools need clampdowns', *Financial Times*, 5 April 2013
5. FCA, 'Barclays fined £38 million for putting £16.5 billion of client assets at risk', 23 September 2014
6. Emma Dunkley, 'RBS to pay £4.2 billion for mis-sold US mortgage-backed securities', *Financial Times*, 12 July 2017
7. Martin Arnold, 'Barclays fined $2.4 billion for Forex rigging', *Financial Times*, 20 May 2015
8. FCA, 'Barclays fined £26 million for failings surrounding the London Gold Fixing'
9. 'Barclays' $453 million fine for US energy market-rigging upheld', bbc.co.uk
10. 'Barclays and Credit Suisse are fined over US "dark pools"', 1 February 2016, bbc.co.uk
11. Roland Gribbens, 'Barclays Wealth division "out of control" says secret report', *Sunday Telegraph*, 20 January 2013
12. Jill Treanor, 'US justice department accuses Barclays over mortgage mis-selling', *Guardian*, 22 December 2016
13. Anthony Salz, 'Salz Review: an independent review of Barclays' business practices', Barclays, London, 2013, pp. 6–7. The report cost £14.8 million, ibid., p. 172.
14. Ibid., p. 6
15. Barclays Annual Report 2013, p. 340
16. Ibid.
17. 'Antony Jenkins to staff: adopt new values or leave Barclays', 17 January 2013, telegraph.co.uk
18. Martin Arnold, 'Knives come out after Jenkins outstays his welcome', *Financial Times*, 9 July 2015
19. Barclays Annual Report 2013, p. 48
20. Tom King, Barclays Global Financial Services Conference, 8 September 2014, Barclays/Barclays-investor-relations.com
21. Barclays Annual Report 2014, p. 32

22. Independent Commission on Banking, Final recommendation, September 2011, webarchive.nationalarchives.gov.uk
23. Barclays Annual Report 2012, p. 18; Martin Arnold, 'Diamond eyes Barclays Africa assets', *Financial Times*, 4 March 2016
24. Martin Arnold, 'Mack the Knife loses shine amid Barclays' woes', *Financial Times*, 18 July 2015

24. The Second Coming of Jes Staley, 2016

1. Kate Kelly, 'James Staley's series of unfortunate events', *New York Times*, 26 August 2017
2. Martin Arnold, 'Barclays: Captain Credible', *Financial Times*, 16 October 2015
3. Martin Arnold and Kadhim Shubber, 'Barclays tightens email security after Jes Staley hoax', *Financial Times*, 21 May 2017
4. The case will begin in January 2019. 'The four Barclays men charged with fraud by the SFO', *Financial Times*, 20 June 2017
5. Caroline Binham, '$1 billion lawsuit against Barclays postponed', *Financial Times*, 9 November 2017; Barclays Annual Report 2017, p. 286. In May 2018 the Crown Court dismissed all charges brought by the Serious Fraud Office against Barclays in the context of the capital raisings of 2008. Barclays said: 'The SFO is likely to seek to reinstate these charges by applying to a High Court Judge to re-commence proceedings via a new indictment of the same charges.' Dismissal of SFO charges against Barclays PLC and Barclays Bank PLC, Barclays press release, 21 May 2018.

Epilogue: And Then

1. Barclays Annual Report 2017, p. 2, chairman's letter
2. Martin Arnold and Miles Johnson, 'Hedge fund makes $1 billion bet on Barclays rebound', *Financial Times*, 22 January 2018; Neil Collins, 'Barclays has been a miserable investment so it's no surprise a raider has appeared', *Financial Times*, 24 March 2018

Index

Abdullah, King of Jordan 228
ABN AMRO
  acquisition by RBS 165–6, 168
  proposed merger with 154–8,
    164, 165–6, 168
Abrahams, Iain 76, 260
ABSA, South African bank 353,
    364
Abu Dhabi 228–9, 230, 233–41
Aceco company 360, 370
advertising 7, 35
  2000 campaign 111
advisory services agreements, SFO
    investigation 342
Africa
  Jenkins' proposals for 353
  part sale of assets 364–5, 367–8
Agius, Marcus, chairman 151–2,
    205, 215, 376
  and ABN deal 157, 168
  and Abu Dhabi deal 239, 241
  and AGM (2012) 305
  and appointment of Diamond
    268–71, 273
  and Carnwath 291, 292, 298–9
  and Diamond's pay 301–2
  FSA letter to 302–4
  and Lehman bid 189

and letter to shareholders (2009)
    246–7
  and Libor investigation 307–9,
    315–16
  and recapitalization 214, 219–20
  resignation 316–18, 328
  and share price 243–4
  and Varley 267–8
Ahmed, Kamal 335
AIG insurance company 181, 198,
    202
Aitken, John 233–4
Alex Brown investment bank 72
Allen & Overy 236
Allvey, David 110
Andrew, Prince 228
Arculus, David, non-executive
    board member 89, 90, 129
Ashley, Michael 349, 350, 351
Asia
  capital markets 62
  financial crisis (1997) 75, 82, 83
asset management, passive (index
    funds) 212
Asset Protection Scheme 244
Association of British Insurers
    237
AstraZeneca 158

Atlas Merchant Capital 367
Avendis Group 164

Bailey, Andrew, Bank of England
    300–301, 315, 358, 374
  and Agius 319–20, 322
  and Diamond 302, 316, 317, 323
Baker, Mary, non-executive board
    member 72, 89
Baldwin, Robert, Morgan Stanley 15
Ball, Charles, Barclays merchant
    bank 9
Band, David
  and Bott 50
  chief executive of BZW 26–7, 47,
    53, 54, 55
  death 68, 375
  and restructuring of BZW 29–30
  and Taylor 54–5
Bank of America 147, 244, 340,
    363
  and Lehman 183, 186
  and Lehman bankruptcy 198
  merger proposal 139
Bank of Credit and Commerce
    International 40
Bank of England 40
  and Barclays' exposure in
    Russia 85
  controls 7, 11
  emergency funding 203, 205,
    207–8
  interest rates 114
  as lender of last resort 166–8
  'lifeboat' bank rescues (1974–78) 8
  powers of 207
  and quantitative easing 244
  relationship with FSA 251
Bank of International Settlements
    223

Bank of Montreal 106, 108–9
  Institute for Learning 109
Bank One 363, 364
Bank of Scotland 98
Bankers Trust 61, 75
  acquisition of Alex Brown 72
Barber, Anthony, chancellor of the
    exchequer 7
Barber, Brendan, TUC 285
Barclaycard 69, 122, 211
  Jenkins at 140–42
Barclays 5–7
  2017 results 377
  and Abu Dhabi deal 233–41
  acquisitions (2007) 160–66
  AGM (2012) 304–6
  appointment of chief executive
    (1994) 42–5
  audit of business practices (2013)
    341
  bad debts 38–9, 110–111
  capital reserve 47
  Charter of Expectations 152
  and competition 34–5
  Credit Committee (1998 meeting)
    81–3
  criticisms of 259, 284–6
  and financial crisis (2008) 204–210
  formal Warning Notices from
    FCA 341–2
  growth and complexity (by 2006)
    149–50, 152–3
  imposition of fines by US 274–5,
    310–311, 339–40
  and Libor 223–5
  merger proposals 139, 147
  move to Canary Wharf 140
  Nominations Committee 109
  profits 37, 38–9, 42, 46–7, 123,
    137–8, 146

and Protium deal 259–61
and recapitalization 220–21
regulators' concerns about 319–21
reputational damage 314–16,
    328–9
rights issue (1988) 36
rights issue (2013) 345, 352
Risk Committee 163, 164
strategic uncertainty (1999) 105
and suggestion of Treasury
    funding 218–20
Taylor's policies 46–7
Varley's reorganization 142–4
see also Barclays board; Barclays
    Capital Group
Barclays Bank, Dominion, Colonial
    and Overseas (DCO) 6, 73
Barclays board 13, 37–8, 71, 150
2006 meeting (Brocket Hall)
    146–50
2013 meeting 299–302
and ABN AMRO negotiations
    156–7, 164, 165–6
and appointment of Varley
    129–30
board committees 293–4
and BZW 47–8
Carnwath's view of 293–4
choice of Jenkins 334–6
commitment to universal banking
    137, 263–4, 274, 332–4
decision against removal of
    Diamond 314–16
disfunctional relations 99,
    100–101
and incentives 295, 296–7,
    302–3, 340
investors' loss of faith in 105, 303
leaks to press 71, 74
and McFarlane's strategy 351–5

non-executive directors 150, 152,
    321, 378
and Protium deal 260–61
Remuneration Committee 294,
    295, 297–9, 301, 341
role of chairman 150–51
and Staley 361–2
and sub-prime exposure 163
Taylor and 88–92, 93–4, 97
Barclays Capital Group 77, 152,
    268, 376
acquisitions (2008) 173
and 'Alpha Plan' 135, 146
ambitions for 135, 153
and bid for Lehman Brothers
    179–98
capital consumption review 118
difficulties 285–6
expansion 117–19, 137–8, 161–2
exposure to bad debt 165, 172
and Libor manipulation 308–9
long-term incentive plans 295,
    296–7, 302–3, 340
New York board meeting (1998)
    88–93
profits 118, 285
proposed cuts 345–7, 348
reduction of risk weighted assets
    351, 353–4
Risk Solutions Group 254–5, 286
and Russian markets 81–3, 84–6
strategy meeting (2010) 279–83
warning about 159–60
Barclays Corporate and Investment
    Bank 376
Barclays Global Investors (BGI) 84,
    92, 129, 211–14
sale to BlackRock 255–6, 266
Barclays Global Retail and
    Commercial Banking 264–5

Barclays International 365
Barclays Merchant Bank 5, 6–7, 9
Barclays UK 365
Barclays Wealth 340
Barings bank 54
Barrett, Matt 106–9, 138, 146, 376
    appointment as chief executive
        110–12
    and BGI 213
    and branch sales management
        124–6
    as chairman 127–8, 138, 139
    and choice of Varley 131–2
    and customers 126
    and Diamond 116–17, 131–2
    early career 108–9
    private life 107, 110
    and retail banking 119–24, 340
    staff presentations 112
Basel 2 Regulations 243
Basel 3 Regulations 346
BBC Today Business Lecture 287–8
Beale, Graham, Nationwide 206
Bear Stearns 164, 172, 177, 363
Bernanke, Ben, US Federal Reserve
    164, 201
Bevan, Sir Timothy, chairman 5,
    34–5, 375
    and Camoys's plan 11–12
Bews, Caroline 64
Big Bang (October 1986) 4, 14, 25–7
    problems of 28–9
Big Society Bank 294
Birkin, Sir Derek 38, 42, 71
Birmingham see Edwards, Karl
Black Monday (October 1987) 28
BlackRock 238
    sale of BGI to 255–6
Blair, Tony, Prime Minister 147
    and 'Cool Britannia' 112–15

Blankfein, Lloyd 191
BNP Paribas 164
Boath, Richard, SFO and 371
Bommensath, Eric, Barclays Capital
    344, 345
bond issues 8, 47
bond markets 57, 69, 117
    European 62
bonuses 51, 66–7, 302–3
    for branch staff 125, 126, 171
    government restraints on 295
    and incentive plans 295, 296–7,
        302–3, 340
    Jenkins' reforms 344
    performance 125
    public outcry against 257–8,
        269–70
    rises 345
Booth, David 173, 285–6, 292, 299,
    301–2, 334
Bott, Sally 49–53, 110, 377
    and Carnwath 297
    and Diamond 63, 295–6, 325
    return to Barclays 294–5
    and Taylor 53–4
    view of BZW 51–2, 65
Bradford & Bingley 204, 205
Bramson, Edward 378
branch closures 111–12
branches, as marketing units 124–6
Brand and Reputation Committee
    126, 341
Brazier, Alex 322
Brazil 370
Breedon, Tim 349, 350, 351
British Banking Association (BBA)
    223, 307
Broadbent, Sir Richard 129, 150,
    151, 260, 292
    and Risk Committee 163, 172

Brown, Alan 82
Brown, Gordon
  and 2010 election 272
  chancellor of the exchequer 113,
    131, 146–8, 157
  and financial crisis (2008)
    199–204, 208–9
  meeting with Bush 203
  and nationalization of banks
    220–21
  as prime minister 157, 199, 258
  reputation 200–201, 222,
    271–2
  and Vadera 248
  and Walker 329
Brown, Sarah 201
Brydon, Donald 68
BGI 212
Buffett, Warren 193, 230
building societies, transformation
  to companies 120
Bull, Wendy Lucas 351
Bully Banks pressure group 313
Burt, Peter 103
Bush, George W., US President 180,
  203
Buxton, Andrew 35, 42, 375
  at BZW 37
  and Camoys' plan 12–13
  as chairman of Barclays 43–4, 47
  and Qatar 178
  and resignation of Taylor 97, 99
  retirement 103
  and sale of BZW 74
  and Taylor 70, 88–9, 90–91,
    93–4
  as vice-chairman of Barclays 37
Buxton, Jane 44
Bycroft, Charles 20–22, 23, 30, 42,
  66, 378

  and Band 26, 27
  and Bott 49–50
  and Diamond 55–6, 57–8, 62–3
BZW (Barclays De Zoete Wedd)
  14, 64, 212, 376
  annual compensation meeting
    50–51
  and Big Bang 25
  and bonuses 66–7
  compared with Citigroup 51–3
  fixed income business 57–8, 63
  integration problems 22–3
  Kleinwort raid on 24–5
  poor performance 29, 47–8,
    65–6, 69, 72
  restructuring 29–30
  review of (1996) 55, 70–71
  Structured Capital Markets 231
  Taylor's plans for disposal 71–3
  tribalism 64, 65
  see also Barclays Capital Group;
    Barclays Global Investors

Cable, Vince 237, 258, 358
  on bonuses 270, 303
  as business secretary 272–3
Cadbury Committee, report
    on corporate governance 38,
    42, 70
Cahill, Edward 164
Cambridge Science Park 227–8
Cameron, David, Prime Minister
    201, 292, 312, 374
  and Big Society Bank 294
  coalition government 272
Camoys, Thomas Stonor, Baron
    4–5, 9, 149, 375
  and Bott 50
  and capital markets 9–10
  and establishment of BZW 22–3

Camoys, Thomas – *cont.*
  plan for transformation of
    Barclays 10–14, 363
  and Stock Exchange reforms 3–4
  stroke (1987) 26
Canada, deregulation 106–7
capital markets 8, 9–10, 13
  Asia 62
  British lack of experience in 26
  newer 117
  US dominance 69
Carney, Mark, governor of the
    Bank of England 358, 374
Carnwath, Alison 151, 291–2
  and 2012 board meeting 299–302
  and AGM (2012) 305–6
  and Barclays board 293–4, 327
  and bonus culture 296–7
  and Bott 297
  opposition to Diamond's bonus
    297, 298–9, 327–8
  Remuneration Committee 297–9
'Carol' 169–71
Carpenter, Michael 43
Carrington, Lord 5
cash machines 123
Cazenove, broking firm 14, 207
Chambers, Peter 238, 239
Chase bank 134, 363, 364
China Development Bank 157
China Investment Corporation 238
Citigroup 9, 49, 136, 363
  acquisition of Schroders 134
  and Lehman bid 192
  losses 171, 244
City of London 4, 53
  American banks in 53–4
  confidence (2007) 157, 199–200
  deregulation 25
  mass redundancies (1974) 8, 22

and New Labour 113–14
reputation 147–8
and resignation of Diamond
  325–6
Clegg, Nick, coalition government
  272
Cleghorn, John 106
Clifford Chance 233–4
collateralized debt obligations 152
Combined Code of Corporate
  Governance (1998) 148–9
Commodity Futures Trading
  Commission (CFTC) (US) 307,
  310–11
competition 11–12, 34–5, 123
  from building societies 119–20
  from retail banks 34, 111
  from US investment banks 10
Competition Commission 122, 123
Compton, Paul 362
computers 19, 23
  integrated technology 118
  risk management models 46
  TAPS (automated share trading) 16
Connect, debit card 35
Conti, Fulvio 292
Cook, William Bernard 15–19, 22
  and Diamond 17–18, 59, 280, 366
  and graduate recruitment scheme
    117–18
  TAPS 16, 19
Corbat, Michael 104
corporate finance 69, 73
corporate governance
  Cadbury report on 38, 42, 70
  Combined Code (1998) 148–9
  and non-executive directors 150
  reforms (1990s) 340–41
Countrywide Financial (US) 164
Courtaulds 33, 43, 45

Cox, Archie 197
credit cards, charges 122–3
credit default swaps 152, 162
credit ratings 164, 365
Credit Suisse Financial Products
    (CSFP) 61
Credit Suisse First Boston (CSFB)
    59–61, 76, 119, 221, 232
    purchase of BZW 75
Crocker Bank (US) 37
Croft, Jane 252
Cropper, Hilary, non-executive
    board member 89, 130
Cruickshank, Donald, report on
    banks 111–12
customer service 35
CVC Capital Partners 255–6

Daniels, Eric, Lloyds 206
Darling, Alistair, chancellor of the
    Exchequer 167–8, 192, 215,
    373
    and Barclays' bid for Lehman
    186–7, 195–6
    and financial crisis 204
    and nationalization of banks
    220–21
    and Treasury meeting 205
    and Varley 274
Davey, Ben 350
Davie, Jonathan 74
Davis, Peter, Prudential 101
Davis, Roger 129, 130, 139
Dawson, Professor Sandra 130, 150
De Zoete & Bryan 14
Dean Witter bank 72
debt and borrowing 121
    see also leverage
del Missier, Jerry 66, 76, 117, 133,
    138, 376

co-head of Barclays Capital 280,
    285, 311
    and Lehman bid 182, 184, 188,
    196
    resignation 323
Deloitte 344
deregulation 21, 25, 28
    Canada 106–7
    United States 19, 28
derivatives
    equity 70–71, 76, 117
    interest rate 65–6
    mortgage linked 161
    over-the-counter 61
    and risk exposure 149–50
    to hedge against Russian
    exposure 83, 86
    see also structured collar option
Deutsche Bank 240
Dexia, Belgium 203
Diamond, Robert E. (Bob) 56, 57,
    365–8, 376
    and acquisitions 173, 177–8, 216
    and Barclays Africa 367–8
    and Barclays board 293–4
    and Barclays Capital 82–3,
    100–101, 116–19, 135, 268
    at BZW 64–7, 68, 76–7
    as candidate for CEO 105
    career 16–17, 58–63
    and choice of chief executive 129,
    130, 131–3
    confidence 281–3
    and Cook 17–18, 59, 280, 366
    criticism of Bank of England 166
    at CSFB 59–61
    and financial crisis (2008) 215–17
    and Fuld 187–8
    Governor King's demand for
    resignation 317–23, 367

Diamond, Robert E. – *cont.*
  and interview with John
    Humphrys 286–90
  and Jenkins 331
  and Lehman bid 179–80, 181–2,
    189–98
  and Libor 224–5, 309–310,
    311–12, 366
  at Morgan Stanley 58–9, 60
  and pay 138, 269–70, 295–6,
    297–9, 305–6
  as president of Barclays 138
  reputation 119, 129, 137–8,
    269, 271
  resignation 323–5
  and restructuring of BZW
    76–7
  Ricci's video 281
  rule on initiatives 118, 161
  and Russian market 81–3, 86–7,
    90, 91
  and sale of BGI 366
  and Staveley proposal 234–5
  and sub-prime crisis 165
  and Treasury Committee 323–5,
    373
  and universal bank strategy
    282–4, 367
  and Vadera 248–9
  and Varley 133, 134–5, 150–51
Dibb, Gary 110
Dickinson, Lawrence 327
Dimon, Jamie 72, 191, 332–3, 359
Distillers 42
Dodd-Frank Act (2010) (USA),
  'Volcker Rule' 346, 364
Donini, Jerry 189, 190
dot.com revolution 113
  crash 114, 123
Dougan, Brady 191

Dow Jones index, falls (2008) 204,
  230
Dresdner bank 54
Dubai, IMF and World Bank
  meeting 131
Dunn, Pattie 92, 255
  and BGI 212–14

Eadie, Craig 229–30
Earle, Glenn 234
Eastern Europe, emerging markets
  81–2
Economist, on Libor scandal 312
economy
  1992-3: 31
  2006 boom conditions 148
  'Barber boom' inflation 7–8
  global 121–2, 123, 146, 172
  influence of financial service
    sector 200
  recession (1974) 8
  recession (from 2009) 257–8
  recovery (1990s) 46–7
Edwards, Karl, October House
  Records 115–16, 144–6,
    168–71, 210–211
  compensation 337–8
  and derivatives charges 249–50,
    253–5, 312–13
  liquidation 312–14
  and October House Wines 378
  and Risk Solutions Group 254–5,
    286
  structured collar option 169, 170,
    254, 312, 337
Eisman, Steve 162–3
elections
  1974: 8
  2010: 258, 272
Electric Storage Battery company 15

Ellwood, Peter 122
emerging markets 81–2, 87
    see also Russia
Enron 148
EquiFirst 161, 164
equity capital 146
equity trading 70, 73
euro, launch of 62
Euromoney 118–19
Europe, and financial crisis 203
European Central Bank, provision
    of emergency credit 165
European Commission, and Libor
    enquiry 307
European monetary union (1999) 62
Exchange Atlas Mara 368
executive search 30, 42–3, 359
    origins of 21–2
    for successor to Taylor 101, 102–3
    see also recruitment; Spencer
    Stuart partnership

Fairbrother, Jeremy 227
Fannie Mae, US mortgage company
    180, 181
Financial Conduct Authority (FCA)
    272, 337, 374–5
    formal Warning Notices 341–2
financial crisis (2008) 199–204, 373–4
    bank rescues 230
financial instruments 149, 152
Financial Services Act (2012) 320
Financial Services Authority (FSA)
    84–5, 114, 374–5
    and Barclays recapitalization
    211–14
    concern about Barclays 261,
    272–3, 300, 302–4, 328–9
    and Libor investigation 310–11
    and light-touch regulation 148

and PPI 262–3
    and recapitalization 209
    split 272
    stress tests 250–53
    see also McCarthy, Callum;
        Sants, Hector; Turner, Lord
Financial Services and Markets Act
    (2000) 270
Financial Times 252–3, 357, 361–2
    Alphaville column 244
    Lex column 32, 371
Fink, Larry 256
Firstplus, and PPI 262
Fisher, Dick, president of Morgan
    Stanley 18–19
fixed income bonds 69, 76–7
football, cheating and gaming in
    338–9
foreign exchange controls, abolition
    11
foreign exchange markets,
    manipulation 338
Forster, Malcolm, risk department
    82, 85
Fortis Group, Belgium 203
Franklin, Sir Michael 37
Fraser, Simon 292, 298–9, 334
Freddie Mac, US mortgage
    company 180, 181
Fuld, Dick, Lehman Brothers 178,
    184, 187–8
fund managers, money-making 147,
    159

Galley, Carol 41, 121
Geithner, Timothy, US Federal
    Reserve 181–2, 183, 223, 374
    and Barclays' bid for Lehman
    185, 187–8, 191–2, 194, 195
    and Brown 203

George, Eddie, governor of the
    Bank of England 37, 88, 92
Germany, bank rescues 208
Gieve, John, Bank of England
    185–6, 198
Gillette 147
Gillies, Crawford 349, 350, 351
Glass-Steagall Act (1933) 361
Global Retail and Commercial
    Banking 143
gold market, rigging 338
Goldman Sachs 53, 239
    and Lehman bankruptcy 197
    recapitalization 230
    and sale of BZW 74, 75
    and sub-prime exposure 162
Goodwin, Fred, RBS 122, 123, 206
    and bid for ABN 156, 157
    retirement 220
Greenspan, Alan 121–2
Groenink, Rijkman, ABN AMRO
    154–6
Grossmann, Blake, and BGI 213
Guardian 312
Guinness plc, and Distillers 42

Hance, James 139
Harding, David 377
Harding, Mark 190, 191, 193,
    282, 307
Harrington, Noreen 82, 85–6
Harris Bank 108
Harrison, Bill 68–9, 71–3, 375
    remuneration 72–3, 75
    and sale of BZW 74, 116
Hart, Chris 359, 360, 378
Haviland, Christopher 82
Hawkes, Michael 24
HBOS 148, 203
Heath, Edward, Prime Minister 7

hedge funds 19
Henderson, Sir Denys 38, 42, 71
    and Taylor 43, 44–5
Hennessy, Jack 59–60
Herbert, Gill 95–6, 128
Heywood, Jeremy 201, 374
    and Libor 223–4
    and Tucker 222–5
Higgs, Derek, accounting review
    148
Hoffman, Gary 129, 130, 139, 140,
    141
    group vice-chairman 144
    and Jenkins 142
Hogg, Christopher 32–3, 45
HomEq, US mortgage servicing 162
Hopkins, Sir Anthony 111
Horrocks, Mark 234
Horta Osório, António, Santander
    206
House of Commons, Treasury
    Select Committee (2002) 122
Household International (US) 172
Howe, Geoffrey, chancellor of the
    exchequer 11
HSBC 206
    bad debts 163, 172
Humphrys, John, and Diamond
    interview 286–90
Hypo Real Estate, Germany 208

Iceland, Glitnir bank 203
ICI 43
Idzik, Paul 140, 142
IMF/World Bank, autumn meeting
    (2008) 214–15
incentives 295, 296–7, 302–3, 340
    and sales techniques 125
Independent Commission on
    Banking 282, 350

Industrial Bank of Japan 8
insurance policies 125
inter-bank lending market 200, 203
    see also Libor
Interest Rate Hedging Product
    (IRHP) 170
interest rates
    New Labour period 114, 147
    record low 257, 313
    rise (1988) 36
    US rise 53
International Emergency Economic
    Powers Act (US) 275
International Financing Review 138
International Nickel company 15
internet banking 111
    'Open Plan' platform 120
investment banks
    crisis (1995) 54
    ringfencing 350, 352–3, 365
    risk-taking 135
    US 10
IPIC (International Petroleum
    Investment Company) 230,
    232, 233

J. P. Morgan bank 4, 15, 27, 153,
    340
    acquisition of Bear Stearns 172,
    177, 363
    sold to Chase 134
    Staley and 359–61, 364
    and sub-prime exposure 162
    and Washington Mutual 202
Jacomb, Martin, chairman of BZW
    23–4
James, Howell 252
Jarvis, Peter, non-executive board
    member 89, 97–8
Jassim, Ali 235–6

Jeeps, Dickie 226–7
Jeffrey, Reuben, the Third 286,
    291–2, 335
Jenkins, Amanda 136, 141, 142
Jenkins, Antony 139–40, 265–6, 377
    appointment as CEO 330–32
    Barclaycard 140–42
    at Citigroup 136
    conflict with investment bankers
    343–4
    reform strategy 332, 341, 343–5,
    347–9
    relations with King 350–51, 353–6
    resignation 355–6, 357–8, 362
    values tablets 344–5, 362, 368
Jenkins, Sir Brian 127, 129–30
Jenkins, Roger 76, 217, 231–3
    and SCM 260
    SFO and 371, 378
    and Staveley 230, 232–5
John, Dyfrig, HSBC 206
Johnson Matthey bank 40
Jones, Stephen 217–18, 233
Joss, Robert, Westpac 101

Kalaris, Tom 117, 376
    and Lehman bid 184, 188
    resignation 344
    SFO and 371
    and Staveley 230
Kapito, Robert 256
Keegan, Mike 66–7
Keeley, Michael 259
Kelly, Robert 191
Kheraj, Naguib 117, 150, 213, 249
Killian, James Rhyne 360
Kimbell, David 43, 45
    and successor to Barrett 151
    and successor to Taylor 101, 103,
    105, 108

King, Mervyn, governor of Bank of
    England 166–8, 215, 374
  and Brown 201
  demand for Diamond's
    resignation 318–21
  and Libor 223
  and Rake 320–21
  and recapitalization 204, 206
  and Treasury meeting 205–6
King, Stephen 259
King, Tom, Barclays Capital 344,
    345
  and Jenkins 350–51, 353–6
  'Project Colours' 353–4, 364
  on proposed cuts 348–9
Kingman, John 205, 217
KKR private equity firm 370–71
Klein, Michael 192, 198
Kleinwort Benson 10, 54
  poaching of Wedd Durlacher
    traders 24–5
Kvalheim, Grant 138, 161–2

La Salle bank (US) 155
Lagarde, Christine 187
Large, Sir Andrew, executive
    director 89, 91, 137
  and Taylor 93, 94
Larsen, Peter Thal 252–3
Lawson, Nigel, Baron 38, 89, 98
Lazards 255
Le Blanc, Robert 172, 204, 248–9,
    282
  and Risk Committee 163
Leadsom, Andrea, MP 284, 325
Leeson, Nick 54
Legal & General 125
Legal & General Investment
    Management 238, 239
Lehman Brothers 165

bankruptcy 196, 197–8, 202
  Barclays' interest in 178–98
  conditions of deal 190–92
  imminent collapse 183–4, 185
  losses 179, 180
  sale of equities and corporate
    finance to Barclays 198
  toxic assets 188–9
  and US government liquidity
    guarantee 191–4
Leigh Pemberton, James 158, 165,
    314, 378
Leigh Pemberton, Sir Robin 40
lending
  Barclays policy 35, 36
  Birmingham 115–16
  government 'corset' restraint
    (1973) 7–8, 11
  increased 9, 46
Lendrum, Chris, head of corporate
    banking 90, 91, 98
leverage
  ended 350
  falls 250, 263, 347–8
  high level 243–4
  increased 121, 122, 146, 162
Lewis, Ken 139
Libor (inter-bank lending rate)
  Barclays Capital and 308–9
  enquiry into manipulation 270
  global investigation into 307–8
  imposition of US fines 310–311
  manipulations 222–5
  traders' chat room messages
    309–310, 311
Likierman, Sir Andrew 150, 260, 292
Link consortium 111
Lloyd, Jerry, Morgan Stanley 18
Lloyds Bank 37, 47, 73, 124, 340
  and HBOS 203, 205, 218

Lombard Street, 54, Barclays head
  office 5
Long Term Capital Management
  (LTCM) 87, 92
Lucas, Christopher, finance director
  197, 204, 282, 291, 311, 330

McCarthy, Sir Callum 148, 186,
  187, 194, 258–9, 374–5
McDade, Bart 189, 190, 196, 198
McDermott, Tracey 311
McDermott Will & Emery 307
McFall, John, MP 167, 258,
  269–70, 283
McFarlane, John, chairman 377
  2017 results 377
  appointment 347
  and Jenkins 349–56, 357, 358
  and Staley 361, 370
McGee, Skip 346
Mack, John 60, 119, 191, 196
McKillop, Sir Tom, RBS 208
Macpherson, Nicholas 205
Main, Tim 369–70
Major, John, Prime Minister 31, 112
Mandelson, Peter, Lord 113, 376
Mansour bin Zayed al Nahyan,
  Sheikh 228–9, 232–3, 235–6
  and IPIC 230, 238–40
marking-to-market 303–4
Marrone, Sam 58, 76
Martin, Paul, Canadian finance
  minister 106
Mathewson, George, RBS 86, 103
Maughan, Deryck 143
Maxwell, Robert 148
May, Theresa, Prime Minister 369,
  374
Mayhew, David 42, 207, 218, 317,
  378

MBNA 147
Meddings, Richard 118
media 253–4
  inaccurate reporting in 208
  on Libor scandal 312, 321
  and PPI misselling 262–3
  view of Diamond 285
Melzer, Thomas C. 15–16, 18, 59
merchant banks, expansion of 10
Merck Finck, sale of 111
Mercury Asset Management 41
mergers, multinationals 147
Merrill Lynch 54, 171, 363
Mickelson, Phil 269
Middleton, Sir Peter 37, 70, 123,
  376
  and appointment of Varley as
    chief executive 127–33, 267–8
  and Barrett 109
  and board 100
  and Bott 50
  chairman of BZW 47
  as chief executive and chairman
    98, 99–101
  and Diamond 100–101
  'Middleton's Law' 98, 100
  non-executive board member 89,
    90
  and O'Neill 102, 103
  and resignation of Taylor 95–9
  and sale of BZW 74
  and successor to Taylor 105
Midland Bank 34
  rescue 37
Miliband, David 201
Miller Smith, Charles 43
Mobbs, Sir Nigel 38, 42, 71, 127
  non-executive board member 89,
    90, 92
  and resignation of Taylor 96–7

money-making
  changed attitude to 28, 30
  hedge fund managers 147, 159
  investment banking 62
Moreno, Glen 329
Morgan, John Pierpont 4, 27
Morgan Grenfell 10
Morgan Stanley 8, 340
  Cook and 17–18
  Diamond at 58–9, 60
  and Lehman bankruptcy 197
  merger with Dean Witter 72
  as model 14–15
  and Warburg 54
Morse, Sir Jeremy, Lloyds 37
mortgage lending 148
mortgage market, US sub-prime
  161–6
mortgage-backed securities 152,
  161
  corrupt trading of 338
  and Protium 259–61
Morzaria, Tushar, finance director
  349, 355, 356, 362
Moyo, Dambisa 292, 305
Muehlemann, Lukas 75
Munk, Peter 107
Myners, Paul, Lord 205, 209–210,
  217, 219, 373–4
  and pressure on Barclays 245–6,
  248

Nadir, Asil 148
National Health Service 113
Nationwide building society 206
NatWest bank 8, 34, 47
  and investment bank 73, 75
  merger with RBS 120
Nesbitt Burns bank 108
New Century Financial (US) 164

New Labour, and 'Cool Britannia'
  112–13
New York, Racquet and Tennis
  Club 56, 57, 62
Newmarch, Mick, Prudential 41,
  121
Nitzan, Jorge 370
Northern Rock 148, 157, 250
  failure of 199
  nationalized 171–2
  run on 167

O2 147
Oakeshott, Lord 312
Obama, Barack, US President 373
October House Records 115–16,
  144–6, 337
  liquidation 313–14
Odey, Crispin 91
Ogden, Dayton 43, 108
oil crisis (1973) 8
one-stop banking 137
O'Neal, Stan, Merrill Lynch 171
O'Neill, Michael, chief executive
  101–2, 103–4
Osborne, George, chancellor of the
  exchequer 272, 294, 358
  and Agius 319
  and Diamond 321, 324

Pandit, Vikram 104, 191
Paribas bank 72
Parker, Alan 252, 309, 335–6, 378
Parker, George 252, 253
Paulson, Hank, US Treasury 177,
  181, 183–4, 373
  and Lehman 186, 190–91,
  194–6
Paulson, John 163
pay, executives 111

Payment Protection Insurance (PPI) 125, 261–3
PCP Partners 228, 232, 235, 238
Performance Incentive Plan 125
Perry, Patrick 81, 84, 85
Peston, Robert 167, 208, 317
Phillips & Drew, brokers 182
Pitman, Brian, Lloyds 37
Polly Peck 148
Pratley, Nils, *Guardian* 312, 327
Prince, Chuck, Citigroup 171
private securities exchanges ('dark pools') 338, 340
privatizations 25–6, 28, 47
Proctor & Gamble 147
profits 37, 38–9, 42, 46–7, 123, 137–8, 146
 falls 285, 299
 rising 164, 345
'Project Colours' 353–4, 364
'Project Electra', investment bank redesign 345–7, 352, 364
'Project Mango' 344, 346
'Project Sesame' 368
proprietary trading 87, 100
Protium, transfer of mortgage backed securities to 259–61
Prudential, fund management 41
Prudential Regulatory Authority 272, 374
public opinion
 anger towards bankers 257–8, 281, 339
 and blame for recession 284–5
public relations, errors 111–12, 123

Qatar
 and Barclays share issue 178–9
 funding for Barclays 217–18, 221, 232

Qatar Holding LLC 315, 341–2
Qatar Investment Authority 178
Q.ton conference centre, Cambridge 227–8, 235
quantitative easing 244, 266, 343
Al-Qubaisi, Khadem 240
Quinton, John, chairman 35–7, 38, 375

Rake, Sir Michael 173, 260, 292, 297, 350
 and Agius 316–17
 candidate for chairman 329, 347
 and choice of Jenkins 335–6
 and Diamond 322–3
 and King 320–21
 McFarlane and 349, 351
 resignation 358
 and resignation of Jenkins 356
recapitalization of banks 201, 204, 206, 282–3
 new rules 350
recruitment
 Barclays Capital Group 117
 hiring frenzy (1980s) 21–2
 super-league of headhunters 42–3
 see also executive search
Renaissance, Russian financial institution 85
Reserve Primary fund (US) 202–3
residential mortgage backed securities (RMBS) 161, 162
retail banking
 Barrett's reforms 119–24, 340
 branch closures 111–12
 changes (1990s) 124–6
 competition 34, 111, 119–20
 excessive profits 122
 ringfencing 350, 352–3, 365
Rhoner, Marcel, UBS 178

Ricci, Rich 256, 296, 311, 376
  and BGI 213
  co-head of Barclays Capital
    280–81, 285
  investment bank plan 344
  and Lehman bid 182, 184, 188,
    196
  resignation 344
Ridley, Dr Matt 167
rights issues
  (1988) 36
  (2013) 345, 352
Risk Appetite process 163
Roberts, David 129, 130, 144
Robin Hood Tax Campaign 305
Robinson, Alastair 47
'Roger' 64–5
Royal Bank of Canada 106
Royal Bank of Scotland (RBS) 86,
    98, 148
  bid for ABN 156, 157, 165–6,
    168
  liquidity 216
  merger with NatWest 120
  takeover speculation 103
  and Treasury funds 218, 219
Rudd, Sir Nigel 74–5, 92, 127,
    128, 129
  and ABN deal 157
  Buxton and 89, 90
  and successor to Barrett
    150–51
Rudloff, Hans-Joerg 192, 281
Russell, Stephen 130
Russia
  Barclays' exposure to 83–7
  credit limits for trading 82–3
  financial crisis (1998) 83
Ryan, Anthony, US Treasury
    Department 181–2

Sachsen LB bnak 164
Saint Victor, Diane de 351
sales techniques
  cross-selling 170
  and incentives 125
Salomon Brothers 75
Salz, Anthony, audit 341
Samuels, Simon 154
Sands, Peter, Standard Chartered
    bank 206
Santander 206
Sants, Hector, FSA 375
  and choice of Jenkins 334–5
  and Lehman bid 182, 185–6,
    193, 197
  and recapitalization of Barclays
    210
  and sale of BGI 255
  and stress tests 250–53
  view of Diamond 273, 315
Sarbanes-Oxley Act (USA) 148
Sarkozy, Nicolas, French President
    220
scandals 338–42
  accounting and business 148
  see also Libor
Schlosstein, Ralph 256
Scholar, Tom 185, 224, 248, 253,
    374
Schroders, and Citigroup 134
Schueneman, Diane 351
securitization 70–71
  sub-prime mortgages 161
Seegers, Frits 136, 143
  and acquisitions 173, 216
  management style 264–5
  overseas expansion 264–5
  and pay 340
Senior Managers Regime (2016)
    349

Serious Fraud Office (SFO)
    and Barclay's Qatar relationship
        315, 371
    investigation into advisory
        services agreements 342
share dealing 16
    abolition of fixed commissions
        4, 10
    automation 19, 25
share price, Barclays' 85, 87, 90,
        236–7, 243–4
    after BGI sale 256
    and appointment of Diamond
        271
    falls 165, 168, 240, 299, 311–12,
        314
    and Jenkins's reforms 345, 348,
        352
share prices, global falls (2008)
        172
shareholder value 147
    increases 121, 122
    revolution 34
shareholders
    and 2012 AGM 305–6
    demands of 339
Shaw, David E. 19
Sheinwald, Sir Nigel 220
Sherman, Watts 4, 153
shops and shopping, online 113
shorting (of stock) 136, 160, 267
Simpson, Thacher & Bartlett 184
Skirton, Andrew, and BGI 213
Smart, Brad, *Topgrading* 280
Smith Barney brokers 75
Smith, Heidi 282, 287, 377
Smith New Court 54
Société Générale 139
Solent Capital Partners 164
Spence, Geoffrey 205

Spencer Stuart partnership 42–3,
        44, 101, 334, 335, 359
    recruitment of Barrett 107, 109
sports sponsorships 35–6
Spottiswoode, Claire 272
'stakeholder economy' 113
Staley, Jes 377
    candidate for CEO 332, 333,
        334–6, 359–61
    career 360–61
    as CEO 361–2, 369, 369–72
    influence of J. P. Morgan 362–4,
        369–70
    reputation 370–71
    and universal banking 362, 363–4
Standard Chartered bank 206
Staveley, Amanda 226–41, 378
    and Abu Dhabi investors 232–41
    early career 226–30
    lawsuit against Barclays 342,
        368, 371
    and Roger Jenkins 230, 232–5
Stealth Group 348
Steel, Robert 150, 151, 332
    and acquisitions 177–8
    and Lehman bid 19, 181–2
    at Wachovia 180–81, 202
Sten, Anne-Marie 107, 110
Stewart, John 120–21
Stock Exchange
    and automated trading 25
    firms purchased 14
    reforms 3–4, 10
stock markets
    Black Friday 216
    booming (2006) 147
    falls (2008) 204, 215
    global 28
    reaction to Lehman bankruptcy
        197–8

Stocken, Oliver, executive director 47, 89–90, 91, 98
stress tests 249, 250–53
Structured Capital Markets 76, 260
  closure 344
structured collar option
  compensation 337–8
  mis-selling of 169, 170, 254, 312, 337
structured investment vehicles (SIVs) 162, 163, 165
sub-prime crisis 171–3
  central bank interventions 166, 172
  US resignations 171
Sunday Times, leak about ABN AMRO offer 156
Sunderland, Sir John 150, 292, 298–9
  and Agius's successor 318, 328–30
  and choice of Jenkins 335
  Remuneration Committee 344
Sure Start children's programme 113
Swiss Bank Corporation 54

TAPS (Trade Analysis and Processing System) 16
TARP (Troubled Assets Relief Program) (USA) 203–4, 208, 230
tax schemes 47, 117, 231, 260
Taylor, (John) Martin 31–2, 375–6
  appointment as chief executive 43–5
  and Barclays 33–4
  and Barclays Capital Group 86–7, 88–9
  and Bott 53–4

  and Buxton 70, 88–9, 90–91, 93–4
  and concerns about BZW 54–5, 58, 68–71
  decision on sale of BZW 73–5
  and Diamond 63, 86–7, 94
  and Hogg 32–3, 70
  and Large 94
  and Independent Banking Commission 272
  management style 92–3, 99
  plans for disposal of BZW 71–3
  and possible demerger 90
  reforms at Barclays 46–7
  relations with Barclays board 88–92, 93–4, 97
  report on Russian crisis 90–92
  resignation 96–9
  risk and credit analysis modelling 46, 99
  and Russia 82–3, 84–6
Telefonica 147
telephone banking 111
Temasek Holdings (Singapore) 157
Thain, John 191
al Thani, Sheikh Hamad bin Jassim bin Jabr (HBJ) 178–9, 232
Thatcher, Margaret, Prime Minister 3, 11, 28, 34
Thieke, Steve 351
Throsby, Tim 362–3
Today programme, Humphrys' interview with Diamond 286–90
Trading with the Enemy Act (US) 275
Travelers Group 72, 75, 136
Treasury Committee, Diamond and (2012) 323–5, 373

Treasury meeting (September 2008)
205–6
Treasury meeting (October 2008)
208–210
Tucker, Paul, Bank of England 221,
222–5, 374
and Diamond 224–5
Tuke, Anthony Favill, chairman of
Barclays 5, 8–9, 153
Turner, Adair, Lord 205, 258–9,
269, 374–5
and Agius 302–4, 322
and Agius's successor 328–9
and appointment of Walker 330
concerns about Barclays 272,
301, 302, 315–16
and Diamond 273, 321–2
Turner, Cathy 140
Tyco 148
Tyrie, Andrew, Treasury
Committee 283, 325

UBS, Barclays interest in 177–8
UN General Assembly 203
Ungern-Sternberg, Alex von 64, 76
Unicredit 139
United States
banking system 15, 18–19
deregulation 19, 28
and financial crisis 202–4
and investigation into Libor 307–8
regulatory reforms 346, 352–3
Sarbanes-Oxley Act 148
sub-prime crisis 171–3
and sub-prime mortgage markets
161–6, 180
and super-banks 134
universal banking 137
commitment of board to 332–4
Diamond and 282–4

Staley and 362, 363–4
Varley's vision 263–4, 274
US Federal Reserve
and LTCM rescue 87
provision of emergency credit 165
US Surgical Corporation 15, 17–18
US Treasury
direct support for banks 221, 244
and TARP fund 203–4, 208

Vadera, Shriti, Baroness 202, 217,
248–9, 373–4
and stress tests 240, 251
Vander Weyer, Deryk 11
Varley, John 98, 150–51, 376
and Abu Dhabi proposal 235–6,
239
annual report (2009) 265
and appointment as chief
executive 105, 128–33, 137
and Barrett 110, 111, 112, 128
and bid for ABN AMRO 154–8,
168, 171
and Diamond 133, 134–5, 140,
142–3
executive director 90, 91, 92
as finance director 120, 136–7
and financial crisis (2008) 204–5
and FSA stress tests 251–3
and government pressure (2009)
245–9
and Jenkins 140–42, 143–4
and Lehman bid 179–80, 182–5,
189–90, 193–4, 196–8
presentation to investors (2009)
250
and recapitalization 209, 210,
216, 217–18
retirement 267–71
and Seegers 265–6

Varley, John – *cont.*
  SFO and 371
  strategy 139–44, 152–3
  and Treasury 206, 218–19
  and vision of universal bank
    263–4, 274
Vasari Global 238
Venkatakrishnan, C. S. 362
Vickers, Sir John 272, 350
Vix (Volatility Index) 135
'Volcker Rule' 346, 364
Vorderman, Carol 262

Wachovia, US financial services
  company 181, 202
Walker, Sir David, chairman
    329–30, 377
  and Jenkins 334–5, 336, 344
  retirement 347
  review of business model 333–6,
    346–7
Wall Street Crash (1929) 279
Wall Street, New York 147
  and dot.com bubble 114
  reforms (1975) 15
Warburg 8, 14, 54
Warburg Investment Management 41
warrants 230, 233
Washington Mutual 202, 363, 364
Weatherstone, Dennis, J. P. Morgan
    5, 68, 153, 360–61, 363

Wedd Durlacher 14, 24
Weill, Sandy 72, 75, 136, 139
Welch, 'Neutron Jack' 34
Wells Fargo bank 202
Wells Fargo Nikko Investment
    Advisers 212
West LB Asset Management 164
Wheat, Allen 60–61, 76, 119
Wheatcroft, Patience 173
Wheatley, Martin 358
Which? magazine 262–3, 281
'William' (The Thinker), fund
    manager 378
  analysis of Barclays 158–60,
    242–3, 266–7, 368–72
Wilson, Harold, Prime Minister 7
Wilson, Ken, US Treasury 183
Winters, Bill 207, 272, 286, 332–3
Wolf, Martin 272
Wolfe, Tom, *The Bonfire of the
    Vanities* 62
Woolwich building society 120–21,
    123
World Development Movement 305
World Trade Center, 2001 terrorist
    attacks 114–15
WorldCom accounting scandal 148
Wright, Sir Peter 37–8
Wriston, Walter, Citigroup 9, 153

Zech, Jurgen 130